Lee's Bold Plan
for Point Lookout

Lee's Bold Plan for Point Lookout

The Rescue of Confederate Prisoners That Never Happened

JACK E. SCHAIRER

McFarland & Company, Inc., Publishers
Jefferson, North Carolina, and London

LIBRARY OF CONGRESS CATALOGUING-IN-PUBLICATION DATA

Schairer, Jack E., 1943–
Lee's bold plan for Point Lookout : the rescue of Confederate prisoners that never happened / Jack E. Schairer.
    p.   cm.
Includes bibliographical references and index.

ISBN 978-0-7864-3555-5
(softcover : 50# alkaline paper)

1. Point Lookout Prison Camp for Confederates.   2. Prisoners of war—Maryland—Point Lookout—History—19th century.   3. Prisoners of war—United States—History—19th century.   4. Lee, Robert E. (Robert Edward), 1807–1870—Military leadership.   5. Maryland—History—Civil War, 1861–1865—Prisoners and prisons.   6. United States—History—Civil War, 1861–1865—Prisoners and prisons, Confederate.   7. Maryland—History—Civil War, 1861–1865—Campaigns.   8. Washington (D.C.)—History—Civil War, 1861–1865—Campaigns.   9. United States—History—Civil War, 1861–1865—Campaigns.   I. Title.
E616.L8S33   2008
973.7'71—dc22   2008033133

British Library cataloguing data are available

©2008 Jack E. Schairer. All rights reserved

No part of this book may be reproduced or transmitted in any form or by any means, electronic or mechanical, including photocopying or recording, or by any information storage and retrieval system, without permission in writing from the publisher.

On the cover: (background) Print of Point Lookout, Maryland (Library of Congress); (top, inset) Generals Early and Lee (W. Duke & Sons and Co., Duke University Library); (foreground) Confederate soldier (Jones Bros. Pub. Co., New York Public Library). Front cover by TG Design.

Manufactured in the United States of America

McFarland & Company, Inc., Publishers
Box 611, Jefferson, North Carolina 28640
www.mcfarlandpub.com

To my wife, Marilyn

Table of Contents

Preface 1

1 Introduction 3
2 Lee Was an Audacious Man 8
3 Plans to Capture Washington and Point Lookout 23
4 Trevilian Station 29
5 General Hunter Fails to Move in the Shenandoah Valley as Directed 36
6 Lee's Bold Plan, Phase I 53
7 Early's Fateful Decision 70
8 Washington's Defenses Undermanned 74
9 Point Lookout Prison Camp Vulnerable to Attack 89
10 Early Tarries on the Upper Potomac 98
11 A Lack of Shoes Causes Delay 110
12 Grant Fails to Meet Early's Threat 113
13 Early Hindered by Lack of Cooperation with Mosby 122
14 Washington's Defenses Depleted by Removal of Troops to Maryland Heights 126
15 Seaborne Attack on Point Lookout in Conjunction with Early's Forces Called Off 130
16 Wallace Aggressively Contests Early's Move to Frederick 136
17 General Ransom Costs Early Time 143
18 Hunter and Howe Fail to Move to Threaten Early 147
19 Confederates Fail to Secure Bridge at Monocacy Junction 154
20 Early Delayed by Battle of the Monocacy 157
21 Johnson-Gilmor Raid Toward Baltimore and Point Lookout 164
22 Wallace's Retreat to Baltimore Aids Early's Advance on Washington 170
23 Hot Weather Slows Early's Move on Washington 173
24 Early Loses Opportunity to Enter Washington at Fort Stevens 176

25	Veteran Reserve Troops and Convalescing Officers Help Defend Washington	185
26	Quartermaster Employees Serve in Washington's Defense	192
27	Lack of Intelligence on Washington Defenses Handicaps Early	196
28	Actions at the Blair Mansions a Minor Factor in Early's Failure to Enter Washington	200
29	McCook's Force Outside Fort Stevens Deters Early's Assault	205
30	Convalescing Union Troops Help Defend Washington	207
31	Lincoln Under Fire at Fort Stevens	210
32	Foreign Recognition of the Confederacy and Lincoln's Problematic Reelection	213
33	Epilogue: Early Reconsidered	221

Chapter Notes 225

Bibliography 243

Index 251

Preface

This story has a beginning for me as a child spending summers in Saint Mary's County, Maryland, and going to Point Lookout, the site of a Union Civil War prison. There I saw a large monument to the thousands of men who died there. Although most Civil War era things were gone, there were still some vestiges of what once had been. I remember as a boy in the 1950s talking to a man in Dameron, Maryland, who said his grandfather had been in that prison camp.

What continued to interest me these many years later were the unanswered questions of how Point Lookout fit into the larger picture of what happened in the Civil War. Encouraged by a mentor, John Driscoll, who has been reading and writing about the Civil War for many decades, I looked into the story of not only what happened but why it happened and why it turned out as it did.

What I found was that in a very short period of time while hemmed in by Grant at Richmond, General Robert E. Lee had undertaken a bold plan to relieve Lynchburg and, if possible, to move on Washington to keep open his supply lines and divert Grant. While Jubal Early's Confederate army was on the march, it became much more — an additional plan to release the almost 15,000 Confederate prisoners at Point Lookout.

The plan was as audacious as Lee. It could have and should have succeeded, and it might have changed everything. Contributing factors of many types influenced the outcome and are the fabric from which this story is woven.

I particularly want to thank the marvelous staff at the Wisconsin Historical Society Library for their very helpful assistance. I again want to thank John Driscoll for his patience, insights and very valuable help in many aspects of this project.

Jack E. Schairer • Madison, Wisconsin

Chapter 1

Introduction

The High Tide of the Confederacy is generally regarded as being at Gettysburg. It can be fairly said, however, that the high tide should have been at Washington in July 1864 with General Jubal Early commanding Stonewall Jackson's old corps, taking and burning the city and injuring or capturing the president, possibly with the assistance of liberated Confederate prisoners from the Point Lookout prison camp—evacuating before the 6th corps veterans from Grant's army and the 19th corps veterans diverted from Grant's army could prevent it.

General Robert E. Lee, commanding the Army of Northern Virginia, was fighting a war of attrition with the Union Army of the Potomac and Army of the James under the overall command of Lieutenant General Ulysses S. Grant. Grant had been named a lieutenant-general by President Lincoln in March 1864. He had lost over 40,000 men in a series of flanking moves toward Richmond by June.[1]

Grant was able to replace his losses, in part by stripping the defenses of Washington, Point Lookout and other places of veteran troops. Lee was not able to replace his, absent a prisoner exchange, which had been suspended for a substantial period. But Lee was an audacious man.

General Lee sought to turn the tables on Grant by releasing a corps of troops totaling between 12,500 and 15,000 men from the defenses of Richmond under the command of General Jubal A. Early in June 1864 to first go to protect the vital logistical center of Lynchburg in the Shenandoah Valley, which was being threatened by Union general David Hunter and an army of about 18,000 men. There Early was to join forces with those of General John Breckinridge and those under General John D. Imboden and General John C. Vaughn to attack Hunter. Hunter had destroyed much property, particularly civilian property in the Shenandoah Valley, the breadbasket of the Confederacy. If circumstances permitted, General Jubal A. Early, commanding this Confederate force, was to move down the Valley, secure it, go into Maryland and on to Washington.[2]

Union cavalry raids on Richmond in the spring of 1864 demonstrated the potential feasibility of such actions. Wade Hampton's defeat of Sheridan at Trevilian Station made the success of Lee's gamble possible by preventing Sheridan from joining General David Hunter in the Shenandoah Valley and forcing him back to the Union lines at Richmond. This opened the way for General Early to proceed to execute Lee's imaginative plan, which was being undertaken at a time when General Grant was involved in the execution of a brilliant plan of his own designed to place Lee in a conundrum. Grant was trying to seize the crucial rail center at Petersburg, forcing Lee to either defend Richmond or move 20 miles south and defend his vital source of supplies. In an elaborate series of maneuvers around June 12 and 13, 1864, Grant, in a series of masked movements, was moving large bodies of troops from their lines before Richmond to try to accomplish his objective. Ultimately, due to the failure of execution of Grant's well-conceived plan by General "Baldy" Smith and others and the timely action of General Beauregard to frustrate the Union plans, Lee was able to have both Richmond and Petersburg.

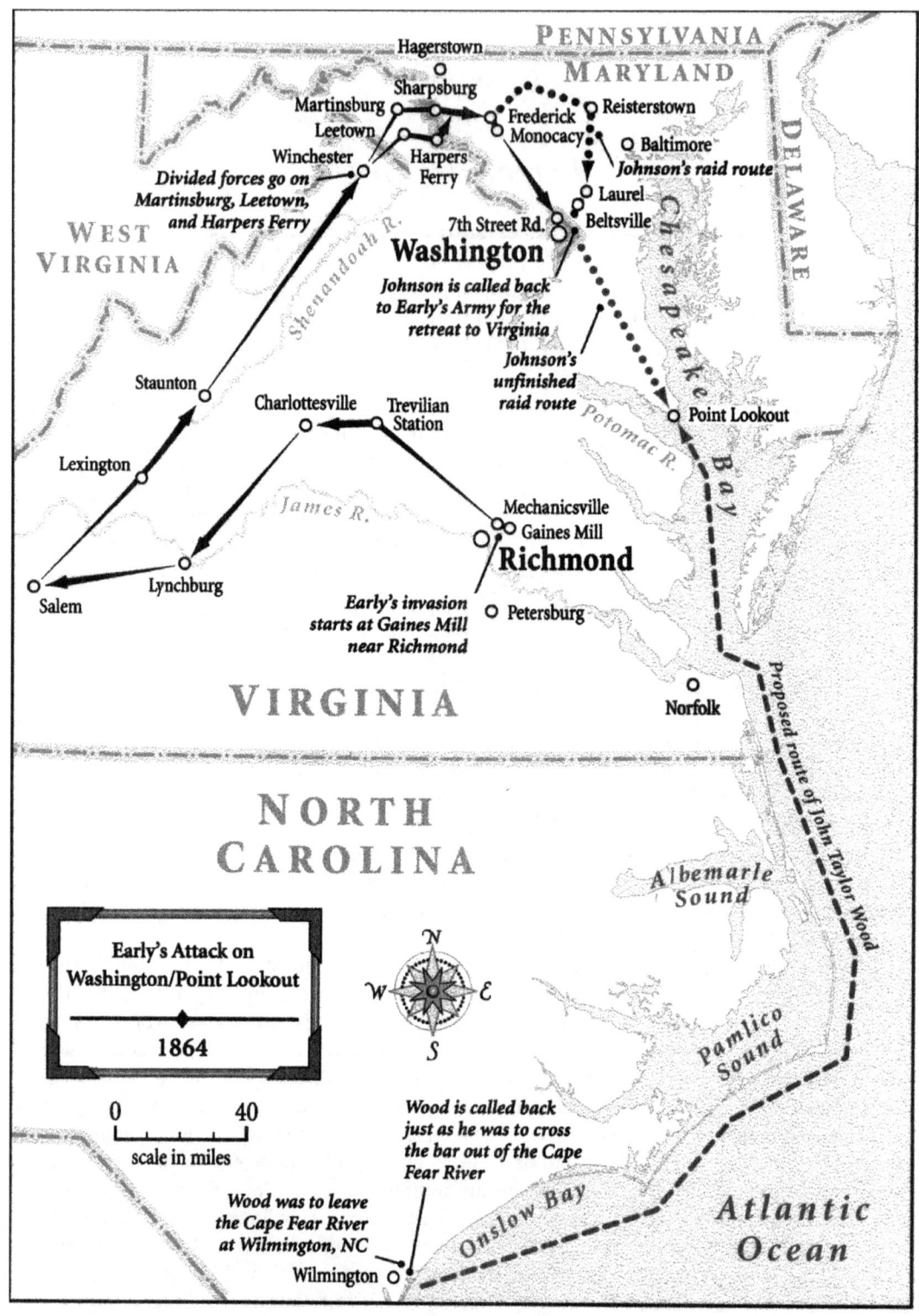

MAP OF JUBAL EARLY'S RAID IN JUNE AND JULY 1864. ATTACK ROUTE OF EARLY, JOHNSON AND WOOD (MAP BY DAVID DEIS).

Meanwhile, while these maneuvers were going on, Early was able to slip out of the Confederate lines from Gaines Mill near Richmond, march to Lynchburg, defeat Hunter, get down the Valley and into Maryland before Grant and the War Department understood where he was. This was, in part, due to the greatest intelligence failure of the Civil War.[3] While Early was marching in the Valley, Lee was in correspondence with Confederate president Jefferson Davis regarding liberating the prisoners at Point Lookout, the largest Union prison camp, which was located at the confluence of the Potomac River and the Chesapeake Bay about 90 miles southeast of Washington. The Point Lookout phase of this plan, developed on the fly while Early was on the march, was to be done in cooperation with an amphibious operation by John Taylor Wood, who would be bringing ships, rifles and Marines to Point Lookout from Wilmington, North Carolina. Once at Point Lookout, Wood was to effectuate a landing in coordination with a cavalry attack by Brigadier General Bradley T. Johnson of Early's command. He would be coming from the area near Baltimore after cutting rail and telegraph communications between Washington and the North. Davis agreed to the modification of the plan to include Point Lookout, and this phase of the plan was communicated to Early on July 6, 1864, by Captain Robert E. Lee, Jr.

Lee's gamble should have been successful. That it was not was due in part to the loss of time en route and hesitancy on the part of General Jubal A. Early, an excellent military officer remembered as the man who did not encourage General Ewell to attack at the end of the first day at Gettysburg, which may well have cost the Confederates a victory. There were a number of other factors which militated in favor of the success of the plan and a number which militated against it.

Factors which supported the success of the mission included Early's quick movement to Lynchburg and defeat of Hunter, followed by his expeditious movement down the Shenandoah Valley to Winchester; General David Hunter's taking of his entire army through West Virginia in June and July 1864 out of the theater of military operation so as not to be an impediment to Early's invasion; the stripping of the defenses of Washington of veteran troops and artillerists in the spring and summer of 1864 sent to Grant's army, leaving minimal numbers to defend the city along with convalescing troops, militia and armed civilians. Another factor favoring the success of Early's mission was Chief of Staff Henry Halleck's unusual move of dispatching troops to Harpers Ferry as Early was passing, further diminishing troop strength in the defenses of Washington. Grant's lack of an effective and timely response to the threat, in part due to lack of proper intelligence and in part due to his refusal to timely credit and act on the intelligence information he did have, was also of great assistance to the Confederate operation. General Lew Wallace's retreat toward Baltimore rather than Washington after the Battle of the Monocacy opened the door to Washington for Early.

A number of factors worked to the detriment of the proper execution of Lee's plan. First, Early chose at Winchester not to take, as authorized, the most direct route to Washington through Leesburg. Instead, he took the longer route through Harpers Ferry. Further, Early's forces were held up at Leetown on July 3 by the stubborn defense of Colonel James Mulligan and a relatively small force. General Early spent from the afternoon of July 3 to the evening of July 4 on the Upper Potomac at Martinsburg, West Virginia, and Harpers Ferry, West Virginia with his troops, feasting on captured Union stores and liquor. General Early's forces also failed to cut off the retreat of Generals Sigel and Weber to Maryland Heights, which commanded the main route to Washington.

Early also spent several more days demonstrating and making ineffectual troops movements before Maryland Heights, where the Union force was in a practically impregnable position. After this was done, Early took the same route through Frederick he could have taken days before. Another factor militating against the success of Lee's bold plan was the slowness of Early getting his army up through Frederick, Maryland, to Monocacy Junction, a key communications link to Washington, from July 6 through July 8, 1864. This was in part due to delays involved in Early's extorting money from the citizens of Hagerstown, Maryland, and Frederick, Maryland, in return for not burning those cities. The need to forage to feed the army, delays waiting for shoes and timid action by the cavalry division commander, General Robert Ransom, in actions west of Frederick also contributed to the pace of the Confederate movement from the Upper Potomac.

Also a factor was the aggressive action by Union general Lew Wallace in appreciating the threat that Early posed; in marshaling available home guards, militia and cavalry units in contesting Early's movements to and beyond Frederick; and in getting Brigadier General James Ricketts' 6th corps units to provide an aggressive defense to the Confederate actions. Another factor militating against Lee's gamble was the capable and aggressive action of Lew Wallace and Ricketts in the Battle of the Monocacy in holding Early up for a full day in a major battle against great odds, which could probably have been avoided had Early taken the Buckeystown Road around Monocacy Junction. The oppressive heat at that time was debilitating to Early's marching army. In spite of everything, Early arguably could still have taken and burned Washington on the afternoon of July 11 when the forts were lightly defended; Early himself recognized this, but hesitated and lost his final opportunity.

Another factor operating against Early's success was the strong leadership of one of the ablest officers in the Union army, Quartermaster General Montgomery Meigs. Meigs, himself born in the South, organized about 1,800 armed quartermaster employees and put them in the line at the point of attack at Fort Stevens, where he led them effectively and well.

A similar and related factor was the fine and effective service provided by the Veteran Reserve troops, who served capably under difficult circumstances. Some of the able leadership in the crucial northern defenses of Washington was provided by convalescing wounded officers who stepped forward when needed. Also, the 2,800 men of Price's Provisional Brigade, consisting of men from almost every regiment of the Army of the Potomac in the hospitals of Washington who could fire a gun, constituted a substantial reserve force.

Another factor going against the proper execution of Lee's gamble was the unorthodox strategy of Major General Alexander McD. McCook, who had been relieved after Chickamagua, and was in Washington before returning to Ohio, commanding a group of armed civilians, hospitalized veterans, militia, veteran reserves and a smattering of dismounted cavalry and other troops. McCook put some of his troops out of his main defensive work at Fort Stevens and hotly skirmished with Early's troops on the afternoon of July 11, creating the appearance of greater numbers than he had. A Stonewall Jackson Early was not. He hesitated and was lost.

Perhaps Early was simply unlucky. President Lincoln, a tall man wearing a stove-pipe hat, was standing on the parapet of Fort Stevens on July 12 against the advice of those around him, when a Confederate sharpshooter shot a surgeon standing next to him. Obviously, if the president had been shot instead of the surgeon, the course of history would have been different.

On the Point Lookout aspect of the Lee's plan, a major factor in favor of it was that the camp was lightly defended, mainly by inexperienced troops. Most of the veteran troops had been stripped from the garrison and sent to Grant's army in the spring and summer of 1864. Also, the defensive works were incomplete in mid–July 1864.

Factors militating against the success of the raid to Point Lookout were articles in the press, delays in getting weaponry to John Taylor Wood and concerns about knowledge by Union naval and other military authorities which contributed to the last-minute cancellation of Colonel and Commander John Taylor Wood's amphibious operation from Wilmington, North Carolina. Other factors were the two-day delay in Early's communicating to Brigadier General Bradley T. Johnson, leader of the Point Lookout cavalry raid, about having Johnson be responsible for numerous military operations around Baltimore in addition to the raid and delays by Johnson and Col. Harry Gilmor's taking time to see friends.

There was also some delay in Lee's communicating with Early after Davis approved the plan, owing to the personal communication from Capt. Robert E. Lee, Jr., to Early while he was on the march in Maryland, making execution of the Point Lookout aspect of the plan more difficult.

The timing of Early's attack on Washington and the planned raid on the Point Lookout prison camp was optimal. Lincoln's re-election was no sure thing. There was substantial war weariness in the North. Grant had taken staggering casualties in his spring campaign in the Wilderness, Spottsylvania, the North Ana and Cold Harbor. His army was in a stalemated siege in Petersburg. The Atlanta campaign in the summer of 1864 was inconclusive. Recognition by England and France hinged on a battlefield demonstration of the Confederacy's independence. The entry into Washington, even for a short time, and the return of a corps-sized group of Confederate prisoners to Lee's army could have been that demonstration.

In the end, Lee's plan for Point Lookout failed not for want of brilliance of conception or imagination in the plan itself but, in part, for want of effective execution on the Confederate side and effective response and execution by most of those in Early's path under very difficult circumstances, holding the line until veteran troops could arrive. Lee almost turned the tables on Grant. If he had, perhaps he, not Grant, would have ended up being president of a nation.

Chapter 2

Lee Was an Audacious Man

While the concept of an attack on Washington in mid–1864 may have developed in part as a response to the Union cavalry attacks on Richmond, the initiative to undertake it as a large-scale operation came from General Robert E. Lee. He was a blood relative of Thomas Jefferson and Chief Justice John Marshall and was a very aggressive general. Colonel Joseph Ives of Lee's staff had said that Lee would "take more desperate chances and take them quicker than any other general in this country, North or South."[1] Lee's chief of artillery, General Edward Porter Alexander, said of him, "Military critics will rank Gen. Lee as decidedly the most audacious commander who has lived since Napoleon, & I am not at all sure that Napoleon in his whole career will be held to have overmatched some of the deeds of audacity to which Gen. Lee committed himself." Napoleon described Marshal Turinne as the only general he knew who got bolder as he got older. The campaigns of General Robert E. Lee show that his audacity intensified through to Appomattox.[2] Once called the King of Spades early in the Civil War for his work on defensive positions, Lee was the only man Stonewall Jackson, himself a bold man, said he would follow blindfolded.[3] Lee's battlefield audacity was remarkable. His division of force in the face of McClellan's larger army at the Seven Days Battles in the Peninsular Campaign, his detachment of Stonewall Jackson to strike General Pope's communications at Second Manassas (Bull Run) and his use of Jackson's forces to strike Hooker's flank at Chancellorsville were marked by "singular boldness."[4]

Lee's daring had earlier shown itself during his service in the Mexican War as a captain of engineers. At Cerro Gordo, the Mexican commander, Santa Anna, held a strong position in mountainous terrain supported by artillery. General Winfield Scott, commanding the United States forces, ordered a full reconnaissance. Robert E. Lee was directed to conduct that reconnaissance and determine whether the Mexican position could be turned. Lee worked his way through very difficult ground on the Mexican left and determined that a road could be cut through on which troops could advance with caution.

Scott provided Lee with a working party to cut a trail. With Lee as a guide, General Twigg's division was sent around Santa Anna's left. The attack on Cerro Gordo was successful. Santa Anna suffered a serious defeat, having 3,000 men captured and losing most of his artillery.[5]

General Winfield Scott said, "I am impelled to make a special mention of the services of Captain R.E. Lee, engineers. This officer, greatly distinguished at the siege of Vera Cruz, was again indefatigable, during these operations, in reconnaissance as daring as laborious, and of the utmost value. Nor was he less conspicuous in planting batteries, and in conducting columns to their stations under heavy fire of the enemy."[6]

After Cerro Gordo, Robert E. Lee entered Jalapa, which was 93 miles from Mexico City. General Winfield Scott directed Lee and Major William Turnbull, his chief topographical engineer, to each make their own study of the approaches to Mexico City. Information was gathered from indigenous Mexicans and travelers in the area which verified information going on a map. After the arrival of Franklin Pierce with 2,500 reinforcements on August 7, 1848, General Winfield Scott made the bold move of abandoning his line of communications. He started to move toward Mexico City, living off the land. General Twigg's division started for Mexico City on August 7.[7]

Captain Robert E. Lee was being used on reconnaissance missions. He was able to ascer-

LEE: AN AUDACIOUS MAN (NATIONAL ARCHIVES).

tain the strength of the principal Mexican defensive work by a causeway in a lake where Santa Anna had 7,000 troops in a formidable defensive position. General Scott determined to take what he thought to be a more practicable route to Mexico City to the south of Lake Chalco. Scott expected to meet the Mexican army in the area of San Augustin. San Antonio in that area was heavily fortified. East of San Antonio was soft ground prohibiting the passage of wheeled vehicles. To the west was a great lava field 5 miles wide and 3 miles long, consisting of blocks and fissures of lava, called the Pedregal.[8]

General Scott assigned Captain Lee to the 11th infantry and two companies of dragoons under Captain Phil Kearny, later a Union general who faced Lee in the Peninsular Campaign, to see if there was any way across the Pedregal. Lee found a road to the west of San Angel which followed the edge of the Pedregal. This road would allow passage of infantry and could be made passable for artillery as well.[9]

Lee's force came in contact with a Mexican force with whom they exchanged fire. Lee could see that the Mexican soldiers had crossed the western part of the Pedregal. He reasonably concluded that Scott's army could also cross the western part of the Pedregal, allowing them to skirt the strong Mexican fortifications at San Antonio. Deciding not to pursue the plan of action of another engineer of considerable ability named Mason, General Winfield Scott determined to attack by way of the San Angel Road as Captain Lee had suggested.[10]

In doing so, Scott's forces ended up between two Mexican armies. General Percival Smith conferred with Lee and General Cadwalader. Two engineers had found the rear approach to Podierna unprotected. Lee crossed the Pedregal to carry to General Smith the plan of General Smith to attack the Mexican position at Podierna at daylight. Smith planned to attack regardless of whether Lee returned from talking to Scott.[11]

Crossing the Pedregal for the second time on August 19 in pitch darkness, Lee encountered General Shield's forces moving up to join General Smith. Lee directed one of his men to guide Shields to Smith's position. Lee then walked the three remaining miles across the lava fields, being bruised and cut by the lava. He arrived at Scott's camp at 11:00 P.M. Lee met with Generals Scott, Twiggs and Pillow. Twiggs had been injured.

Lee crossed the Pedregal for the third time that day leading General Twiggs to that part of his force east of the San Angel road who were to participate in the demonstration in front of the Mexican defenses. At 1:00 A.M. Captain Lee then guided Colonel T.B. Ransom, serving in place of Franklin Pierce, who had been injured by the fall of his horse, to what Lee believed to be the most favorable place for a demonstration to mask the main attack. Pierce's men moved slowly over the lava to take their positions at dawn when the fighting began.[12]

The United States forces soon attacked successfully from the rear. Both Mexican armies fled in disarray. The men of Scott's forces pursued their advantage. Scott then diverted General Worth to attack San Antonio from the front while Pillow and Twiggs attacked the fortification from the rear. Lee was on reconnaissance with Pillow when the Mexican army evacuated San Antonio to avoid being enveloped and fled to Mexico City.[13]

Lee was then instructed by General Scott to lead troops to the area of the Churubusco River where there was a bridgehead. After an engagement involving troops of Generals Worth, Pierce and Shields, the bridgehead was taken and another Mexican fortification stormed.

At this point, Captain Lee had been up for 36 hours. He had crossed the Pedregal three times in one day. He had also been instrumental in positioning troops at Scott's direction and leading forces in the dark through the lava field.[14]

General Twiggs thanked Captain Lee for his exceedingly valuable services during the whole operation. General Percival Smith found Lee's reconnaissance to have been conducted with great skill and the results to have had great value. He credited Lee with sound judgment and great personal daring. General Pillow also commended Lee for gallantry and valuable service. General

General Winfield Scott, Lee's commander in the Mexican War (Massachusetts Commandery Military Order of the Loyal Legion and the United States Army Military History Institute).

Shields said he had confidence in Lee's judgment and positioned his troops in line with his recommendations. General Winfield Scott described Lee's crossing the Pedregal on the night of August 19–20, 1848, as the greatest feat of physical and moral courage he had seen in the campaign.[15]

Once again, Lee was called upon to conduct a reconnaissance as to the approaches to Mexico City. He was involved in the construction of four batteries to be used against Chapultepec. Lee was involved in the actions concerning the storming of Chapultepec and entry into Mexico City.[16]

Lee's audacity carried forward to his civil war service. Colonel Ives said of Lee, "His name might be Audacity."[17] Lieutenant-General Jubal A. Early, in his address at Washington and Lee University on the second anniversary celebration of General Robert E. Lee's birthday after his death, given on January 19, 1872, described Lee's battlefield daring during the Seven Days Battles of 1862 in detail based on the knowledge of one who had served as a general officer under him. Early pointed out that Lee was not in command of the Confederate armies operating on the peninsula before the Seven Days Battles but only took command upon the serious wounding of General Joe Johnston at Seven Pines and became the South's leading general by relying on offensive action:

> In March, 1862, he was called to Richmond and charged with the conduct of military operations in the armies of the Confederacy, under the direction of the President. Just before that time, the evacuation of Manassas took place; and subsequently, the transfer of the bulk of the opposing armies in Virginia to the Peninsula, the evacuation of Yorktown and the evacuation of the Warwick River, the battle of Williamsburg, and the transfer of the seat of war to the Chickahominy, in the vicinity of Richmond occurred.
>
> On the 31st of May and the 1st of June, the battle of Seven Pines was fought, and General Johnston was so severely wounded as to be disabled for duty in the field for some time. Fortunately, the eminent and patriotic statesman who was at the head of Government well knew the merits of General Lee, and at once assigned him to the vacant command; and, then in fact began that career to which I invite your attention.[18]

When he took command of the army he renamed the Army of Northern Virginia, General Lee was facing the Army of the Potomac under McClellan with twice his force, or 100,000 men, in front of Richmond.

Early described General Lee as then conceiving of a strategic movement to relieve Richmond. Lee would be making an attack on McClellan's army with a combined movement with forces in the Valley:

> General Jackson, by his rapid movements and brilliant operations in the Valley, had prevented the march of a column of about forty thousand men, under McDowell, from Fredericksburg on Richmond, to unite with the besieging army; and a part of McDowell's force, and Fremont's army from Northwestern Virginia, had been sent to the Valley, for the purpose of crushing Jackson. It was very apparent that Jackson's force, then consisting of his own command proper, Johnson's command from Allegheny Mountain, and Ewell's division, could not long withstand the heavy forces concentrated against it; and that, when it was overwhelmed, the enemy's troops operating in the Valley, and covering Washington would be at liberty to move on Richmond; while the detachment of the army defending that city, of a force large enough to allow Jackson to defend successfully, in a protracted campaign with forces accumulating against him, would probably assure the fall of the Confederate capital. Preparations were, therefore made to attack the besieging army, with the forces covering Richmond and in the Valley, by a combined movement. Some forces were brought in from the South, and three brigades were sent to the Valley, for the purpose of deceiving the enemy, and facilitating the withdrawal of General Jackson.[19]

Early then recounted that Stonewall Jackson had prevented McDowell's army from joining with Fremont's army and had defeated both armies in succession. Those armies had retreated down the Valley, with the Union generals believing Washington to be threatened. Jackson then left his cavalry and a small force of infantry in the Valley and moved his army to join Lee at Richmond. On June 26, 1862, Lee then attacked McClellan's right flank causing him to change his base and move in a series of engagements down the peninsula to Harrison's Landing under cover of gunboats on the James River.

> To give you some idea of the boldness and daring of this movement, and the impression it made on the enemy, I will call your attention to some facts and figures.
> In his report, dated August, 1863, and printed in 1864, McClellan gives the strength of the troops under his command at Washington, on the Potomac, and within reach on the 1st of March, 1862 as—
> "Present for duty, one hundred and ninety-three thousand one hundred and forty-two."
> A portion of this force had been left to operate in the Valley, another to cover Washington; and he puts the strength of the "Army of the Potomac," which designation his army bore, on the 10th of June, 1862 — just six days before the battles began, at —
> "Present for duty, one hundred and five thousand eight hundred and twenty-five."
> He further says that he had sixty batteries with his army, aggregating three hundred and forty field-pieces. Besides these he had a large train of siege guns.
> General Lee's whole force, of all arms, including the troops of Magruder, Huger, Holmes and Jackson, when the latter arrived, did not reach eighty thousand effective men, and of these, Holmes command, over six thousand strong, did not actively engage in any of the battles.[20]

Early estimated that the Confederate army contained about 75,000 infantry including a number of batteries attached to the brigades. There were about 5,000 cavalry and less than half as many guns as possessed by the opposing Union armies. Early also indicated that the Union troops possessed better firearms.

General Early went on in his address to point out that in addition to his use of brilliant tactics while fighting with a far smaller force, General Lee's strategy would have inflicted a more substantial defeat on the Union forces under McClellan had General Lee's orders been promptly carried out.

> From the data I have give you, you will perceive that I have not under-estimated the strength of the forces at General Lee's command; and this was the largest army he ever commanded. The idea of relieving Richmond, by an attack on McClellan's flank and rear, was a masterly conception, and the boldness, not say audacity, of it will appear when we take into consideration the relative strength of the two armies, and the fact that, in swinging around the enemy's flank, General Lee had left very little over twenty-five thousand men between the capital and the besieging army. Timid minds might regard this as rashness, but it was the very perfection of a profound and daring strategy. Had McClellan advanced to the assault of the city, through the open plains around it, his destruction would have been insured. As it was, his only chance for escape was in a retreat through the swamps and forests, which concealed and sheltered his columns on their flight to the banks of the James. Notwithstanding the favorable nature of the country for his escape, McClellan's army would have been annihilated, had General Lee's orders been promptly and rigidly carried out by his subordinates.[21]

General Early carefully pointed out that General McClellan had always exaggerated the number of troops arrayed against him. On the 25th of June, 1862, just before Lee's attack, McClellan had telegraphed the War Department to Secretary of War Stanton telling him that Lee, Jackson and Beauregard had forces totaling 200,000 against him, asserting he was operating against vastly superior numbers when the opposite was true.[22]

The boldness of the actions of General Robert E. Lee in the Seven Days Battles was remarkable. The *Historical Times Illustrated Encyclopedia of the Civil War* put it this way:

> The southern commander, in what would become the hall-mark of his generalship, fashioned a bold plan. Leaving only 25,000 men south of the Chickahominy to confront McClellan's 70,000, Lee

prepared to strike Porter with 47,000. To deceive the Federals, he sent 1 division westward toward the Shenandoah Valley, while at the same time recalling Maj. Gen. Thomas J. "Stonewall" Jackson and his 18,000 troops from the valley to a point north of Porter's unsupported right flank. Jackson, riding ahead of his men, conferred with Lee and other generals. The Confederate officers scheduled the offensive for 26 June.[23]

After discussing the nature of the operations on the peninsula, the authors found:

> The Union commander, surprised by Lee's boldness, had become a beaten man, ordering a change of base from the York River to the James River. McClellan described it as a strategic withdrawal, while others, less generous, called it a "great skedaddle." Once Lee took the initiative 26 June, he never relinquished it during he campaign....
> The Seven Day's Campaign changed the course of the war in Virginia. Lee had relieved the Confederate capital and had seized the initiative in the East, which he maintained until the battle of Antietam in September.[24]

Edward Pollard found that Lee's aggressive performance in the Seven Days Battles and thereafter were so well received in the South that he could have become a dictator.[25]

Alan T. Nolan noted, "Lee from the beginning embraced the offensive. Appointed to command the Army of Northern Virginia on June 1, 1862, he turned to the offensive, beginning with major engagements on the Peninsula-Mechanicsville, Gaines Mill, Frayser's Farm and Malvern Hill."[26]

Nolan cited Grady McWhiney for the proposition that the aggressiveness of Lee cost the Confederates dearly, with his losses in his first six battles being six percent greater than the Union casualties. He also cited another eminent Civil War historian, Frank Vandiver, for Lee's high casualty ratios. Nolan went on to say, "He [Lee] does not want to relinquish the offensive. He does not want to cease to be audacious."[27] In a similar vein, Thomas Connelly criticized Lee for amassing over 50,000 casualties in his first three months as head of the Army of Northern Virginia.[28]

These men were saying audacity has a price. Lee's army suffered substantial casualties, more than taken by the Army of the Potomac, in driving McClellan from the peninsula and in defeating the forces arrayed against him in the Shenandoah Valley. Nolan has taken the position the tactical defensive was needed to give the Confederates their best chance of winning the war, owing to the huge disparity of men and resources between the parties.

Regardless of whether Lee's generalship offered the best ultimate opportunity for independence, the daring that marked it was certainly his hallmark, as reflected in his military operations in the Civil War.

After preventing McClellan's moving on Richmond in conjunction with McDowell's forces from Fredericksburg with a brilliant series of maneuvers and chasing McClellan down the peninsula, Lee then succeeded in driving the Union forces back to the Washington area by a remarkable strategic operation also marked by boldness.

The Union forces in the Shenandoah Valley were brought under command of Major General John Pope. McClellan still had about 90,000 men near Richmond. Pope had about 75,000 men north of the Rappahannock, which he started moving toward Charlottesville and Gordonsville. In between was Lee with his 80,000 man army.

Pope needed to protect not only Washington but also his lines of communications with McClellan's army in the Richmond area. By moving in the direction of Gordonsville and Charlottesville, Pope would potentially be able to draw Lee away from Richmond and cut communications with the Valley.[29]

Jackson moved north toward Gordonsville. A force under A.P. Hill was also sent to support Jackson. Jackson attacked Pope's advance under General Nathaniel Banks in a hard-fought battle at Cedar Mountain on August 9, 1862. Lee, being aware that McClellan was drawing forces from the Peninsula to join Pope, moved to prevent the joining of the Union armies. He sent Longstreet to join Jackson. His purpose was to attack Pope's flank. Such a maneuver would cut off his line of retreat and also interfere with McClellan's movements. Because General J.E.B. Stuart had captured Pope's headquarters at Catlett's Station on August 22, Lee was aware of Pope's plans.[30]

Substantially outnumbered, Lee undertook the dangerous plan of splitting his army. On August 25, 1862, Stonewall Jackson with part of Lee's army marched around Pope's right flank to sever his supply lines and communications. After marching 50 miles, Jackson's forces attacked the Confederate supply depot at Manassas Junction on the 26th and 27th. On the 27th Pope abandoned his position.

Pope let Lee and Longstreet move to join Jackson.[31] Pope reached Manassas Junction about noon on the 28th. On the evening of the 28th, Jackson's men became involved in a fierce fight with General John Gibbon's Iron Brigade forces at Groveton with substantial casualties on both sides. The Stonewall brigade and Gibbon's forces each lost about one third of their men.[32]

Pope could have withdrawn across Bull Run and awaited the arrival of Sumner's and Franklin's corps and Cox's division. If he had consolidated his forces, he would have been in a better position to fight Lee. Instead Pope launched a series of piecemeal attacks against Jackson's position behind an unfinished railroad cut on August 29. The Union attacks were repulsed with heavy casualties on both sides. Pope attacked again on August 30 and was again repulsed with great loss. Longstreet then counterattacked, crushing Pope's left flank, and driving his forces back to Bull Run. In the fighting, Pope incurred about 16,000 casualties to Lee's 9,200.[33]

By acting with imagination, Lee had achieved a major tactical victory and had prevented the joinder of Pope's and McClellan's armies to create an overwhelming force against him. Lee's splitting his army, putting part of his army between Pope and Washington and putting Jackson in a strong defensive position on his flank, had confused Pope and led to a major Confederate triumph and Union defeat.

Lieutenant General Jubal A. Early, in his 1872 address at Washington and Lee, discussed Lee's boldness in the Second Bull Run (Manassas) campaign:

> Lee, noting that General Burnside had arrived at Fredericksburg with 13,000 men from North Carolina and South Carolina with all but 5,000 of that force going to Pope, was determined to move against Pope to crush him before he could be reinforced. Lee left D.H. Hill's and McLaw's divisions, two brigades under J.G. Walker, a brigade of cavalry under Wade Hampton, and some other troops at Drury's and Chaffin's bluffs to watch McClellan near Richmond. Lee moved to the Rapidan with the major part of his army. Due to the capture of a dispatch to Gen. Stuart, Pope became aware of the intended movement against his army.
>
> Jackson, having already destroyed Pope's supply depot and having threatened his line of communications and retreat, with three divisions withstood two days of attacks from Pope's forces, who had been reinforced by Porter and Heintzelman's corps from McClellan and by Reno's men from Burnside's force.

Early felt, "Never did General Jackson display his leading characteristics more conspicuously than on this occasion, and he fully justified the confidence of the commanding general."[34]

Jackson had been involved in the fight at Groveton with the Iron Brigade on the 28th, did most of the fighting in throwing back Union attacks on the 29th and also repulsed renewed attacks on the 30th.

Jackson engaged in another flanking movement against the retreating Confederate army at Chantilly or Ox Hill under orders from Lee who was trying to keep Pope's forces from getting back to the defenses of Washington. Jackson was able to defeat the Union force, inflicting substantial casualties, including General Phil Kearny and General Isaac I. Stevens, who died in the fighting.[35]

Both Lee and Jackson felt that a decisive victory on Northern soil would assure independence for the Confederacy. The time appeared ripe for such a movement north.[36] Joseph L. Harsh found that with limited resources the South could not simply outlast the North and could not win a protracted defense-oriented struggle. Lee took command in the field as a pragmatist. During the first year of the war he had the time and opportunity to form a comprehensive view of the struggle. He came to recognize that the Confederacy had at best a long shot to gain independence. He knew that the imbalance of manpower and resources that existed between the North and the South, coupled with the laws of mathematics, worked inexorably against the Confederacy. He recognized that as long as the North remained determined to subdue the South, the Confederacy could not win the war. Confederate victory would only come from a Union abandonment of the conflict.[37]

Going north into Maryland would be one of the greatest strategic decisions of the war. There was substantial sentiment in the governments of England and France for the recognition of the Confederacy. After Second Bull Run (Manassas) Lord Palmerston planned an October 1862 cabinet meeting to hammer out with France a proposed armistice and cessation of the blockade to be followed by diplomatic recognition. The Palmerston government wanted to see a showing on the battlefield that the South would not be subdued and that their independence would be demonstrated.[38]

Peter Carmichael takes the position that "between 1862 and mid–1863 offensive campaigns as implemented by Lee offered the South its best chance of success during the period beginning with the Seven Days and culminating with his tactical masterpiece at Chancellorsville. Lee emerged as the South's premier general by relying on offensive action. During the Pennsylvania and Maryland raids, Lee took calculated risks, both strategically and tactically." He went on to state that these actions had a reasonable chance of securing a peace settlement or European recognition.[39]

The *Historical Times Illustrated Encyclopedia of the Civil War* described the Antietam Campaign as a bold movement by Lee:

> On 4 Sept. 1864 the Army of Northern Virginia forded The Potomac River in an invasion of Union territory. Confident after their smashing victory at Second Bull Run, the ragged Confederates, many of whom were barefoot, spilled into western Maryland, concentrating 3 days later at Frederick. Gen. Robert E. Lee proposed with this bold movement to relieve war-ravaged Virginia during the fall harvest, acquire thousands of Maryland recruits, earn European diplomatic recognition for the Confederacy, and perhaps force the Union to sue for peace.
>
> At Frederick, Lee formulated the details of his audacious campaign. In Special Order No. 191 the Confederate general divided his army for the third time in as many campaigns. Shielded by South Mountain, Lee planned to move his army north into Pennsylvania. To open a supply line into the Shenandoah Valley, he sent Maj. Gen. Thomas J. "Stonewall" Jackson against the Union garrison at Harper's Ferry. After capturing this force Jackson was to reunite with Maj. Gen. James Longstreet's 3 divisions for the thrust northward. Lee believed he could combine his divided command before his troops could be overtaken by the pursuing reunited Army of the Potomac.[40]

General George B. McClellan had been restored to command of the Army of the Potomac on September 2, 1862, and had left Washington to pursue Lee on September 7, getting to Frederick several days after the Confederates had vacated the city. On September 13, 1862, two Union soldiers in an abandoned Confederate camp found a paper wrapped around three cigars. That paper was Lee's Special Order No. 191. This order was transmitted to McClellan.

Two of Longstreet's divisions were near Hagerstown. Jackson's troops were moving on Harpers Ferry. Lee had one infantry division at Boonesboro and Stuart's cavalry at South Mountain. McClellan waited almost a day before moving against Lee's divided army. Lee learned of the lost order within a day. He had to determine whether to continue the invasion and how to defend against an anticipated Union attack against his divided army.

After defending his supply lines at Fox's and Crampton's gaps on September 14, Lee was preparing to retreat the following day when he found that on the morning of the 15th Stonewall Jackson had captured Harpers Ferry along with 10,000 men, 73 cannon and 13,000 small arms. The Union commander, Colonel Dixon Miles, was killed in the waning moments of his inept defense. Lee, on the verge of retreat, gambled once more and ordered a concentration of his troops at Sharpsburg, Maryland.[41]

In his 1872 address at Washington and Lee University, General Jubal A. Early described General Lee's masterful troop maneuvers:

> As soon as General Lee heard of the success at Harper's Ferry, he ordered all of the troops operating against that place to move to Sharpsburg as soon as practicable, leaving A.P. Hill, with his division, to dispose of the prisoners and property captured at Harper's Ferry. General Jackson, late in the afternoon of the 15th, ordered his own division and Ewell's, the latter now under Lawton, to Sharpsburg, where they arrived on the morning of the 16th. Walker's two brigades came up later in the day. The ten brigades brought by Jackson and Walker made twenty-four brigades of infantry, with the fourteen already on the ground, which General Lee had with him when the battle of Sharpsburg opened on the morning of the 17th of September. Jackson's division was placed on the left flank, and Hood's two brigades, which were next to it on the right, were relieved by two brigades of Ewell's division during the night of the 16th, and these were reinforced by another very early the next morning. General Jackson's whole force on the field consisted of five thousand infantry and very few batteries of his own division. One brigade, my own, numbering about one thousand men and officers, was detached, at light, toward the Potomac on our left to support some artillery which Stuart was operating; so that General Jackson had only four thousand infantry in line, and D.H. Hill was immediately on his right, holding the centre and left centre with his division, then three thousand strong. General Lee's whole infantry force on the field, at the beginning of the battle, did not exceed fifteen thousand men, including Jackson's and Walker's commands. On the left and centre, McClellan hurled, in succession the four corps of Hooker, Mansfield, Sumner and Franklin, numbering, in the aggregate fifty-six thousand and ninety-five men, according to his report; and a sanguinary battle raged for several hours, during which, Hood's two brigades, my brigade, Walker's two brigades, Anderson's brigade of D.R. Jones's division, and McLaws and Anderson's divisions successively went to support the part of the line assailed, at different points, the last two divisions arriving late in the morning during the progress of the battle. And all the troops engaged, from first to last, with the enemy's fifty-six thousand and ninety-five men, on that wing, did not exceed eighteen thousand men. At the close of the fighting there, our left was advanced beyond where it rested in the morning, while the centre had been forced back some two hundred yards.[42]

Lee had taken a gamble to fight at Antietam. Yet Lee was able by skillful maneuvering to take his smaller force and shift it to meet Union attacks. This ability was helped by Burnside's failure to attack on the Confederate right. Lee retreated into Maryland, having sustained 13,609 casualties to 27,767 for the Union forces, including those captured at Harpers Ferry.[43]

Lee has been criticized, as discussed by Douglas Southall Freeman, for dividing his army to take Harpers Ferry rather than securing Harpers Ferry before invading Maryland. He also has been challenged for sending Longstreet to Hagerstown based on inaccurate information which further reconnaissance might have revealed and for deciding to go into battle against a far larger force on September 17 at Antietam.[44]

Yet Lee's tactics were courageous. He gambled and seized the initiative. Through superb tactical management of the battlefield at Antietam, Lee was able to secure what was in effect a tactical draw, considered a defeat owing to his retreat from the field. However, there was no recognition from European powers, and Lincoln was soon to issue the Emancipation Proclamation. There is considerable scholarly disagreement as to whether Lee's movement north was a reasonable tactical choice or whether conserving his manpower and fighting from the tactical defensive would have been a more prudent course.[45] Regardless, Antietam showed that Lee continued to be an audacious man.

Lee next was dealing with General Ambrose Burnside, who had taken over the Army of the Potomac in the late fall of 1862 and was moving his army toward the Rappahannock River. Lee had a sprawling twenty-mile line from Fredericksburg to Port Royal. Lee was preparing to cover Fredericksburg as well as a major turning operation further down the Rappahannock, should it be made.

Burnside was delayed waiting for pontoon bridges to arrive and then chose to attack directly at Fredericksburg against a heavily fortified position on a steep hill. On December 13, 1862, Franklin's division attacked Jackson's troops on the southern part of the field, finding a gap that was sealed. Sumner's and Hooker's divisions attacked directly at Marye's Heights at their steepest point and against a sunken road. Nine thousand of the 12,653 casualties suffered by the Union forces came at Marye's Heights. The Confederate losses were 5,309.[46]

Lee had fought from the tactical advantage of a superb defensive position. Jackson had wanted to counterattack against the Union forces. However, the order was countermanded due to the Union artillery which covered the open ground between the two armies. Lee proved bold but not rash at Fredericksburg.

General Jubal A. Early described that situation in his address at Washington and Lee University as follows:

> There were some absurd stories about propositions alleged to have been made by General Jackson, for driving the enemy into the river. That great soldier did begin a forward movement about sunset, which I was to have led, but, just as my men were moving off, he countermanded the movement, because the enemy opened such a terrific artillery fire from the Stafford Heights and from behind the heavy embankments on the road leading through the bottoms on the south side of the river, that it was apparent that nothing could have lived in the passage across the plain of about a mile in width, over which we would have had to advance, to reach the enemy massed in that road. According to the statements of himself and officers, before the committee on the conduct of the war, Franklin, who had commanded the enemy's left, had confronting our right, from fifty-five to sixty thousand men, of whom only twenty thousand had been under fire.[47]

After Lee's triumph at Fredericksburg in one of the worst defeats of the war for the Union and the disastrous Mud March that followed, General Burnside was replaced by Fighting Joe Hooker in command of the Army of the Potomac. The Chancellorsville Campaign that followed was a major triumph for Lee.[48]

On April 29, 1863, the Union forces crossed the Rappahannock River. Union forces were moving to turn the left flank of the Confederate army. These Union troops were going to Chancellorsville, a village 14 miles west of Fredericksburg. Lee ordered Stuart to move toward Hooker with the forces of R.H. Anderson and Lafayette McLaws. Lee was given the difficult choice of retreating or striking the Union forces moving toward Chancellorsville.[49]

On April 30, 1863, Hooker had 75,000 men in the rear of the Confederate forces at Chancellorsville and 40,000 men under General Sedgwick threatening the Confederate lines at Fredericksburg. Lee's response was a brilliant gamble that risked disaster if it failed.

Lee initially divided his forces, leaving 10,000 men with General Jubal A. Early at Fredericksburg and keeping nearly 50,000 to strike at the Union forces going to Chancellorsville. On May 1, 1863, Stonewall Jackson's forces marched toward Chancellorsville and were engaged with Hooker's forces. Hooker lost his nerve and abandoned his initiative, withdrawing toward the Wilderness. Late in the day, Lee found out from J.E.B. Stuart and Fitzhugh Lee that Hooker's right wing at Chancellorsville was up in the air, not being anchored to any natural barrier.[50]

General Robert E. Lee and Stonewall Jackson met on the night of May 1, 1863, to discuss how best to proceed. Members of each of their staffs had reconnoitered and discussed whether a frontal assault was practicable. Considering the strength of the Union position, the only viable option was to attack Hooker's right flank or from the Confederate left.

Lee divided his army again. He left General Jubal A. Early with 10,000 men to oppose General Sedgwick at Fredericksburg. Stonewall Jackson was to take 26,000 men through a circuitous route to attack Hooker's exposed right flank at Chancellorsville. Lee with 20,000 men was to face Hooker's Union troops over a 3½ mile wide front.[51]

On May 2, 1863, Lee was involved in personally directing a series of feints by troops under Anderson and McLaws against the Union forces in Lee's front. Meanwhile, Jackson was undertaking an arduous 14 mile march over country roads led by a guide to attack the Union right flank. As members of the Union XI Corps were in camp about 5:30 P.M., Jackson attacked unexpectedly. Hooker's flank was pushed back 2 miles with substantial loss.

However, that night General Jackson rode out beyond his lines to reconnoiter for a subsequent attack. He was shot by his own men, who mistook him for Union cavalry. His left arm had to be amputated, and he died 8 days later.[52]

General J.E.B. Stuart took over for Jackson on May 3. Stuart took the offensive as did Anderson and McLaws, fighting to close the gap between their forces.

A Confederate shell struck a column of the Chancellor House against which General Hooker was leaning, stunning him. The Union forces then withdrew to a line closer to the Rappahannock River.[53]

Meanwhile, General Sedgwick at Fredericksburg had moved General Early from the heights there and was going forward to join Hooker at Chancellorsville.

General Jubal A. Early described the breakthrough of Union troops concentrated in a spot in the 5 mile long line he was charged with holding against forces three times as great — although there has been some criticism of how Early handled that situation.

> In the mean time, Sedgwick, whose corps numbered about twenty-four thousand men, and who had a division of another corps with him, making his whole force about thirty thousand, had crossed the river, at and below Fredericksburg, with the portion of his troops not already over, and, by concentrating three of his divisions at one point on the long line, of five or six miles, held by my forces, had on the 3d of May, after repeated repulses, broken through, immediately in the rear of Fredericksburg, where the stone wall was held by one regiment and four companies of another, the whole not exceeding five hundred men.[54]

General Cadmus Wilcox's forces were able to slow Sedgwick at Salem Church, several miles from Fredericksburg. Reinforcements from McLaw's division stabilized the Confederate line of the forces facing Sedgwick. On the 4th and 5th of May, 1863, moves by Early, Anderson and McLaws forced Sedgwick back across the river.[55]

Lee's aide, Walter Taylor, felt that Chancellorsville stood first among the battles.[56] Lee's strategy had unquestionably been audacious in the face of a far larger force and immense odds. Hooker had initially stolen a march on the Confederates and had put Lee's entire army in jeopardy, only to have Lee gamble, regain the initiative and achieve a decisive victory.

The Confederate victory at Chancellorsville did not allay the pressure on the Confederacy from the North's superiority in men and materials and Grant's threat to envelop Vicksburg and destroy the main Confederate force in the west. The recognition of the Confederacy by European powers continued to remain a possibility in spite of the Russian fleet's show of force. Efforts to detach troops from Lee's army to be sent to the west were considered and rejected by Confederate president Jefferson Davis and his cabinet. Instead, Lee himself moved his army north.[57]

Douglas Southall Freeman has conceded that Lee's invasion of the North in the Gettysburg campaign was a daring move and politically and militarily it probably was justified. The injudicious use of Confederate cavalry by General J.E.B. Stuart, denying Lee crucial intelligence for which Lee was ultimately responsible, as well as the failure of Ewell to take Cemetary Hill on July 1 and other failures involving the management of the battlefield, contributed to the outcome.[58]

Michael Palmer has questioned the lack on an invasion plan by Lee. He also faulted decentralized command and the decision for Pickett's attack on the third day. Edward H. Bonekemper noted Lee had rejected Longstreet's bleak assessment of the chances for success in an attack on the Union center on the third day and ordered the charge.[59]

Alan Nolan concluded there was an alternative to this campaigns leading to a total defeat — a defensive grand strategy in 1862 and 1863 from which occasional offensive actions could be taken. This strategy would have reduced the Confederate casualties of about 100,000 men and numbers of general officers during this period. Some of the general officers lost at Gettysburg included Lewis Armistead, Dick Garnett and William Barksdale.[60]

Regardless of the myriad of opinions on Gettysburg and the causes of the ultimate result, it can be fairly said that the Gettysburg campaign was a bold initiative fraught from the outset with major problems. Lee was certainly brave. But he was not always correct in his assessments and handling of his military operations.

Lee's courage did not go away in defeat. After Grant was named lieutenant-general in March 1864 and assumed overall command of the forces facing Lee, Lee continued to fight well against great odds in the Wilderness campaign, Spottsylvania, the North Ana and Cold Harbor during May and June 1864. However, Lee lost 32,000 men or 46 percent of his force, while Grant lost 50,000 men or 41 percent of his force. Lee had lost eight general officers killed, twelve wounded and two captured. Lee was also able to thwart Grant's effort to cut his lines of supply and destroy his army by movements to Petersburg in June 1864. However, he could not effectively replace his losses.[61]

In the Wilderness from May 5 through 7, 1864, Grant suffered approximately 17,500 casualties or about 15 percent of his force. Lee only suffered 7,500 casualties, but they constituted about 12 percent of his army. Lee had been outnumbered about two to one and prevented Grant from turning his flank. However, he was unable to stop his continued move south toward Richmond.[62]

Lee had again inflicted major casualties on the Union forces in the hard fighting at Spottsylvania from May 7 through 19, 1864, but lost nearly an entire division in the Mule Shoe Salient. After Grant failed to break Lee's lines at Spottsylvania, he moved toward Hanover Junction, where the Virginia Central Railroad and the Richmond, Fredericksburg and Potomac railroads crossed. After three days of stalemated fighting from May 23 through 26, Grant left the North Ana and moved east toward Cold Harbor.

In the battle of Cold Harbor on June 3, 1864, Grant assaulted a nearly impregnable position and lost 7,000 men to Lee's 1,500. It was perhaps the worst loss that Grant suffered at Lee's hands.[63]

General A.L. Long commended Lee for his effective defense in the Wilderness and the rest of the Overland Campaign against a numerically superior force on whom he inflicted substantial casualties.[64]

General John B. Gordon, who served under Lee, described how fiercely Lee's broken little army fought at that time in response to Lee's direction:

> Fragments of broken iron are welded closest and strongest in the hottest fires. So the shattered corps of Lee's army seemed to be welded together by Grant's hammering — by the blood and the sweat and the fury of the flames that swept over and around them. In the tangled jungles of the Wilderness; through the incessant uproar by day and by night at Spottsylvania; on the reddened banks of the North Ana; amidst the sickening slaughter of Cold Harbor — everywhere, and on every field where the American armies met in deadly grapple, whether behind breastworks or in the open, whether assaulting or repelling, whether broken by the resistless impact of beating back with clubbed muskets the headlong charges of Grant — these worn and battered soldiers of Lee seemed determined to compensate him for his paucity of numbers by a self-immolation and a steadfast valor, never surpassed, if ever equalled.[65]

However, Noah Andre Trudeau was much more critical of Lee's command decisions in the Wilderness campaign. He felt Lee had made some serious miscalculations. "In reviewing Lee's command decisions during the course of the Overland Campaign, it is hard not to conclude that the terrible stresses of the period seriously undermined both his self-confidence and military judgment. His miscalculations on the night of 7 May in the Wilderness and on 10 May at Spottsylvania might have been fatal had not chance and circumstance dictated otherwise."[66]

Alan T. Nolan finds that when Lee "was ultimately forced to resort to the defense in 1864, that strategy was effective even though his army and its leadership by that time had been grievously reduced by the casualties that resulted from his prior offensives.[67]

Peter Carmichael, in an analysis of Lee's generalship during the Overland Campaign, notes that Lee fended off an army double the size of his own with vastly superior weaponry. However, he cites Edward Porter Alexander's comments that if Lee had pulled Ewell and Hill out of their winter quarters, Lee might have obtained a decisive victory.

Carmichael feels that by the spring of 1864 the time had come for a defensive strategy to augment the war weariness and political turmoil before the election. "In the spring of 1864 everything depended on breaking the North's will to fight. Defensive tactics alone could have accomplished this goal."[68]

James Mason's letters of February 19, 1864, and April 13, 1864, to President Jefferson Davis were pessimistic about European intervention.[69] Since 1862, such European involvement had hinged on a decisive confederate victory. Time was running out for the Confederacy. One option was a defensive strategy that Carmichael has suggested would cause the war-weary North to consider discontinuing the conflict. Another was that a decisive battlefield victory of sufficient magnitude to undermine the North's desire to continue the conflict and at the same time demonstrate that the South could maintain its position was needed to turn the tide.

General Robert E. Lee, ever the charismatic gambler, determined in a matter of days to undertake his boldest plan yet: while being hemmed in by Grant at Richmond, to turn the tables and move to attack and take Washington. By doing damage in the city and potentially capturing President Lincoln or forcing him to leave, the Confederacy would be making an powerful statement to the world consistent with the manner in which Lee conducted most of his operations. Lee clearly believed this was possible. He sent his son, Captain Robert E. Lee, Jr., while Early was on the march to add a complex multi-pronged attack to free the Confederate prisoners at Point Lookout, which would also add a corps-sized force to Lee's army.[70]

The immediate impetus for Lee's decision was a note that outlined the situation in the Shenandoah Valley and suggested that Hunter's army could be expelled and the way to Washington opened. President Davis forwarded this note to General Robert E. Lee on June 11. Lee responded that it would take a corps for the desired action. On the 12th, Lee gave verbal orders to Gen. Jubal A. Early to prepare for operations. Written instructions arrived on the 12th for Early to leave at 3:00 A.M. on the 13th.[71]

Lee needed to protect his vital source of supplies at Lynchburg which he did with the dispatch of Early's army — which had the option of returning to Lee or going north. General Wade Hampton's defeat of Sheridan at Trevilian Station had made the enterprise possible. Hunter's retreat through West Virginia opened the opportunity to attack Washington and ultimately Point Lookout. Lee had great expectations for the initiative:

> How large and anxious were Gen. Lee's expectations from this movement may be judged from a letter he wrote to the War Department, on hearing of Early's arrival at Frederick. He desired of the Secretary of War most especially that the newspapers be requested to say nothing of his movements for some time to come, and that the department would not publish any communications from him which might indicate from its date his "distance from Richmond." But while the commander anxiously awaited further news from Early, expecting the possible capture of Washington, and the possi-

ble necessity of his personal presence in a new and towering theater of operations, the report came that Early, after having won the battle of Monocacy Bridge, had delayed to attack Washington, until overawed by reinforcements, and had retreated across the Potomac, satisfied with the success of his spoils.

Gen. Lee was disappointed, more than he cared to express, in the failure of his lieutenant to fulfill the expectations that had been indulged in the direction of Washington.[72]

Union general Martin D. Hardin, involved in the defenses of Washington during Early's attack there, asserted that there was a period of thirty-six hours when the Federal capital might have been taken and said that it might have been that General Early did not move as rapidly as he could have.[73] Had Washington been taken, the outcome of the election and the issue of European recognition could have changed.

Although Gary Gallagher found that Gen. Early had accomplished everything that Gen. Lee had asked in a month's marching and fighting, that clearly was in dispute.[74] By adopting the Point Lookout operation on the fly as part of the plan to capture Washington and free the prisoners, Lee clearly felt much was possible. The unlikeliness of the plan was its strength. No one would believe it could happen. Lee's gamble at least should have resulted in Washington being taken. It was not the risk that failed but its execution under circumstances which make up this story.

Chapter 3

Plans to Capture Washington and Point Lookout

Plans for an attack on Washington and President Lincoln by Colonel Bradley T. Johnson and an attack on the Point Lookout prison camp in Southern Maryland by General Robert E. Lee gradually evolved.[1] Union cavalry operations directed toward Richmond in the winter and spring of 1864 as well as pressure on the lines at Richmond in the Overland Campaign of May and June 1864 from the Wilderness to Cold Harbor gave impetus to plans for such a strike by the Confederates.

During the winter of 1863–1864, Col. Bradley T. Johnson of the Maryland cavalry originated a plan for a cavalry raid to capture President Lincoln at Soldier's Home near Washington, where he frequently stayed. Soldier's Home was Lincoln's summer residence, north of the city of Washington.[2] Johnson suggested the plan to General Wade Hampton. Hampton discussed the plan several times with Johnson and then approved it.[3]

One version of the plan was for Johnson to take the Maryland battalion with 250 troopers and cross the Potomac River above Georgetown. Then men were then to push by a battalion of Union cavalry known to be stationed at Georgetown and go to Soldier's Home, where Lincoln stayed. Having captured Lincoln, the raiding force would then send him across the Potomac River in the custody of a body of picked men. Johnson's main force would cut the wires between Washington and Baltimore. They would then move through western Maryland into the Shenandoah, or, if that was cut off, go up into Pennsylvania before going over into West Virginia near Grafton.[4]

Johnson himself described the plan in 1889 as taking the 1st Maryland Cavalry along the base of the Blue Ride through Culpepper, Madison and Loudon counties. The Confederate force would then cross the Potomac at Muddy Branch. Their plan was to surprise the 2nd Massachusetts Cavalry and move on to Soldier's Home. President Lincoln would then be taken south to Richmond. The command would then be divided with one party to cut the rail and telegraph lines between Baltimore and Washington and then go to White's Ford. The other was to move through Frederick and cross the Potomac at Point of Rocks or Shepherdstown and go north into Pennsylvania, West Virginia or Canada if necessary.[5]

Colonel Bradley T. Johnson's plan was not implemented immediately, as the 1st Maryland Cavalry was in winter quarters and was involved in operations around Richmond. General Robert E. Lee began contemplating a raid under Col. Johnson from Hanover Courthouse to release the prisoners at Point Lookout in January 1864.[6]

In early February 1864, Brig. Gen. Issac J. Wistar led a cavalry force which was to attack Richmond from the northeast. This raid was under the direction of Maj. Gen. Benjamin F. Butler operating as head of the Army of the James. Butler had instructed Wistar to capture public officials, release prisoners, and destroy property and stores. Part of his force was to include the

1st District of Columbia Cavalry under the command of Col. Lafayette C. Baker, who was head of the United States Secret Service. The 1st District of Columbia Cavalry had been at Williamsburg on January 30, 1864. It went on an expedition to Bottoms Bridge, twelve miles from Richmond, on February 5 through 8, 1864, before being back in camp for an extended period. Because of circumstances in the military theater, Wistar's raid had to be called off.[7]

Wistar had been commissioned a lieutenant colonel in the 71st Pennsylvania Infantry in 1861. Later that year he became colonel of the regiment. He was wounded at the Dunker Church at Antietam and became a brigadier general in November 1862. Wounded four times, Wistar resigned from the army on September 15, 1864. He later made a fortune financing railroad building. The commander of the 1st District of Columbia Cavalry, Lafayette C. Baker, was very energetic in trying to find and detain Southern sympathizers under the auspices of the Secret Service. The 1st District of Columbia Cavalry was billeted in Washington, where Baker headed his investigative operations.

On February 28, 1864, a force of Union cavalry under Brig. Gen. Judson Kilpatrick and Col. Ulric Dahlgren undertook an attack to capture Richmond and to destroy property and release Union prisoners at Belle Isle and Libby prisons. Kilpatrick's strategy was to ride around the flank of the Army of Northern Virginia under Gen. Robert E. Lee on the Rapidan and attack Richmond directly. President Lincoln had been involved in the planning of the operation and had requested that the son of Admiral John A. Dahlgren, Ulric Dahlgren, take part.

Kilpatrick's main force crossed the Rappahannock River above Fredericksburg on February 28, 1864, and, as planned, rode around the flank of Lee's army. Dahlgren, with a command of about 500 troopers, was to cross the James River above Richmond. Dahlgren's force consisted of details from the 1st Maine, 1st Vermont, 2nd New York, 5th New York and 5th Michigan cavalry regiments. He was to try to attack Belle Isle Prison on the south side of the James while Kilpatrick was attacking Richmond from the north.[8] On March 1, 1864, Colonel Bradley T. Johnson received a telegram from General Lee that a large body of Union cavalry had moved around his army's flank and was headed for Hanover Junction. Johnson sent out scouts, who discovered that the Union cavalry column had crossed the Virginia Central Railroad and was headed for Richmond.[9]

The Maryland Line under Col. Johnson's command in March 1864 consisted of the 2nd Maryland Infantry, the 1st Maryland Cavalry and the Baltimore Light Artillery.[10] On March 1, 1864, Company A of the 1st Maryland Cavalry pursued the Union cavalry under Kilpatrick and skirmished all day with the rear guard.[11]

Brigadier General Kilpatrick with his force of about 3,500 cavalry went down the Fredericksburg Road toward Richmond on March 1, 1864. Lee's army on the Rapidan depended on supplies from the Shenandoah Valley and the South, which came by rail across six bridges on the North Ana, South Ana and the Middle River. If Kilpatrick's force going toward Hanover Junction destroyed those railroad bridges, Lee's supply line would be cut.[12]

Colonel Bradley T. Johnson had sent orders to his pickets to destroy the boats on the Pamunkey River between Hanover Court House and White House to prevent the passage of the Union forces in that direction. Scouting parties were sent out in an expanding circle to the north and west in an effort to ascertain the location of the Union force. Just before dawn on March 1, Col. Johnson struck a Union picket force at Taylorsville, two miles from Hanover Junction, and found that the main body of Kilpatrick's force had moved on toward Richmond.[13] Johnson moved on to Ashland Station, where he prevented Union forces from burning the depot and destroying the railroad. Johnson found Kilpatrick's troopers at Yellow Tavern, about five miles from Richmond, in a line of battle with artillery fire already going on. Johnson was able to capture five men carrying dispatches from Col. Ulric Dahlgren to Kilpatrick.

Colonel Dahlgren moved to cross the Virginia Central Railroad at Fredericks Mills and went about 20 miles above Richmond on the James. The James River was too high and Dahlgren could not cross it there. The guide who had led them into this situation was hung. Dahlgren thus moved to attack Richmond from the west. After dark, Dahlgren made an attack that drove the Confederates to their inner works before retiring.[14]

The information obtained by the Confederates under Johnson from the capture of Col. Dahlgren's couriers revealed that Dahlgren was planning to attack on the River Road. Dahlgren had asked in the intercepted message for Kilpatrick to attack vigorously in his support.

General Wade Hampton in his report on March 6, 1864, stated he believed that the Union forces probably would have taken Richmond had it not been for Johnson's forces intercepting the dispatch from Col. Dahlgren to Brig. Gen. Kilpatrick concerning a simultaneous attack.[15]

Colonel Bradley T. Johnson then attacked Kilpatrick's pickets in the center of their line of battle on the

GENERAL BRADLEY T. JOHNSON DEVELOPED A PLAN OF ATTACK ON WASHINGTON (LIBRARY OF CONGRESS).

Brooke Turnpike and drove them in to the main force. Kilpatrick, noting a force in his rear and not wanting to be cut off, did not attack Richmond but moved down the peninsula and crossed the Chickahominy River at Meadow Bridge, where he went into camp for the night. Hampton's men attacked Kilpatrick's camp on the night of March 1, 1864. The Union cavalry force was driven off.[16]

On March 2, 1864, Johnson crossed over the Chickahominy River and pursued Kilpatrick's rear guard to Old Church. Johnson attacked the Union rear guard there and took a number of prisoners. Kilpatrick formed a line of battle, and Johnson fell back a half a mile before renewing his attack.

Kilpatrick continued down the peninsula, being harassed by Johnson's cavalry as he went. Four hundred of Kilpatrick's men attacked Johnson's small force on two sides, passing through his line but losing 45 men.[17] An infantry force came up to Tunstall's station from Williamsburg to the aid of Kilpatrick. At Tunstall's Station, Kilpatrick joined forces with men of Major Gen. Butler's command.[18]

Major General Wade Hampton described Col. Bradley Johnson's conduct during the operation against the raiding Union forces as follows:

> I cannot close my report without expressing my appreciation of the conduct of Colonel Bradley T. Johnson and his gallant command. With a mere handful of men he met the enemy at Beaver Dam and he never lost sight of them until they had passed Tunstall's Station, hanging on their rear, striking them constantly, and displaying throughout the very highest qualities of a soldier.[19]

Colonel Ulric Dahlgren, in trying to attack Richmond from the west, was met with stiff resistance from a Richmond city battalion under the command of Brig. Gen. G.W. Custis Lee. Dahlgren broke off his attack and tried to go around Richmond to the north. On the night of March 2, 1864, Col. Dahlgren broke his command into two parts.[20] Dahlgren had only two other commissioned officers and between 75 and 135 men according to various estimates among officers involved. Unable to cross the Pamunkey River at Dabney's Ferry due to Col. Johnson's destruction of the boats, Col. Dahlgren was attacked in King and Queen County by a party under the command of Lieutenant Pollard of Company H of the 9th Virginia Cavalry and Captain Fox of the 5th Virginia Cavalry. Dahlgren was killed and most of his cavalry command captured.

A document was found on Dahlgren's body which expressed some of his purposes.

> Guides, Pioneers (With Oakum, Turpentine and Torpedoes)[,] Signal officer, Commissary, Scouts and Picked Men in Rebel Uniform:
> Men will remain on the north bank and move down with the force on the south bank, not getting ahead of them; and the communications can be kept up without giving an alarm it must be done. Everything depends upon a surprise, and NO ONE must be allowed to pass ahead of the column. Information must be gathered in regard to the crossings of the river, so that should we be repulsed on the south side we will know where to cross at the nearest point. All mills must be burned and the canal destroyed, and also everything which can be used by the rebels must be destroyed, including the boats on the river. Should a ferry-boat be seized and can be worked, have it moved down. Keep the force on the south side posted of any important movement of the enemy, and in case of danger some of the scouts must swim the river and bring us the information. As we approach the city, the party must take great care that they do not get ahead of the other party on the south side, and must conceal themselves and watch our movements. We will try to secure the bridge to the city (one mile below Belle Island) and release our prisoners at the same time. If we do not succeed, then must we dash down, and we will try to carry the bridge from each side. When necessary, the men must be filed through the woods and along the river bank. The bridges once secured and the prisoners loose and over the river, the bridges will be secured and the city destroyed. The men must keep together well in hand, and once in the city, it must be destroyed, and Jeff Davis and his Cabinet killed. Pioneers will go along with combustible material. The officer must use his discretion about the time of assisting us. Horses and cattle which we do not need immediately must be shot rather than left. Everything on the canal and elsewhere of service to the rebels must be destroyed. As General Custer may follow me, be careful not to give a false alarm.[21]

The Kilpatrick and Dahlgren raid had led to a demand for retribution among Southerners. General Wade Hampton was confident that the plan to abduct President Lincoln could be successful. He wanted to undertake the mission himself with a force of about 4,000 cavalry. General Philip Sheridan's subsequent advance on Richmond made Hampton's participation difficult. Meanwhile, in March 1864 the 1st Maryland Cavalry was engaged in some minor cavalry actions at Dabney's Ferry and King William Court House. Much of April 1864 was spent in camp or on picket duty. There were 16 officers and 294 men present or on duty on April 20, 1864.

General Philip H. Sheridan started his raid on Richmond on May 9, 1864, and attacked Beaver Dam Station. This raid followed the furious fighting in the Wilderness from May 5 through 7, 1864, and further heavy fighting at Spottsylvania Court House climaxing on May 12, 1864, when Lee lost about 4,000 men captured in the Mule Shoe Salient.

Colonel Ridgely Brown with 150 men attacked Sheridan's advance force driving in the pickets the night of May 9. General J.E.B. Stuart had Col. Brown harass and delay Sheridan's forces. Brown's force then moved to Hanover Junction and joined the 2nd Maryland Infantry and the Baltimore Light Artillery.[22]

On May 10, Gen. J.E.B. Stuart ordered Col. Bradley T. Johnson to watch General Lee's flank with the 1st Maryland Cavalry. Stuart, with 2,500 men, put himself between Sheridan and Richmond.[23]

Stuart intercepted Sheridan's force at Yellow Tavern. On May 11, 1864, the two forces battled all day with Stuart being killed and Richmond successfully defended.[24] Colonel Johnson with two guns of the Baltimore Light Artillery and the 1st Maryland Cavalry defended a railroad bridge on the South Ana River and other bridges until May 21, 1864. Johnson was involved in ascertaining Grant's movements, discovering the movements of Sheridan and Burnside. On May 27, 1864, Col. Johnson was ordered to report to Gen. Fitzhugh Lee at Hanover Court House.[25]

During the latter part of May and the first weeks of June 1864, Col. Bradley T. Johnson was engaged in numerous cavalry actions. On May 27, 1864, Johnson was ordered by General Lunsford Lomax, to whom Johnson was attached in General Fitzhugh Lee's Cavalry Division, to assist Col. Baker of the 5th N.C. near Dabney's Ferry. At Pollard's Farm, Johnson ran into Gen. George Custer's brigade of about 4,000 men. Johnson lost between 50 and 60 men and had his horse shot out from under him. Further fighting occurred on June 1, 1864, at the South Ana bridges, with Col. Ridgely Brown being killed.[26]

At the Battle of Trevilian Station, the largest all-cavalry battle of the Civil War, Johnson's Maryland Line cavalry force, as part of Gen. Fitzhugh Lee's command, did not appear to be engaged on the first day. Johnson said, "In the battle of Trevilians I had, during the second day, been made to do pretty much the duty of a brigade, for which my force was utterly inadequate." Private Henry Clay Mettan of the 1st Maryland Cavalry, Company E, said that on July 12 at Trevillian Station, Johnson's men took a conspicuous and useful part in the battle.[27] The 1st Maryland Cavalry was engaged on June 12, 1864, in holding the end of the Confederate line to the left of Gen. Wickham's brigade in Fitzhugh Lee's division. Mettan reported the regiment as capturing over 100 horses and men.[28]

After the Battle of Trevilian Station, General Hampton asked Colonel Johnson to prepare for the raid on Washington to abduct President Lincoln. Johnson engaged in picking the best horses and men he could for the enterprise.[29]

Lee felt it was crucial to have the proper person to command the operation against Point Lookout. The person Lee wanted was Bradley T. Johnson, whom he felt was best suited for the task. Being a Marylander, he knew the country.[30]

Johnson had served under Stonewall Jackson in the 1862 Shenandoah Valley campaign. He had also temporarily but effectively commanded a brigade in the Second Bull Run (Manassas) campaign.

Johnson talked to Maj. Gen. Jubal A. Early, who was moving through the Gordonsville area on the way to Lynchburg. After being advised of Johnson's mission, Early told him to go to Waynesboro in the Shenandoah Valley and to guard his rear with them, then to go to Maryland together.[31]

Johnson was then made a brigadier general and named to command the brigade of Gen. William "Grumble" Jones, who had been killed at the Battle of the Piedmont. That force consisted of the 8th and 24th Virginia Cavalry and the 34th, 36th and 37th Virginia battalions of cavalry.[32] Johnson subsequently was in Early's march on Washington and led the raid around Baltimore to free the prisoners at Point Lookout.

After Early's successful defense of Lynchburg after having been dispatched from Lee's army on June 12, 1864, and Gen. David Hunter's withdrawal into West Virginia to the Ohio River, Early met up with now Brigadier General Bradley T. Johnson on his way north in the Shenandoah Valley.

The cavalry division in Early's Army of the Valley was commanded by General Robert Ransom, a former infantry officer with limited experience in leading cavalry. Early's three cavalry brigades were commanded by Brigadier General John McCausland, Brigadier General Bradley T. Johnson and Brigadier General "Mudwall" Jackson.

On July 3, 1864, Johnson spearheaded the Confederate advance to Leetown, a few miles north of Winchester, where he was driven back. After participating in minor cavalry actions in the Martinsburg–Harpers Ferry area from July 3 through July 6, Johnson was in the forefront of the Confederate push toward Frederick.

When General Robert E. Lee added the attack on Point Lookout to the plan to take Washington, Johnson was chosen to lead the planned cavalry attack by land on Point Lookout as well as the destruction of communications links between Washington and Baltimore and the north. In conjunction with Colonel Harry Gilmor, General Johnson wreaked havoc in the Baltimore area, cutting vital rail links, briefly capturing Maj. Gen. William Franklin, and cutting vital telegraph links as well. Ultimately, Johnson was called back while on the road to Point Lookout and helped both with rearguard operations in Early's retreat from Washington and with protecting his crossing of the Potomac.[33] However, even though Lee's plan failed in its execution, the plan to abduct President Lincoln remained in play.

The attack on Washington by Early's forces and the related aborted raid on Point Lookout did not end Confederate efforts to abduct President Lincoln and change the course of the war. Thomas Nelson Conrad, a Confederate spy, was brought to Richmond in August 1864 on an assignment involving President Lincoln.[34]

On September 5, 1864, Col. John Singleton Mosby and Lieutenant Charles Cawood, commander of Confederate Signal Corps operations in King George County, Virginia, were told to cooperate with Conrad. Conrad was sent with $400 in gold to the Northern Neck of Virginia on September 17, 1864, with a group of signal corps men. Conrad arrived in Washington in late September 1864 and observed President Lincoln, trying to ascertain the best place to seize him and determining a route to take home upon his capture.[35]

Conrad devised two alternative escape routes. One was to take the Patuxent River, where a ship would then travel up the Rappahannock River to an area still controlled by the Confederates at Urbanna. The other was to go through Charles County, Maryland, to the Potomac and across to Richmond—a route proximate to that taken by John Wilkes Booth after the assassination of President Lincoln.

General George Washington Custis Lee was to make his troops available as a security force to guard the escape routes once Lincoln was captured.[36]

Conrad explained what he did to further the plot to capture President Lincoln:

> Ten days after securing the order for the War Department at Richmond I had reached Washington safely and began to reconnoiter the White House. I had to ascertain Mr. Lincoln's customary movements First.... Lafayette Square only a stone's throw north of the White House entrance was the very place I needed as a vantage ground. Partially concealed by large trees of the park, I found no difficulty in observing the official's ingress and egress, noting about what hours of the day he might venture forth, size of the accompanying escorts if any; and all other details.... Hours and days of watching were necessary before I learned that he usually left the President's quarters in the cool of the evening on pleasant days, driving and accompanied in his private carriage, straight out Fourteenth Street to Columbia Road then across to the high elevation.... We had to determine at what point it would be the most expedient to capture the carriage and take possession of Mr. Lincoln, and then whether to move him through Maryland to the lower Potomac ... across on the Upper Potomac and deliver the prisoner to Mosby's Confederacy for transportation to Richmond. To secure the points necessary for reaching a proper conclusion about all these things required days of careful work and observation. ... Having scouted the country pretty thoroughly ... we finally concluded to take the lower Potomac route.[37]

The plot to abduct President Lincoln was not undertaken. However, John Wilkes Booth and others in Washington and nearby Clintion, Maryland, later undertook the successful attempt to kill President Lincoln in the spring of 1865 after the Civil War had come to a conclusion.[38]

CHAPTER 4

Trevilian Station

General Jubal A. Early was able to take Stonewall Jackson's old corps from the lines at Richmond and move to Lynchburg by the Virginia Central from Charlottesville because General Wade Hampton and the Confederate cavalry were able to prevent General Philip H. Sheridan from destroying the railroad and uniting with Gen. David Hunter for a coordinated move to Lynchburg or returning to Gen. Ulysses S. Grant's army. Sheridan was soundly defeated at Trevilian Station on June 11 and 12, 1864, and forced to return alone to Grant's army without having accomplished any of his objectives. After his successful defense of Lynchburg, Early thus was also able to move north on Washington and ultimately Point Lookout in implementing Lee's daring strategy.

The Trevilian Station expedition was designed by Gen. Sheridan to draw the Confederate cavalry away from the Army of the Potomac as Grant's forces were moving across the James River to move on Petersburg south of Richmond. Sheridan said:[1]

> There also appeared to be another object, viz., to remove the enemy's cavalry from the south side of the Chicahominy, as, in case we attempted to cross the James River, the large cavalry force could make such resistance at the difficult crossings to give the enemy time to transfer his force to oppose the movement.[2]

Sheridan understood Grant had told Hunter to advance to Charlottesville, where he would unite with Sheridan. Sheridan and Hunter would then destroy the James River Canal and the Virginia Central Railroad and then link up with the Army of the Potomac.[3]

Sheridan was to move along the north bank of the North Ana River. When he reached the point across from Trevilian Station on the Virginia Central Railroad, Sheridan planned to cross the river by bridge or ford it. Upon crossing, Sheridan's objective was to rapidly move to capture the depot at Trevilian Station and tear up the Virginia Central track from Louisa Court House to Gordonsville. Having destroyed the railroad, Sheridan then would move to Charlottesville to locate and join General David Hunter.[4] The two united commands could then move to Lynchburg.

Grant's priority was the destruction of the James River Canal and the Virginia Central Railroad. If General Hunter did not receive his orders until he was in the Shenandoah Valley between Staunton and Lynchburg, he was to turn east until he intersected the Virginia Central's track to Lynchburg and was to continue to move east, thoroughly destroying it, until he met up with Sheridan. After Grant's purposes were accomplished by Sheridan and Hunter, they were to return to the Army of the Potomac.[5]

Hunter failed to follow General Grant's directives and instead went to Lynchburg with inadequate ammunition, destroying civilian property and the Virginia Military Institute. This left both Hunter and Sheridan on their own to their mutual disadvantage.

Grant's strategy was brilliant. While the Army of the Potomac was crossing the James and moving on Petersburg, a critical railroad hub and logistics center for Lee, Sheridan and Hunter

General Philip Sheridan led raid on Trevilian Station (National Archives).

would be interrupting Lee's critical line of supply. This would be accomplished by destruction of important railroad facilities on the Virginia Central and the Orange and Alexandria but also by destroying the crucial logistics center of Lynchburg before returning to help hem in Lee at Petersburg. As with Lee's plan for Point Lookout and attack on Washington, a masterful strategy failed in its execution, both on the part of the forces of Hancock and Baldy Smith attacking Petersburg and on the part of Sheridan and Hunter.

Sheridan did draw the Confederate cavalry away from the James but did not wreak havoc on the railroads. He failed to make the connection with Hunter, to destroy the Virginia Central Railroad — which Early used to get from Charlottesville to Lynchburg to defeat Hunter — to sever Lee's supply line and to bring Hunter back to the Army of the Potomac.[6] Brig. Gen. Thomas L. Rosser of Wade Hampton's cavalry division described the consequences of Hampton's success and Sheridan's failure at Trevilian Station this way: "Had Sheridan won the battle he would have gone on to Lynchburg, or wherever he desired, as there would have been no one to oppose him. He would have destroyed the railroads, canals, depots, and indeed, cut General Lee off and starved him out of Petersburg and Richmond."[7]

Sheridan's cavalry force had been severely depleted from hard campaigning following the start of the Wilderness fighting on May 8, 1864. A substantial number of Union troopers had been killed, wounded or captured. Only part of the cavalrymen who started the Wilderness campaign on May 8 were available to Sheridan as he started out on June 7, 1864, on his raid.

The Union 1st Cavalry Division was commanded by Brig. Gen. Alfred T.A. Torbert, a former infantry officer. The first brigade of that division was commanded by Brig. Gen. George

Armstrong Custer, who had the 1st Michigan Cavalry, the 5th Michigan Cavalry, the 6th Michigan Cavalry and the 7th Michigan Cavalry under his command. Colonel Thomas C. Devin commanded the second brigade, which included the 17th Pennsylvania Cavalry as well as the 4th New York Cavalry, the 6th New York Cavalry and the 9th New York Cavalry. Torbert's third brigade was commanded by Brig. Gen. Wesley Merritt, who had the 1st US Cavalry, the 2nd US Cavalry, the 5th US Cavalry, the 6th Pennsylvania Cavalry and the 19th New York Cavalry in his unit.[8] Captain Theophilus F. Rodenbough, in command of the 2nd US Cavalry regiment, was awarded the Congressional Medal of Honor for distinguished service at Trevilian Station.[9]

Brigadier General David M. Gregg's 2nd Cavalry Division had two brigades of cavalry and one of horse artillery. Brigadier General Henry E. Davies commanded the 1st Massachusetts Cavalry, the 1st New Jersey Cavalry, the 1st Pennsylvania Cavalry, the 6th Ohio Cavalry and the 10th New York Cavalry. Colonel J.I. Gregg of the 2nd Cavalry Division's 2nd Cavalry Brigade commanded the 1st Maine Cavalry, the 2nd Pennsylvania Cavalry, the 4th Pennsylvania Cavalry, the 8th Pennsylvania Cavalry, the 13th Pennsylvania Cavalry and the 16th Pennsylvania Cavalry.[10]

Captain James M. Robertson's Brigade of Horse Artillery contained Batteries H and I of the 1st US Artillery and Batteries B, L and M of the 2nd US Artillery, consisting of 20 guns.

Brigadier General Matthew Butler of Wade Hampton's command estimated Sheridan had 10,337 men at Trevilian Station.[11] Brevet Brigadier General Theophilus Rodenbough of the 2nd US Cavalry believed Sheridan had about 8,000 men.[12] Other estimates were from 7,000 to 8,000 to 10,200.[13]

Sheridan's force started out from New Castle on the Pamunkey River on June 7, 1864, and crossed that river on pontoons. The force moved via New Market and Mt. Pleasant to Young's Store, where they bivouacked on the night of June 9. On June 10, 1864, Sheridan's forces crossed the South Ana River, stopping for the night on the road to Trevilian Station.[14]

General Robert E. Lee sent General Hampton to intercept Sheridan. Thomas Nelson Conrad of the 3rd Virginia Cavalry and the Confederate Secret Service had been scouting on the morning of June 8, 1864, and had come across a mulatto who claimed to have just escaped from Sheridan's headquarters and to have important information. The man claimed to know a lot about the raid including where Sheridan was going. He was sent from General Rosser's command to General Hampton's.[15] On June 7 a scout in General Rooney Lee's division had told Hampton that Sheridan was making a raid.[16]

On the morning of June 9, 1864, Hampton's division marched toward Beaver Dam Station. Clearly Hampton had known precisely where Sheridan was going and made up for the lengthy head start that Sheridan had. Rosser and Young's brigades of Hampton's division were encamped closer to Gordonsville. General Fitzhugh Lee's division was near Louisa Court House.[17]

Brigadier General Wesley Merritt's regular US Cavalry forces camped about 6 miles north of Trevilian Station. Colonel Thomas Devin's brigade was about 5 miles northeast of the station, while Brigadier General George Armstrong Custer was about 3½ miles north of Louisa Court House. Brigadier General David M. Gregg's division was along the roads from Carpenter's Ford. J. Irwin Gregg's brigade was in the rear.[18] There was considerable Confederate scouting activity that night, indicating a sizeable Confederate force was in the vicinity.[19]

There was a six or seven mile distance between the divisions of Hampton and Fitzhugh Lee on the night of June 10. Both Hampton and Sheridan anticipated a battle on the 11th.[20]

General Wade Hampton met on the morning of June 11 with Brigadier General Thomas L. Rosser and Brigadier General Matthew C. Butler. Hampton proposed to fight. His plan was to join with General Fitzhugh Lee's division near Clayton's Store and then face Sheridan's forces.[21]

Sheridan, on the morning of June 11, formed a line of battle with Brig. Gen. Wesley Merritt and his US Cavalry brigade on the right, then Devin, Custer and Gregg going to the left. Gen.

Fitzhugh Lee's advance forces met pickets from Custer's 7th Michigan Cavalry. Sheridan advanced to attack Hampton.[22]

Brig. General Matthew C. Butler engaged the 4th South Carolina to meet the heavy column of Sheridan's men and dismounted his troopers. Butler's men were heavily engaged with a superior force of Sheridan's men for several hours when Butler was informed Custer had gone around his right flank. Fierce fighting took place in dense underbrush. Under orders from General Hampton, he slowly withdrew near the railroad.[23]

General Fitzhugh Lee, coming up from Louisa Court House, had taken another road and had not encountered Custer's forces. There was a gap between his forces and Hampton's. Custer went through the gap and captured Hampton's wagon train and a large number of horses behind the Confederate lines. Hampton then ordered Brigadier General Rosser to attack Custer, with Hampton's other brigades also attacking Custer and threatening to envelope him.[24]

Custer's men were fighting in a hollow circle, being pressed by the Confederate cavalry on all sides. James Kidd, commanding the 6th Michigan, remembered:

> For a time there was a melee which had no parallels in the annals of cavalry fighting in the Civil War, unless it may have been at Brandy Station or Buckland Mills. Custer's line was in the form of a circle and he was fighting an enterprising foe on either flank and both front and rear. Fitzhugh Lee charged and captured a part of Pennington's battery. The Seventh Michigan led by Breuer recaptured it. Fragments of all the regiments in the brigade rallied around Custer for the mounted fighting, of which there was plenty, while the Fourth and Sixth dismounted and took care of the rear. Custer was everywhere present giving directions to his subordinate commanders, and more than one mounted charge was participated by him in person.[25]

The first and second brigades of Gregg's 2nd Division vigorously attacked Gen. Fitzhugh Lee's troops on the afternoon of the 11th to allow Custer's brigade to extricate itself around 5 P.M. Lee faced the Union left flank with the two parts of the Union line forming a right angle.[26]

Custer had taken a fearful beating in his attack in isolation from the rest of the Union cavalry command. The 1st Michigan lost 1 killed, 5 wounded and 59 captured. The 5th Michigan Cavalry had 4 killed, 6 wounded and 136 captured. The 6th Michigan Cavalry had 5 killed, 22 wounded and 60 captured. With 1 killed, 14 wounded and 44 captured, the 7th Michigan cavalry had the fewest losses. All told, Custer lost 361

GENERAL WADE HAMPTON LED CONFEDERATES TO VICTORY AT TREVILIAN STATION (LIBRARY OF CONGRESS).

men or 22 percent of his force engaged on the 11th alone. His losses were over half of the total Union casualties on that date.[27] George Booth described it as follows:

> At one time Custer, with his brigade, broke through our line and captured the horses of Butler's Brigade. The men being engaged at that time on foot, we had just reported to Rosser on our left, when the news of the mishap reached him. At once he started for the scene of the difficulty, charging into Custer's column, now somewhat disordered by their success, and in a little time they were defeated and we had them on the run, recovering Butler's horses and making many captives of the men and horses from the enemy.[28]

The Confederate forces at the end of the day on the 11th fell back along the Gordonsville Road. Sheridan's forces were prepared for a counterattack, which did not come. Sheridan controlled the battlefield and had a tactical victory on the first day even though he had achieved none of his objectives.

Although on the 11th the 4th New York Cavalry had been able to tear up some track on the Virginia Central and Hampton had lost 628 men killed, wounded or captured, Sheridan had not been able to effectively cut Lee's supply lines, destroy the Virginia Central or the James River Canal or unite with Gen. Hunter, who had gone to Lynchburg.

On the morning of June 12, 1864, Brigadier General Matthew C. Butler of Hampton's division was posted about a mile above Trevilian Station.

Young's brigade, commanded by Wright, was in the center and Rosser on the right. The Confederate line was at an obtuse angle on the railroad embankment protected by hastily constructed breastworks of rail fencing and other materials.[29] The point rested on the Gordonsville Road. It was anchored by the railroad cut. Thomson's battery of two Napoleons was to the right of the center of the line. Thomson's other guns as well as Hart's battery were posted at intervals in the Confederate position.[30]

Gregg's division of Union cavalry spent the morning destroying track on the Virginia Central from Louisa Court House to a mile west of Trevilian Station.[31] About 3:00 P.M. on June 12, Sheridan ordered Torbert to take his division on a reconnaissance along the Gordonsville and Charlottesville roads.[32] Custer's Michigan brigade was in the lead and encountered Confederate forces dismounted and behind breastworks. After a reconnaissance showed the breastworks to be heavily manned, Custer ordered his men to dismount and fight on foot. The 6th Michigan Cavalry was on the left of the railroad and the 7th Michigan Cavalry on their left. Several assaults were made by Custer's men on the Confederate position. Each was repulsed. Brigadier General Wesley Merritt's reserve brigade on the right flank took substantial casualties when attacked by men of Fitzhugh Lee's division.[33]

Kidd's 6th Michigan Cavalry troopers and the 7th Michigan Cavalry drove Butler's pickets back to their formidable positions. Private Daniel Eldridge of the 7th Michigan Cavalry called the fight on June 12 one of the hottest he had seen during the war.[34] The 1st Michigan Cavalry was met with a hail of bullets trying to cross the field in front of the Confederate works, where Butler's protected men were using their rifles to good effect.[35] The 7th Michigan exchanged fired with Butler's men in their works for several hours. Custer had elected to remain in a protected line and exchanged fire from there.[36]

The 17th Pennsylvania Cavalry and 4th and 6th New York Cavalry reported to Brigadier General Wesley Merritt. Merritt's regiment along with elements of Devin's command attacked Butler's position. The 4th New York Cavalry took fifty-one casualties in less than two hours. The attack was repulsed, but Merritt continue to attack Butler's line.[37]

Between 1:00 P.M. and the coming of darkness, numerous Union assaults were made upon the entrenched Confederate position at the angle. During the fighting, Williston's horse artillery effectively utilized its guns. Torbert's men also poured substantial fire on the Confederate position.[38] By the time of the last attack, the Confederate and Union lines were only a few yards apart.[39]

Butler's men inside the angle suffered only 50 casualties on June 12, as did another Confederate brigade posted in that line. The casualties were higher in General Fitzhugh Lee's division, with Brigadier General Wickham experiencing 33 casualties and Brigadier General Lunsford Lomax similar numbers.

Custer's brigade lost 52 men; Colonel Thomas C. Devin, 84; and Brigadier General Wesley Merritt, 115. Repeated attacks on a very strong position took a substantial toll on a Union cavalry force that had already suffered major losses the day before. Sheridan had been decisively defeated at Trevilian Station.

After the Battle of Trevilian Station, Sheridan moved out about midnight on June 12, 1864, heading for White House Landing. Hampton's men did not pursue Sheridan aggressively on the 13th. Much of the day was spent attending to the Confederate wounded.[40] Meanwhile, Sheridan continued his slow retreat back to Grant's army. Hampton had shadowed Sheridan's line of march. Union cavalry horses were dropping along the way from overwork and lack of fodder. White House Landing was threatened by Hampton until Sheridan's return on June 21, when Hampton retreated.[41]

The Confederate victory of Sheridan at Trevilian Station was described by Colonel Thomas T. Mumford as the proudest achievement of the Confederate cavalry during the Civil War.[42] Sheridan's field expedition was pushed back to the Union Lines.

Lee, by sending Wade Hampton to intercept Sheridan, had made it possible to continue Lee's initiative. Had Hampton failed, Sheridan could have joined Gen. David Hunter and fulfilled Grant's objectives. As it was, Sheridan returned, having incurred substantial losses, having been decisively defeated and having fulfilled none of his objectives.

Except for destroying some track in the area of Trevilian Station and Louisa Court House, Sheridan had failed in a primary objective, which was to destroy the Virginia Central Railroad as an important means of providing provisions for Lee's army. Moreover, there had been no destruction whatsoever of the James River Canal by Sheridan's forces.

Sheridan had also failed in

Brig. Gen. George Armstrong Custer incurred Heavy Losses at Trevilian Station (National Archives).

his second objective, which was to link up with Gen. David Hunter. However, Hunter had also failed to follow Grant's orders and meet up with Sheridan. Grant had directed that if Hunter did not get his instructions until he was between Staunton and Lynchburg, he was to turn east by the most practicable route until he crossed the Lynchburg line of the Virginia Central. Hunter was to follow that railroad until he reached Sheridan's command.[43]

Hunter did not turn east toward Charlottesville and Gordonsville when at Staunton. Nor did he turn east later, but rather moved on to Lexington. Had Hunter moved to effectuate a junction with Sheridan via the Virginia Central, he might have been able to link up with him or to threaten Hampton's forces from the rear. At least, there might have been communication between the Union commanders, which might have affected Sheridan's tactics and strategy. Gen. David Hunter found out on June 13 about Sheridan's defeat at Trevilian Station.[44] However, had he followed Grant's directions and been in communication with Sheridan prior to that time, he might have been in a position to fulfill the crucial lynchpin of Grant's plan — the unification of the two commands. Had that taken place, Lee's gamble with Early's force could realistically not have been implemented. The third main objective Sheridan failed to accomplish was to bring General Hunter's army of 18,000 men back to the Army of the Potomac.[45] As a result of Trevilian Station, Lynchburg and Lee's supply lines could be saved and the bold move to the north undertaken.

CHAPTER 5

General Hunter Fails to Move in the Shenandoah Valley as Directed

Major General Franz Sigel was defeated at New Market in the Shenandoah Valley on May 15, 1864, by Confederate forces commanded by General John C. Breckinridge.[1] This important victory allowed the Confederates, rather than Sigel, to temporarily control the Shenandoah Valley—a major source for supplies for General Robert E. Lee's Army of Northern Virginia.[2] Lee knew that his army could not afford to lose access to the foodstuffs and supplies of southwestern Virginia and beyond.

Lieutenant General Ulysses S. Grant was informed by Chief of Staff Henry Halleck on May 17, 1864, that Sigel had been defeated and was moving to Strasburg. Halleck also informed Grant that Secretary of War Edwin Stanton was proposing General David Hunter to replace Sigel. Grant agreed to the appointment of Hunter.[3]

Major General David Hunter was an 1822 graduate of the U.S. Military Academy at West Point. He stood 25th in a class of 44. After leaving West Point, Hunter served as a paymaster. He held this position during the Mexican War and subsequently. Before the 1860 election, Hunter wrote Abraham Lincoln in Springfield warning him of an assassination threat. After Lincoln's election, Hunter again warned Lincoln of possible danger from officers at Fort Leavenworth. These contacts developed into a mutual friendship. Hunter was granted leave from Fort Leavenworth and was part of a group of officers Lincoln took with him from Springfield to Washington. By August 1861, Hunter was a major general. Hunter's political connections with President Lincoln and his administration clearly assisted his military career.

After having been seriously wounded at First Bull Run (Manassas), where he commanded General Irwin McDowell's second division, Hunter went to Missouri, where he commanded a division under General John C. Fremont before assuming command of the Western Department.[4] After taking over the Department of the South, Major General David Hunter's forces under Quincy Gillmore captured Fort Pulaski, which guarded the ocean approaches to Savannah, Georgia, in April 1862. On May 9, 1862, Hunter abolished slavery in his department. This action was nullified by President Lincoln as having been in excess of his authority. After being defeated at Secessionville, Hunter was temporarily suspended from military duty. His next command would be in the Shenandoah Valley in 1864.[5]

After traveling from Washington, Hunter arrived at Cedar Creek near Stasburg in the Shenandoah Valley. Major General Franz Sigel was relieved of command and agreed to serve as head of a reserve division at Martinsburg, West Virginia, to guard the Baltimore and Ohio Railroad.[6]

Hunter spoke with Colonel David Hunter Strother, a relative and the department's chief of staff. Colonel Strother recommended that Hunter immediately move up the Valley to Staunton and meet up with Brig. Gen. George Crook and Brig. Gen. William Averell. Their combined forces would then move to Charlottesville.

5. General Hunter Fails to Move in the Shenandoah Valley as Directed

The separate forces under Major General David Hunter and Crook and Averell coming separately from West Virginia to effectuate Grant's orders were a long way from any supply lines and were dependent on wagon trains for supplies, including ammunition. Those trains were subject to constant threat from guerrillas, including Colonel John Singleton Mosby.[7] Thus Hunter, as he undertook operations in the Valley, was aware that he was tethered to a tenuous wagon train supply line for ammunition as he moved further and further away from his base of supplies near the Potomac River in West Virginia.

When Hunter arrived at Cedar Creek in the Valley on May 21, 1864, he had a telegram from Halleck telling him that Gen. Crook had been told to go from Gauley in the Kanawha Valley in West Virginia east to Lynchburg. Alternatively, Crook had been given the option to go to Fincastle and then to Staunton in the Shenandoah Valley. Hunter was given orders to go to Staunton and from there to Gordonsville or Charlottesville, where he would meet forces from the Army of the Potomac.

Major General David Hunter, Union commander during Lynchburg campaign (Library of Congress).

Hunter found out that this predecessor, Major General Sigel, had already ordered Crook to go to Staunton. Major General Averell had joined Crook's infantry with his cavalry unit on May 19, 1864. Hunter ordered Averell to proceed to Staunton as well. Hunter telegraphed the adjutant general on May 21, 1864, that he was prepared to move east to join Grant after his linking up with Crook and Averell at Staunton.[8]

General Grant wished to eliminate the Shenandoah Valley as a breadbasket for Lee and as an invasion corridor to Washington and the North. Grant's plan was for the Union forces to march to Staunton, destroying railroad equipment and military supplies. Hunter was to then move to Charlottesville or Lynchburg, depending on Confederate opposition.[9] Grant stated to Halleck: "On the whole, therefore, I think it would be better of General Hunter to move in that direction; reach Staunton and Gordonsville or Charlottesville, if he does not meet too much opposition."[10]

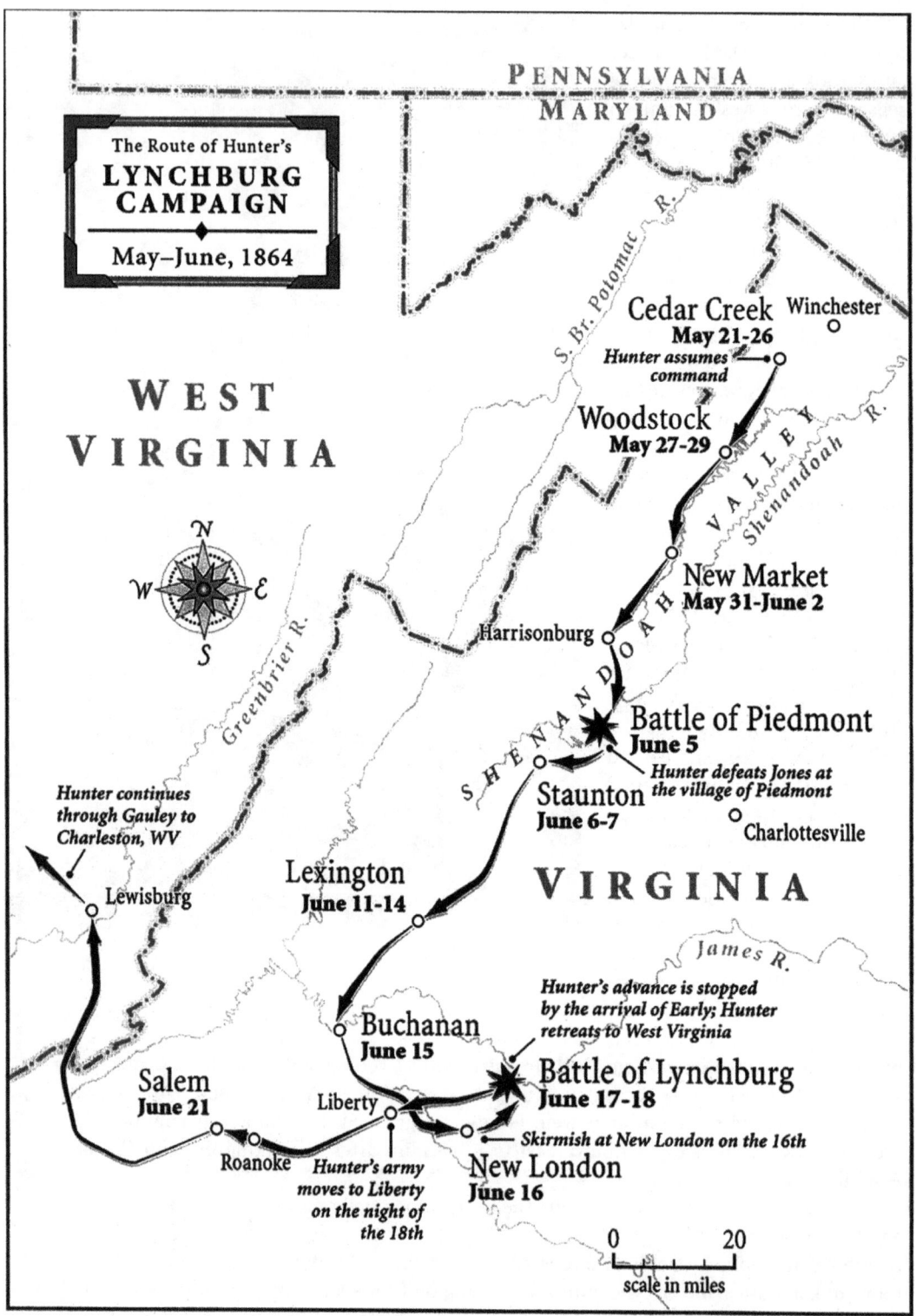

MAP OF GEN. HENTER'S LYNCHBURG CAMPAIGN ROUTE: MOVEMENTS OF HUNTER'S ARMY MAY–JUNE 1864 (MAP BY DAVID DEIS).

Before undertaking an operation in the direction of Staunton to meet up with Crook and Averell, on May 22, 1864, Hunter tried to replace Brigadier General Jeremiah Sullivan of the infantry and cavalry officer Major General Julius Stahel: "General Stahel, in command of the cavalry, has had but little experience as a cavalry officer in this country, nor am I aware that he has had any experience with cavalry elsewhere. General Sullivan, in command of the infantry, may be a very excellent officer, but is also of limited experience, and, I, therefore, urgently need two additional brigadiers of experience, energy and reliability."[11]

Halleck responded that energetic and efficient brigadiers were scarce and none were available. Hunter was told that if he wished Stahel, Duffie or Averell, the cavalry commanders there, mustered out, Halleck would endorse it.[12] This Hunter declined to do. Ironically, Stahel would win the Congressional Medal of Honor for distinguished service in Hunter's victory at the Battle of the Piedmont about two weeks after Hunter assumed command.[13]

Before leaving Cedar Creek for Staunton on May 26, 1864, five days after taking command, Hunter became embroiled in issues relating to attacks on supply trains. Hunter's response was the same whether the attack was from Confederate forces of the 43rd Virginia Battalion under Colonel John Singleton Mosby or from bushwackers or partisans. Captain Henry DuPont, Hunter's chief of artillery, described him as a person subject to fits of sudden anger and dominated by prejudices and antipathies so intense as to make him at times incapable of taking a fair and reasonable view of many military and political situations.[14] After unknown persons fired on a wagon train at Newtown on May 23, 1864, Hunter on May 24, 1864, ordered Major Timothy Quinn of the 1st New York (Lincoln) Cavalry to go to Newtown, ascertain from which houses and outbuildings the firing on the wagon train had taken place, and burn them.[15] Hunter took the position that if the firing happened again, any rebel house within five miles of the firing would be burned.[16]

Hunter's chief of staff, Colonel David Hunter Strother, met with the citizens of Newtown on May 24, 1864, discussing Hunter's directive and advising them to report guerrillas and their supporters. One woman's possessions were burned as well as the houses of three persons.[17] After 12 or 14 wagons in a wagon train were burned by forces of Colonel Mosby at Newtown on May 30, 1864, General Hunter ordered 200 Union cavalry to go to Newtown and burn it except for the church and houses of loyal citizens. This was in spite of the fact that Mosby's men were in a regiment in the Confederate army. Joseph R. Stearns of the 1st New York (Lincoln) Cavalry went to Newtown but refused to carry out Hunter's order. This focus on the destruction of property was to continue to delay Hunter and distract him from Grant's military objectives throughout the Lynchburg campaign.

On May 25, 1864, General Grant telegraphed Halleck with specific orders that if Hunter could get to Charlottesville or Lynchburg, he should do so, but he was to return to his original base or Gordonsville.

Major-General H.W. Halleck
Jericho Ford, Va
May 25, 1864

If Hunter can possibly get to Charlottesville and Lynchburg, he should do, living on the country. The railroads and canals should be destroyed beyond the possibility of repair for weeks. Completing this, he would then find his way back to his original base, or from about Gordonsville, join this army.

U.S. Grant Lieutenant-General[18]

Hunter had been advised on May 24, 1864, that Breckinridge had rejoined Lee's army.[19] Facing Hunter in the Valley was Brig. Gen. John Imboden, commander of the Valley District, which ran from west of the Blue Ridge to the James River in Botetourt County, with a force of about 1,000 men.[20] There were also small cavalry units in the Valley under Brig. Gen. John McCausland and "Mudwall" Jackson.

Imboden asked for reinforcements, telling General Robert E. Lee he was outnumbered four to one in infantry and two to one in cavalry.[21] Actually, Imboden was outnumbered by considerably more than that overall. However, General Lee had his own great need for troops at that time.

Lee's Army of Northern Virginia had been involved in a series of bloody engagements in May 1864. The fighting at the Wilderness from May 5 through 7 had been fierce. Although Lee's army had sustained fewer casualties than Grant, his losses were still substantial. The Wilderness campaign was followed by nearly two weeks of fighting at Spottsylvania from May 7 through 19, 1864. After failing to break Lee's lines at Spottsylvania, Grant moved his army south and east toward Hanover Junction where the Virginia Central and the Richmond, Fredericksburg and Potomac railroads intersect. There they were engaged in fighting in the North Ana campaign from May 23 to May 26, 1864.[22] To address his immediate need for manpower, Lee had been forced to recall General Hoke's and Gen. Pickett's forces from North Carolina. General Breckinridge had been recalled from the Shenandoah Valley on May 18.

Thus, at the time that General John Imboden was calling for reinforcements to supplement his small force facing Hunter in the Valley, Lee had none to give. General Lee did state, however, that he would direct General William E. "Grumble" Jones to come up from southwestern Virginia with the forces he could raise. Lee also ordered Gen. Imboden to call up reserves from Rockingham and Augusta counties in Virginia.[23] Jones was ordered by General Robert E. Lee to join Imboden on May 29, 1864; Imboden asked Jones for aid.[24]

Jones was able to bring about 3,000 troops from southwestern Virginia and eastern Tennessee to aid Imboden in facing Hunter. Although Gen. Imboden estimated that General Jones had only about 2,000 men, Brig. Gen. John C. Vaughn also came up with a force of about 800 cavalry. Included in these forces were the 18th Virginia Cavalry, the 23rd Virginia Cavalry and McClanahan's six-gun battery. Also, on May 27, 1864, a local newspaper had run an announcement calling for troops to support the Confederate armies."[25]

Imboden had warned General Lee on May 25 of rumors that Hunter was amassing troops for a move on Staunton. On the morning of May 26, 1864, General Hunter left Cedar Creek with his Army of the Shenandoah to move toward Staunton, Charlottesville and Lynchburg. Two thousand of Hunter's troops had no shoes or inadequate footgear and were to be resupplied at Woodstock.[26] Hunter ordered each soldier to carry the clothes on his back, 100 rounds of ammunition, extra socks and shoes, and enough basic supplies to last for 5 days. Otherwise, the army was to exist on supplies taken from Valley residents.

The army moved beyond Strasburg and went into camp two and one half miles north of Woodstock.[27] Colonel George Wells of the 34th Massachusetts Regiment en route burned a farmer's home that had been claimed to have been a rendezvous for bushwhackers.[28] Hunter spent from May 27 through May 29 in camp at Woodstock waiting for wagon trains with supplies, particularly shoes.[29]

Hunter's army left Woodstock on May 29, 1864, and moved through Mount Jackson to New Market, where they arrived on May 30.[30] It was thought that the Confederates under General Imboden were retreating through Harrisonburg.

On the 29th, Hunter's chief of staff, Colonel Strother, reported that General Hunter expected cooperation from General Philip H. Sheridan coming from the direction of Richmond. Hunter was assuming that Sheridan had gotten possession of the Virginia Central Railroad.[31]

A great deal of pillaging was going on by the Union troops. General Hunter discussed this in a communication with Major General Julius Stahel on May 30, 1864: "GENERAL. I desire to call your attention to numerous and grave complaints against soldiers of this command for unauthorized pillaging. It is represented that the men sent out in regular foraging parties break away from their officers and straggle into houses, carrying off dresses, ornaments, books, money..."[32]

General Hunter remained at New Market for several days until June 2, 1864. His forces still had not obtained their first objective, which was to reach Staunton. Meanwhile, General Imboden was requesting as many troops as possible from the area. Colonel William L. "Mudwall" Jackson, a relative of Stonewall Jackson, who had been in Covington, was recalled. Captain Thomas Davis with about 50 men of Col. Harry Gilmor's men from the Maryland Line joined Imboden, as did reserves from Rockingham and Augusta counties. Many of these reserve forces reported with shotguns and hunting weapons. Also about 130 miners from southwestern Virginia made it to Staunton to join Imboden's force.

On May 30, 1864, General William E. "Grumble" Jones put the 36th Virginia, the 45th Virginia, the 60th Virginia and Beckley's 45th Volunteer Battalion on a train at Bristol, near the Tennessee line, for Staunton. Bryan's 6-gun battery was also loaded on the train. Jones stopped along the way to conscript men from hospitals and wherever else they could be found.[33]

BRIG. GEN. JOHN IMBODEN COMMANDED CONFEDERATE CAVALRY FORCES OPPOSING HUNTER, MAY 1864 (LIBRARY OF CONGRESS).

Six of the first eight days since Hunter had taken command of the Union forces in the Shenandoah Valley had been spent in camp. This was time that did very little to further Grant's objectives and gave Imboden time to gather his forces. Finally, on June 2, 1864, Hunter's Army of the Shenandoah left New Market after having been there for three days. Hunter's forces encountered Confederate skirmishers near Harrisonburg. The Confederates were driven from Harrisonburg, and Hunter stayed the night near there. Hunter also spent June 3 in Harrisonburg, planning his further operations.[34]

Hunter's inactivity had permitted the Confederate forces to assemble. "Grumble" Jones's forces began to arrive at Staunton from Bristol in the late afternoon of June 3, 1864. They then marched 17 miles to North River. Bryan's artillery arrived but not the horses to serve it, so horses from Staunton were taken.[35] Jones, as senior officer, assumed command. Brigadier General John C. Vaughn's cavalry brigade, which had been serving in southwestern Virginia and eastern Tennessee, arrived on June 4. Vaughn's small brigade included part of the 60th, 61st and 62nd Tennessee, the 3rd, 39th, 43rd and 59th Tennessee Mounted Infantry, and the 1st, 12th and 16th Tennessee Cavalry as well as some men from the 16th Georgia Cavalry Battalion. The total Confederate force including Vaughn's troops was less than 4,500 men.[36] Imboden's purpose was to engage Hunter's forces as soon as possible before they could join up with the forces under Crook and Averell, who were moving to Staunton.

General Imboden described that situation as follows: "Hunter, with eleven thousand superbly-appointed troops of all arms, was only eight miles distant in our front, and Crook and Averell, with seven thousand more, only two days' march in our rear; the two bodies rapidly approaching each other, and we between them ... and with no hope of further assistance. Obviously our policy was to fight Hunter at the earliest moment, and possibly defeat him, and then turn on Crook and Averell and do the best we could."[37]

The Confederate force was organized into a first brigade under Colonel Buehring Jones consisting of the 60th Virginia and the 36th Virginia as well as a regiment of convalescents, guards and men detailed from government shops. Colonel W.H. Browne commanded the second brigade, which included the 45th Virginia Infantry Regiment, Beckley's 45th Virginia Battalion and two regiments of local reserves. A reserve unit of 700 miscellaneous soldiers was placed under the command of Lt. Col. Robertson. There were 6 guns in McClanahan's battery as well as an improvised battery of 6 guns.[38]

Hunter did not attack the Confederate defenses at North River as the Confederates anticipated but moved southeast toward Port Republic. General Imboden was familiar with the country, and General Jones agreed to his plan to try to check Hunter's advance at a hilltop position northeast of Staunton.[39] General Jones changed his mind about defending there and decided to fight at Piedmont, 3 miles in advance of the original position in a strong position between a bend of the Middle River and the East Road.[40]

Hunter's army reached the North River on the 4th of June only to find that the needed pontoon bridge was not there. After spending several hours waiting while the pontoon bridge was put into place, the Union troops were able to cross about 6:00 P.M. The troops were put into a line of battle about a mile south of Piedmont.[41] The Confederate position was on wooded hills commanding an open valley. The left was anchored on a high bluff with the Middle River at its base. On the Confederate right were log and rail fences near a forest from where fire could be directed. The Confederate reserves were spread out on the roads leading to the Valley Pike.[42] The problem with the Confederate position was the gap between General Jones's forces and those of General Vaughn. Vaughn had moved to the right of the East Road connecting Port Republic with Staunton, leaving a gap of several hundred yards between him and Jones's infantry's.[43]

The 18th Connecticut, the 28th Ohio, the 116th Ohio and a position of the 5th New York Heavy Artillery in Colonel Augustus Moor's first brigade of Brigadier General Jeremiah Sullivan's Infantry Division arrived at Piedmont on the morning of June 5, 1864. They formed between the cavalry on their far right and the road from Piedmont to Port Republic. Hunter had personally addressed the 18th Connecticut that morning and asked that they wipe out the stain of their performance at New Market, where Sigel had been defeated.[44] Colonel Joseph Thoburn's second brigade included the 54th Pennsylvania, the 34th Massachusetts and the 12th West Virginia, which was moved to the left of Moor's men near the East Road.[45] About 10:00 A.M. men from Colonel Augustus Moor's first brigade began to charge the Confederate picket line and advance against their main works. The men of the 18th Connecticut and other units came under heavy fire from the Confederate position on the heights.[46] Confederate troops counterattacked. They were yelling "New Market," "New Market."[47] The 21st New York Cavalry and the 14th Pennsylvania Cavalry, fighting dismounted, helped repulse the Confederate counterattack.

The 116th Ohio had come up to help blunt the advance of Jones's forces. Artillery fire from Captain DuPont's battery also had a telling effect. Two more Union attacks against Confederate positions on the heights were repulsed.[48] A Confederate counterattack was also withstood. General William E. "Grumble" Jones tried to close the gap in his line by moving Bryan's two gun battery, withdrawing his troops and bringing up reserves. Jones had sent several couriers to Imboden ordering him to attack Hunter's exposed left flank to help address the problem. Imboden did not attack.[49]

General Hunter ordered Colonel Joseph Thoburn to send two regiments to attack Jones's right where the gap existed between Jones's and Vaughn's Confederate forces. The 54th Pennsylvania and the 34th Massachusetts moved forcefully against Jones.[50]

Colonel Jacob Campbell of the 54th Pennsylvania described the movement of the Union forces overlapping the Confederate position and attacking their flank and rear:

> We advanced to the brow of the hill, where my regiment lay down on the ground, discharging a volley into the enemy, and immediately charged into the woods on the right flank and rear of the enemy's entrenched position. Here for a short time a most desperate struggle took place, bayonets and clubbed guns were used on both sides, and many hand-to-hand encounters took place. So sudden and apparently so unexpected to the enemy was our movement on their flank that they were compelled to give way in great confusion, despite all of the efforts of their officers to rally them.[51]

"Grumble" Jones had tried to bring his reserves forward to meet the Union attack. He was killed trying to rally his troops along a fence to protect their flank about a hundred yards from the woods from where the Union troops were coming.[52] Confederate reserve troops had inflicted numerous casualties on the 34th Massachusetts. However, the Confederate line was unable to hold. The 14th Pennsylvania Cavalry, the 116th Ohio and the 18th Connecticut enveloped Jones's lines and forced his forces to retreat in confusion after his death.

Brigadier General John C. Vaughn, whose forces were nearby, did not come up. Nor did the force under Brigadier General John D. Imboden. Historian Robert Krick states, "Jones fell victim to the criminal indolence of two subordinates at the disastrous Battle of Piedmont. A Federal bullet struck him down after cavalry generals John C. Vaughn and John D. Imboden stolidly watched the enemy advance unhindered across their front at the crisis of the battle."[53]

Contributing to the Confederate defeat was the failure of almost half its force on the right wing to take part in the battle. General Jones also reacted too late to the problem of the gap in his lines. Vaughn and Imboden's failing to close the gap in front of them was another problem.[54] One Confederate trooper present stated, "These two generals stood by, silent spectators of this flank movement, absolutely regardless of the orders of General Jones."[55]

While Colonel Joseph Thoburn was attacking the gap in the Confederate line, Colonel Augustus Moor and his First Brigade troops breached Jones's defenses in their front. They forced the Confederates back in hand-to-hand fighting.[56] Colonel Waddell of a West Virginia regiment described the Union advance: "The men responded with a cheer, and steadily the regiment advanced, increasing the pace to the double quick, and, as the distance decreased, into a run, arriving at the fortifications, jumping and clambering over them and gaining the inside of the works, giving the defenders little or no time to rally, commenced a hand-to-hand contest, pushing them back and putting them to flight in a short time."[57]

Hunter reported losses of 500. He also estimated Confederate losses as being 600 killed and wounded and 1,000 prisoners. Confederate losses were not less than 1,500 men as stated by Imboden.[58] The Confederate forces, now commanded by General Vaughn, retreated toward Waynesboro and Rockfish Gap to cover Gordonsville and Charlottesville. They fell back in good order and were about eleven miles from Staunton. However, the way to Staunton was now open for the Union forces. Staunton was an important rail and supply center. Its occupation exposed Lee's left flank.[59]

At Piedmont, Hunter's chief of staff reported the Confederates to be in full retreat at 3:00 P.M. on June 5, 1864.[60] Hunter did not pursue the fleeing Confederates but ordered his army to camp on the battlefield.[61] Meanwhile, nearby in Staunton, Colonel Edwin G. Lee had received news of the Confederate defeat and was evacuating military supplies. These supplies were being transported south by rail and wagon. Lee managed to save all of the ammunition stored there.

He was also able to save bacon, quartermaster's supplies and salt.[62] The failure of Hunter to timely reach Staunton and resupply his ammunition proved important in the Lynchburg campaign, as Hunter was low on ammunition. He was also dependent on a tenuous supply line back to Martinsburg and Harpers Ferry which became more difficult to maintain the further he advanced.

On June 6, 1864, Hunter moved his army from the Piedmont battlefield toward Staunton. When they reached the road to Waynesboro, Hunter rejected the suggestion of his chief of staff to pursue and destroy Vaughn and Imboden. He then moved into Staunton.[63]

The Union's control of the Valley would have a major effect on the strategy of both Grant and Lee. Grant's month-long offensive of attrition in May 1864 had incurred enormous casualties. He had used the available pool of troops, including those from the defenses of Washington.

Grant was advised of Hunter's victory at the Battle of Piedmont on June 6. He contacted Hunter on that date and advised him of his modified strategy. Grant was sending General Sheridan with two cavalry divisions to Charlottesville. He was to destroy the Virginia Central Railroad and the James River Canal as he went. Hunter was to join Sheridan on the railroad connecting Charlottesville and Lynchburg. Hunter was to use his discretion about taking Lynchburg. He and Sheridan were then to rejoin the Army of the Potomac.

> The direction I would now give is, that if this letter reaches you in the Valley between Staunton and Lynchburg, you immediately turn east by the most practicable road until you strike the Lynchburg branch of the Va. Central road. From thence move eastward along the line of the road, destroying it completely and thoroughly until you join Sheridan.[64]

Grant had also explicitly stated in his memoirs that he had told Hunter that Sheridan was coming.

On June 7, 1864, Hunter ordered the burning of railroad installations and the depot at Staunton. A steam mill, a woolen mill, a wagon shop, government stables and storehouses were also destroyed. Military equipment included 3 guns, 1,000 firearms and 1,000 cavalry saddles.[65]

Colonel David Hunter Strother reported on June 7, 1864, that Hunter was determined to move directly on Charlottesville. Strother supported Hunter's plan. Other staff members opposed it. On that day, Hunter did move his army west a few miles to try to catch Brigadier General John McCausland's remaining Confederate cavalry force. However, he returned to Staunton later on June 7.[66]

On June 8, 1864, General George Crook's infantry force along with General William Averell's cavalry arrived at Staunton. Hunter met with his generals to determine how to proceed on June 9. General Crook wanted to make a forced march to Lynchburg before it could be reinforced. Crook had sufficient ammunition. He felt action should be undertaken immediately and rapidly. General Averell was to make a detailed plan to get to Lynchburg in 5 days. After considering his options, General Hunter decided to move his army south.[67]

Meanwhile, actions were taking place affecting Hunter's own ammunition problem. After the Battle of Piedmont, Hunter was aware that another day of heavy fighting would nearly exhaust his supply of ammunition. The ammunition he would have found at Staunton had he rapidly moved from the battlefield had been transported south by the Confederates. So, Hunter sent Major General Julius Stahel of his cavalry to Martinsburg, West Virginia, a supply center on the Baltimore and Ohio Railroad. Stahel was to obtain troops and ammunition and bring it back to Hunter's army as it was on the move. This objective was not accomplished.[68]

Colonel David Hunter Strother went to see Brigadier General George Crook on June 9, 1864, to get his additional views on how to proceed and to share Hunter's and his staff's thinking. Crook had been a brigadier at South Mountain and Sharpsburg. He then had served in Gen-

5. General Hunter Fails to Move in the Shenandoah Valley as Directed

eral George H. Thomas's Army of the Cumberland in the Chickamauga campaign. Strother found:

> He was drier and less sanguine than either Averell or myself. He asked what we proposed by moving on Lynchburg. I told him we hoped thereby to drive Lee out of Richmond by seizing and threatening all his Southern and Western communications and sources of supply.[69]

Hunter's views, expressed to Crook, about forcing Lee out of Richmond were not consistent with Grant's often and clearly expressed desire to have Hunter's forces go to Charlottesville to damage both Lee's supply and communications infrastructure and to come back to the Army of the Potomac with Sheridan. Hunter's force would provide about 20,000 additional troops that could operate to fulfill Grant's objective of pressuring and containing Lee until he was unable to continue the war.

Strother's discussion with General Crook continued:

> He asked if we thought we could accomplish it with our present force. I replied that we could easily beat all the force that the enemy had in the Valley and in West Virginia combined, that we hoped Lee would not be able to reinforce the Valley, being too closely pressed by Grant, that in the event of his detailing a division or two it would be cut off by Sheridan who was marching his cavalry toward Gordonsville and would cooperate with us.[70]

Strother revealed that Hunter assumed that Grant would contain Lee and prevent reinforcements from coming to the Shenandoah Valley. Further, if reinforcements were sent, they

Top: BRIG. GEN. WILLIAM AVERELL JOINED HUNTER AT STAUNTON, COMMANDED A CAVALRY BRIGADE (LIBRARY OF CONGRESS). *Bottom:* BRIG. GEN. GEORGE CROOK JOINED HUNTER AT STAUNTON, EXPRESSED NEED FOR RAPID ADVANCE (LIBRARY OF CONGRESS).

would be cut off by Sheridan. This was in spite of the fact that Grant on June 6, 1864, after the Battle of Piedmont, had directed Hunter to join forces with Sheridan. As recently as June 7, Colonel Strother had reported that Hunter was determined to go to Charlottesville.

General Hunter had not been in communication with either Grant or Sheridan while at Staunton. He does not appear to have appreciated or understood the enormous casualties Grant had incurred in his month-long campaign from the Wilderness to Cold Harbor. Nor did he seem to grasp Grant's need for Hunter's nearly 20,000 troops to join him soon in the Richmond theater of operations, destroying supply and communication links for Lee in the process.

In talking to Strother, General George Crook addressed the problems of communications and supplies and the need for rapid action.

> Crook said we might take Lynchburg, but, depend on it, Lee would not permit us to hold it long, nor could we do so for want of supplies. If we expected to take Lynchburg at all we must move upon it immediately and rapidly. I agreed with him that such be our proper and safe course but mentioned our lack of ammunition. Crook said he had plenty of it and if permitted would march on Lynchburg with his division alone, saying that celerity was more important than numbers or ammunition. This conversation was reported to the General, giving force to General Crook's views in regard to the danger of delay.[71]

Thus, in order to move on Lynchburg at all as a precursor to going to Charlottesville, the problem of lack of ammunition and supplies was a major concern. The long supply line by wagon had to travel through country infested with Confederate partisans and guerrillas. These trains traveled slowly, and there was an absolute need for speedy movement. However, Lynchburg itself was a supply center. Having delayed entering Staunton and having lost critical supplies and ammunition as a result, Hunter could not afford to have the same thing happen at Lynchburg, even further removed from his supply base.

In exercising his discretion to move south on Lynchburg, Hunter was leaving Sheridan to fend for himself. He was thus disregarding Grant's desire for him to join Sheridan and return to the Army of the Potomac. He was fully aware that quick movement was of the essence in the Lynchburg campaign. He declined to let Crook make a forced march, which would have gotten to the city when it was lightly defended before it was reinforced by Early. He also failed to move at a reasonable pace that would make success more likely, instead being diverted by the destruction of property.

Lee at Richmond was faced with at least four possible threats. Grant could continue to hammer his Army of Northern Virginia with 100,000 men while Lee defended with 45,000 and 7,400 garrison forces in Petersburg. He could cross the James River and attack General Pierre G. Beauregard's 7,900-man force at the vital rail center of Petersburg, south of Richmond. Hunter could sweep the Confederate forces from the Shenandoah Valley and move east on Richmond with between 15,000 and 20,000 men. Also, Sheridan could cut the Virginia Central Railroad and destroy Lee's supply and communications lines with the Shenandoah Valley, which would allow Hunter to return to the lines at Richmond.

There were other possibilities. Grant could undertake simultaneous operations on both sides of the James River. In doing so, he could use Major General Benjamin F. Butler's Army of the James at Bermuda Hundred. Grant could also move south of the Chickahominy and lay siege to Richmond from there. Lee had stated that if it became a siege then it was a mere question of time, with Lee fighting the Union forces, facing starvation, disease and ultimately being unable to continue.[72] Thus at the time he was contemplating his gamble, Lee was being pressed from all sides.

By detaching Major General John C. Breckinridge back to the Valley with his 2,100 men and by sending Early's 2nd Corps to relieve Lynchburg with his over 8,000 men, Lee would be losing a sizeable part of his army at a time he faced the most substantial pressure from Grant. In one of the great coincidences of history, when Early's force was being detached to undertake Lee's plan, Grant's army was moving from its trenches to go south of the James and did not know it.

Lee's dilemma after the Battle of Piedmont was the need to protect Lynchburg and the lack of forces to do it. Most of the soldiers available for defense of the city were from General Hospital No. 3, authorized early in 1864. There were about 4,000 convalescents there as of March 1, 1864. Many more wounded came in during May 1864, during the Wilderness campaign and related actions. At Camp Nicholls outside of Lynchburg on the Salem Pike, wounded soldiers were divided in companies by Captain Van R. Otey and prepared to man Lynchburg's defenses The camp was named after General Francis R. Nicholls, who had participated in Stonewall Jackson's Shenandoah Valley campaign of 1862; he had been wounded at Winchester, losing an arm. He had commanded the District of Lynchburg.[73]

After the Battle of Piedmont, General Vaughn and General Imboden together had about 2,000 men. Confederate cavalry were posted at New Hope to gather up Jones's fleeing troops and to organize them for a retreat to Fishersville. Jones's men initially coming off the battlefield were taken to the main Confederate force. Colonel O'Ferrall was left at New Hope on the evening of June 5, 1864, with two squadrons of cavalry, who were locating more retreating troops.[74] Brigadier General Vaughn telegraphed General Robert E. Lee on the night of June 5, saying, "I will try to protect Staunton, but unless reenforcements come at once, I cannot do it."[75] That night Vaughn also reported to Confederate secretary of war James Seddon that Staunton could not be held. Late on the evening of the 5th, Imboden and Vaughn telegraphed Richmond and found out that Lee had informed General Jones earlier that no reinforcements could be sent. By this time, about 1,000 men of Jones's force had reached Fishersville, making a total Confederate force of about 3,000. Vaughn and Imboden planned to retreat through Waynesboro to Rockfish Gap. Brigadier General John McCausland and Colonel "Mudwall" Jackson also had small cavalry forces in the Valley which joined those of Imboden and Vaughn at Rockfish Gap. Jackson commanded the 19th Virginia Cavalry. Jackson had a small brigade since May 1864. McCausland's force totaled about 1,500 men.[76]

On June 6, 1864, Confederate president Jefferson Davis was advised that Brigadier General John C. Vaughn had communicated with Confederate secretary of war James Seddon about the death of General Jones and the defeat at Piedmont. General Lee had contacted Davis about sending Wharton's and Echol's brigades totaling 2,100 men under Breckinridge back to the Shenandoah Valley, where they had been posted before being recalled to Richmond during the Overland Campaign. Lee noted, "It is apparent that if Grant cannot be successfully resisted here we cannot hold the Valley — If he is defeated it can be recovered."[77] Lee was also concerned about having a capable commander in the Valley. Breckinridge had been injured at Cold Harbor and still had not recovered. Lee also considered Echols to still be unfit.[78]

Lee was also having to deal with a somewhat contentious command problem in the Army of Northern Virginia's 2nd Corps. General Richard Ewell, who had been ill, had been forced to ask Lieutenant General Jubal A. Early to take over command of the 2nd Corps. On May 29, 1864, during the Cold Harbor campaign, General Robert E. Lee relieved General Ewell and put Early temporarily in command of the 2nd Corps.[79] Ewell was dissatisfied with being replaced. He went to see Confederate president Jefferson about the matter, to no avail.[80]

On June 9, 1864, General Lee advised Davis that he believed that Sheridan intended to join General David Hunter and that Wade Hampton's and Fitzhugh Lee's cavalry divisions had been sent to Hanover Court House to engage Sheridan.[81] On June 10, 1864, General Braxton Bragg, military advisor to Confederate president Jefferson Davis, wrote to Davis that it seemed to him very important that the Union force be expelled from the Shenandoah Valley. If the Union force were crushed, Washington would be open to the small force that could be employed. Davis referred Bragg's letter to Robert E. Lee without comment.[82]

General Ulysses S. Grant, hoping to open communications with Hunter, sent General Sheridan with Torbert's and Gregg's divisions of the Army of the Potomac Cavalry Corps to move toward Charlottesville and Gordonsville. The plan was for Sheridan to destroy the railroad as he went. He was to join Hunter if he could and come back with Hunter's army to Richmond.[83] Grant's plan was for Sheridan to destroy the James River Canal and Virginia Central Railroad links to Lee at Richmond. Fitzhugh Lee and Wade Hampton encountered Sheridan's forces in the vicinity of Louisa Court House at Trevilian Station on the Virginia Central Railroad.[84] In a fierce two-day cavalry battle, Sheridan was defeated at Trevilian Station without accomplishing his objectives. He was forced to return to Grant's army and his base of operations.[85]

In order to effectuate Grant's plan, Hunter would preferably move quickly to Charlottesville along the rail lines to link up with Sheridan. Otherwise, he was to move quickly in his discretion to Lynchburg. Hunter did neither. He moved slowly on Lynchburg, was defeated and ultimately fled to West Virginia out of the entire theater of military operations.

After linking up with General Crook and General Averell at Staunton on June 8, 1864, Hunter set out for Lexington on June 10. Brigadier General Jeremiah Sullivan commanded the 1st Infantry Division, while Brigadier General George Crook headed the 2nd Infantry Division. The 1st Cavalry Division was led by Brigadier General Alfred Duffie, who succeeded the wounded General Julius Stahel in command. Brigadier General William Averell led the 2nd Cavalry Division.[86]

Hunter divided his army into four columns which were to meet in Lexington. Averell had the right; Crook took the main Valley road; Sullivan was on the roads to the left of Crook; and Duffie went on the roads at the base of the Blue Ridge.[87] Hunter's chief of staff estimated the strength of Hunter's forces leaving Staunton as follows: "The Army of the Shenandoah, which had come with General Hunter was here with about eight thousand effectives. The Army of the Kanawha under Crook brought about twelve thousand. The Army of West Virginia (as I named it in general orders of the day of the junction) moved from Staunton with twenty thousand men, thirty-six canon. Our cavalry numbered about five thousand."[88]

General John C. Breckinridge had directed Brigadier General John McCausland with his 1,500-man cavalry force to get in front of Hunter and obstruct his march as much as possible. McCausland was to report to Breckinridge on Hunter's daily progress.

Breckinridge was moving all the other Confederate forces in the Valley to Lynchburg to defend it. The 13th West Virginia of Crook's division tangled with the cavalry force under Brigadier General John McCausland on June 10. However, Crook's men were not significantly delayed. They were able to march 24 miles to Brownsburg on the 10th.[89] Sullivan's division burned large mills at Greenville and Fairfield on June 10. They camped after also having made significant progress.[90]

Grant had sent further word to Hunter that if he did not receive his orders until he was in the Shenandoah Valley between Staunton and Lexington, he was to turn east until he intersected the Virginia Central track between Charlottesville and Lynchburg. He was then to move east on the railroad, thoroughly destroying it, until he met up with Sheridan.[91] Hunter did not communicate with Sheridan, who was at Trevilian Station facing Wade Hampton's and Fitzhugh Lee's cavalry divisions; he needed Hunter's assistance or at least that of his cavalry. Nor did Hunter attempt to turn east as Grant had wanted. Rather, Hunter would delay his movements for three more days at Lexington while engaged in the destruction of both private and government property, which did very little to further Grant's military objectives and actually worked to counter them.

Although Hunter did not move his army to cut the rail links to Lynchburg as Grant so clearly wanted, he did send a brigade of cavalry on a raid in that direction which included some attacks against railroad property. One of the most significant aspects of General Hunter's move toward Lexington on June 10, 1864, was the failure of his cavalry under Brigadier General Alfred Duffie to destroy the railroad bridges connecting Charlottesville and Lynchburg.

Brigadier General Alfred N. Duffie, a French-born officer, had succeeded Major General Julius Stahel in command of the 1st Cavalry Division after Stahel had been wounded at the Battle of Piedmont. Born in Paris in 1835, the son of a French count, and educated at the French military academy at St. Cyr, Duffie had been a lieutenant in the French army in the Crimean War. Duffie's troopers followed the Blue Ridge and then moved to the Tye River Gap to reach rail lines linking Lynchburg and Charlottesville as well as Richmond and Petersburg. Hunter's objectives were to destroy the Orange and Alexandria Railroad, military stores at Amherst Court House and the South Side Railroad. Before starting off on their raid, Duffie's forces had been advancing on the left flank of Hunter's army as it moved toward Lexington.[92]

Duffie's cavalry was vigorously opposed near Waynesboro and had moved south and later east to the Tye River. Part of Duffie's cavalry force was a detachment of the 1st Maryland Regiment, Potomac Home Brigade, under Major Townsend Daniel of Cole's Cavalry. Daniel, with part of Duffie's split force, was trailing a Confederate wagon train which had left Staunton on June 5, 1864, ahead of the advancing Union forces. On June 8, 1864, the wagon train had gone to Arrington on the Orange and Alexandria Railroad about midway between Charlottesville and Lynchburg.[93] Most of the wagons had proceeded by way of Rockfish pursuant to orders from General Vaughn. A small group remained at Arrington under Captain R.H. Phillips. Major Daniel with his Union cavalry force had followed the wagon train to Arrington by following the wheel ruts. Daniel's forces on June 11, 1864, attacked the 7 Confederate wagons, captured 41 prisoners and destroyed the depot.[94] The railroad bridges were not destroyed and the rail link between Charlottesville and Lynchburg remained open. Duffie's men had only damaged five miles of track, which was repaired in two days.

Captain Henry C. Douthat of the Botetourt Artillery, part of Lynchburg's defense forces, was en route to join General Breckinridge at Rockfish Gap.[95] Douthat and his men were able to see the fire at the depot. Obtaining arms on the train, Douthat was able to move by rail part of the way to meet the threat of the Union cavalry to the bridge over the Tye River. After getting to Amherst Station, Douthat was able to get within several miles of Arrington. He then marched his men on the double quick, arriving before the Union cavalry. His men, armed with Enfields, were posted as pickets. The Union cavalry force from Duffie's command arrived before midnight. They were fired on by Douthat's men. Believing a superior Confederate force to be before them, the Union cavalry unit retired back to Amherst Court House, where they reported back to General Duffie's force. Hunter had ordered Duffie to move toward Lexington, where they did not arrive until late on the 13th.[96] Thus, the Tye River Railroad bridge remained open for the passage of Early's troops to relieve Lynchburg.

Douthat, by his forceful action, had been able to protect the Orange and Alexandria bridge. Had this small Confederate force not been able to accomplish their successful defense and had Duffie's forces brought more manpower to bear to achieve the destruction of the bridge, the result of General Jubal A. Early's march to Lynchburg might well have been different. Early's army and artillery would have had to cross a river and march an additional 30 miles. As it was, part of his army arrived just as Hunter was getting there, with the remainder coming up to join them hours later. Thus Hunter's cavalry failed him at a small but critical juncture. It was the railroad bridge over the Tye River, not the 7 Confederate wagons, which was strategically important.

Another part of Brigadier General Duffie's cavalry force attempted to go to Amherst Court House to destroy the Orange and Alexandria railroad there. The Union cavalry met Confederate cavalry forces there from Brigadier General John Imboden's command and were not able to accomplish their objectives.[97]

Another part of Brigadier General Alfred N. Duffie's small detachments destroyed two iron furnaces near the Tye River Gap. They also clashed with units of Imboden's cavalry command in that area. The various units of Duffie's cavalry division did not return to Hunter's army until June 13, 1864, in the area of Lexington. They had not done anything of strategic importance and had failed to damage the Confederate communications infrastructure in any meaningful way. General George Crook thought that General Duffie's delay was due to misconduct and caused the Union forces to arrive a day later at Lynchburg.[98] Thus Duffie's raid not only failed to cut the vital rail links that allowed Early to get to Lynchburg but also delayed Hunter in getting there, giving Early more time — time that he desperately needed.

On the morning of June 11, 1864, Brigadier General William Averell's 2nd Cavalry Division crossed the North Fork of the James River above Lexington.[99] Some VMI cadets and men from the Lexington Home Guard burned a bridge across the James. General Crook's forces and the cavalry force under General William Averell arrived at Lexington about noon on June 11, 1864.[100]

Brigadier General John McCausland with his small force attempted to defend Lexington. He took a position behind the North River, a branch of the James, and his men fired some musket and canon shots at the Union troops across the river in Lexington. Confederate sharpshooters were in a thicket and some buildings attached to the Virginia Military Institute. Part of the Confederate force was about 250 VMI cadets under Colonel Francis H. Smith. Colonel Smith, superintendent of VMI, protested to McCausland against making a futile defense which endangered both the citizens of Lexington and the Virginia Military Institute.[101] General David Hunter rode to the scene and ordered Averell to cross the river north of Lexington to outflank the Confederate forces. He also ordered Captain Henry DuPont to fired on the VMI barracks in the area of McCausland's position. DuPont fired one round from each of the 6 guns he served at the VMI barracks, which caused the Confederates to retreat.[102]

General Averell crossed the river by a ford above Lexington and flanked the Confederate force. McCausland retreated toward Buchanon, and the VMI cadets marched toward Lynchburg. General Crook blamed Averell's slowness in effectuating his movement as allowing McCausland's Confederate force to escape Lexington virtually unscathed. Hunter himself felt Averell's late and somewhat timid action in his flank movement had prevented the capture or dispersal of McCausland's force.[103]

The 14th Pennsylvania Cavalry under Colonel John M. Schoomaker of Averell's division put the Virginia Military Institute buildings under guard. Although there was considerable looting on June 11, 1864,[104] Colonel David Hunter Strother noted: "We rode directly to the Institute and found the sack already advanced, soldiers, Negroes, and riffraff disputing over the plunder. The private trunks of the cadets seemed quite fat and renumerative, and I heard that one soldier got one hundred dollars in gold from one of them. The plunderers came out loaded with beds, carpets, cut velvet chairs, mathematical glasses and instruments, stuffed birds, charts, bowls, papers, arms, cadet uniforms and hats in most ridiculous confusion."[105] A supply of ordinance and small arms was found at the institute. Some iron furnaces east of Lexington were also burned on the 11th. General Hunter made his headquarters at the home of VMI superintendent Colonel Francis Smith.[106]

Thus, at a time when both Hunter and his subordinate officers had agreed that a speedy movement to Lynchburg was of the utmost necessity if Hunter were to undertake the campaign at all in his discretion rather than go to Charlottesville, Hunter had already delayed part of the day on the 11th for the sacking of VMI. He was to continue his delay in Lexington for two more days, primarily for the destruction of property, much of it private property. These delays did nothing to further Grant's military objectives and contributed ultimately to the disastrous failure of Hunter's Lynchburg campaign.

5. General Hunter Fails to Move in the Shenandoah Valley as Directed

June 12, 1864, was taken up with further delays by Hunter's army in Lexington involving the destruction of property. General Hunter had discussed with Colonel Strother, his chief of staff, the destruction of the Virginia Military Institute.[107] Strother had recommended that it be burned, as treason had systematically been taught there, in his opinion; VMI taught that allegiance was to the state of Virginia alone. Also, VMI had furnished numerous capable officers to fight against the government of the United States. Strother also had found military reasons for its destruction: "There were military reasons besides. The professors and cadets had taken to the field against government troops, as an organized corps. The buildings had been used as a Rebel arsenal and recently as a fortress. Professor Smith, who understood the liabilities incurred by the use of the building, protested against McCausland's appropriation of it for defensive purposes, hoping that otherwise it might be spared **** The order was given to fire the building and all the houses and outbuildings."[108] Hunter also ordered the burning of the house of ex–Virginia governor John Letcher on June 12, 1864: "He had been given by an officer a violent and inflammatory proclamation from John Letcher, lately Governor of Virginia, inciting the people of the country to rise and wage a guerilla warfare on his troops. Hunter ascertained that after having advised his fellow-citizens to the course the ex-Governor had himself taken flight and ordered his property to be burned under his order against persons practicing or abetting such unlawful and unauthorized warfare."[109]

The buildings burned at VMI on June 12, 1864, were the barracks, some faculty quarters occupied by Major Gilham and Colonel Thomas Williamson, and possibly the cadet hospital. General Hunter, General Averell, Colonel Strother and others viewed the burning of the buildings at VMI from a nearby hill. Hunter was reported to seemingly be enjoying the scene.[110]

Hunter's actions in this respect were not approved of by many of his officers. General George Crook stated: "I did all in my power to dissuade him from burning the school."[111] Colonel Rutherford B. Hayes, a brigade commander under General Crook and future president of the United States, wrote in his diary, "General Hunter burns the Virginia Military Institute. This does not suit many of us. General Crook, I know, disapproves. It is surely bad."[112] Captain Henry DuPont, Hunter's chief of artillery, wrote:

> In my judgment, as well as in that of every other Union officer who expressed himself on the subject, the destruction of the cadet barracks was fully justified by the laws of war, but the burning of the buildings containing the library, the philosophical apparatus, the large and extensive mineralogical collection and other objects used solely for educational purposes, was extremely unnecessary besides being contrary to the conventions of civilized warfare which respect as far as possible the property of institutions of learning.[113]

General Crook issued an order to his brigade commanders to hold officers responsible for the conduct of their troops involving private property which he felt were disgraceful to the command:

> The general commanding regrets to learn of so many acts committed by our troops that are disgraceful to the command, such as breaking open trunks of private citizens & with disregard of General Orders, No. 11, by troops of this command. Brigade commanders must hold their officers responsible that this order is enforced. Supplies must not be taken by individuals, their supplies are being collected by division quartermasters for issue.[114]

Colonel Strother had been contacted by a trustee of Washington College on June 12, 1864, and advised that soldiers were sacking the building and asked for a guard to protect the property. Strother ordered the Washington College property to be protected, advising that it would be treated differently than the property at VMI.[115] Colonel Strother also went to Stonewall Jackson's gravesite. "I rode out around town, and passing the cemetery, saw Stonewall Jackson's grave in the midst of an enclosure, with a tall staff near it. A number of curious men and officers from our army were collected around it."[116]

The supply train from General Sigel from Martinsburg arrived at Lexington on June 12, 1864. Very little essential munitions were received. What was brought was a lot of forage and clothing. That same day, Hunter ordered Sigel to send nothing but ammunition in any future train except a supply of subsistence goods for the escort.[117] Hunter also received several pieces of intelligence on the 12th. A Confederate prisoner, Major Bell, a scout from Imboden's command, stated that Imboden was still at Waynesboro. He also stated that Lee had defeated Grant.[118]

Lynchburg was about 44 miles from Lexington. Hunter's delay was giving the Confederates time to reinforce Lynchburg with Breckinridge's two brigades of infantry, Wharton's and Echol's, and consolidate the remnants of the Confederate army defeated at the Battle of Piedmont as well as other smaller units. General Vaughn and General Imboden were at Waynesboro. Colonel Smith and the cadets from VMI were marching from Lexington to Lynchburg. Brigadier General McCausland was in Hunter's front, continuing to delay him as long as possible.

By not going immediately from Staunton to Charlottesville to join Sheridan or to Lynchburg, while Confederate forces were weak, Hunter was undertaking a course of inaction which would allow the Confederates to defeat the Union forces piecemeal—first Sheridan at Trevilian Station and then Hunter at Lynchburg.

General Grant said of the situation: "Had General Hunter moved by way of Charlottesville, instead of Lexington, as his instructions contemplated, he would have been in a position to have covered the Shenandoah Valley against the enemy should the force he met have seemed to endanger it. If it did not, he would have been within easy distance of the James River Canal, on the line of communications between Lynchburg and the force sent forth for its defense."[119]

Chapter 6

Lee's Bold Plan, Phase I

On June 10, 1864, General John C. Breckinridge communicated to General Braxton Bragg, military advisor to Confederate president Jefferson Davis, that he was of the opinion that the Valley should be cleared of Union forces. Bragg added that although it seemed very important to him to expel Union forces from the Valley, if their forces could be crushed, Washington would be open to the Confederate forces.[1] Jefferson Davis forwarded this message to General Robert E. Lee without suggestion. General Lee replied on June 11, 1864, that it would be desirable to do this but it would entail detaching a corps or two from Lee's army. Lee told Davis that he would do it if it were deemed prudent in terms of the defense of Richmond. Lee felt that Grant would like this but that a Confederate victory would relieve the situation. Bragg told Davis on June 12, 1864, that the Confederate forces in western Virginia would need reinforcement by at least 6,000 men.[2]

On June 12, 1864, General Lee got word that General Hunter had occupied Lexington on June 11. Hunter was now free to join Grant's army at Richmond, which concerned Lee. Lee decided to undertake a bold initiative to remove the Union forces in the Valley and strike north to Washington and Baltimore if possible.

> Finding that it would be necessary to detach some troops to repel the force under General Hunter, which was threatening Lynchburg, I resolved to send one that would be adequate to accomplish the purpose, effectively, and, if possible, strike a decisive blow. At the same time that General Early was instructed, if his success justified it, and the enemy retreated down the Valley, to pursue him, and if opportunity offered, to follow him into Maryland. It was believed that the Valley could then be effectively freed from the presence of the enemy, and it was hoped that by threatening Washington and Baltimore General Grant would be compelled either to weaken himself so much for their protection as to afford us an opportunity to attack him, or that he may be induced to attack us.... In addition to these considerations there were other collateral results, such as obtaining military stores and supplies, that were deemed of sufficient importance to warrant the attempt.[3]

Grant had to replace stunning losses. Lee had been able to learn that troops in the control of the United States were being sent to Grant for his army. Thus there would be little or no opposition by the Union forces that were at Washington.[4]

In Lee, Grant had found an opponent capable of turning the tables. "When it came to taking a risk, the Confederate commander had few equals."[5]

The man that General Robert E. Lee had chosen to lead this undertaking was Lieutenant General Jubal A. Early—a contentious and feisty man whom Lee felt had the ability to handle the assignment. Early had entered West Point in 1834. By June 1835, he stood 8th on merit in a class of 76. On conduct he stood 223rd out of a cadet corps of 240.

> Jubal's conduct rating may have suffered, at least partly, from an dispute with a cadet named Lewis A. Armistead. Early made some scathing remark to Armistead on the parade ground as the cadets marched to mess; the quarrel continued at the meal, and Armistead ended by breaking a plate over

Early's head. For this Armistead was dismissed from the Academy (he was to die at Gettysburg during Pickett's charge).⁶

After his second year at West Point, Early stood 11th in his class on general merit out of a total of 58 cadets still remaining at the academy. Early had 196 demerit points, 4 short of what would be required for expulsion from West Point. Early barely made it through the conduct requirements.

A substantial number of demerits may have flowed from a further display of pugnacity and ill temper. The incident seems to have pitted Early against his classmate Joseph Hooker, who would be known during the Civil War as "Fighting Joe." Early was in the audience at a debating society contest in which the topic was slavery. Hooker, a native of Hadley, Massachusetts, asserted that owners of slaves killed them when they were too old or sick to work.

Early leaped to his feat and denounced the statement as an outrageous lie. Hooker objected to the interruption, and Early said nothing more. But after the debate, he waited for Hooker outside and kicked him. Hooker, whether scared of Early or prudent in avoiding trouble, did not fight back.⁷

After graduating from West Point in 1837 and service against the Seminoles, Early began practicing law in Rocky Mount, Virginia. Early was appointed a major in the First Regiment of Volunteer Infantry of Virginia. His unit was mainly used on garrison duty in northern Mexico. Early was appointed military governor of Monterey. He served with distinction in that post. At the conclusion of the Mexican War in 1848, Early returned to civilian life and his law practice.⁸

After the Civil War broke out, Early had accepted a commission and served as colonel in the 24th Virginia. Early performed well at First Bull Run (Manassas) and was appointed a brigadier general after the battle. He served in the Peninsular Campaign, being wounded at Williamsburg. Subsequently, he led a brigade under General Thomas J. "Stonewall" Jackson at Malvern Hill. Early fought well at Cedar Mountain, Second Bull Run (Manassas) and at Antietam. At Fredericksburg, he again fought with distinction. Early has been criticized for failing to reconnoiter properly in the Chancellorsville campaign.⁹

However, Early's involvement on the first day at Gettysburg in the crucial failure to take Cemetery Ridge had been the subject of controversy:

LIEUTENANT-GENERAL JUBAL A. EARLY, CHOSEN TO LEAD ATTACK ON LYNCHBURG AND NORTH (LIBRARY OF CONGRESS).

> On the first day of the battle, when it was essential for the South to take control of Cemetery Ridge, Ewell would not commit the forces to do it. Lee had given him discretionary orders, telling him to make the assault "if possible." Ewell decided it wasn't. Moreover, he persuaded the normally combative Early that this was

the right course. Early indicated later that he had wanted to make the attack, but at the critical hour he did not argue forcefully for it and acquiesced to Ewell's decision.[10]

Early also participated in the Mine Run Campaign in late 1863 and the May 1864 Overland Campaign that included the Wilderness, Spottsylvania, North Ana and the Cold Harbor battle of early June 1864.[11]

Major Charles R. Bowery, Jr., in *Lee and Grant: Profiles in Leadership on the Battlefields of Virginia*, discussed Lee's masterful reorganization of his decimated officer corps after the wounding of General James Longstreet on May 6, 1864, while fighting Grant at Spottsylvania. Based purely on military ability, the ablest man to take Longstreet's place as he recovered from his wounds was Lieutenant General Jubal A. Early—Lee's "Bad Old Man." Early was feisty, extremely profane, combative and could generally be relied on to follow Lee's aggressive orders aggressively. However, he had a history of problems listening to subordinate officers and interacting well with them.[12]

General Lee had consulted staff officer Moxley Sorel about who should take over for Longstreet during his recuperation. Sorel felt Early would be objectionable to the officers and men of the corps. The man Sorel preferred was General Richard Anderson—a vigorous and capable officer. Lee listened to Sorel and did name Anderson to fill in until Longstreet returned to command. This Anderson did quite well. Lee determined to use Early in a role where his daring would be utilized to the fullest—the command of the Army of the Valley, which Lee would use to relieve Lynchburg and attack the North. Artillerist Robert Stiles also described Lee's confidence in Jubal Early to fulfill difficult and demanding roles:

> The commanding general reposed the utmost confidence in him. This he indicated by selecting so frequently for independent command, and to fill the most critical, difficult, and I had almost said hopeless, positions, in the execution of his own great plans; as for example, when he left him at Fredericksburg [During the Chancellorsville campaign] with nine thousand men to neutralize Sedgwick with thirty thousand.[13]

The talent pool that Lee had to choose from had somewhat diminished. There were twelve brigadier generals in the 2nd Corps of the Army of Northern Virginia at the commencement of the Wilderness campaign. After Cold Harbor, there was one brigadier left. Gordon and Ramseur had been promoted to the rank of major general. The other nine had been killed, wounded or captured. Ewell had turned over command of the corps to Early. Then Ewell had been relieved and assigned to the defenses of Richmond. Longstreet had failed at independent command at Knoxville in 1863 and was recovering from wounds received in the Wilderness. A.P. Hill had been confined to an ambulance at Spottsylvania and was resuming command of his division on May 20, 1864.[14] Early had a good record and was well regarded by both Lee and Confederate president Jefferson Davis, who found Early was "a man of independent mind, entirely self-reliant and with an aptitude for strategy."[15] Millard Kessler Bushong states, "He [Early] was bold and aggressive. According to President Jefferson Davis, General Lee and he agreed that, in the absence of Stonewall Jackson, 'Early was the living man who like Jackson could be relied on to carry out the purposes intrusted to him without asking for additional instructions."[16] Speaking of Early in his military capacity, Davis regarded him as the nearest to Stonewall Jackson of all of Lee's subordinate officers.[17]

However, Henry Kyd Douglas, who served under Early, although echoing similar sentiments to those of Lee and Davis regarding Early's military ability, also found him difficult for subordinate officers to deal with. "He received with impatience and never acted upon, either advice or suggestion from his subordinates. Arbitrary, cynical, with strong prejudices, he was personally disagreeable; he made few admirers or friends either by his manners or his habits." Early himself stated that he was not blessed with popular and captivating manners and had been viewed as being haughty and disdainful.[18]

On the afternoon of June 12, 1864, General Robert E. Lee summoned Early to his headquarters for a conference. Lee gave Early orders to prepare his 2nd Corps for an operation in the Shenandoah Valley. The 2nd Corps, which Early was now permanently commanding after Ewell was relieved, was near Gaines Mill and Cold Harbor on June 12, 1864. Nelson's and Braxton's artillery battalions were added under the command of Brigadier General Armistead Long.[19] The bold plan outlined by General Lee and put into writing later on the night of the 12th was for Early "to strike Hunter's force in the rear, and if possible, destroy it, then to move down the Valley ... and threaten Washington."[20] Lee hoped that Early's attack would force Grant to weaken himself and allow an attack on him or force an attack by him.[21] Jeffrey D. Wert stated:

> Lee viewed the proposed operation as a gamble. While Hunter's threat to Lynchburg had to be eliminated, Lee hoped to gain the strategic initiative in the Old Dominion with his army locked in place outside Richmond by George G. Meade's Army of the Potomac [under the direction of General in Chief Ulysses S. Grant]. Lee saw in Early's operations and opportunity to break the stalemate. He believed that such a strike across the Potomac River would compel Grant to detach units from Meades's army and timely provide an opening to launch an offensive against the weakened Federals."[22]

He also found Early to have been burdened by a strategy with a numerically inferior command. He also had to deal with the legacy of Stonewall Jackson.

To be able to effectuate Lee's initiative, Early would have to be able to overcome those problems plus problems in relationships with subordinate officers. At least Lee had given Early some outstanding combat officers to be Early's subordinates in his Army of the Valley — including Rodes, Ramseur, Gordon and Breckinridge.

Early described Lee's written directions:

> I [Early] was directed to move with the force designated, a 3 o'clock next morning for the Valley by way of Louisa Court House and Charlottesville, and through Brown's or Swift Run Gap into the Blue Ridge, as I might find most advisable, to strike Hunter's forces in the rear, and, if possible, destroy it; then move down the Valley, cross the Potomac near Leesburg, or at or above Harper's Ferry, as I find most practicable, and threaten Washington City. I was further directed to communicate with General Breckinridge, who would cooperate with me in the attack on Hunter and the expedition to Maryland.[23]

On June 12, 1864, General Robert Ransom was ordered to turn over his command near Richmond to General G.W.C. Lee and to report to Richmond as soon as circumstances permitted. He was assigned to command the cavalry division in Western Virginia, which would be with Early's army.[24]

Early's forces, as they prepared to leave the Richmond area, had seen hard service from the Wilderness to Cold Harbor as their commander described:

> The 2d Corps now numbered a little over 8,000 muskets for duty. It had been on active and arduous service in the field for forty days and had been engaged in all of the great battles from the Wilderness to Cold Harbor, sustaining very heavy losses at Spottsylvania Court-House, where it lost nearly an entire division, including its commander, Major General Johnson, who was made prisoner. Of the brigadier generals with it at the commencement of the campaign, only one remained in command of his brigade. Two (Gordon and Ramseur) had been made Major-Generals; one (G.H. Stewart) had been captured; four (Pegram, Hays, J.A. Walker and R.D. Johnston) had been severely wounded; and four (Stafford, J.M. Jones, Daniel and Doles) had been killed in action. Constant exposure to the weather, a limited supply of provisions, and two weeks' service in the swamps north of the Chickahominy had told on the health of the men. Divisions were not stronger than brigades ought to have been, nor brigades than regiments.[25]

On the route to the Valley, Early's infantry divisions in the 2nd Corps would be led by Major Generals Ramseur and Gordon. The cavalry would be under the command of General Ransom and the artillery, Brigadier General Long.[26] An arduous march awaited the Confederate forces, which had been through such protracted and heavy action for so long. Starting before 3:00 A.M. on the morning of June 13, 1864, Early's forces had left their lines and started their movement. They marched 25 miles on June 13, 1864, to Auburn Mills on the South Ana River.[27]

Of crucial importance was that Jefferson Davis, at Lee's request, had kept news of the movement of Early's army from the newspapers.[28] His army marched through Mechanicsville and reached Trevilian Station beyond Louisa Court House on June 15, 1864. By June 16, Early's forces had reached Charlottesville, having marched 80 miles in four days.[29]

Major General John C. Breckinridge, with the brigades of John Echols and Gabriel Wharton, numbering about 2,100 men, had already left Lee's army and had moved toward Lynchburg. Wharton's brigade consisted of the 30th Virginia Infantry Battalion Sharpshooters, the 45th Virginia Infantry and the 51st Virginia Infantry. Echol's brigade included the 22nd Virginia Infantry, the 23rd Virginia Infantry Battalion and the 26th Virginia Infantry Battalion. Breckinridge initially also ordered General Vaughn to go to Lynchburg. Lee had ordered Breckinridge to concentrate all available troops there.

Vaughn and Imboden were ordered by General Breckinridge to temporarily remain by Rockfish Gap. General D.H. Hill was put temporarily in charge of preparing the defensive works at Lynchburg. General Breckinridge was hospitalized due to an injury caused by the fall of his horse at Cold Harbor.[30]

On June 12, 1864, the Confederate commander mobilized his small force available for the defense of Lynchburg. His forces consisted of home guards and men recruited from the hospitals in the city. All convalescents capable of holding a gun were organized at Camp Nicholls, outside of Lynchburg. The militia forces were posted at Amherst Heights, across the James River from the city. After Captain Douthat's engagement on the Tye River with General Duffie's cavalry forces, his 100-man unit joined the garrison at Lynchburg. Citizens also volunteered. These men ranged from 15-year-old E.C. Hamner to 81-year-old Mike McConnell.[31]

While Early was in the process of getting up to Charlottesville on the way to Lynchburg and the Confederates were otherwise concentrating their other limited, available forces to defend Lynchburg, General David Hunter had finally started to move out of Lexington. At 2:00 A.M. on the morning of June 13, Hunter sent Averell's cavalry in advance to Buchanon with the purpose of keeping McCausland's small Confederate force from destroying the bridge there over the James River.[32] Averell also had sent a 200-man cavalry force on a reconnaissance mission around Lynchburg.[33] On the afternoon of June 13, Duffie's cavalry force rejoined Hunter's army at Lexington, bringing in a number of prisoners, who were interrogated. Colonel David Hunter Strother reported that

> while it was important that we should have moved from Lexington without delay, we were detained, awaiting the arrival of General Duffie's column of cavalry, which marched on the road next to the Blue Ridge, and which did not report until the thirteenth in the afternoon. He had crossed the bridge at the Tye River Gap, struck the Charlottesville and Lynchburg railroad near Amherst Court House, destroyed it to some extent, making considerable captures of men, horses and material. He was confused and detained by the difficult and intricate character of the country.[34]

Averell sent a dispatch on the thirteenth that he was within 4 miles of Buchanon engaging McCausland's cavalry, which were falling back.[35]

Meanwhile, Hunter was slowly preparing to move his army toward Lynchburg without being in effective communication with Grant. Messengers back to Harpers Ferry had a very long distance to travel and were in constant danger of capture. Captain John McEntee, the lone Bureau of Military Information operative in the Shenandoah Valley, found General Hunter to be very little interested in intelligence information.[36] Hunter was moving forward to attack Lynchburg aware he had inadequate munitions and that he was getting farther and farther away from his supply lines. The Union forces under Hunter also did not know that General Early had left the Confederate lines at Richmond to move to Lynchburg.[37]

Hunter left Lexington on the morning of June 14 on an all-day march to Buchanon. McCausland's men slowed the Union advance by ambushing advance units and blocking the roads with felled trees.[38] McCausland had destroyed the bridge over the James River at Buchanon, Brigadier General Averell having been unsuccessful in his task of preventing the destruction of the bridge. However, this did not seriously delay the crossing by the troops.[39] A number of iron works in the vicinity of Buchanon were also destroyed by Union forces.

By going to Lynchburg by way of Buchanon, Hunter was not taking the most direct route. He was going about 23 miles south before cutting east, rather than going southeast through Buena Vista or east through Amherst Court House and then south. Hunter had been advised on June 13 by prisoners taken by General Duffie that Ewell was advancing with a powerful force. The prisoners also stated that Sheridan had been defeated.[40] Hunter, marching through hostile country with extended supply lines and a lack of ammunition, now faced the prospect of having to deal with Confederate forces from Richmond without Sheridan's help. General George Crook had also reported that he had heard that General Breckinridge was at Lynchburg with 10,000 men, some of whom were from Lee's army.[41]

On June 15, 1864, Hunter moved his army across the Blue Ridge from Buchanon to Liberty (now Bedford) via the Peaks of Otter—a march of about 23 miles. McCausland burned the bridge over the James River just as the Union cavalry was arriving, causing Hunter substantial delay. He was still 24 miles from Lynchburg. However, his army spent time in the area of Liberty destroying the railroad, causing further delay.

General Hunter did not seem to fully appreciate that Lynchburg was a major supply center, the capture of which would help solve his ammunition and provisions problems. Nor did he seem to appreciate the importance of getting to Lynchburg by the most direct and timely means possible. Instead, he had spent three days at Lexington and had been further delayed by McCausland's actions in harassing his forces. McCausland and a small brigade of his command under Colonel William Peters would alternately fight and then fall back. Also, Hunter had further delayed his movements by the time spent on the destruction of property en route.

On June 16, 1864, Hunter's forces did not undertake a rapid movement toward Lynchburg as would be expected when the Union army needed the munitions and supplies there. Hunter was on his own, as Sheridan had been defeated. Hunter also knew that Lee had sent reinforcements from Richmond. Yet on the 16th, when Lynchburg was still most vulnerable to attack, Hunter tarried as he had done at Staunton, Lexington and other places en route. His army spent the day destroying railroad track on a line that was not the main line from Charlottesville to Lynchburg.

Brigadier General William Averell, in Hunter's advance, was moving toward Lynchburg on the Bedford Pike. He was checked by McCausland's Confederate cavalry and made it just across the Big Otter River. Brigadier General Jeremiah Sullivan's infantry division was behind Averell. Sullivan had served 6 years as a midshipman in the navy prior to the Civil War. After serving under General Shields at Kernstown in 1862, he had gone west and was at Iuka and Corinth under General Rosecrans before going to the Department of West Virginia in September of 1863.[42] On June 16, 1864, General George Crook was marching toward Lynchburg along the Virginia and Tennessee Railroad, tearing up track. General Duffie was scouting Lynchburg's approaches. All told, Hunter's army got 7 miles closer to Lynchburg on the 16th—destroying property at a time when hard marching was needed.[43] Had he made alacritous movements east, Hunter could have been in a position to move on Lynchburg before Early's arrival. Hard marching could have put Hunter in the vicinity of Lynchburg of June 16th when it was lightly defended. Had he moved east to Amherst Court House and the Virginia Central Railroad in the first place, he would have been in a position to intercept Early's forces from Richmond, which he knew (from prisoners) were coming.

General Early himself questioned whether it could be believed that Hunter would have set out on so important an expedition without a sufficient supply of ammunition.[44] He also stated, "Had Hunter moved to Lynchburg with energy, that place would have fallen before it was possible for me to get there. But he tarried on the way and when he reached there, there was discovered 'a want of ammunition to give battle.'"[45] In his autobiographical work, Early called Hunter's delay in moving the 100 miles between Staunton and Lynchburg remarkable:

> Hunter's delay in advancing from Staunton had been most remarkable. He had defeated Jones' small force at Piedmont, about 10 miles from Staunton, on the 5th, and united with Crook on the 8th, yet he did not arrive in front of Lynchburg until near the night of the 17th. The route from Staunton to Lynchburg, by which he moved, which was by Lexington, Buchanon, the Peaks of Otter and Liberty is about one hundred miles in distance. It is true that McCausland delayed his progress by keeping constantly in his front, but an energetic advance would have brushed away McCausland's small force, and Lynchburg, with all its manufacturing establishments and stores, would have fallen before assistance arrived.[46]

When Early moved down the Valley covering much of Hunter' route, he found evidence of the atrocities which he felt had delayed Hunter from timely getting up to Lynchburg. Early had found houses burned and women and children left without shelter. The countryside had been stripped of provisions by the foraging Union troops, leaving the persons in their wake little or nothing to eat. The Virginia Military Institute had been burned, as well as the house of ex-governor Letcher. This marauding conduct by Hunter's forces at his direction in Early's view had diverted his attention from military objectives and had ultimately caused his campaign to fail.

Early's view of General Hunter's dilatoriness was shared by Captain Porter of the Union army. He stated, "Hunter made the fatal mistake of tarrying too long at Lexington; he lost two full days there. If he had utilized them it seems almost certain he would have been in Lynchburg for one day at least."[47]

While Hunter was delaying his move on Lynchburg, Early and his army were continuing to move rapidly to reinforce Breckinridge and other Confederate forces at Lynchburg. Early arrived at Charlottesville on the 16th and received a telegram from Breckinridge that Hunter was about 20 miles from Lynchburg.[48] Early sent a message to Breckinridge about 11:40 A.M. on the 16th, telling him, "Send off at once all engines and cars of Orange and Alexandria Railroad to this place, including everything at its disposal. I will send troops as soon as I get cars."[49] Charlottesville was about sixty miles from Lynchburg. It was too far to march there in time to reinforce the city before Hunter arrived. So, Early had to come by rail to relieve the city.

Early had found that the railroad and telegraph lines between Charlottesville and Lynchburg had been cut by a cavalry force from Hunter and those from Richmond to Charlottesville by Sheridan. The rail and telegraph lines had been only slightly damaged and had been repaired.

After sending a message to General Breckinridge about his situation, General Early set about obtaining all the rail cars he could find.[50] Almost two hours after his first message Early sent another message to Breckinridge telling him everything depended on promptness, energy and dispatch. "I have authority to direct your movements and I will take responsibility for what you find it necessary to do. I will hold all rail agents and employees responsible with their lives for hearty co-operation with us."[51] Early stated, "There were no trains at Charlottesville except one which belonged to the Central road, and was about starting for Waynesboro. I ordered this to be detained, and immediately directed, by telegram, all the trains of the two roads be sent to me with all dispatch, for the purpose of transporting my troops to Lynchburg."[52] In the early afternoon, at 2:20 P.M., Early told Breckinridge that his troops had marched 20 miles on the

16th to get to Charlottesville and that he would come as soon as the trains from Lynchburg arrived. "If you can hold out all morning and the railroad does not fail, all will be well."[53] Early remained in Charlottesville on the night of the 16th, as the trains were not ready to transport the troops until early the next day.[54] General D.H Hill, who was in Lynchburg convalescing and awaiting assignment, was assigned along with convalescing 2nd Corps brigadier Harry Thompson Hayes by Breckinridge to work on the city's defenses. Determining Hunter would approach and attack from the west, the generals supervised the construction of redoubts and trenches on College Hill in the western part of the city. These works were mainly manned by militia.[55] Breckinridge had initially turned over command duties to General D.H. Hill.[56]

Breckinridge's two brigades were in the city on June 15 and 16, 1864, and were in a position to meet Hunter's forces should they arrive.[57] John Worsham of the 21st Virginia Regiment found Lynchburg in a state of excitement when Confederate forces arrived, as Hunter's forces were then near to the city. There was only a skeletal garrison defending against the Union advance before the reinforcements arrived. The arrival of the reinforcements cheered the citizens of Lynchburg.[58]

When Brigadier General John Imboden arrived in Lynchburg, he and about 2,000 men under his command were sent to join Brigadier General John McCausland, who was impeding the Union advance on Lynchburg. Imboden had been ordered to take his own force and troopers of "Mudwall" Jackson's brigade of cavalry and move 10 miles southwest to New London. Imboden was to reinforce McCausland there and take command. Their purpose was to delay Hunter as long as possible to give Early's troops time to come up.[59] McCausland's and Imboden's forces skirmished with Union forces near New London. By nightfall, Sullivan's infantry moved to attack McCausland, and the Confederates fell back.[60] Averell reported to Hunter a sharp fight at New London on June 16. That night the Confederate cavalry forces moved back to the Quaker Meeting House about 4 miles from Lynchburg.

Thus at this point on the night of the 16th, McCausland and Imboden had a combined force of about 3,500 men southwest of Lynchburg facing what Hunter's chief of staff described as a force of over 20,000 men. In Lynchburg, there were Echol's and Wharton's brigades with some artillery, totaling about 2,100 men. There were 250 cadets from VMI as well as Douthat's 100-man force. Other militia and invalids from the hospitals and local units were mobilized, probably totaling less than 1,000. Douthat's force, the VMI cadets, the remnants of Jones's force and Breckinridge's brigades occupied the College Hill works on the 16th.

Lynchburg was vulnerable from many directions, and its defensive works were limited, primarily on the western side of the city. Thus, Early's arrival at Lynchburg with his army of over 8,000 men was crucial to an effective defense of the city. Brigadier General Duffie had been sent on the morning of the 16th to scout the approaches to Lynchburg but had not yet reported his findings to Hunter.[61]

Slow progress had been made on the 16th even though Brigadier General Averell had talked to a Confederate soldier's wife on the morning of the 15th and had ascertained from her that Lynchburg was not strongly defended. The only works in the Union line of march were rifle pits.[62] Colonel David Hunter Strother recognized the situation thusly: "I have a vague uneasiness as to the result of our move. Lee will certainly relieve Lynchburg if he can. If he cannot, the Confederacy is gone up. If he does succeed in detailing a force, our situation is most hazardous."[63]

At 2:00 A.M. on June 17, 1864, Major General David Hunter ordered Colonel David Hunter Strother to go to Brigadier General Jeremiah Sullivan, in charge of the Infantry Division, and order him to move immediately to New London.[64] Hunter's forces moved out early, but the bridge crossing the Great Otter River was not prepared to permit the artillery and baggage to cross. This delayed Hunter's movement most of the day on the 17th.[65]

At about 4:00 P.M. on the 17th, Averell found Confederate forces in position near the Quaker Meeting House about 4 miles from Lynchburg on the Salem Pike. Imboden's Confederates were fighting dismounted from behind rail fences. Averell called for support. Crook's infantry came up, making a combined Union force of about 10,000 facing a few thousand Confederate cavalry. The Union forces attacked and drove the Confederates back.[66] Crook's infantry division engaged the Confederate forces from about 6:30 P.M. to 7:30 P.M. They captured about 70 prisoners and took one gun. Although the men were ready to march on Lynchburg at that point, General Hunter decided to camp there for the night.[67] The cumulative effect of the repeated delays Hunter's army incurred at Lexington and on the road to Lynchburg had allowed the Confederates to concentrate their forces.

On the morning of June 17, 1864, Early had only enough rail cars to transport about half of his infantry. Ramseur's division, one brigade of Gordon's division and a part of another of Gordon's brigades were embarked on the trains and taken to Lynchburg. Rodes' division and the rest of Gordon's were ordered to march along the railroad, with the artillery and wagons moving by highway.

COLONEL RUTHERFORD B. HAYES LED A BRIGADE IN THE LYNCHBURG CAMPAIGN (LIBRARY OF CONGRESS).

Lieutenant General Early himself was at the front of the train. This part of Early's Confederate force arrived at Lynchburg about 1:00 P.M. on June 17, 1864. They had had a five hour journey on the 60 miles from Charlottesville due to the deteriorated condition of the track. The rear car of one of the trains had derailed on a bridge near Lynchburg, resulting in injury or death to a number of men.[68]

General Early stated that after his arrival, he found General Breckinridge in bed suffering from a severe wound that resulted from the fall of a horse killed under him at Cold Harbor. Breckinridge was an able soldier. He had commanded a corps at Shiloh and had served at Stone's River. He had also been at Chickamauga and had commanded a corps at Missionary Ridge before taking over the Department of Southwestern Virginia in 1864. General Breckinridge had defeated General Sigel's army at New Market before joining Lee's Army of Northern Virginia at Cold Harbor. At Lynchburg, Breckinridge agreed to cooperate with Early and agreed to serve under him.[69] Early directed military operations there.[70]

General Early and D.H. Hill went out to examine the Lynchburg defenses. The Confederate forces there included Wharton's and Echol's brigades of Breckinridge's force, the VMI cadets, the remnants of Jones's force, convalescents and militia. A few works were in place on College Hill, covering the Forest Road and the Salem Pike. Early ordered the defensive lines moved further out so as not to expose the town of Lynchburg to Union artillery fire. Ramseur's and Gor-

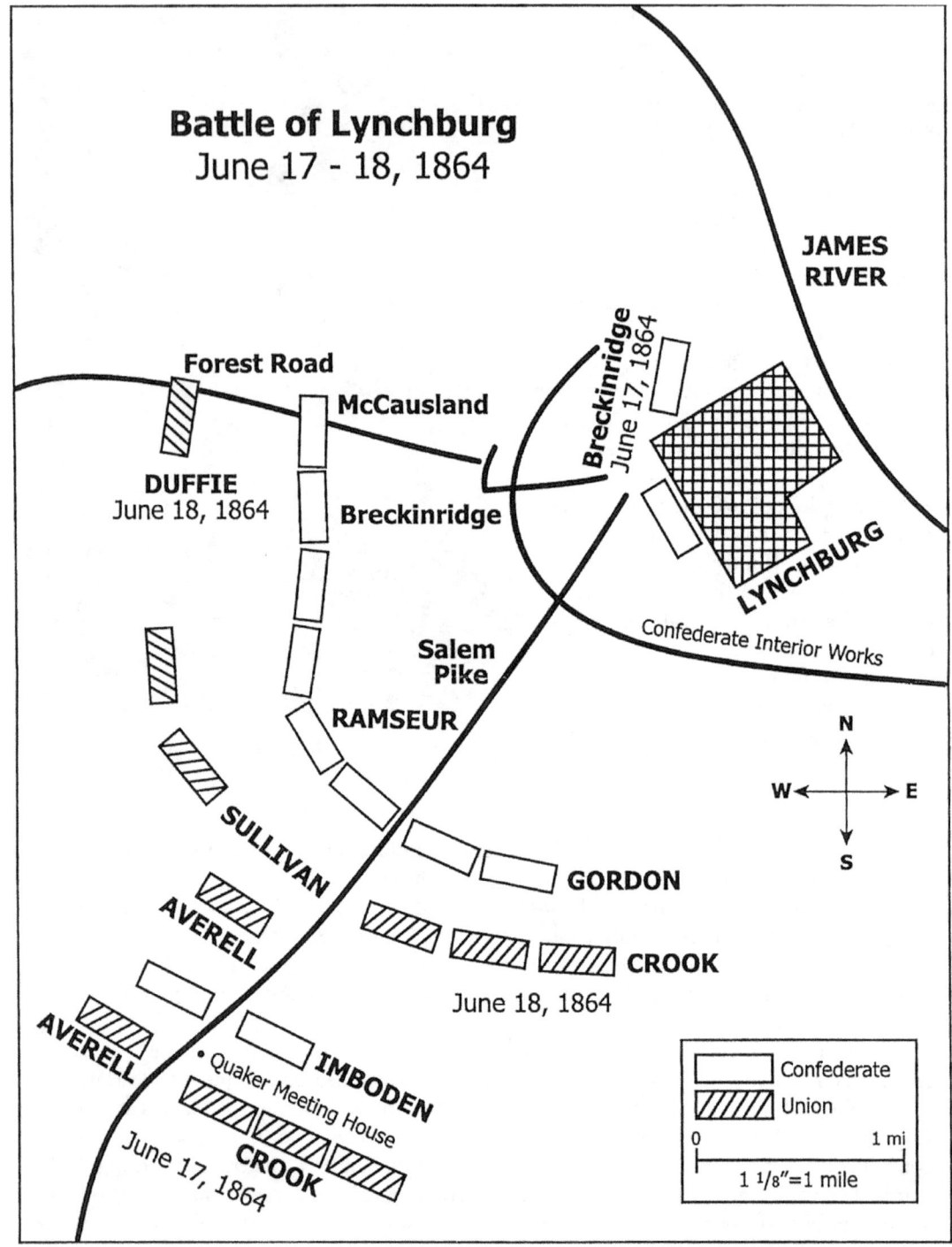

Diagram of Battle of Lynchburg: positions of opposing forces (Deb Josephs from drawing by author).

don's men were moved to the new lines. General Imboden had his cavalry brigade at the Quaker Meeting House further out, where he had already been actively engaged with the advancing Union forces.[71]

Imboden's Confederate cavalry were being pushed back by the Union forces in their front. Early then ordered Gordon's and Ramseur's men to move out on the Salem Pike near a redoubt about 2 miles from Lynchburg. The Confederate forces stopped the Union advance.[72]

Major John Warwick Daniel described the situation as follows:

> As Hunter's skirmishers were pushing close to the town, and as the cavalry were falling back before them, a few pieces of artillery near the toll-gate, under Lieutenant Carter Beckley, were doing their best to stop the oncomers. In these conditions, Tinsley, the bugler of the Stonewall Brigade [Second Corps], came trotting up the road, sounding the advance, and behind him came the skirmishers of Ramseur's Division with rapid strides. Just then the artillerists saw through the smoke the broad, white slouch hat and the black feather of "Old Jube" who rode amongst them and looking toward the enemy exclaimed "No buttermilk rangers after you now, damn you."[73]

Earlier on the 17th, Brigadier General John Imboden had sent Brigadier General John McCausland to check the Union cavalry advance to the north on the Forest Road where Brigadier General Alfred Duffie was engaged.[74] Imboden had served under Stonewall Jackson at Cross Keys and Port Republic. He had also been in large part responsible for saving the trains of the Confederate army at Williamsport after Gettysburg.[75]

Duffie said he met the Confederate force about 1:30 P.M. on the 17th in position in a woods near the Forest Road. "I immediately engaged him, with my men dismounted in the woods so dense as to forbid the use of cavalry. The engagement of my division lasted about two hours, during which we drove the enemy a short distance. Meantime, the infantry immediately on my right became engaged, and the firing was heavy along the whole line. The enemy fell back slowly."[76] At Backwater Creek, Duffie broke off the attack in the face of a strong Confederate position on high ground.[77]

As he faced the Confederate forces near Lynchburg on the night of June 17, 1864, Hunter had a formidable army of about 18,000 men. General Jeremiah P. Sullivan's 1st Division contained the 18th Connecticut commanded by Colonel William G. Ely, the 2nd Maryland Eastern Shore Infantry, the 28th Ohio, the 116th Ohio, the 123rd Ohio and a battalion of the 5th New York Heavy Artillery. Colonel Joseph Thoburn's 2nd Brigade consisted of the 34th Massachusetts, the 1st West Virginia, the 12th West Virginia and four companies of the 5th New York Heavy Artillery.[78]

Brigadier General George Crook's 2nd Division's first brigade was commanded by future United States president Rutherford B. Hayes. His brigade contained the 23rd Ohio, the 36th Ohio, the 5th West Virginia, and the 13th West Virginia.[79] A captain in the 23rd Ohio, William McKinley, later became the 25th president of the United States.[80]

WILLIAM McKINLEY, OFFICER SERVING IN 23RD OHIO UNDER HAYES (LIBRARY OF CONGRESS).

Carr B. White's 2nd Brigade consisted of the 13th Ohio, the 91st Ohio, the 9th West Virginia and the 14th West Virginia. Colonel Jacob Campbell's 3rd Brigade included the 54th Pennsylvania, six companies of the 3rd and 4th Pennsylvania Reserve Corps, the 11th West Virginia and the 15th West Virginia. There was also the 1st Battery of Kentucky Light Artillery and the 1st Battery of Ohio Light Artillery.

Brigadier General Alfred N. Duffie's 1st Cavalry Division's 1st brigade, under the command of Colonel William Tibbetts, contained the 1st Maryland Home Brigade, the 1st New York (Lincoln) Cavalry, the 1st New York (Veteran) Cavalry and the 21st New York Cavalry. Colonel John Olney's 2nd Brigade had the 1st, 3rd and 7th West Virginia Cavalry. The 3rd brigade had the 2nd West Virginia Cavalry and the 34th Ohio Mounted Infantry. Captain Henry DuPont's Artillery Brigade contained the 30th Battery New York Light Artillery, Battery B of the Maryland Light Artillery, Battery D of the West Virginia Light Artillery and Battery B of the 5th U.S. Artillery.[81]

During the night of the 17th, the Confederates worked to extend and strengthen their fortifications. Then men of Rodes's and part of Gordon's divisions had yet to come up to Charlottesville by train.[82] Early had less than 8,000 men at Lynchburg facing a Union army over twice that size. Early ordered an engine and a few cars to run in and out of Lynchburg that night to create an illusion that more troops were arriving. Hunter stated, "During the night the trains in the different railroads were heard running without intermission, while repeated cheers and the beating of drums indicated the arrival of large bodies of troops to the town."[83]

Colonel David Hunter Strother also had spoken on the 18th with Brigadier General Sullivan and Colonel Thoburn, who had similar impressions:

> Sullivan said he had heard railroad trains coming and going all night, also cheering and military music which indicated the arrival of troops in the town. Since the morning the lines were much strengthened and were pressing him hard. He was sustaining himself with difficulty. He said he was ready to attack if ordered but he felt assured that it would be a disaster. Thoburn spoke in the same strain and in somewhat more decided language. I said I had begun to suspect that they were right and that I would represent their views to the General. At the same time if an attack were ordered, I wanted to know where he would advise attacking. He had no choice and would not suggest, so convinced was he that the enemy was strongly reinforced. I reported to General Hunter Sullivan's views as I heard them.[84]

On the morning of June 18, 1864, about 9:00 A.M., Brigadier General Alfred N. Duffie attacked cavalry forces under Brigadier General John McCausland and infantry under Brigadier General Gabriel Wharton of Breckinridge's command, forcing the Confederates back toward Lynchburg. On the extreme right of the Confederate line was the 3rd Battalion of Virginia Infantry. The dismounted cavalry under Duffie moved in three columns. One was on the Forest Road, one in the woods on the left, and one in the woods on the right. When Duffie got to Backwater Bridge about 2 miles from Lynchburg, he told Hunter he had attacked.[85] By 12:30 P.M., he had driven the Confederates into their fortifications. Duffie also told Hunter that he was engaged with a superior force.[86]

There was skirmishing in the morning in the area of the Union center under Sullivan.[87] Crook helped bolster the center, where the Confederates made a determined attack, which was repulsed.[88] The line of battle ran from above the toll-gate, about two and a half miles down the Salem Pike from Lynchburg, two or three miles to the north and west up to the Forest Road. Ramseur and Gordon launched an attack on the Union lines about 1:00 P.M. on the 18th. Colonel Strother described the assault as follows:

> The Rebel yell of attack sounded along out whole front. All sprang into the saddle. The storm of yells and musketry rapidly approached and groups of fugitives began to appear through the woods. The General and staff drew their swords and rushed in, rallying these men with shouts and vitupera-

tions. Further on we met Sullivan's line retiring in good order but in haste. The General immediately faced them about and waving his sword led them back to their original position.[89]

Captain H.A. DuPont, Hunter's chief of artillery, said, "Leaping over their defenses, the enemy's infantry, with terrific yells, assaulted the Union left center."[90]

General Crook, who had been moving to the right to flank the Confederate position, returned and dispatched reinforcements to the left to aid in the repulse of the Confederate attack. The Confederates were driven back. The 116th Ohio pursued the Confederate troops into their works but, being unsupported, fell back to their original position.[91]

Averell's cavalry skirmished with Confederate forces on the Union right during the afternoon without making any substantial headway.[92] On the Union left on the Forest Road, Brigadier General Duffie's forces had moved the Confederate forces back until about 5:00 P.M. Then Confederate small arms and artillery fire forced Duffie to take a defensive position about 2 miles from Lynchburg. Duffie could see from his position that reinforcements were moving to the Confederate lines from the city.[93] About 5:00 P.M., McCausland attacked Duffie, driving back Duffie's skirmishers along Backwater Creek. He was also trying to flank the Union forces on the left. Duffie was able to hold his position.[94]

The reinforcements Duffie was seeing were men from Rodes's division and the rest of Gordon's division. They had left Charlottesville about 10:00 A.M. on the morning of the 18th. They arrived in Lynchburg in the middle of the afternoon and were moved up to the front lines at the end of the day.[95] General Rodes, made a major general for his role in Stonewall Jackson's famous march at Chancellorsville, was coming to defend Lynchburg — the city of his birth. Among those arriving was General Robert Ransom, who had been assigned to command the cavalry.[96]

That afternoon, prisoners captured by Sullivan's forces stated that they had come in on the night of the 17th from Charlottesville by rail. They had estimated the Confederate forces in Lynchburg to be about 30,000. Hunter, Crook and Averell discussed the situation, as did Colonel Strother. Hunter determined that the Union army should retreat.[97]

Hunter later reported that, based on reports from captured prisoners, he believed that part of Ewell's corps and that a whole corps under Early were now before him at Lynchburg:

> From prisoners captured we obtained positive information that a portion of Ewell's Corps was engaged in the action, and that the whole corps, 20,000 strong, under the command of Lieutenant-General Early, was either already in Lynchburg or near at hand. The detachment sent by General Averell to operate on our right had returned, reporting that they had encountered a large body of rebel cavalry in the quarter, while Duffie, although holding his position, sent word that he was pressed by a superior force. It had now become sufficiently evident that the enemy had concentrated a force at least double the numerical strength of mine, and what added to the gravity of the situation was the fact that my troops has [sic] scarcely enough ammunition left to sustain another well contested battle.[98]

Captain Henry DuPont described Hunter's situation on the night of June 18, 1864: "With but little ammunition and less food, we now found ourselves in a hostile country several hundred miles from our base, from which we were entirely cut off.... It was perfectly clear to me that our safety lay in an exceedingly prompt and rapid retreat."[99]

Hunter had a serious problem of his own making. He was almost 200 miles away from his supply base at Martinsburg. His supply of ammunition was nearly exhausted. He was short on food with a veteran force opposing him. His own delays had cost him not only the stores he needed at Lynchburg, but also the opportunity to cripple Lee's supply lines.[100]

After dark, Hunter's army began to withdraw from their lines. There were no fires, and a picket line kept in contact with the Confederates until midnight. Hunter ordered his baggage and supply trains to retire by way of the Bedford Pike. His army bivouacked for the night west of Lynchburg.

Early had made plans to attack Hunter at daybreak on the 19th. During the night, he realized the Union forces were moving. Many of his forces had just come up, and a night attack had risks. Also, Hunter might have been moving to attack Lynchburg from the south. If Early launched an attack that was unsuccessful, he could lose the city. If he took large casualties, he might not be able to undertake a march north. Thus, Early stayed in his lines that night.[101] Early said of the situation:

> Sometime after midnight, it was discovered that he [Hunter] was moving, though it was not known whether he was retreating, or moving so as to attack Lynchburg on the south, where it was vulnerable, or to attempt to join Grant on the south side of the James River. Pursuit could not, therefore, be made at once, as a mistake, if either of the last two objects had been contemplated, would have been fatal.[102]

The night of the 18th, Hunter left Duffie's cavalry division on the Forest Road. Duffie was told to protect the flank of Hunter's withdrawing army until notified that he could himself withdraw. Duffie's force was almost out of ammunition. About 10:00 P.M., having received no further order from General Hunter, Duffie fell back about 3 miles. After a staff officer sent to find Hunter could not find him but reported the army gone, Duffie marched all night and met up with the rear guard of the army at Liberty.[103]

One Union soldier, William Watson, said that the men were told they were retreating because General Lee had sent a large force from Richmond that was trying to surround them. There was not enough ammunition for another day of fighting.[104]

Private William Stark of the 34th Massachusetts said, "At half past 8 pm we were right about faced and marched by the flank. We had not marched 10 minutes until we saw enough to satisfy us that we were retreating. Everything moved with caution and in perfect order. It was a very bad place to get an army from without alarming the enemy."[105]

Unlike Chickamauga, where General Rosecrans and other general officers of his command lost their nerve and fled the field, here Hunter fled the entire theater of military operations by going with his army to West Virginia, leaving a major Confederate army free to threaten the North and Washington. Hunter did not return to Harpers Ferry until July, when the attack on Washington was over and Early was back in Virginia. This approach by Hunter was anticipated by neither General Early or General Lee.

Early had considered that Hunter was possibly moving to attack Lynchburg from the south, where it was more vulnerable, or moving to join Grant on the James.[106] General Robert E. Lee expected Hunter to refit and reorganize in Lewisburg, West Virginia, and then return to the Shenandoah Valley.[107]

Hunter also had the possibility of retreating back toward his base of operations at Martinsburg and Harpers Ferry where General Max Weber's and General Franz Sigel's forces could potentially come to his aid. Early initially believed that Hunter would withdraw down the Shenandoah Valley the way he came.[108] Hunter could also take the Valley of the South Branch of the Potomac River, paralleling the Shenandoah Valley, which would allow him to get some supplies in West Virginia while shadowing Early and remaining in proximity to him.

Another option was for Hunter to fall back into southwestern Virginia, where there were abundant supplies. Early stated that he would have been obliged to follow Hunter there.[109]

One of Grant's main concerns was to shut down the Shenandoah Valley as an invasion route to the north. To do that, Hunter had to adopt a strategy to accommodate that concern. He had already destroyed much property in the Valley, which was another of Grant's objectives for him. Hunter picked the only strategy that both opened the Valley and the North to a Confederate invasion, at a time when the war was going very badly for the Union and Lincoln's reelection was very uncertain, and took his army out of the theater of operations as a deterrent force. Hunter had handed Lee the opportunity to turn the tables and the possibility of temporarily seizing and burning Washington, which almost changed everything.

In proceeding with his withdrawal, Hunter occupied Liberty, about 10 miles west of Lynchburg, on June 19. General William Averell fought a rearguard action with the Confederate advance of cavalry in that area. Private William Stark of the 34th Massachusetts said of the action:

> The Rebs come up on our rear this afternoon and attacted [sic] us with spirit. They wacked our Cavlry [sic] badly and drove them through Liberty. Averell met them with heavy columns and checked them. Everything moved lively now. The waggon [sic] trains started pm; hundreds were set to chopping down trees and throwing down fences. Such a hammering as you never heard was kept up until midnight. The noise was to deceive them and deaden the sound of our trains. The trees were felled to obstruct progress in filling up our rear.[110]

General Early had telegraphed General Lee about the outcome of the Battle of Lynchburg on June 19.

> Last evening the enemy assaulted my lines in front of Lynchburg and was repulsed by the part of my command which was up. On the arrival of the rest of the command I made arrangements to attack this morning at light, but it was discovered that the enemy was retreating, and I am now pursuing. The enemy is retreating in confusion, and if the cavalry does its duty, we will destroy him.[111]

The Confederate cavalry pursuit of Hunter's retreating army was delayed. Brigadier General John Imboden, who was on the road to Campbell Court House in a direction opposite to that which Hunter was going, did not receive the order to move toward Liberty in time to get there before the Union forces. Brigadier General John McCausland took the wrong road and did not get to Liberty until after the Union army had passed. However, Ramseur's infantry division did make a 25 mile march to Liberty and overtook Averell's rear guard there.[112] Averell was driven back through Liberty losing at least 100 killed and wounded. The Union army was on the march again at midnight.

While being pursued by Early, Hunter continued his retreat on June 20 toward Salem. The Union army had been on the road part of the night and kept moving on the 20th. Averell advised at 2:00 P.M. that the Confederates were advancing on the Union rear in force. Brigadier General George Crook reported at 2:30 P.M. on June 20 that the Confederates were pressing on his flank. The army continued its march to Salem, entering there at sunrise.[113]

On the morning of June 21, 1864, McCausland's Confederate cavalry got behind Duffie's Union cavalry force and attacked the Union wagons and artillery. Duffie had neglected to protect important road crossing which had allowed the Confederate access to the Union wagons and artillery near Hanging Rock. The Confederate forces captured and disabled two batteries, cutting up the carriages with axes and taking the horses. Numerous prisoners were taken. Sullivan and Averell were ordered up.[114]

Colonel David Hunter Strother noted, "The road was blocked with our disabled artillery, their carriages hacked to pieces, guns spiked, horses and harnesses gone, Captain DuPont was fitting some of them up and succeeded in restoring four pieces. We abandoned eight pieces, destroying them completely."[115]

The 34th Massachusetts was part of Sullivan's force which came up. Private Stark noted:

> We hurried to the rescue on the double quick. The sun shone down upon us in that narrow gorge with uncommon heat, and men went on and on, on a run. We soon came up to the Cavlry [sic] and Artilry [sic] men. There former were working around and trying to catch the raiders. The Artillerymen were idle, some of them had escaped from the Rebs. They were mostly Germans, great strong swarthy men that you would think would not have any feeling for anything. Some lay bleeding whilst others were lamenting for their poor horses and lost guns. There were waggons [sic] burning with

ammunition in them. They were cut, burned and hacked to pieces for the space of about three miles, thrown over the bank, &c. We got to the front at last, 7 miles in 85 minutes by the watch.

Ninety of the Artilry [sic] horses were found and shot as they had to be left. The Rebels took perhaps 100 prisoners. We captured some.[116]

Grant had telegraphed Major General George G. Meade on June 21, "The only word I would sent [sic] Hunter would be verbal simply let him know where we are & tell him to save his army in the way he thinks best whether by getting back into his own Dept or by joining us. If we had the enemy driven north of the Appomattox I think he would have no difficulty joining us."[117]

On June 22, 1864, Colonel David Hunter Strother wrote, "Our position will be a gloomy one if the reports we hear are confirmed. Worn out with fatigue, without support in a country producing little at best and already washed by war, the troops are beginning to show signs of demoralization and short of ammunition. We will hardly save our army if the enemy is as far ahead as it appears and occupies the positions reported."[118]

By the 23rd, the Union army had reached Sweet Springs in West Virginia. Hunter had rejected a suggestion to move northward through the Valley of the South Branch of the Potomac, running parallel to the Shenandoah Valley, to reach the Baltimore and Ohio at New Creek and Cumberland. This was due to lack of supplies and the risk of being cut off by Confederate forces from Staunton and Harrisonburg in the Shenandoah Valley. Hunter decided to go through Meadow Bluff and Gauley and ultimately to reach Charleston, West Virginia.[119]

Early had decided to discontinue pursuit once Hunter was in the mountains, which was a desolate region which would furnish little or nothing by way of provisions for his army once the Union army had passed.[120]

As Hunter was passing into West Virginia and taking himself out of the path of Lee's invasion plan, Early was turning north on a path that would take him to Winchester by July 2.[121] Hunter's incongruous action was not lost on Early. On June 23, Early wired Lee that since Hunter had temporarily taken himself out of the war, he would proceed with his original instructions, which were to secure the Shenandoah Valley and cross into Maryland and attack Washington if circumstances permitted.[122] On June 26, 1864, General Lee confirmed to Confederate president Jefferson Davis that Early should proceed with his original plan after taking note that Hunter had made good on his retreat but was still a threat.[123]

> General Hunter has escaped Early, and will make good his retreat, as far as I can understand, to Lewisburg. Although his expedition has been particularly interrupted, I fear he has not been much punished except for the demoralization of his troops and the loss of some artillery. From his present position he can easily be reorganized and re-equipped, and, unless we have sufficient force to resist him, will repeat his expedition.[124]

Lee felt that Early should move down the Valley and draw Hunter after him. If circumstances proved favorable, Lee thought Early should cross the Potomac. Lee was confident he could maintain his lines at Richmond against Grant while Early was undertaking the gamble.[125]

The Union and Confederate armies were marching in opposite directions. On the 23rd, Hunter moved to Sweet Springs.[126] Having already rejected going north through the Valley of the South Branch of the Potomac, Hunter continued his move into West Virginia. He moved to White Sulphur Springs on the 24th, Lewisburg on the 25th, Gauley on the 27th and Charleston on the 30th.[127]

Private William Stark of the 34th Massachusetts characterized conditions on Hunter's retreat as follows:

> Everything that was eatable ... was eaten, such as roots and herbs. We pealed [sic] the black birch trees and ate the bark.... The men and teams continued to give out. What ammunition we had left was thrown away to lighten our burthen [sic].... Trunk valises, Knapsacks and all kinds of baggage was thrown from the train and left or burned.[128]

Hunter took three days in Charleston to reorganize and refit his troops. They took steamers to Parkersburg on July 3 and arrived on July 4. Hunter's army was in Parkersburg until July 8. Then he took his army to Cumberland, where he remained until July 14 before going by rail to Martinsburg.[129]

After Hunter removed himself from the theater of operations, the Confederates had a commander described as self-reliant, of independent mind and with an aptitude for strategy.[130] Early was believed by Davis to be a man who could operate on a mission without needing additional instructions as to what to do.[131] Early had received a telegram from Lee at Lynchburg giving him the option of returning to Lee's army at Richmond or proceeding with his original instructions.[132] After his pursuit of Hunter had ceased, Lee sent another dispatch submitting it to Early's judgment if the condition of his troops would permit the expedition north across the Potomac to be carried out. Early advised Lee he was determined to continue with his original plan of operations.[133] On June 23 Brigadier General Bradley T. Johnson joined Early with a brigade of Maryland cavalry. On the twenty-sixth, Early's men got to Staunton. At Staunton, Lee again telegraphed Early, submitting to his judgment whether the movements to the Potomac should be made. Early again responded that it was his purpose to continue.

On June 26, 1864, Early and his staff distributed the small amount of supplies obtained from Richmond. Fruits and grains were stocked in. Broken equipment was discarded. The forces were reorganized. Early started north again on the twenty-eighth. The only contact with Union troops Early's army encountered was contact with a small cavalry unit near Front Royal by the 31st Georgia of Evans's brigade on July 1. By July 2, Early had reached Winchester at the head of the Shenandoah Valley. His men had traversed about 200 miles in 10 days, a pace reminiscent of Jackson's foot cavalry. Some of the men, like John O. Caster of the Stonewall Brigade, had to be hospitalized due to sore feet and ended up being held at Winchester.[134]

On June 28, 1864, Grant received his first report from General David Hunter and Captain John McEntee of the Bureau of Military Information, which informed Grant that Hunter had withdrawn in the face of a superior force at Lynchburg and speculated that Early's forces had probably returned to Richmond.[135]

John Garrett, president of the Baltimore and Ohio Railroad, telegraphed Secretary of War Stanton on June 29, 1864, that there were reports of Confederates moving down the Shenandoah Valley. On July 1 Chief of Staff Halleck notified Grant of conflicting reports of Confederates in the Valley. On that date, Grant replied that Early's corps had returned to Richmond. On July 2, 1863, Franz Sigel, the Union commander at Martinsburg, reported that Confederate forces had been seen near Strasburg.[136]

At Winchester on July 2, Early received a dispatch from Lee telling him to remain in the lower Valley until everything was in readiness to cross the Potomac and to destroy the Baltimore and Ohio Railroad and the C and O Canal as far as possible. On July 2, McCausland's cavalry was sent on the road to North Mountain toward Martinsburg, with Bradley Johnson being sent to Leetown on July 3 to try to cut off the retreat of Sigel from Martinsburg.[137]

With Hunter's vacating of the theater of operations, all that remained between Early and Washington were the small armies of Franz Sigel at Martinsburg and Max Weber at Harpers Ferry. Grant did not know this or credit information suggesting it.

Hunter showed little insight into the potential catastrophe his actions had created as Lee's plan was unfolding. In a letter to Grant, Hunter said he was not informed that he had anything to do with the defense of Washington and assumed Halleck had made provisions for that purpose.[138] A Confederate threat that need not have been was continuing to be undertaken at the Union's great peril.

Chapter 7

Early's Fateful Decision

According to Lieutenant General Jubal A. Early, General Lee had given him orders on June 12, 1864, to take the 2nd Corps of the Army of Northern Virginia to the Shenandoah Valley to strike General David Hunter's force and destroy it, if possible. Early was then to move down the Shenandoah Valley toward the Potomac and cross near Leesburg in Loudon County, Virginia, or at or above Harpers Ferry—whichever Early deemed more practicable. After this, he would move on Washington.[1] Lee telegraphed Early on the 26th at Staunton, where the Confederate Army of the Valley was being resupplied and taking a brief respite from hard marching. Many of the men were barefoot or had inadequate footwear. Lee again left it to Early's judgment whether to proceed down the Valley and cross the Potomac.[2] On June 30, 1864, when Early had reached Mount Jackson, he telegraphed Lee about the rich grain crops in the Valley. He told Lee he hoped he could do something shortly for Lee's relief. Early was determined to proceed on an immediate invasion of Maryland and advance to Washington.[3] He had been given discretion to adopt the best plan of action from a military and political point of view.

After his expeditious move north from the Lynchburg area subsequent to saving the city and disposing of Hunter, Early left Staunton in the Valley on June 28, 1864, with five days' rations for his troops in wagons and two days' rations in haversacks. Early said, "On the 2d of July we reached Winchester, and have received a dispatch from General Lee, directing me to remain in the lower Valley until everything was in readiness to cross the Potomac and destroy the Baltimore and Ohio Railroad and the Chesapeake and Ohio Canal as far as possible."[4] When Early's army reached Winchester at the head of the Shenandoah Valley on July 2, his provisions were exhausted.[5]

When Early was at Winchester on July 2, 1864, he was about 37 miles from Leesburg on the Potomac River in Loudon County, Virginia, and another 20 miles or so from Washington. Lee had given Early authorization to proceed either through Loudon County or north through Harpers Ferry and Martinsburg, a route that was approximately twice as long. Time was of the essence in executing Lee's plan.

Loudon and Clarke counties in Virginia were part of "Mosby's Confederacy." This was an area largely under the control of Colonel John Singleton Mosby and the 43rd Virginia Battalion of cavalry. The primary Union force in this area was the cavalry brigade of Brigadier General Gustavus A. DeRussy commanded by Colonel Charles Russell Lowell, Jr. This unit consisted of the 2nd Massachusetts Cavalry, the 13th New York Cavalry and the 16th New York Cavalry. Also, there were the Loudon (Va.) Rangers, an irregular group that often clashed with Mosby's forces.

The next Union force that would be between Early and Washington if he crossed the Potomac at Poolesville, Maryland, were the troops in the division commanded by Lieutenant Colonel Joseph A. Haskins, which manned Batteries Cameron and Reno and Forts Baker, Bunker Hill, Davis, DuPont, Foote, Greble, Lincoln, Mahan, Meigs, Reno, Ricketts, Slocum, Snyder,

MEMBERS OF MOSBY'S RANGERS (NATIONAL ARCHIVES).

Stanton, Stevens, Sumner, Totten and Wagner in the northern and western defenses in Washington and Montgomery County, Maryland, as well as the eastern defenses in Washington and Prince George's County, Maryland.

The 1st Brigade under Colonel William Hayward consisted of the 4th U.S. Artillery, Battery A, the 1st Rhode Island Light Artillery, Battery D, four companies of the 1st Pennsylvania Artillery Battalion, the 13th Michigan Battery, the 14th Michigan Battery and the 150th Ohio National Guard.

Colonel J.M. Marble's 2nd Brigade consisted of the 2nd U.S. Artillery, Battery I, Battery L of the 1st Ohio Light Artillery, the 1st company of the New Hampshire Heavy Artillery, the 151st Ohio National Guard and the 170th Ohio National Guard. Lieutenant Colonel John Oberteuffer commanded the 3rd Massachusetts Heavy Artillery and the 6th through the 14th independent companies.

Brigadier General DeRussy had two brigades consisting of artillery units and national guard regiments manning the forts near the Potomac River in Virginia on June 30, 1864. The 1st Brigade under Colonel John Lee garrisoned Forts Cass, C.E. Smith, Craig, Corcoran, Ethan Allen, Marcy, Tillinghast, Whipple and Woodbury. The 2nd Brigade under Colonel W. Smith Irwin manned Battery Rodgers and Forts Barnard, Berry, Ellsworth, Farnesworth, Garesche, Lyon, O'Rourke, Reynolds, Richardson, Scott, Ward, Weed, Williams, Willard and Worth.[6]

Thus there was no substantial Union force to block Early's path to Washington through Leesburg and Poolesville. The short distance would make it very difficult for Grant, who at that time was unsure that Early was not in the lines at Petersburg, to bring up forces to protect Washington in time.[7]

However, on the northern route he chose, Early faced Major General Franz Sigel's Reserve Division at Martinsburg and Brigadier General Max Weber's garrison force at Harpers Ferry.

The total forces under Sigel's command were over 5,000. Sigel had the 10th West Virginia and the 23rd Pennsylvania of Colonel Thomas Maley Harris's forces along with 1,000 dismounted cavalry under the command of Colonel James A. Mulligan at Leetown, just north of Winchester.[8] Sigel's other forces were posted at Maryland and Bolivar Heights, Monocacy, Point of Rocks, Frederick, Duffield's Depot and Sleepy Creek. His additional units included the 135th Ohio National Guard, the 152nd Ohio National Guard, the 160th Ohio National Guard, and the 161st Ohio National Guard, as well as the 1st Maryland Potomac Home Brigade, the 132nd Company U.S. Veteran Reserve Corps and four companies of the Loudon Rangers.

The 17th Indiana Light Artillery, eight companies of the 5th New York Heavy Artillery, the 32nd New York Independent Battery, Battery A of the 1st West Virginia Light Artillery and Battery D of the 1st Pennsylvania Light Artillery were also under Sigel's command.[9]

Major General Lew Wallace, commanding the 8th Corps at Baltimore, had under his command the 1st Separate Brigade under Brigadier General Erastus Tyler, the 2nd Separate Brigade under Colonel William O. Morris and the 3rd Separate Brigade under Brigadier General John R. Kenly. Wallace had 265 officers and 6,027 men under his command on June 30, 1864, including forces at Annapolis and in the District of Delaware.[10]

Thus by taking a more northerly route crossing the Potomac, General Early faced substantial Union forces and a longer route. His army was travelling light and living off the land to a large extent. Early had stated that he would have had to thresh grain to feed his army if he moved through Loudon County. However, Loudon County was an area known to be sympathetic to the Confederacy and was farm country—country through which Early returned to the Valley after his attack on Washington.

The other consideration Early faced in terms of what route to take was General Lee's orders for destruction of the B & O Railroad and the C & O Canal. Both ran to Washington. The B & O could have been attacked by cavalry forces on raids as could the C & O Canal, to keep reinforcements from arriving from the west to threaten Early's rear. Such attacks would also interrupt major Union supply lines. Also, Washington itself was the major supply center for Union operations in the east.

Thus, Lee had give General Early a very important alternative by allowing him to proceed through Loudon County at his discretion.

There was a meeting on July 2, 1864, between some of Colonel John Singleton Mosby's partisans and members of Early's staff. One of Early's quartermasters, Hugh Schwartz, was in attendance. Schwartz was informed that the Loudon County area lacked sufficient provisions for a large army.[11] On the night of the 2nd, Captain George Booth of Johnson's cavalry advised Mosby of Early's desire to cooperate with him.[12] Early, finding the provisions problem out at Winchester, elected to proceed to Martinsburg and Harpers Ferry, where Union supplies were stored, and ultimately to cross the Potomac at Shepherdstown and other sites near Harpers Ferry.

Early stated, "My provisions were nearly exhausted, and if I had moved through Loudon, it would have been necessary for me to halt and thresh wheat and have it ground, as neither bread nor flour could otherwise be obtained, which would have caused greater delay than was required by the other route, where we could take provisions from the enemy."[13]

However, Martinsburg and Harpers Ferry were major Union supply centers which were relatively close to Winchester. Also, Early, after his attack on Washington in July 1864 went to Poolesville, chose to cross the Potomac at White's Ferry in Loudon County near Leesburg and return to the Shenandoah Valley by that route without apparent concern for his ability to supply his army in that relatively small area.[14]

There were other factors affecting Early's decision to proceed from Winchester to Harpers Ferry. He was under orders from Lee to destroy the B & O Railroad and the C & O Canal. Early was also concerned about reinforcements from the west arriving by rail in his rear. He was also concerned about General Franz Sigel's Reserve Division at Martinsburg and his other forces.[15] Early also had left empty wagons at Staunton to bring up shoes for his troops, who badly needed them. The shoes did not arrive until July 7.[16]

Major General Lew Wallace, who aggressively held up Early on his way to Frederick, and on the Monocacy on the more northerly route which Early chose, told Brigadier General James Ricketts at the Monocacy that Early should already be in Washington. Wallace stated, "He [Early] had only to cross the Potomac at Edwards Ferry below Harper's Ferry. No power on earth could have saved the city from him. As it is, he has fooled away his time and chances, and an opportunity which, if now lost by him, the Confederacy can never hope for again."[17]

In hindsight, Early, having been resupplied at Winchester, except for shoes, might well have been able to cross the Potomac and proceed more directly to Loudon County through Leesburg, territory patrolled by Mosby. This area would have been in support of a Confederate force. Early's decision to forego the option Lee had given him was certainly a factor in his ability to execute Lee's plan.

Chapter 8

Washington's Defenses Undermanned

On May 17, 1864, Brigadier General Albion P. Howe reported to Major General Henry Halleck, chief of staff, regarding the state of the defenses of Washington based upon his personal inspection. Those defenses consisted of over 60 separate forts and works with over 868 guns and mortars.[1] These fortifications consisted of an immense interconnected system of batteries, rifle trenches, abbatis, forts and cleared fields of fire.

Brigadier General John G. Barnard, chief engineer of the defenses of Washington, who also was to serve as Grant's chief engineer of all armies in the field, described their composition this way:

> From a few isolated works covering bridges or commanding a few especially important points, was developed a system of fortifications by which every prominent point, at intervals of 800 to 1,000 yards, was occupied by an enclosed field-fort, every important approach or depression or ground unseen by the forts, swept by a battery of field guns, and the whole connected by rifle trenches which were in fact lines of infantry parapet, furnishing emplacement for two ranks of men and affording communications along the line, while roads were opened wherever necessary, so that troops and artillery could by moved rapidly from one point of the immense periphery to another, or under cover, from point to point along the line.[2]

The guns in the Defenses of Washington, as described by Cooling and Owen in *Mr. Lincoln's Forts: A Guide to the Civil War Defenses of Washington*, ranged from 6-pounder field guns to 200-pounder Parrotts. The armaments include 24- and 32-pounder seacoast guns, 10- to 100-pounder Parrotts, 42-pounder James Rifles, 30-pounder rifles, 24-pounder flank defense howitzers, 24-pounder siege guns, and 24-pounder Coehorn mortars. Smaller guns included the 12-pounder Whitworth breechloading rifles, 12-pounder James rifles, 12-pounder heavy guns, 12-pounder mountain howitzers, 12-pounder field howitzers, 12-pounder light Napoleon field guns, 10-inch siege mortars, 8-inch siege howitzers, 8-inch seacoast howitzers, 6-pounder James guns, and the 4-inch rifles.[3]

The 12-pounder Napoleon, used in the Washington defenses, was a smoothbore muzzle-loading field gun adopted by the U.S. Army in 1856. It had a maximum range of 1680 yards, but its maximum effective range was between 800 and 1,000 yards. It was the standard field piece of the army and fired solid shot, spherical case shot and canister.

The Parrott guns were rifled, muzzle-loading cannons with a heavy iron band around the breech to take the pressure during firing. The 20-pounder Parrott had a maximum range of 3,500 yards; the 30-pounder, 4,400 yards. Their effective range was only about 2,500 yards. They took shells ranging from 10 to 250 pounds, depending on the size of the gun. Coehorn mortars were muzzle-loading, smoothbore guns mounted on a block or platform. The guns were portable and were often used in sieges. James rifles were guns developed by Charles T. James of Rhode Island and used specially-rifled projectiles.[4] The northern defenses consisted of Fort Marcy and Fort Ethan Allen west of the Potomac, with Fort Sumner, Battery Alexander and

Battery Vermont east of the Potomac River near the Chesapeake & Ohio Canal. Outer works on the northwest were Fort Mansfield, Fort Simmons and Fort Bayard, with Battery Kemble, Fort Gaines and Fort Reno, astride the Military Road with the Georgetown Pike, behind them. In the north central area were a small work, Fort Kearny, and a larger work, Fort DeRussy, near Wisconsin Avenue, a north-south road. To the east along the Seventh Street Road was Fort Stevens, where General Early's attack on Washington would later focus.

Running from northwest to southeast from Fort Stevens were Fort Slocum, Fort Totten, Fort Slemmer, Fort Bunker Hill, Fort Saratoga, Fort Thayer and Fort Lincoln[5] (see map of Civil War defenses of Washington).

Defending the southeastern section of the city east of the Anacostia and Potomac rivers were Fort Mahon, and southward were Fort Chaplin, Fort Meigs, Fort DuPont, Fort Davis, Fort Baker, Fort Wagner, Fort Ricketts, Fort Stanton, Fort Snyder, Fort Carroll and Fort Greble.

GENERAL JOHN G. BARNARD, CHIEF ENGINEER OF THE DEFENSES OF WASHINGTON (LIBRARY OF CONGRESS).

Down along the Potomac were Fort Foote and Battery Rodgers on the west side of the river in Alexandria, Virginia. Fort Washington was south of the city of Washington on the east side of the Potomac.[6]

Brigadier General Albion Howe, inspector of artillery, made a report on the status of the defenses of Washington on May 20, 1864. In that report he discussed the works north and east of the Potomac and made some recommendations:

> The works on the north side of the Potomac are a continuous line of forts from Fort Sumner, on the river above the city, to Fort Greble, on the river below the city. The forts in this line are in

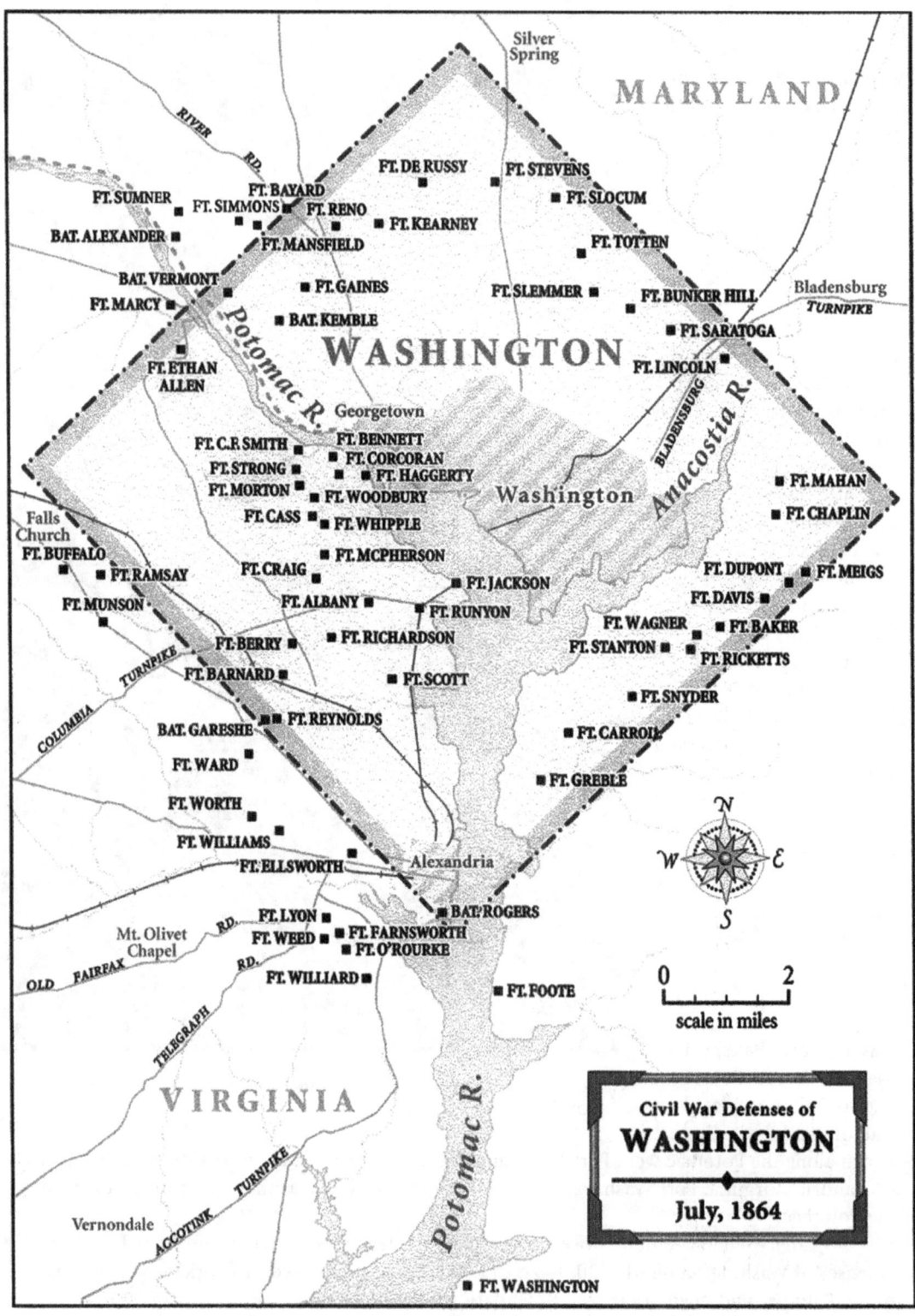

Map of Civil War defenses of Washington, showing location of forts (map by David Deis).

artillery support of each other, and connected throughout by earthern epaulements. Fort Gaines is an interior work. The most important position in this line is that part included between Forts Sumner and Slocum, as it covers the approaches to the city on the river line of roads. The most important works in the portion of the line are Forts Steves, Reno, Sumner, and Slocum. The portion of the line between Fort Slocum and the Eastern Branch is less liable to be assailed, and that portion of the line east of the Eastern Branch the least liable to attack of any part of the whole defenses. The most important works between Fort Slocum and the Eastern Branch are Forts Lincoln, Bunker Hill and Totten.

The most important works east of the Eastern Branch are Forts Stanton, Carroll and Greble, which, from their position, are in range of the Arsenal and Navy-Yard, and Fort Stanton in easy command of both. With a view to guard these works from surprise, I recommend that regiments of the Reserve Corps be stationed at the following points: One regiment between Forts Sumner and Mansfield, one regiment near Fort Reno, one regiment near Fort Stevens, one regiment between Forts Slocum and Totten, and regiment between Forts Lincoln and Bunker Hill; the officer commanding the division north of the Potomac to establish a picket -line from this force. The cavalry force at the fords of the Potomac, beginning at Great Falls and extending to the Monocacy, is sufficient, as is the force on the south side to guard the railroad. The forts throughout the line are advanced to completion, sufficient for defensive purposes, except Forts Ward and Stanton, in which I found but few guns mounted, and the work on them progressing but slowly.[7]

Howe found a vulnerability in these works as well as in those west of the Potomac River in Virginia, due in large part due to the manner in which the men manning them were posted.

> The weakest feature in this line of works, and it obtains more or less throughout the whole line of the defenses, is their liability to be surprised. The garrisons of the works, with the exception of small guards, are quartered outside the works. No infantry force has been kept between and near the line of the works. The outpost guards have been very weak. The character of the topography of the country for miles outside of the works, with the numerous roads, all favor and invite a sudden and covered dash upon the works.[8]

Further west of the Potomac in the Virginia defenses of Washington from south to north, were Fort Willard, Fort Ward, Fort O'Rourke, Fort Farnesworth, Fort Lyon, Fort Ellsworth, Fort Williams and Fort Worth, with Fort Ward being the major work. The main western defenses of Washington north of Fort Ward consisted of Battery Garesche, Fort Reynolds, Fort Barnard, Fort Berry, Fort Richardson, Fort Albany, Fort Craig, Fort Tillinghast, Fort Cass, Fort Woodbury, Fort Morton, Fort Strong and Fort C.F. Smith. Outer western defenses were Fort Ramsey, Fort Munson, Fort Buffalo and Fort Taylor. Inner defenses near the Potomac were Fort Scott, Fort Runyon, Fort Jackson, Fort McPherson, Fort Whipple, Fort Corcoran, Fort Haggerty and Fort Bennett.[9] The garrison requested to man the works at two men per yard of fort perimeter and per yard of interior work perimeter in March 1863 was 20,000 and by April 1865 was 22,800, making the total perimeter nearly 13 miles.[10]

The works in the defenses of Washington in May 1864 were found sufficient in their engineering and artillery strength: "After careful examination of the line of works, I am of the opinion that they are ample in their engineering and artillery strength for the purpose for which they were intended—the defense of Washington."[11] However, this strong system of defensive works was dangerously undermanned. The defenses had been stripped of veteran artillerists, sent to fight as infantry in Grant's army before Richmond.

The Report of the Commission ordered by Secretary of War Stanton to report on the defenses of Washington stated a total infantry garrison of 25,000 men and 9,000 artillerymen were required for the defenses. Brigadier General J.G. Barnard reported in 1871, "When Early marched on Washington in 1864 the defenses had been stripped of disciplined and instructed artillery regiments (number about 18,000) which had constituted their garrison, and their places supplied by newly raised 100-day regiments (Ohio National Guard), insufficient in numbers and quite uninstructed." This assessment was borne out by reports of the troop movements in the months prior to Early's raid. By May 17, 1864, according to General Howe's report, garrisons had been withdrawn and the following forts were not reported as being garrisoned by artillery units: Fort Saratoga, Fort Lincoln, Battery Jameson, Fort Bunker Hill and Fort Thayer.[12]

By May and June 1864, nearly all of the able-bodied men in the defenses of Washington had been sent to reinforce Grant before Richmond. Most of the men on guard duty in Washington were Veteran Reserve troops. Most of the experienced artillerists in the garrison force had been sent to the Army of the Potomac as infantry, as well as dismounted batteries of field-artillery and the men serving them.

As reported by General Howe on May 17, 1864, Fort Marcy on the northwest defenses of Washington south of the Potomac River by the Chain Bridge was garrisoned by three companies of the 2nd Pennsylvania Heavy Artillery with 10 officers and 430 men manning two 12-pound mountain howitzers, three 20-pounder Parrotts, three 10-pounder Parrotts, three 24-pounder siege guns, six 30-pounder Parrotts, two 24-pounder Coehorn mortars and one 10-inch siege mortar. Fort Ethan Allen was commanded by Colonel Gibson with 29 commissioned officers and ordinance sergeant and 1,346 men serving nine 6-pounder field guns, three 10-pounder Parrotts, three 32-pounder bronze howitzers, four 24-pounder siege guns, two 8-inch Sea Coast howitzers, eleven 30-pounder Parrotts, six 24-pounder Coehorn mortars and four 10-inch siege guns. One company of the 13th New York Cavalry was also garrisoned at the fort.[13]

The 2nd Pennsylvania Heavy Artillery had served in the defenses of Washington since 1862. The regiment was involved in expanding Fort Massachusetts along the Seventh Street Road into Fort Stevens, which was the place where General Early attacked in 1864. The unit also manned Forts Slemmer, Bunker Hill, Saratoga, Thayer and Lincoln as well as northern and eastern defenses in 1862 and northern defenses in 1863. On March 18, 1864, the units were transferred to Forts Marcy and Ethan Allen near the Chain Bridge. On May 27, 1864, the original regiment was transferred to Grant's army and served at Cold Harbor and in the siege of Richmond. Captain Norris and some 2nd Pennsylvania Heavy Artillery troops performed well at Fort DeRussy during Early's attack.[14]

However, at the time of Early's attack, Fort Marcy was garrisoned by four companies of the 147th Ohio under Lt. Col. John K. Woodward. Fort Ethan Allen was garrisoned by the 169th Ohio and the remaining companies of the 147th Ohio.[15] Batteries Kemble and Parrott had huge rifled cannon to protect the Chain Bridge.

The works in the northwest, being Fort Sumner, Battery Vermont, Fort Mansfield, and Fort Simmons as well as Battery Kemble and Battery Parrott were manned in May 1864 by the 1st Maine Heavy Artillery. The largest work, Fort Sumner, was commanded by Colonel Daniel Chaplin with 30 commissioned officers, an ordnance sergeant and 868 men. They served six 6-pounder field guns, four 12-pounder field guns, eight 30-pounder barbette guns, three 8-inch howitzers, two Coehorn mortars, one 10-inch mortar, six 4-inch rifled cannon and two 100-pounder Parrotts. Fort Mansfield was staffed in May 1864 by nine commissioned officers, an ordnance sergeant and 281 men serving two 12-pounder howitzers, four 6-pounder James rifled cannon, one 8-inch siege howitzer and four 4-inch rifled guns. Fort Simmons had five 30-pounder Parrotts, one 8-inch siege howitzer, and two 12-pounder rifled howitzers, commanded by Lieutenant Colonel Thomas Talbot with 9 commissioned officers, an ordnance sergeant and 289 men. Battery Parrott had two 100-pounder Parrotts and was served by Captain Frederick Shaw, one commissioned officer, an ordnance sergeant and 46 men. Battery Cameron had two 42-pounder James rifled cannon and two 100-pounder Parrotts served by Major George Sabine, five commissioned officers, an ordnance sergeant and 146 men. Smaller Battery Vermont had three 32-pounders with a garrison of one commissioned officer, an ordnance sergeant and 27 men.[16]

The 1st Maine Heavy Artillery was an experienced unit, having served in the defenses of

Washington from September 1862 until May 1864, when they were transferred to Grant's army. This regiment ended up having more battlefield casualties than any other regiment in the Union army. They reached the North Ana on May 23, 1864, and served at Cold Harbor and other engagements through to Appomattox. The veteran artillerists at Fort Sumner (named after Union General Edwin Vose Sumner, a veteran of the Black Hawk War, the Mexican War and the Civil War), Fort Mansfield and Fort Simmons were replaced by 100-days men from the 151st Ohio in May 1862.[17]

This line of fortifications provided protection from the area of Rock Creek west to the Potomac. Brigadier General John Wilson described the importance of roads west of Rock Creek in the defenses of Washington:

> Rock Creek nearly bisects the area between the Potomac and the Anacostia River and along the ridge between the Creek and the Potomac was an important carriage road from Washington, passing through Georgetown and following the crest of the ridge to Tennallytown where it divided into the Rockville Rd., River Rd. and Brookville Rds.[18]

The contiguous forts on the northern perimeter covering the main roads from the northwest leading into Washington were manned by the 7th New York Heavy Artillery. The primary work was Fort Reno, commanded by Colonel Lewis O. Morris with four companies of the 7th New York Heavy Artillery with 21 officers and 602 men handling one 100-pounder Parrott, nine 24-pounder guns in barbettes, one 24-pounder howitzer, four 30-pounder Parrotts and four mortars.

Morris's artillery force was replaced by a number of other units by July 1864. Colonel John C. Marble commanded companies C and G of the 151st Ohio National Guard, Company H of the 1st New Hampshire Heavy Artillery, Colonel Dayton's Veteran Reserve regiment, Company L of the 9th New York Heavy Artillery, and a newly-arrived regiment of the 19th Corps. At Fort Reno, General Hardin reported having Colonel Gile with the 1st Veteran Reserve Regiment, the 6th Veteran Reserve Regiment and the 2nd Massachusetts Cavalry under Colonel Charles Russell Lowell, Jr., operating in that area. The 1st Veteran Reserve Regiment was in the rifle pits to the right of Fort Reno. The 19th and 24th Veteran Reserve regiments were moved in column behind Fort Reno. The 6th Veteran Reserve Regiment was in the rifle pits to the right of Fort Reno.[19]

The 7th New York Heavy Artillery was also pulled out of the defenses of Washington in 1864 before Early's attack. The unit was sent to serve with Grant's army at Petersburg. The defenses of Washington had been virtually stripped of experienced artillerists prior to Early's arrival and attack. General John G. Barnard, chief engineer, wrote that in July 1864 all experienced artillery garrisons had been withdrawn and their places taken by a few regiments of 100-days men just mustered into service, with forts also being manned by teamsters, quartermaster's men and civilians. He felt that militia regiments manning the forts scarcely knew how to load and fire the guns.[20]

Fort Reno was originally named Fort Pennsylvania after troops who built it. The fort was renamed Fort Reno after Major General Jesse L. Reno, who was killed at South Mountain in September 1862. The fort rested at the highest point in the Washington defensive line at 429 feet above sea level. It had a perimeter of 517 yards with 27 guns and mortars and 22 additional platforms for field guns. Fort Reno commanded three major roads running into Tennallytown which then joined to run into Georgetown and then into Washington, including the River Road.[21]

The 2nd Massachusetts Cavalry provided support in the Tennallytown area near Fort Reno before Early's attack on July 1864.

Fort DeRussy, on the east-west Military Road east of Fort Reno, had 12 officers and 289 men serving a total of 11 guns. Fort Bayard, commanded by Major J.M. Murphy, had seven officers and 129 men serving two 12-pounder field howitzers and four 20-pounder Parrotts. It was high on the edge of the Rock Creek Valley. Its rifled guns had ranges of up to 4,500 yards. The fort was named for Brigadier General Gustavus A. DeRussy, commander of one of the divisions of the 22nd Corps at Washington. Also, DeRussy's 4th New York Heavy Artillery provided the men to build the fort.[22]

The fort helped command the Milkhouse Ford Road, which crossed Rock Creek. It was a trapezoidal work with a perimeter of 190 yards, and it had a line of rifle pits in front.

> Fort DeRussy was designed for an effective garrison of 11 officers and 283 enlisted men. Ample ammunition supply was considered to be 1.287 prepared "cartridges" for the large artillery, 960 pounds of case shot, 112 grape shot, 190 canister shells, 1011 had grenades, plus 17,842 ball cartridges for small arms. Such was the state of the fort's readiness in March, 1864.[23]

At the time of Jubal Early's raid in July 1864, Fort DeRussy was garrisoned by Spear's Company A of the 1st Wisconsin Heavy Artillery, Howe's Company L of the 9th New York Heavy Artillery, detachments of the 163rd Ohio National Guard and Captain John Norris's provisional regiment of Pennsylvania Artillery. A division of the 6th Corps bivouacked in the area behind the fort during the Battle of Fort Stevens.

During that battle, the 100-pounder Parrott alone fired 32 shells on the Confederate forces at a range of 4,200 to 4,500 yards. The smaller guns of the fort aided the artillery and infantry at Fort Stevens helping to contain the Confederate skirmish lines and prevent an assault on the fort.[24]

There were nine officers and 289 men at Fort Kearny serving 10 guns. The 7th New York Heavy Artillery in May 1864 also garrisoned Battery Smead and Fort Gaines with a total of eight officers and 293 men serving a total of 10 guns in the two works. The 147th Ohio provided garrison troops at Fort Reno on July 11, 1864, and Co. I of the 151st Ohio at Battery Smead.[25]

Fort Stevens, the fort guarding the Seventh Street Road entrance to Washington from the north, was the center of the northern defenses and the place where Jubal Early focused his attack on Washington in July 1864. It was 5.2 miles from the capital and was 321 feet above sea level. The fort was named after Brigadier General Isaac I. Stevens, who was killed at Chantilly, Va., on September 1, 1862.

> Fort Stevens was described in 1864 as a "large enclosed work, situated on high ground" overlooking the terrain to its front for several miles. It commanded the vital artery of the Seventh Street Road or turnpike leading directly into Washington from Silver Spring. It was enclosed by abatis and behind the fort lay a hollow able to mask large bodies of troops from enemy artillery fire. The fort contained two magazines (one in the original section, one in the expanded part of the fort), and a bomb-proof for a garrison now calculated at 423 officers and men, but note merely "fair" in combat readiness.[26]

The field of fire in front of Fort Stevens was aided by the requirement, in place in July 1864, that all of the grassy surfaces be frequently mowed. The grass was not allowed to be more than a few inches high.[27]

Fort Stevens was garrisoned in May 1864 by two companies of the 1st Vermont Heavy Artillery and one company of New Hampshire Heavy Artillery (Unattached) commanded by Lieutenant Colonel R.C. Benton. There were 15 officers, including an ordnance sergeant and 423 men from the unit manning four 24-pounder barbette guns, five 30-pounder Parrotts, six 24-pounder siege guns, two 8-inch siege howitzers, one Coehorn mortar and one 10-inch mortar.[28] Companies B and D of the 1st Vermont Heavy Artillery were at Fort Stevens until March 1864. Subsequently these units were called to Grant's army near Richmond before Early's attack. Companies of the 150th Ohio were at Fort Stevens as replacement troops in July 1864.[29]

To the right of Fort Stevens in the northern defenses of Washington was Fort Slocum. The fort was named after Colonel John S. Slocum, who had been killed at First Bull Run (Manassas).

The fort had a perimeter of 653 yards and provided auxiliary fire for Fort Stevens to the west while covering Rock Creek Church Road's two forks. There were hills to its front. The work had 25 guns and mortars, with 15 platforms for field and siege guns. It had six 10-pounder rifled Parrotts, two 24-pounder seacoast guns, two 24-pounder siege guns, four 24-pounder howitzers, an 8-inch siege howitzer, seven 4-inch rifles, a 10-pounder siege gun and two 24-pounder Coehorn mortars.[30]

The 2nd Pennsylvania Heavy Artillery was at Fort Slocum in July 1864 during Early's attack. Captain J.N. Holly ordered the opening shot of the Battle of Fort Stevens fired at 11:30 A.M. on July 11, 1864. Both Brigadier General Montgomery Meig's quartermaster forces and Colonel Francis Price's Provisional Brigade of convalescents served near Fort Slocum.[31] Two companies of the 1st Vermont Heavy Artillery had served at Fort Slocum until May 1864. Then they were replaced by units of the 150th Ohio National Guard.[32]

To the right of Fort Slocum was Fort Totten, in the area where Early's attack was to come. The fort was named after Brigadier General Joseph Totten, chief engineer of the U.S. Army. The fort had a perimeter of 272 yards and controlled a valley and country in front of it to the north and east.[33] It also was in front of the Soldier's Home, where President Lincoln had been staying until 10:00 P.M. on the night of July 10, 1864, as Early was moving to Washington at Rockville.[34]

Fort Totten was armed with two 8-inch siege howitzers, eight 32-pounder Parrotts, three 30-pounder Parrotts, four 6-pounder James field guns, one 10-inch and one 24-piunder Coehorn mortar and one 100-pounder Parrott.[35] Brigadier General Wilson described the position:

FORT TOTTEN, NORTHERN DEFENSES OF WASHINGTON NEAR FORT STEVENS (LIBRARY OF CONGRESS).

Fort Totten occupies a commanding and strong position and exercises a powerful influence upon the approaches from the northward and those through the valley between it and Fort Lincoln; it's well adapted to its position, well built and armed, amply supplied with magazines and bombproofs. The 100-pounder here will sweep the section from Fort DeRussy to Fort Totten.[36]

Company B of the 1st Vermont Heavy Artillery served at Fort Totten until May 1864. Company M was also at Fort Totten until May 1864, when it was transferred to Grant's army at Petersburg. Fort Totten was commanded by Major Charles Hunsdon in May 1864 with eight commissioned officers, an ordnance sergeant and 206 men.[37] Further down the line southeast of Fort Stevens beyond Fort Totten were Fort Bunker Hill, Fort Saratoga, Fort Thayer and Fort Lincoln.

Company D of the 1st Vermont Heavy Artillery was at Fort Saratoga from March until May 1864; this was five forts to the southeast of Fort Stevens (see diagram of northern defenses of Washington near Fort Stevens). It had six 32-pounder-in barbette guns, one 8-inch howitzer and one Coehorn mortar.

Company F of the 1st Vermont Heavy Artillery was at Fort Thayer in May 1864. Fort Thayer had four 24-pounders in barbette guns, one 24-pounder siege gun, two 8-inch siege howitzers and one 24-pounder Coehorn mortar.

GENERAL JOSEPH TOTTEN COMMANDED THE U.S. ARMY CORPS OF ENGINEERS (THE UNITED STATES ARMY MILITARY HISTORY INSTITUTE).

As with most of the other heavy artillery units garrisoned in Washington, these companies of the 1st Vermont Heavy Artillery were sent to Grant's army a short time before Early's attack. Units of the 150th Ohio replaced the Vermont troops at Forts Totten, Saratoga, Slocum and Thayer in May 1864.[38]

Fort Bunker Hill's artillery garrison was withdrawn on May 12, 1864, being Companies H, I and M of the 1st Vermont Heavy Artillery.[39] The fort had eight 32-pounder-in-barbette guns, two 30-pounder Parrotts, one 10-inch siege mortar, one Coehorn mortar and one 8-inch siege howitzer.[40] Replacement troops at Fort Bunker Hill were 100-days men from the 150th Ohio.[41]

The forts along the southeast perimeter east of the Anacostia River included Fort Mahan, garrisoned in May 1864 by one company of Unattached Massachusetts Heavy Artillery serving 18 guns including four 15-inch Rodman guns and four

24-pounder and two 30-pounder Parrotts. Fort Davis had two officers and 32 men from the 9th Unattached Company of Massachusetts Volunteer Artillery and served 12 guns, including three 24-pounder barbette guns. Fort Ricketts in May 1864 had two officers and 32 men from the 12th Unattached Massachusetts Heavy Artillery serving three 12-pounder field guns and one 8-inch siege howitzer.

Fort Davis was commanded in May 1864 by Lieutenant D.D. Dana of the 9th Unattached Massachusetts Heavy Artillery with a total of 33 men serving five 6-pounder field guns, three 24-pounder-in-barbette guns, three 8-inch siege howitzers and one Coehorn mortar. Fort Wagner had three 12-pounder field guns, one 8-inch siege gun and one Coehorn mortar served by two officers and 32 men of the 12th Unattached Massachusetts Heavy Artillery in May 1864. Fort Ricketts had the same staffing and complement of guns in May 1864.

Fort Stanton was garrisoned by one company of the Massachusetts Volunteer Heavy Artillery with two commissioned officers, an ordnance sergeant and 128 men in May 1864 serving six 32-pounder barbette guns, three 24-pounder howitzers and six other guns. Fort Snyder, a small work to the southwest of Fort Stanton and southeast of the Anacostia River, had a total of 72 officers and men of the 12th Company of Massachusetts Heavy Artillery with nine guns. Fort Baker had eight 10-pounder Parrotts, seven 24-pounder barbette guns and seven other guns served by two officers and 136 men of the 6th Massachusetts Unattached Heavy Artillery. Fort Greble to the southwest of Fort Snyder in the line of forts facing southeast from across the Anacostia River had 16 guns in May 1864 with five officers and 120 men from the 7th Unattached Massachusetts Heavy Artillery. Fort Foote to south of the city of Washington had one 15-inch Rodman gun and two 200-pounder Parrotts with six officers and 110 men of the Unattached Massachusetts Volunteer Heavy Artillery.[42]

This whole fort line was made up of isolated forts without support from intersecting rifle pits or trenches. Company sized units were stretched over one to three times their normal area of responsibilities.[43] This was the area that the prisoners, if liberated from the Point Lookout prison camp, would likely hit first coming in a northwesterly direction from that place to Washington.

In the time immediately before Early's attack on the northern defenses of Washington, Brigadier General John G. Barnard requested that Halleck return the much-needed artillerists serving as infantry in Grant's army to the defenses of Washington. These defenses in July 1864 lacked experienced artillery units, with many of the militia units not knowing how to fire the guns in the forts.

WASHINGTON, July 9, 1864.

Maj. Gen. H.Wl. Halleck:

GENERAL: In view of any conceivable probability of an attack on Washington, I feel it my duty to say that the most important re-enforcement we could have, and one to be obtained at least expense in proportion to its importance to the Army of the Potomac, would be the heavy artillery regiments formerly serving here. The First and Second Connecticut regiments are serving as artillery regiments with that army and should not be disturbed, but the others, or most of them, are very much reduced in numbers, and through loss of field officers and numerical weakness very much injured in efficiency as infantry regiments. They are at best worth only so much infantry to General Grant. To the defenses of Washington they would be of value not to be estimated. The militia regiments now garrisoning the forts scarcely know how to load or fire the guns. These artillery regiments are experienced and skillful gunners; know the guns and know the localities. The remnant of these regiments would furnish a full complement of experienced gunners to all the forts, and impart confidence to the militia troops now in the forts, and give to the defense a reliability which it cannot have, do what we may without them.

J.G. BARNARD
Bvt. Maj. Gen, Chief Engineer
Defenses of Washington

P.S.—I am aware that one regiment, the New York Ninth, has been ordered back, but would wish that the other and far better regiments should likewise come so as to have in each fort gunners and officers familiar with the localities.[44]

Lieutenant Colonel Alexander, aide to General J.G. Barnard, chief engineer of the defenses of Washington, and later the armies in the field under Grant, was disturbed that the batteries on the Washington side of the Potomac River along Chain Bridge were in charge of Private Spink of the 147th Ohio National Guard. He knew nothing about ordnance or artillery. No one at Chain Bridge even knew how to load the cannon.[45]

The situation was much the same across the Potomac. West of the Potomac in Virginia (see map of Civil War defenses of Washington), the 10th New York Heavy Artillery in May 1864 garrisoned Fort Lyon with five companies with 20 officers and 627 men serving five 30-pounder rifled Parrotts, ten 32-pounder seacoast guns and 23 other guns. Fort Weed had three 24-pounder siege guns, six 30-pounder Parrotts and two other guns manned by six officers and 122 men of the 10th New York Heavy Artillery. Fort Farnsworth with 10 guns had four officers and 128 men. Two companies of the 10th New York Heavy Artillery manned six 20-pounder rifled Parrotts and seven other guns at Fort O'Rourke in May 1864. Fort Willard had 12 officers and 358 men of the 10th New York Heavy Artillery serving 16 guns.[46]

The 10th New York Heavy Artillery left the defenses of Washington on May 24, 1864. The unit would serve from June 5, 1864, to June 25, 1864, in the 4th Brigade, 2nd Division of the 18th Corps and from June 24, 1864, until August 1864 (during the time of Early's attack on Washington) in the 1st Brigade on the 2nd Division of the 18th Corps.[47]

Much of the middle of the western defenses of Washington in May 1864 was garrisoned by the 2nd Connecticut Heavy Artillery (see map of Civil War defenses of Washington). Like the other defenses of Washington, these works were stripped of veteran troops and artillerists sent to Grant's army in the spring and early summer of 1864, leaving the defenses very vulnerable.

Fort Ellsworth had 20 officers and 522 men serving one 100-pounder rifled Parrott, three 30-pounder Parrots and 16 other guns. Fort Williams had 20 officers and 562 men manning 15 guns, including four 10-pounder Parrotts. Two companies of the 2nd Connecticut Heavy Artillery garrisoned Fort Worth with two 100-pounder Parrotts, two 20-pounder Parrotts, five 12-pounder Napoleons and 19 other guns. There were three companies of the 1st Connecticut Heavy Artillery at Fort Ward with 14 officers and 401 men handling one 100-pounder Parrott gun, siege guns and numerous other guns in May 1864.[48]

The 2nd Connecticut Heavy Artillery numbered 1,800 men on March 1, 1864. On May 17, 1864, it was ordered from the defenses of Washington to the Army of the Potomac. The 2nd Connecticut joined units of the Army of the Potomac near Fredericksburg on May 20, 1864, and was assigned to General Emory Upton's 2nd Brigade, 1st Division, 6th Corps. The 2nd Connecticut Heavy Artillery was involved on the North Ana, Cold Harbor and various other engagements in the Richmond theater during the rest of war.[49] Men from the 136th Ohio 100-days regiment were sent as replacement troops to Fort Ellsworth in May 1864.[50]

Battery Garesche, across the Potomac in Virginia, commanded by Lieutenant Logan of the 1st Connecticut Heavy Artillery in May 1864, had five officers and 144 men serving 11 guns. There were four 32-pounder seacoast guns, three 30-pounder Parrotts and six other guns at Fort Reynolds under four officers and 147 men of the 1st Connecticut Heavy Artillery. Fort Barnard had two companies from that regiment serving 19 guns, including six 32-pounder seacoast guns. Fort Berry had one company of artillerists from the regiment serving eight guns.[51]

Fort Richardson had 14 officers and 412 men. Three companies of the 1st Connecticut Heavy Artillery were handling two 24-pounder field howitzers, six smoothbore 24-pounder siege guns, one 100-pound rifled Parrott, three 30-pounder rifled Parrotts, two Coehorn mortars and a 10-inch mortar. The 1st Connecticut Heavy Artillery also had one company in the western defenses in Virginia at Fort Scott in May 1864 with five officers and 137 men manning two 12-pounder mountain howitzers and two 6-pounder heavy James rifled cannons.[52] Around May 10, 1864, the companies from the surrounding forts gathered at Fort Richardson. At noon they marched to Alexandria and took steamers to Bermuda Hundred. There they joined the Army of the James and served in the Petersburg theater for 11 months. Troops of the 166th Ohio were assigned to garrison duty at Fort Richardson in May 1864.[53]

Two Companies of the 1st Massachusetts Heavy Artillery with 12 officers and 256 men were at Fort Woodbury (see map of Civil War defenses of Washington), which had 13 guns, including three 30-pounder rifled Parrotts. Major Shatswell in May 1864 also commanded the garrison at Fort Cass with nine officers and 220 men. The work had five 20-pounder rifled Parrotts, three 24-pounder siege guns and other guns. Major Rolfe of the 1st Massachusetts Heavy Artillery in May 1864 commanded three companies of artillerists at Fort Whipple with 14 officers and 414 men manning 29 guns including eight 12-pounder James rifled guns. He also commanded two companies with eight officers and 220 men at Fort Tillinghast — a fort with four 30-pounder Parrotts and nine other guns. There were two artillery companies of the 1st Massachusetts at Fort Craig with 16 officers and 280 men serving five 30-pounder Parrotts and seven other guns. Fort Albany had one company of artillerists (six officers, 145 men) handling two 24-pounder field howitzers, four 24-pounder siege guns and two 30-pound Parrotts.[54]

The 1st Massachusetts Heavy Artillery had been ordered from the defenses of Washington to the Army of the Potomac at Belle Plain, Virginia, in May 1864. The heavy artillery which the regiment was to serve before Petersburg were sent by steamer and rail to that area. At Belle Plain, the 1st Massachusetts Heavy Artillery became part of the 2nd Brigade, 3rd Division, of the 2nd Army Corps under General Andrew Humphreys. Serving in the Army of the Potomac from May 1864 until May 1865, the artillery regiment was under the command of Brigadier General Byron R. Pierce in General Mott's division.[55]

The works west of the Potomac in Virginia north of Fort Richardson and other forts in that

LARGE ORDNANCE AT THE DEFENSES OF WASHINGTON (NATIONAL ARCHIVES).

area were garrisoned by the 2nd New York Heavy Artillery in May 1864. Lieutenant Colonel J. Palmer at Fort Corcoran had three companies (nine officers and 396 men) manning eleven lighter guns. One company of the Second New York was at Fort Haggerty with five officers and 164 men serving four 24-pounder siege guns.[56]

The 2nd New York Heavy Artillery was ordered to join the Army of the Potomac in the field on May 15, 1864. It participated at Spottsylvania, the North Ana, Cold Harbor and other engagements in the area of Richmond.[57] Fort Bennett also was guarded by one company of the 2nd New York Heavy Artillery (three officers, 117 men) serving two 8-inch seacoast howitzers and three 24-pounder siege guns. There were three companies at Fort Strong (12 officers, 410 men) serving four 24-pounder siege guns, four 30-pounder Parrotts and six other guns. Fort C.F. Smith had four companies of the 2nd New York Heavy Artillery garrisoning it in May 1864 (16 officers, 548 men), handling three 12-pounder field howitzers, two 6-pounder field guns, four 24-pounder siege guns, an 8-inch seacoast howitzer and six 4-inch and four 8-inch mortars.[58]

The Second New York Heavy Artillery was ordered to join the Army of the Potomac in the field as of May 15, 1865. The regiment participated at Spottsylvania, the North Ana and other engagements in the Richmond theater of operations.[59]

On June 30, 1864, an inspection report showed the 22nd Corps (garrisons north of the Potomac) were in a division commanded by Lieutenant-Colonel Joseph A. Haskins. Haskins had three brigades. Colonel William Hayward commanded the First Brigade which included the 13th and 14th Michigan batteries, four companies of the Pennsylvania Artillery Battalion, Battery D of the First Rhode Island Light Artillery and Battery A of the 4th U.S. Artillery. Colonel John Marble's Second Brigade included the first company New Hampshire Heavy Artillery, Battery L of the First Ohio Light Artillery and Battery I of the 2nd U.S. Artillery. The Third Brigade under Lieutenant-Colonel John Oberteuffer consisted of eight companies of the 3rd Massachusetts Heavy Artillery.[60]

By the end of May 1864, most of the artillerists in the brigade had been transferred to Grant's army. So had the artillerists from the 1st Maine Heavy Artillery from the 1st Brigade, the 7th New York Heavy Artillery from the 2nd Brigade and the 10th New York Heavy Artillery from the 3rd Brigade. Henry W. Halleck, chief of staff, on April 17, 1864, estimated abut 13,000 troops available for the defenses of Washington.[61] In July 1864, an estimated 9,500 men were available to fight Early.[62] Of these, slightly over 5,800 were south of the Potomac. Overall command of the 22nd Corps was under General Christopher Augur. Augur had previously served under General Nathaniel Banks at Cedar Mountain and in the siege of Port Hudson.

South of the Potomac the 22nd Corps had one division under the command of Brigadier General Gustavus A. DeRussy as reported by the inspection report of March 8, 1864. These were 11,011 men at that time under Colonels John C. Tidball, Thomas Tannatt, Henry L. Abbott and L. Schermer.[63] Colonel Tannatt and the 1st Massachusetts Heavy Artillery had been transferred out of Washington by May 1864, as had many other units. The 4th New York Heavy Artillery had been part of the 3rd brigade of DeRussy's division of the 22nd Corps in March 1864, when it was transferred to the Army of the Potomac.[64]

On July 10, 1864, Brigadier General De Russy had only 4,000 infantry, 1,800 artillerists and 50 cavalrymen to man the defenses south of the Potomac.[65] Halleck had telegraphed Major General George Cadwalader in Philadelphia to send General Auger in Washington all convalescents capable of defending forts or rifle pits and also to send officers capable of such duty. Three brigades of the troops defending were the Pennsylvania Reserves, consisting of nine regiments of about 1,200 invalids taken from the hospitals in Philadelphia and moved by train and by steamer to get to the battle fronts in the Washington area.[66]

From Fort Sumner on the northwest on the Potomac to Fort Foote, south of the Anacostia River, Brigadier General Martin A. Hardin, the thrice wounded veteran brigadier of Grant's army taken to lead from his convalescent bed in Washington, had only a 1,000 man brigade: 750 men from the 151st Ohio, 150 men from two volunteer artillery regiments and 100 men from two U.S. Artillery regiments.[67]

Hardin also had four companies of the 151st Ohio National Guard, five companies of light artillery and one company of regular U.S. artillerists under convalescing Colonel J.M. Warner of the 1st Vermont Heavy Artillery.[68] They were in forts DeRussy, Reno, Kearny, Bayard, Sumner and Simmons.[69] From Rock Creek to the Anacostia River (see map of Civil War defenses of Washington) were about 1,250 men from the 150th, 151st and 170th Ohio National Guards, two companies of volunteer heavy artillerists plus invalids from the Veteran Reserve Corps manning forts totaling perhaps 126 guns.[70]

Five miles of line stretching from Fort DeRussy to Bladensburg were manned by one militia regiment.[71] At Fort Stevens, there were men from Captain Stafford's Co. F, the 150th Ohio National Guard, some men from the 13th Michigan Battery under Captain Charles DuPont and convalescents gathered by Lieutenant Turner, totaling 209 men.

Major General Alexander McD. McCook was initially assigned to command the reserve corps on Piney Branch Creek between Washington and Fort Stevens on its outskirts and in the northernmost part of its defenses. Originally at Fort Stevens was one company of the 150th Ohio with a battery of artillerymen and some convalescents. The 150th Ohio was responsible for the whole line from Rock Creek to Bladensburg — about half of the northern defensive perimeter.

The 2nd District of Columbia, a Veteran Reserve regiment and two batteries subsequently reported to the reserve corps on the night of July 10. They were subsequently used as skirmishers. McCook moved his troops forward on the morning of July 11 into Fort Stevens and the adjacent rifle pits. Dismounted cavalry, more national guard troops and some invalids also joined the forces at Fort Stevens.[72]

Also present were men from the 150th Ohio National Guard and the 25th New York Cavalry.[73] Only about 500 men of the 2,500 men of Sheridan's dismounted cavalry sent to Washington were fit for duty. Most of these men were in the 25th New York Cavalry.

The Aqueduct Bridge in Georgetown was defended by 58 veteran reserves, who were headed by a captain who did not know where the bars for securing the gates were or if they would fit.[74] The Aqueduct Bridge was one of the main bridges connecting Washington with the defenses in Virginia.

There were several regiments of District of Columbia militia, totaling about 600 men, involved in the defense of Washington. The Chronicle of July 11, 1864, reported that General Thomas had called out the militia. Brigadier General Peter Bacon, a grocer, commanded the District of Columbia militia.[75]

The 2nd District of Columbia infantry participated in the defenses of Washington and Alexandria between 1862 and 1865. The regiment was involved in the repulse of Early's attack on Washington from July 11 to 13, 1864. The 2nd District of Columbia Infantry served in the 1st Division, Tyler's Brigade of the 22nd Corps in the defenses of Washington until May 1864 and then went to the District of Alexandria.[76]

Admiral Goldsborough had marshaled the sailors and marines in Washington to serve as troops in its defense.[77] These men included workers and naval personnel. The commander of the Blockading Squadron reported that men from the New York and Washington navy yards had been called to serve in the defenses of Washington.

> The defenses of Washington, 30 or 40 miles in length owing to the reinforcements sent thence to the Army of the Potomac, were, it was understood, to depend upon a small garrison mostly of green troops. This defense has been strengthened by a detachment from the Washington Navy Yard, and as represented in the rifle pits, by a detachment from the New York Navy Yard also sent to man the fortifications around Washington.[78]

Admiral Goldsborough was placed in charge of Navy Yard personnel in the rifle pits at Fort Lincoln. Goldsborough had contacted General Henry Halleck while serving at Fort Lincoln. "We require 500 cups and spoons. Can they be sent." Halleck replied that the government did not provide such items.[79]

Colonel N.P. Chapman reported to Headquarters on July 12, 1864, the disposition of troops under the command of Major General McCook, who held the critical area of Fort Stevens and points to the east and west. Of his total force of 7,886, one of the largest groups were 1,800 quartermaster employees and civilians. Nine hundred came from Colonel Farnsworth's 12th Veteran Reserve regiment and the 9th U.S. Veteran Reserve Corps. A group of 465 were 100-day men in the 147th Ohio. Convalescents numbering 2,800 in Price's Provisional Brigade were taken primarily from hospitals.

HEADQUARTERS U.S. FORCES
Fort Stevens, July 12, 1864

SIR: Agreeably to your verbal order communicated to me last night, I have the honor to submit the following observations with regard to the status of the forces within the command of Major General McCook:

Headquarters are located in the rear of Fort Stevens from the right of Stevens to Totten inclusive, the line is held by the forces of Major General McCook as follows:

Provisional Brigade, Colonel Price (approximately)	2800
Second District, Colonel Alexander (approximately)	550
12th Veteran Reserve, Colonel Farnsworth (approximately)	550
Quartermaster employees (approximately)	1800
Detachment of 7th Michigan Cavalry, Major Darling, operating between Fort Stevens and Bladensburg, only portion under General McCook's command	450
Total	6150

From Fort Stevens' left to Fort DeRussy troops of Major-General Wright and Major-General McCook are intermixed, those reporting to Major-General McCook as follows:

2nd Vermont Volunteers (approximately)	232
3d Vermont Volunteers (approximately)	272
147th Ohio Volunteers (100-day men)	465
9th U.S. Veteran Reserve Corps	350
157th Ohio	184
Total	1503
Amount brought forward	6150
Total	7653
Between Forts Stevens and Slocum there is a section (92 guns)	
1st Ohio Battery (L, 1st Ohio)	121
Between Forts Stevens and DeRussy, section (2 guns)	
1st Maine Battery	223
Grand total under General McCook	7886[80]

This hodgepodge mixture was what was facing Stonewall Jackson's old corps under Early. They performed remarkably well and assured Washington was defended with McCook's unconventional tactic of putting available men outside Fort Stevens as skirmishers to make Early think a larger force was defending the forts before him. Early failed to attack and carry the defenses on July 11 before arrival of the 6th and 19th Corps troops precluded such an attack. The defenses of Washington had been stripped by Grant to the bare bones to assist in prosecution of the war in the Petersburg area. Those militia, invalid, civilian and veteran regiments who were there performed well under difficult circumstances—being very ably led in the process by Martin Hardin, Alexander McCook, Montgomery Meigs and others.

CHAPTER 9

Point Lookout Prison Camp Vulnerable to Attack

On June 26, 1864, after Early was already on the march north, General Robert E. Lee wrote Confederate president Jefferson Davis suggesting that Early cross the Potomac with his forces and effectuate the release of the prisoners at Point Lookout. He requested that the mission be led by Bradley Johnson in conjunction with a naval expedition to be led by John Taylor Wood. Lee and Davis were contemplating an army-navy operation to release the Confederate prisoners at Point Lookout. Early's army was an important part of these discussions. In Lee's judgment, Point Lookout was feebly defended. The prisoners could take the guns captured at Point Lookout and the prisoners could then march to Washington to assist Early or cross the Upper Potomac if need be. Lee suggested that the operation be conducted as expeditiously as possible. If Early could put into doubt the Union's ability to put down the rebellion, their thought was that the chance for Confederate independence would be enhanced.

On June 29, Lee wrote Davis again, reiterating that the liberation of the prisoners at Point Lookout would be useful. Davis wrote on July 2 concerning the operation and Lee replied on the 3rd suggesting that no information about the plan be communicated to the prisoners. On July 4, Davis wrote Wood advising him to execute his orders and instructions. Davis also wrote Lee on the 4th, and Lee replied on the 5th that General Whiting in Wilmington, N.C., had been directed to supply 20-pounder Parrott guns and help Wood in every way.[1]

Thus action to implement the plan to take Point Lookout had been undertaken before its communication to Early. On July 6, 1864, Lee's son communicated the plan to him, expanding the scope of the expedition to include the release of the prisoners and the return of the equivalent of a corps in soldiers to Lee's army.[2]

Originally, Point Lookout had been a military hospital. Hammond General Hospital, named after Surgeon General W.A. Hammond, was located on the peninsula where the Potomac River joins the Chesapeake Bay at Point Lookout. The hospital complex had twenty wooden buildings arranged like spokes on a wheel and had space for 1,400 beds. There were fifteen 175' by 25' wards and one 175' by 50' building used as headquarters for the doctors and for linens and stores, all connected by a circular-roofed corridor eight feet wide.[3]

As prison populations increased after the Battle of Gettysburg, it became increasingly apparent that existing facilities were inadequate to house the number of soldiers being taken captive. One such prisoner was Private Francis Oswalt, Company E, 11th North Carolina, of General James Johnston Pettigrew's command. Pettigrew, upon the wounding of Harry Heth, had led his division in the attack on the Union center at Gettysburg and had been killed covering the Confederate retreat from Gettysburg. Oswalt had been sent to Pea Island, Delaware, awaiting transfer to the new Point Lookout facility, which was to handle prisoners taken at Gettysburg.[4]

COLONEL WILLIAM HOFFMAN, UNION COMMISSARY GENERAL OF PRISONERS, AND STAFF (LIBRARY OF CONGRESS).

On July 17, 1862, Quartermaster General Montgomery C. Meigs, after correspondence with Surgeon General W.A. Hammond, authorized the construction of a military hospital at the confluence of the Potomac River and the Chesapeake Bay in Southern Maryland. The first sick and wounded soldiers arrived in August 1862.

Secretary of War Stanton wanted prisons to be constructed as cheaply as possible. The 40-acre site of Point Lookout, on low land where the Potomac joined the Chesapeake, was isolated, able to be secured from attack and in a place where costs would not be high.

However, the site was also subject to flooding, had problems with fresh water and heat in the summer and cold and wind in the winter. These conditions would be particularly difficult for prisoners housed in tents. The variety of tents provided were old and had been rejected for use by Union forces. Stanton rejected having barracks at Point Lookout. He ordered tents to house the prisoners. The prison population housed in these tents reached 14,479 in July 1864 at the time of Early's raid and 20,000 in April 1865.[5] The need to so house the prisoners was a foreseeable response to Quartermaster General Meigs's order of July 20, 1863, for the establishment of a camp for 10,000 prisoners at Point Lookout using old tents.[6] Point Lookout was a clear example of the problems in using tents to house prisoners.

Chief of Staff Halleck ordered Brigadier General Gilman Marston to Point Lookout to take command and prepare a camp on a 40 acre site north of the hospital complex surrounded by a high fence.[7] At 6:00 P.M. on July 30, 1863, Marston with the 2nd New Hampshire and 12th New Hampshire and also with about 200 prisoners embarked on the steamer *John Brooks* at the Seventh Street Wharf in Washington to go to Point Lookout. After the regimental camp was laid

9. Point Lookout Prison Camp Vulnerable to Attack

BRIG. GEN. GILMAN MARSTON, FIRST COMMANDER AT POINT LOOKOUT PRISON CAMP (LIBRARY OF CONGRESS).

out, a stockade was built of split pine logs ten to twelve feet above the ground or perhaps a few feet taller, with a walkway for sentries, as well as quarters for the prisoners. Confederate prisoner E.M. Colvin said there were three forts north of the prison ground. The prison was surrounded by the Potomac, Chesapeake and Lookout Creek.[8]

Colonel William Hoffman, commissary general of prisoners, on August 6, 1863, ordered more Confederate prisoners transferred to Point Lookout and, after commandant Gilman Marston had informed Hoffman that the camp could receive prisoners, transferred more.[9] The Point Lookout prison camp was officially named Camp Hoffman.[10] The prison camp enclosure was along the shore of the Chesapeake Bay where the Potomac River joined it. The prison camp was a quadrangle, faced on three sides with a plant fence about 14 feet high. A parapet was on the outside about four feet from the top, extending completely around the three

LITHOGRAPH OF POINT LOOKOUT PRISON CAMP, SHOWING LAYOUT OF FACILITY (NATONAL ARCHIVES).

fenced sides. Sentries with loaded rifles patrolled the parapet night and day. A much lower fence ran around the waterfront side. There were armed guards where gunboats stood by in the Chesapeake Bay.[11]

Marston's forces, which started serving at Point Lookout on July 26, 1863, were veteran forces from the Army of the Potomac which had been decimated in combat. His own 2nd New Hampshire had been at First Bull Run (Manassas) in General Joseph Hooker's division and had fought in much of the Peninsular Campaign of 1862. The regiment had also fought in General Daniel Sickle's brigade in General John Pope's campaign in Northern Virginia that had followed, Burnside's Fredericksburg campaign at the end of 1862 and the Gettysburg campaign.[12] The 12th New Hampshire had been at Fredericksburg, Chancellorsville and Gettysburg.[13]

The 2nd and 12th New Hampshire were joined by the 5th New Hampshire, which came to Point Lookout in November 1863, staying until May 26, 1864. It had lost heavily at Fair Oaks (Seven Pines) in McClellan's Peninsular Campaign. The 5th New Hampshire then had been involved in the heavy fighting at the Sunken Road at Antietam where its losses were 125 men and 10 officers. The 5th New Hampshire faced the stone wall at Marye's Heights. The regiment suffered 157 casualties. After being held in reserve at Chancellorsville, the 5th New Hampshire was involved the battle for the wheat field at Gettysburg on July 2, 1863, losing 79 men out of the 179 present for duty.[14] The veteran New Hampshire troops guarding Point Lookout in 1863 had seen hard service.

By September 1863, Point Lookout housed about 4,000 Confederate prisoners. Marston was advised in October 1864 that another 1,000 men were en route to the camp and that another 2,000 would be sent as soon as tents could be sent. In October 1863, Secretary of War Stanton ordered tents to accommodate 10,000 prisoners. There was overcrowding and conditions were very difficult.

Anthony M. Keiley of Company E of the 12th Virginia Infantry described the tent camp at the Point Lookout Prison as being

> but a few inches above ordinary high tide, and visited in winter by blasts whose severity caused death. The case of the prisoners was pitiable indeed. The supply of wood issued to them during the winter was not enough to keep up the most moderate fires for two hours out of the twenty-four, and the only possible way of avoiding freezing was by unremitting devotion to blankets. This, however, became impossible when everything was afloat.[15]

Nor would the mainly open and unfortified grounds be easy to defend against a determined attack. At the prison camp, the point where the Potomac and Chesapeake merged, was a lighthouse. The Hammond General Hospital complex was north and west of it.

FRANCIS OSTWALT, CO. E, 11TH NORTH CAROLINA, DIED AT THE PRISON CAMP (COURTESY OF THOMAS MCANEAR).

Up the peninsula north along the Chesapeake were officer's quarters, surgeon's quarters, the laundry, the guard's ward, the post office, houses for employees and cottages used for the hospital. The commander's quarters, quartermaster's office and a dispensary were located in a woods north of the officer's quarters. There were no works or gun emplacements in these areas.

North of the woods, a narrow body of water running southwest widened considerably before entering the Potomac. Along the shore northwest of the egress into the Potomac were a series of wharves and warehouses.

A five-gun battery was located in some open land northwest of the watercourse. Along the Potomac northwest of the battery and up the river from the wharves was a fort, known as Fort Lincoln. This fort was square, with gun emplacements at each corner. It was not yet armed with cannon at the time that Brigadier General James Barnes took command in early July 1864.

The 2nd New Hampshire was housed north of a road running northwest from the Potomac toward the prison camp. Immediately northwest of the 2nd New Hampshire was the camp of the 12th New Hampshire. Running from southwest to northeast was a large body of inland water which was located near the Chesapeake Bay, north of the prison camp.

Along the Chesapeake Bay north of the woods containing the prison commander's quarters was a cow yard, a carpenter's shop, a contraband camp and a wagon site. Immediately north of that on the bay was a gated, rectangular officer's camp, which was part of the prison enclosure. The prison hospital was north of these facilities on the Chesapeake in the prison

FORT LINCOLN: SALLY PORT AND SOUTHERN DEFENSES (HOWARD FENHAGEN).

camp. The Confederate prisoners were housed in five rectangular tent camps, the tents two-deep in long rows. The prison pen had a gate facing the southwest and another gate facing the Chesapeake.

Immediately north of the prison pen was the camp of the 5th New Hampshire along the Chesapeake. North of that camp was the camp of the 1st U.S. Colored Volunteers. A bridge crossed the watercourse north of these camps to the camps of the colored regiments to the other side on the north.[16]

Thus the prison facility had a limited complement of troops. The works were limited and incomplete. There were only a few guns, which could not cover most approaches, and the prison camp itself. The watercourses around the camp and to the north of it across the land provided important barriers to invasion but could be crossed. The ships in the naval squadron assigned to duty at the prison also provided important protection.

The troops at Point Lookout, with proper vigilance and the assistance of the gunboats, could prevent a successful attack on the prison. Colonel James Barnes and Colonel Hoffman in early July 1864 agreed to further fortify Point Lookout. Hoffman was present on July 12, 1864, when Early's attack was planned.[17] On July 31, 1863, before Point Lookout received any Confederate prisoners, the secretary of the navy, Gideon Welles, had told Commodore A.A. Harwood, heading the Washington Navy Yard, that sufficient naval forces were always to be in close vicinity of the prison camp and to be in communication with the senior officer there. This directive was

Gun emplacements at the Potomac defenses of Fort Lincoln (Howard Fenhagen).

followed throughout the war. On July 8 and 9, 1864, the naval force off Point Lookout was placed on increased alert.

The increases in prison population and difficulties with conditions, along with the departure of veteran troops before Early's raid, made a successful defense by inexperienced troops difficult.[18] On November 9, 1863, another 2,261 men were sent to Point Lookout.[19] This increase would swell the prison population at that time to over 9,000. Edwin Beitzell put the population at 11,104.[20]

A United States surgeon general's inspection report negatively described conditions at the prison. Many of the prisoners in the camp were ragged, dirty and thinly clad. Many were also without blankets and were being inadequately fed.[21]

Frederick Law Olmstead, one of the great architects of the 19th century, was general secretary of the U.S. Sanitary Commission. He took the position that the Union was morally bound to operate its prison camps as humanely as it could. The discontinuance of the exchange of prisoners had taken place in the summer of 1863, causing more overcrowding.[22]

Major General Benjamin F. Butler toured Point Lookout, which was within his jurisdiction as commander of the Army of the James, on December 24, 1863. He found concern about the hospital, the basic needs of the prisoners and the maintenance of the prison.[23] The water source, supply and quantity was also bad. This finding was not surprising as the prison camp was located on low ground on a sand spit between two large bodies of salt water. By mid–June, 1864, the camp surgeon at Point Lookout, James H. Thompson, protested that the big prison population prevented prisoners from being humanely confined. The risk of disease was greatly increased, particularly by bad water. Surgeon C.T. Alexander, a medical inspector, came to the same conclusion.[24]

The 2nd New Hampshire and 12th New Hampshire were pulled from duty at Point Lookout and sent to Grant's army in April 1864, where they participated in numerous battles including Cold Harbor and the seige of Petersburg. On April 11, 1864, the 12th New Hampshire shipped out for Yorktown on the steamer *Thomas A. Morgan*.[25] The 5th New Hampshire was relieved by a regiment from the Veteran Reserve Corps and left for Richmond in May 1864.

Bartlett Yancey Malone of the 6th North Carolina recorded in his diary, "We was guarded at Point Lookout by the second, fifth and twelfth New Hampshire Regiments untell the 25th of Feb; And the 26th North Carolina Negro Regiment was placed over us."[26]

Also at Point Lookout under Brigadier General Marston was the 4th Rhode Island Infantry. That regiment had been involved in Burnside's North Carolina Expedition in 1862 and then with the 9th Corps under Burnside in the Peninsular Campaign, Second Manassas (Bull Run), South Mountain, Antietam and Fredericksburg. On April 24, 1864, the regiment embarked on the steamer *George Leary* at Norfolk and came to Point Lookout. On June 26, 1864, the 4th Rhode Island received orders for Bermuda Hundred and was replaced by the 10th Veteran Reserve regiment.[27]

Even some of the regiments at Point Lookout prison camp with limited experience were pulled out in the spring and summer of 1864 to serve in Grant's army before Richmond. The 4th U.S. Colored was a Maryland regiment organized in Baltimore in the summer of 1863. After training at Yorktown, Virginia, the regiment was sent to Point Lookout to guard Confederate prisoners.

In the spring of 1864, the 4th U.S. Colored was pulled from guard duty at the prison camp at Point Lookout and transferred to the Army of the James under General Benjamin F. Butler. At the Battle of New Market Heights on September 29, 1864, Christian A. Fleetwood, Alfred Hilton and Charles Veul of the regiment received the Congressional Medal of Honor.[28]

The 36th U.S. Colored Infantry was organized on February 8, 1864, and came to Point Lookout on February 23, 1864. After service in Norfolk and Portsmouth, Virginia, the regiment was sent from April until June 1864 to the District of St. Mary's in St. Mary's County, Maryland, where Point Lookout was located. The regiment was sent to the Army of the James as well. The 36th U.S. Colored was at Point Lookout until July 1, 1864. As of June 30, 1864, it had 661 men in the unit. They were replaced by the 5th Massachusetts Dismounted Cavalry (Colored). An inspection on July 12, 1864, showed the 5th Massachusetts was outside the stockade in a vulnerable and isolated position.[29] This was at the time of the planned attack by Bradley Johnson. In their place were colored regiments and 100-day National Guard troops of limited experience. The 139th Ohio was mustered in on May 11, 1864. It went to Point Lookout from June 1, 1864, to August 22, 1864, and was mustered out on August 26, 1864.[30] The 29th U.S. Colored from Pennsylvania served at Point Lookout from June until August 1864 and left after Early's attack into Maryland.[31] These regiments were part of the inexperienced defense contingent at Point Lookout and would have had to face Bradley Johnson's land attack and John Taylor Wood's amphibious assault, had they been made, without much training or ever having been under fire.

However, the somewhat veteran 5th Massachusetts Colored Cavalry, which had served in numerous engagements in the Petersburg theater of operations in May and June 1864, was transferred to Point Lookout at the end of June 1864. The regiment served the remainder of 1864 at the prison camp.

On June 26, 1864, Major General "Baldy" Smith had advised General Benjamin Butler that in Brigadier General Hincks's division there were three regiments of dismounted cavalry and one of infantry not yet drilled in loading muskets, which Hincks felt rendered them unfit for service in the field. Particular mention was made of the 5th Massachusetts Colored Cavalry. Thus, this regiment was being sent to Point Lookout as being unfit to serve in the field. How such a force would fare under an attack from a veteran Confederate force suggests the difficulty of withstanding at attack at Point Lookout if it were made.[32]

Some Veteran Reserve regiments also were sent to Point Lookout. In May 1864, the 20th Veteran Reserve Regiment was sent from Alexandria in the defenses of Washington to Point Lookout. Major Allen G. Brady of that regiment served as provost marshal of the prison camp.[33]

In addition to the transfer of numerous veteran units, the command at the Point Lookout prison camp was also in a state of flux in the spring of 1864. Brigadier General Gilman Marston was replaced by Brigadier General Hincks, who then went to the Army of the James in April 1864. Hincks was replaced by Colonel Alonzo Draper. Hincks had received a debilitating wound at Antietam and had been promoted to be a brigadier general while on convalescent leave. He had been given recruiting duties until assigned to command at Point Lookout in March 1864. On June 30, 1864, General Benjamin Butler assigned Hinks back to command of Point Lookout, while Secretary of War Stanton assigned Brigadier General James Barnes. Barnes arrived at Point Lookout on July 6, 1864, just before Early's attack, and Hincks was reassigned to Washington.[34] The changes in command in addition to the raw troops complicated the Union defense of the camp.

As a further problem, the fortifications were not complete[35] General Robert E. Lee, in communications with Confederate president Jefferson Davis in late June 1864, had stated that he believed Point Lookout to be lightly defended by colored troops and to be vulnerable to attack.[36] By July 1864, there were 14,489 Confederate prisoners at Point Lookout to be guarded in case of an attack. Without substantial numbers of veteran troops, the prison camp would be difficult to defend. Yancey Bartlett Malone of the 6th North Carolina at Point Lookout said, "The 13th day of July 13 of our men died at the Hospital And it was reported that General Ewel was a fiting at Washington And our Cavalry was in 4 miles of this place the Yanks was hurried up sent in all Details at 2 O'clock in the evening and run their atilery out in frunt of the Block house and placed it in position."[37]

Had John Taylor Wood's amphibious assault and Brigadier General Bradley T. Johnson's cavalry raid succeeded in mounting an attack, the probability of Point Lookout being taken and the prisoners released was high. However, such was not to be.

After Bradley Johnson's command had wreaked havoc in the Baltimore area and severely damaged rail and telegraph communications and proceeding toward Point Lookout, its attack on the prison camp was called off on July 12, 1864. Logistical problems with obtaining sufficient weapons for the amphibious assault coming up from Wilmington, North Carolina, under John Taylor Wood, leaks of the plans for the Point Lookout attack which appeared in northern newspapers delays in Early's getting his army up to be in a position to mount his attack on Washington, and his delays in mounting Johnson' cavalry operation against the prison camp all contributed to the attack on Point Lookout being called off.[38] A daring plan went for naught. The prison camp was never attacked and remained open until the summer of 1865 after the Civil War had ended.

CHAPTER 10

Early Tarries on the Upper Potomac

A Stonewall Jackson Early was not. Glenn Worthington in a careful analysis has posited that Lew Wallace and James Ricketts's hard fought battle on the Monocacy on July 9, 1864, against Early's vastly superior forces saved Washington.[1] Although that battle certainly had a substantial effect in delaying Early, what may well have contributed more significantly in his failure to take and burn Washington and successfully proceed with the raid to liberate the approximately 15,000 Confederate prisoners at Point Lookout in July, 1864 was Early's dilatory actions at Martinsburg and Harpers Ferry from July 3 through July 6, 1864. During that period, his troops looted captured Union stores, liquor and supplies that General Sigel had been unable to destroy before his retreat to Maryland Heights. They were also waiting to be re-supplied with much-needed shoes.[2] Moreover, Early spent several days probing very strong Union defensive positions on Maryland Heights which were not vulnerable to attack, which delayed his movement toward Washington via South Mountain and Frederick — the route he was destined to take since the direct route was controlled by the Union guns on Maryland Heights.

After a very expeditious movement up the Shenandoah Valley from the area west of Lynchburg, Early's men got to Winchester on July 2, 1864. Early then moved his army out of Winchester toward Leetown on the way to Martinsburg, West Virginia. Captain Robert E. Park of the 12th Alabama recalled that they "marched through the historic old town of Winchester, and encamped at Smithfield. The good people of W. received us very kindly and enthusiastically." Part of his army had also gone to Charlestown. Early had received a telegram from General Lee on July 2 asking him to destroy the Baltimore & Ohio Railroad and the Chesapeake and Ohio Canal as far as possible.[3]

Early's plan was to attack Major General Franz Sigel, commanding the Union Reserve Division at Martinsburg, and cut him off from Harpers Ferry, where he also intended to capture the garrison. Franz Sigel had graduated from the Karlsruhe Military Academy in 1843 and had been minister of war for the revolutionary forces in Baden in 1848. After coming to the United States, he was involved in military actions in Missouri for the Union in 1861 and later contributed to the Union victory at Pea Ridge. After being defeated by General John Breckinridge at New Market on May 15, 1864, Sigel was given command of the Reserve Division at Martinsburg. Harpers Ferry is where the Shenandoah and Potomac rivers met. The city commanded the rail, highway and canal routes between Washington and the west.[4]

Brigadier General John McCausland was to be sent to burn the railroad bridge at the mouth of Back Creek, then move to the North Mountain Depot and unite with Brigadier General Bradley Johnson's cavalry force at Haynesville, east of Martinsburg, and cut off General Sigel's retreat from that place.

McCausland was at the top of his class at VMI and taught mathematics there. He had served under General Floyd in western Virginia and under General Albert Sidney Johnson in Kentucky. He escaped capture at Fort Donelson. McCausland commanded a cavalry brigade in the Department of Western Virginia from 1862 to 1864 and then with Early's Army of the Valley.[5]

Previously, Union forces had been concentrated at Martinsburg which included Colonel Thomas Maley Harris's brigade, being the 10th West Virginia and the 23rd Illinois, as well as 1,900 cavalry and 1,500 dismounted cavalry for a total force of 4,650. The 10th West Virginia left Beverly, West Virginia, on June 16, 1864, under directions from Major General Julius Stahel, commander of the 1st Infantry Division and the 1st Cavalry Division of the Department of West Virginia, to move toward Martinsburg. The force marched for three days through Philippi into Maryland, where they took the Baltimore & Ohio to Martinsburg. The infantry was moved to Smithfield, West Virginia, on June 27. Stahel had also posted about 600 cavalry at Darkesville. He also had about 600 cavalry at Big Springs and a detachment of men at Bunker Hill, West Virginia.[6]

The 10th West Virginia had arrived at Martinsburg on June 19, 1864, and was sent with some cavalry to Leetown on June 28, 1864. Colonel Harris was ill and remained in Beverly, West Virginia, until returning to his brigade at Leetown on July 1.[7] Command of Harris's brigade and the troops at Leetown was given to Colonel James A. Mulligan. Mulligan had been involved with the Union army in Missouri in 1861, where he was captured near Lexington, Missouri, in September after essentially being abandoned by General Fremont. He raised the 23rd Illinois "Irish Brigade," which he led as part of his force at Leetown.[8]

The Union troops at Leetown had been digging trenches since July 1.[9] Mulligan had originally started a supply train for the relief of Hunter's army. Facing the advance of the Confederate forces, the supply train returned to Harpers Ferry. Mulligan prepared to fight.

On July 3, Bradley Johnson was ordered to move to Leetown to try to cut off the retreat of the Union garrison at Martinsburg.[10] He was directed to attack the Union position at Leetown by the Confederate cavalry commander, Major General Robert Ransom.

Colonel James A. Mulligan was holding the Union position at Leetown, anchored by his 23rd Illinois "Irish Brigade" and the 10th West Virginia. Mulligan had been in effect abandoned by Sigel and left to hold off the van of the Confederate army while Sigel went to Maryland Heights.

Men from Cole's cavalry had gone to Charlestown and were moving east toward Berryville when Lieutenant Sam Sigler of Company D with a scouting party met a farmer who advised them that Early was at Winchester and would be moving toward Charlestown. Cole's men captured a Confederate mounted infantryman who confirmed Early was moving from Winchester. Cole's cavalry force then moved to Leetown and took the Confederate prisoner to Colonel Mulligan. Scarcely had Cole's men arrived when there was firing by the pickets in the outposts, signaling that the Confederate advance was upon them. Mulligan put Cole's men out in front of his brigade as skirmishers.

Colonel James Mulligan held up the Confederates at the Battle of Leetown (Library of Congress).

Colonel Mulligan with Harris's brigade, cavalry, dismounted cavalry and two Ohio national guard units fought stubbornly all day, after having led his men out of the trenches to attack Johnson after the Confederates' initial cavalry charge and slowly giving ground.[11] The 22nd Pennsylvania Cavalry was in the forefront of the fight. Colonel Mulligan had been ordered to do the best he could to cover the retreat of the main army while falling back slowly.[12]

When Bradley Johnson had been initially forced back by Mulligan, who had a superior position on a hill, the men of Ramseur's Division and Rodes's Division, having marched twenty miles from Winchester, had not been in a position to support him for a counterattack.[13] Mulligan's attack had broken Johnson's front line and forced the Confederates back toward Leetown, while preserving Sigel's path of escape.[14]

Mulligan informed Sigel he was retreating. Sigel realized the precarious position he was in at Martinsburg and prepared to retreat to Harpers Ferry.[15] Sigel directed Mulligan to retire as slowly as he could to Kearneysville and Shepherdstown, where it would be possible for his men to ford the Potomac. Mulligan staged a fighting withdrawal to Shepherdstown and Maryland Heights, overlooking Harpers Ferry.[16] Sigel also moved the 160th Ohio, the 135th Ohio, the 161st Ohio, a battalion of dismounted cavalry and the battery of the 135th Ohio under Colonel Reasoner to Harpers Ferry by way of Shepherdstown on July 3.[17] Sigel was sending stores off by rail from Martinsburg for Shepherdstown and wagons were also loaded.[18] He continued to withdraw his troops from Martinsburg to Harpers Ferry to join the garrison force of General Max Weber ahead of the advancing Confederates.[19] Sigel crossed the Potomac at Shepherdstown.[20] Before the telegraph at Martinsburg was cut, the operator had telegraphed to Washington that a large body of Confederates, supposedly the same body as had fought Hunter, was nearby.[21]

Terry's brigade of Early's army reached and occupied Martinsburg on the afternoon of July 3, 1864. Lieutenant John H. Worsham of the 21st Virginia Infantry claimed that the retreating Union forces had not had time to remove their stores and described consuming them:

> On the afternoon of July 3d we reached Martinsburg, running in on the Yankees who were there, so suddenly, that they did not have time to move any of their stores. They were making big preparations to celebrate the Fourth, and many of the men had received boxes of good things from home and friends. The depot and express office were filled with articles of this kind. A guard was place around these buildings and their storehouses. The express office was put in charge of a quartermaster who was an old friend of mine. At night I went there and inquired of the guard for him and he let me go into the building. He was very glad to see me, as he had only one man to help him get these articles in shape, and asked me to help him; this I consented to do, if he would give me a barrel of cakes. He said "all right." I found one and carried it out and turned it over to my company ... who were profuse in their thanks for the cakes, and soon fell asleep — dreaming of little cakes, big cakes, and a mountain of cakes.[22]

Private George H. Lester of Company E of the 38th Georgia of Evans's brigade recounted Sigel's "Dutchmen's Bar-b-que."[23] Private E.T. Morrow of the 8th Louisiana said, "They had all kinds of fruits, precious sardines, oysters, wines & liquors & any amount of meats, our boys enjoyed the delicacies as well on the substantials [sic] it was a great treat."[24]

Meanwhile, McCausland was executing his part of Early's plan on July 3 by taking his cavalry brigade to burn the railroad bridge at Back Creek and to attack the North Mountain Depot.[25] McCausland had the 14th, 16th, 17th and 22nd Virginia cavalry in his brigade. At North Mountain Depot they captured about 200 Union troops from the 135th Ohio and valuable stores.[26] The Confederates destroyed railroad bridges including that at the mouth of Patterson's Creek, the bridge at Back Creek and the trestling of the Opequon bridge as well as station platforms and culverts.[27] McCausland then entered Martinsburg on July 3.[28] Brigadier General John Imboden's cavalry brigade's mission on the 3rd was to destroy the Baltimore & Ohio Railroad's bridge

Battle of Leetown and Evacuation of Martinsburg and Harpers Ferry
July 3 - 4, 1864

THE BATTLE OF LEETOWN: LEETOWN AND MOVEMENT TO MARYLAND HEIGHTS (DEB JOSEPHS BASED ON AUTHOR'S DRAWING).

over the South Branch of the Potomac, which was heavily guarded by a blockhouse and an armored railroad car. Imboden blew up the armored railroad car with an artillery shell but was unable to take the bridge on the 3rd and broke off his attack.[29] A Union cavalry force at Darkesville near Martinsburg had also been attacked on July 3 without decisive results.[30] Lieutenant Ashley of Vaughn's brigade of Wharton's Division said they camped at Darkesville on the night of July 3, getting to Martinsburg on July 4. There was still plenty of plunder, and the Confederate troops rested on July 4 before tearing up some sections of the Baltimore & Ohio Railroad later that day. Private George Quinn Peyton of the 13th Virginia Infantry of Pegram's brigade of Ramseur's Division observed in his journal that his regiment had gone to Halltown, about five miles from Harpers Ferry, on the 3rd.[31] They did not intercept Sigel on his retreat or capture Harpers Ferry or Maryland Heights although they were nearby.

Time was of the essence for Early. Lee told Confederate president Davis on the 3rd he would alert Early that no corps had left Grant's army. Even though Grant did not choose to believe the reports of Early's activities at this point, he was clearly aware that there was great concern, which made timely action by Early imperative. His inaction on the afternoon and evening of July 3 and limited action on July 4 contributed substantially to his missed opportunity to take and burn Washington and otherwise execute Lee's audacious plan.

Early was concerned about the taking of property and alcohol consumption by his troops of the 4th of July.[32] On the 4th, Breckinridge's men continued to enjoy the captured Union stores. Lieutenant John H. Worsham of the 21st Virginia Infantry said that the captured goods were divided on July 4 among the men. His company got a few oranges, lemons, cakes, candy and a bottle of wine. After celebrating, his unit and the rest of Terry's brigade moved out of Martinsburg.[33] Later on the 4th Breckinridge's men burned railroad bridges and moved within five miles of Harpers Ferry, destroying the railroad as they went. Part of Ransom's cavalry moved to Shepherdstown on the 4th.[34]

About 2,000 Confederate cavalry advanced on the Harpers Ferry–Charlestown Road toward Harpers Ferry on the early morning of the 4th, arriving about 10 A.M. at Bolivar Heights, which overlooks Harpers Ferry. The Union troops in the town and on Maryland Heights overlooking it could be observed. Rodes's and Ramseur's divisions had moved at Halltown, several miles from Harpers Ferry, on the morning of the 4th. Ramseur on the left was on the Baltimore & Ohio west of Harpers Ferry by 9:00 A.M. on the 4th, and he and Rodes on the right had control of Bolivar Heights by 10:00 A.M. Artillery firing went on. The Confederate forces skirmished with Union pickets all day.[35] Yet no serious attack was made on General Max Weber and his small garrison in Harpers Ferry or to gain access to Maryland Heights, which controlled the direct route to Washington.

As Charles H. Moulton of the 34th Massachusetts described, the Union forces at Harpers Ferry awoke on the morning of July 4 to find a large force of Confederates on the other side of Bolivar Heights near Harpers Ferry. The main force was at Halltown, about four miles away. Confederate sharpshooters hid in housed and behind fences and in other places in the town of Bolivar, keeping up a fire on the Union forces. Skirmishers were sent out to meet the Confederates. The 2nd battery of the 5th New York Heavy Artillery as well as the heavy guns on Maryland Heights kept up fire all day on the 4th.[36] The Union troops were driven by Confederate troops from their rifle pits on Camp Hill on Bolivar Heights by Ramseur's troops.[37]

The Union garrison at Harpers Ferry was commanded by Brigadier General Max Weber. He was born in Baden in 1824 and graduated in the same class as Major General Franz Sigel in the Karlsruhe Military Academy in 1843. Weber rendered distinguished service at Antietam (Sharpsburg) and served as a brigade commander in Sumner's corps at Fredericksburg. He was seriously wounded at Fredericksburg, losing permanently the use of his right arm. After being assigned to limited duty in Washington, Weber was sent to command the garrison force at

Harpers Ferry in 1864. Weber had fought with Mieroslwski and Sigel in the 1848 Baden revolution in Germany. Weber had about 800 troops at his command holding Harpers Ferry.[38] General Weber's staff advised him that he could not hold Harpers Ferry and that he should retreat to Maryland Heights.[39] Before doing that, Weber took weapons and stores across the river. The Union Signal Station reported a large Confederate force approaching Harpers Ferry from Halltown. He vacated Harpers Ferry about 7:00 P.M. on the 4th and went to Maryland Heights.[40] The railroad and pontoon bridges were burned by the retreating Union troops.[41]

Halleck had sent Weber a message about 12:30 P.M. on the 4th that he should be prepared to defend his works and that the first man proposing to surrender or retreat should be hung. Weber did not receive this message until after he was already occupying Maryland Heights.[42]

On the night of July 3, General Franz Sigel, upon being advised that Weber would be vacating Harpers Ferry to go to Maryland Heights, crossed the Potomac at Shepherdstown and marched his force to Maryland Heights to join Weber. Sigel and Weber evacuated at least four train loads of supplies before going to Maryland Heights and destroying the bridges at Harpers Ferry.[43] Weber's evacuation of Martinsburg had been going on for some time.[44]

While Weber was burning bridges and crossing the Potomac to Maryland Heights on the evening of July 4, Rodes's Division was moving into Harpers Ferry.[45] Captain Robert E. Park of the 12th Alabama of Cook's Brigade of Rodes's Division recalled pillaging in Harpers Ferry being carried on all night on the 4th:

MAJOR GENERAL FRANZ SIGEL, COMMANDER AT MARTINSBURG AND MARYLAND HEIGHTS (LIBRARY OF CONGRESS).

> We marched through Halltown and Charlestown, near the old field where that fanatical murderer and abolitionist, John Brown, was hung, and halted under a heavy cannonading at Bolivar Heights, near Harper's Ferry. This place on the Baltimore and Ohio Railroad, and on the Potomac river, surrounded by lofty mountains, was once a United States Arsenal and government foundry. The Yankee camps had been hastily forsaken, and our men quickly took possession of them and their contents. After dark General Rhodes took his old Alabama brigade (now Battle's) into the town, where a universal pillaging of United States government property, especially commissary stores, was carried on all night. The town was thoroughly relieved of its stores, and the 4th of July was passed pleasantly.[46]

He also reported the arrival of shoes by wagon from the south.[47] George Lester of the 38th Georgia of Gordon's Division described the festivities with plundered foods.[48]

Sigel's men continued their retreat to Maryland Heights on the 4th. The 160th Ohio was moving toward Sharpsburg on the morning of the 4th, protecting their wagons from Confederate cavalry. About 9:00 P.M., these men reached Maryland Heights.

Maryland Heights controlled Harpers Ferry (National Archives).

Sanford Kellogg found it remarkable that Sigel should have been able to retire a small garrison at Harpers Ferry and a relatively small force at Martinsburg with little loss of personnel or stores in the presence of four Confederate infantry divisions and one cavalry division.[49] Moreover, Sigel had concentrated his troops in a nearly impregnable position. He had Thomas Maley Harris's brigade, four other infantry regiments and two battalions of the 5th New York Heavy Artillery.[50] Sigel and Weber had not been pressed and had been allowed to escape to a position from which they could not easily be dislodged.

The Confederate cavalry had been at Harpers Ferry along with Rodes's and Ramseur's infantry divisions since 10:00 A.M. on July 4, but neither had vigorously attacked or tried to take Maryland Heights, controlling the direct route to Washington, which neither Weber or Sigel had yet reached. Early's inaction on the 4th, following the lack of aggressive action against Sigel on the 3rd, contributed substantially to the missed opportunity to execute Lee's initiative.

The combined forces of Weber and Sigel on Maryland Heights had inadvertently created a conundrum for Early by their actions. Early could attack them in a strong defensive position or bypass them and have them in his rear as a threat to his communications or to his forces. The most direct path to Washington lay via rail to the highways to that city controlled by the Union guns on Maryland Heights. Rather than take decisive action on July 3 or July 4 to move toward Washington by a less direct route through South Mountain and Frederick, which he eventually took several days later, Early hesitated and missed his opportunity to seize the initiative to forcefully execute Lee's plan to take Washington and soon-to-be communicated plan to free the prisoners at Point Lookout and return them to Lee's army. His continued lack of decisive action on July 5 and 6 compounded the problem caused by earlier delays.

Very little was accomplished by Early's army on July 5 other than some units' crossing the Potomac and a serious breakdown of discipline the previous two days. Early was clearly aware that a lack of discipline in his army on July 3 and July 4 had occurred. He advised Breckinridge on July 5 that he had heard deplorable accounts of plundering and confusion in Martinsburg and stated that it was absolutely necessary that rigid discipline be enforced.[51] Early issued a general order to his army that the strictest discipline would be imposed and threatened arrest and summary punishment for unauthorized appropriation of property.[52]

PROJECTILES FOUND IN AREA OF UNION LINES ON MARYLAND HEIGHTS, BETWEEN HOFFMASTER AND HARPERS FERRY ROADS (PHOTOGRAPH BY THE AUTHOR).

With Sigel in control of the most direct route to Washington in a strong defensive position, Early spent crucial time on July 5 demonstrating at Maryland Heights with Rodes's and Ramseur's divisions, without any real possibility of a successful attack. Private George Quinn Peyton of the 13th Virginia Infantry of Ramseur's Division observed that he spent nearly all day on the 5th talking with a lady in the town of Boliver near Harpers Ferry.[53] With the Confederate attacks on the Baltimore & Ohio Railroad and with their attack on Martinsburg, the element of surprise was fast dissipating. There was considerable communication on July 5 about Early involving Grant and authorities in Washington.[54] Yet, Early continued to hesitate for no reasonable tactical objective.

His move to the Potomac was piecemeal. On July 5, Gordon's division including Terry's brigade started to march toward the Potomac to cross at Boteler's Ford, near Shepherdstown.[55] Terry's force consisted of fragments of thirteen regiments: the 2nd, 4th, 5th, 10th 14th, 21st, 23rd, 25th, 37th, 42nd, 44th, 48th and 50th Virginia Infantry.[56] Rodes's and Ramseur's troops crossed the Potomac near Shepherdstown on July 6.[57] Gordon's division had crossed the Antietam on July 5 and moved toward Maryland Heights on July 6.[58] Lieutenant John H. Worsham of the 21st Virginia of Terry's brigade recalled fording the Potomac with a bundle of clothes around his neck, his bare feet being cut by sharp shells adhering to the rocks.[59] Early's forces were scattered, some staying at Harpers Ferry and some moving east, going at different times.

Ramseur had left Lewis's brigade to occupy Harpers Ferry. Ramseur, wounded at Malvern Hill, Chancellorsville and Spottsylvania, was made a major general after his 27th birthday. He was the youngest man to attain that rank in the Confederate service. He was wounded for the fourth time, this time fatally, at Cedar Creek in October 1864.[60]

Terry's forces moved in reconnaissance before Maryland Heights on the 6th before moving toward Frederick with the rest of Early's forces.[61] Echol's division moved to Sharpsburg, Maryland on the 5th. General Clement Evans's brigade crossed the Potomac from Shepherdstown that day.[62] Rodes, Ramseur, Breckinridge and Early dined at the home of staff officer Henry Kyd Douglas at Shepherdstown on the way to Sharpsburg on the 5th.[63] The whole process was fragmented and time consuming.

The Union guns on Maryland Heights opened up on the Confederates. General McCausland's mounted infantry and other troops faced Sigel's immediate front. McCausland then moved on to Hagerstown, Maryland, with orders to burn it or collect $200,000. McCausland engaged units of the 6th U.S. Cavalry there with limited casualties. The Union garrison and much rolling stock and supplies were evacuated.[64]

While Early was spending substantial time on the Upper Potomac, Lew Wallace, in command of the Middle District at Baltimore, was aggressively moving to address the Confederate threat. As early as July 2, Wallace had been warned by John Garrett, president of the Baltimore & Ohio Railroad, about the movements of Early into Maryland.[65] On July 3, while Early was still at Leetown, Wallace had been told by his adjutant, Colonel Lawrence, that Hunter was reported in the newspapers to have crossed the Kanawa Valley into West Virginia.[66]

Wallace immediately understood the immediacy and gravity of the threat to Washington and Baltimore. He told Brigadier General E.B. Tyler, posted at the Relay House near Baltimore, to get his entire command in readiness to move with three days' rations and one hundred rounds of ammunition per man.[67] Tyler, as of June 30, had two companies of the 1st Maryland Eastern Shore Infantry, the 3rd Maryland Potomac Home Brigade and the 144th Ohio Infantry.[68] Subsequently, he was joined by seven companies of the 149th Ohio, the Baltimore Battery under Captain Frederic Alexander, consisting of six pieces of three-inch rifled guns, a howitzer under Captain William Wiegel and the 11th Maryland under Colonel William Landstreet.[69] Wallace also told Colonel Root at Annapolis on July 3 to have his six companies of Ohio militia and Co. I of the 1st Maryland Eastern Shore to be ready to move with three days' rations and one hundred rounds of ammunition per man. Tyler was also told to proceed in person to Monocacy Junction with his entire command to reinforce companies already at the blockhouse and to dig rifle pits. Tyler took the train to Monocacy Junction on the night of July 3.[70] The small force that Wallace was concentrating fifty miles west of Baltimore and sixty miles northwest of Washington was to find out where the Confederates were and where they intended to go, and to block them.[71] Thus, Wallace was moving aggressively to move to meet Early with the small forces available to contest his movements at a time Early was still demonstrating at Harpers Ferry and slowly moving on toward Frederick. On July 3, John Garrett, president of the Baltimore & Ohio Railroad, telegraphed Secretary of State Edwin M. Stanton that his earlier warning of Confederate forces in the Shenandoah Valley was about to be proven correct.[72] Wallace and Garrett conferred on July 3, and Wallace agreed to protect the Monocacy and started to concentrate his forces to do it. Meanwhile confusion still reigned in Washington.[73] Grant informed Halleck that Early's corps had returned to Richmond.[74] Wallace, acting without orders, was taking aggressive action to ascertain Early's whereabouts and intentions absent information from Halleck or Grant to concentrate his command.[75]

Benjamin F. Cooling noted, "It was actually the abrupt action of an unsung departmental commander that uncovered the Confederate's intention and seriously dislocated his timetable. Lew Wallace acted without the knowledge and approval of the War Department in trying to ascertain whether Baltimore

MAJOR GENERAL ROBERT RODES DEMONSTRATED AT MARYLAND HEIGHTS (LIBRARY OF CONGRESS).

or Washington was Early's real objective."[76] Nineteenth century historian George Pond found that "Wallace's merit is that he went to the right place at the right time, and did the best he could with such force as he had, not seeking to postpone the task of planting an obstacle in the enemy's path."[77]

Lew Wallace, commander of the Middle Department at Baltimore, had received a report from Major General Darius Couch at Chambersburg, Pennsylvania, that Martinsburg had been evacuated and Sigel was falling back to Harpers Ferry while General Weber at Harpers Ferry reported Confederate strength to be between ten and twenty thousand men. Wallace telegraphed Halleck on July 4 that Weber had been attacked at Harpers Ferry and probably would have to withdraw. He also informed Halleck that Sigel and Mulligan were falling back to Harpers Ferry on the Maryland side of the Potomac River. Wallace also told Halleck that he had concentrated troops equal to two regiments of infantry at Monrovia. He had a good ground at Monocacy Junction and was doing all he could to concentrate his command.[78] With the assistance of John Garrett, General Wallace left Baltimore after midnight in the early hours of July 4 to go to Monocacy Junction.[79] Garrett had telegraphed Secretary of War Stanton and Chief of Staff Halleck that General Max Weber had telegraphed him from Harpers Ferry at 10:48 A.M. on July 4 that 2,000 cavalry and a force of Confederate infantry were in sight and, if pressed, he would have to withdraw to Maryland Heights.[80]

On July 5, 1864, Brigadier General Erastus Tyler gave Wallace a report that Early's position was not then known and that he had between 5,000 and 30,000 men. Troopers from the 12th Pennsylvania Cavalry, the Loudon Independent Rangers and Cole's Independent Cavalry were sent across the Catoctin Mountains west of Frederick toward South Mountain. Units of the 6th U.S. Cavalry were engaged with McCausland's cavalry at Hagerstown.

On orders from the War Department, Colonel David Clendenin of the 8th Illinois Cavalry was on the move from Washington to Point of Rocks, which had been attacked. There was difficulty in the telegraphic communication between Sandy Hook near Harpers Ferry as Colonel John Mosby had crossed the Potomac at Point of Rocks and had cut telegraphic communication between Harpers Ferry and Washington.[81]

As a precaution, Grant directed General Meade to send one good division and dismounted cavalry to Washington. Meade sent Brigadier General James Ricketts's 3rd Division, 6th Corps and dismounted cavalry from the Cavalry Corps 2nd Division.[82]

Gordon's Division was demonstrating before Maryland Heights on July 6 with Brigadier General Clement Evans's troops, including the 25th Virginia and 9th Battalion of Virginia Infantry and the rest of Jones's old brigade, driving in the Union pickets.[83]

Sigel reported that the Confederate advance on his left was frustrated by a counterattack, estimating about 3,000 infantry in his front with an extensive Confederate line running from the Potomac to Elk Ridge Mountain. Some prisoners were taken from the 12th Georgia. An artillery duel was ongoing. Also, Stahel's cavalry was engaged on the west side of Elk Ridge Mountain.[84]

Rodes and Ramseur continued their movement across the Potomac.[85] Brigadier General William Lewis's brigade of Ramseur's Division was involved in destroying the stores at Harpers Ferry the Confederates could not take.[86]

Early was little closer to his objective on July 5 than he had been on July 3. Although he was in a race against time as Grant and Halleck were finally responding to his threat, as Benjamin Franklin Cooling succinctly put it: "Jubal Early soon proved that he was no equal to Stonewall Jackson in the foot-race department. If Washington's capture was truly the Confederate objective, then Early and his men tarried far too long on the Upper Potomac."[87]

Also, Early's effort to extract money from the townspeople and banks of Hagerstown had taken up further valuable time. On the morning of July 6, 1864, McCausland entered Hagerstown with 1,500 men from the 14th, 16th, 17th, 25th and 37th Virginia cavalry regiments facing a detachment of Union cavalry from the Carlisle Barracks in Pennsylvania under Lieutenant H.T. McLean.[88] McCausland was seeking $200,000 and a large supply of clothing and threatening to burn the city in retaliation for General Hunter's destruction of property in the Shenandoah Valley. The Hagerstown Bank, the Bank of Williamsport and the Hagerstown Savings Bank came up with $20,000.[89] McCausland had missed a decimal point in the note. This undertaking in Hagerstown took part of a day.

Major General Lew Wallace, the Union commander at Baltimore, on July 5, 1864, traveled to Monocacy Junction with 2,500 Potomac Home Brigade and Ohio militia troops to put himself between Early and Washington. Wallace ascertained he would be facing substantial Confederate forces. The acute need for quick action was amplified on the 6th when Early met with Captain R.E. Lee Jr., son of General Robert E. Lee, near Shepherdstown. Lee ordered Early to cooperate in an expedition to liberate Confederate prisoners at Point Lookout:

> Captain Lee later recalled the secrecy surrounding the mission and his meeting both with his father, General Robert E. Lee, and with General Early. During the summer, I had occasion, once or twice, to report to him at his headquarters, once about July 1st by his special order. I remember how we all racked our brains to account for this order, which was for me to report "at once to the commanding general," and many wild guesses were made by my young companions, as to what was to become of me. Their surmises extended to my being shot for unlawful foraging to my being sent on a mission abroad to solicit for the recognition of our independence. I reported at once, and found my father expecting me, with a bed prepared. It was characteristic of him that he never said a word about what I was wanted for until he was ready with full instructions. I was fed at once, for I was still hungry, my bed was shown me, and I was told to rest and sleep well, as he wanted me in the morning, and that I would need all my strength.
>
> The next morning he gave me a letter to General Early, who, with his command, was at that time in Maryland, threatening Washington. My mission was to carry this letter to him. As Early had cut loose with his communications with Virginia, and there was a chance of any messenger to him being caught by raiding parties, my father gave me verbally the contents of his letter, and told me that if I saw any chance of my capture, to destroy it, then, if I did reach the General, I should be able to tell him what he had written. He cautioned me to keep my own counsel, and to say nothing to anyone as to my destination. Orders for a relay of horses from Staunton, where the railroad terminated, to the Potomac had been telegraphed, and I was to start at once. This I did, seeing my sisters and mother in Richmond while waiting for the train in Staunton, and having very great difficulty keeping from them my destination. But I did, and riding night and day, came up with General Early at a point in Maryland some miles

CAPTAIN ROBERT E. LEE, JR., PERSONALLY DELIVERED POINT LOOKOUT ORDERS TO EARLY JULY 6, 1864 (VIRGINIA HISTORICAL SOCIETY).

beyond the old battlefield of Sharpsburg. I delivered the letter to him, returned to Petersburg, and reported to my father. Much gratified by the evident pleasure of the General at my diligence and at the news I had brought from Early and his men, after a night's rest and two good meals I returned to my command, never telling my comrades until long afterward what had been done to me by the commanding general.[90]

Brigadier General Bradley T. Johnson and his cavalry from Early's command were to be dispatched for that purpose. They were to combine with John Taylor Wood, who was leading a naval expedition to Point Lookout.[91] This daring plan had been discussed with President Jefferson during the last week of June 1864 and added a broader dimension to the already ambitious plan.[92]

Early was finally on the road to Washington. However, the window of opportunity was closing. There still was no strong, aggressive push toward Washington by Early. Although the Confederate army was on the move, Rodes's men only got to Crampton's Gap. Breckenridge went to Fox's gap and Ramseur's to Boonesboro gap. Valuable time had been lost on the Upper Potomac and was continuing to be lost by Early's slow movement toward Frederick.

CHAPTER 11

A Lack of Shoes Causes Delay

An order for shoes for Early's army had been given to the Confederate Quartermaster's Department in Richmond before his army moved down the Valley after the Lynchburg Campaign, as a substantial part of Early's force had inadequate footgear. The 2nd Corps of the Army of Northern Virginia, which constituted Early's Army of the Valley, had seen hard service in the Overland Campaign of May and June 1864 before marching 80 miles to Charlottesville, chasing Hunter's army to beyond Hanging Rock and marching down the Valley to Staunton, where they were resupplied. Wagons were left in Staunton to transport the shoes when they arrived.[1]

The provisioning of shoes in the Civil War had been a constant problem. Stonewall Jackson's "Foot Cavalry" in the Valley Campaign of 1862 had marched long distances quickly with many of the troops barefoot. Confederate general Harry Heth had moved into Gettysburg looking for shoes for his men, precipitating a major battle. General David Hunter, after having taken over from Sigel, had stayed several days at Woodstock in the Valley, in part waiting to be resupplied with shoes for his men, many of whom were barefoot or had inadequate footgear.[2] The Confederate Quartermaster Department had done remarkable service to this point in the war in providing articles for the men under difficult circumstances. A clothing manufactory had been set up in Richmond in 1861, which included a shoe manufactory. Supplies of items such as shoes were also obtained from families or purchased as part of a clothing allowance, coming from contractors or manufactories or furnished by the volunteers themselves. Not enough boots were able to be provided by the quartermasters for the army.[3] The Confederates were operating with a number of significant disadvantages that the Union forces did not face.

The blockade, developed at the beginning of the Civil War under the auspices of General Winfield Scott, had gradually operated to choke off the flow of goods and commerce from abroad. By June and July 1864, Wilmington, North Carolina, was one of the few ports where ships regularly ran the blockade. Fort Fisher, at the mouth of the Cape Fear River, was still in Confederate hands. Moreover, New Bern and other cities in that part of North Carolina were still controlled by the Confederates. Thus, vital supply links by rail with Richmond had been maintained. Still, an estimated 100,000 pairs of shoes were lost by failing to get through the blockade in the fall and winter of 1863.[4]

The obtaining of a large number of English army shoes had occurred in 1863 due to the work of procurement officer Major J.B. Ferguson. This flow of shoes continued into 1864. In fact, in the last six months of 1864 and up to January 31, 1865, the Army of Northern Virginia had been supplied with 167,862 pairs of shoes.[5] The maximum effective strength of the army during that period was not precisely known.[6] The obtaining of shoes from England had been a factor in this result.

In addition, there was an enormous disparity between the North and the South in resources and factories. The North had shoe factories in New England as well as in almost all other areas of the Union. The factories were operating under government contracts and were well able to produce the shoes and related goods required to resupply the Union armies. The South had been largely an agrarian society prior to the Civil War. There were a limited number of factories. One such factory in the Shenandoah Valley was the Staunton Boot and Shoe Factory. However, much of the manufacture was by 2,000 workers in Richmond, who were provided the hides and paid a set price per shoe.[7]

As the Civil War progressed, the Mississippi River came under Union control. Large cities with their factories, such as New Orleans and Memphis and later Atlanta, were lost to the Confederacy. The flow of commerce and the ability to produce and transport goods such as shoes lessened.

Further, it was not just the ability to operate and maintain factories that had been in issue but also the ability to secure the necessary raw materials. The Shenandoah Valley had been a source of cattle and hides. However, the operation of a Union army in the Valley of approximately 20,000 men living off the land to a large extent had an effect on the flow of necessary raw material such as hides to Richmond.

Compounding these problems for General Early was the problem of logistics. Shoes from Richmond could be shipped on the Virginia Central Railroad to Charlottesville and then on the Orange & Alexandria Railroad to Lynchburg—a distance of about 140 miles. With the track being frequently damaged and the railroad in a state of disrepair, the time taken for shipment had increased. This was also true of the Southside Railroad, which connected Petersburg with Lynchburg. The rails lines down the Shenandoah Valley north of Staunton had been destroyed earlier in the war. Thus, shoes arriving at Lynchburg from Richmond had to be transshipped by wagon down the Valley. As the Confederate army in the Valley marched north, the distance to be covered by the wagon masters and teamsters to reach them increased, as did the time necessary to cover the distance. Thus, it took from June 13, 1864, when Early left the Confederate lines at Gaines Mill, until July 7, when the wagons reached Early's army in Maryland, for the necessary shoes for his army to be properly fitted for marching to arrive. Mrs. Blackford of Lynchburg had written that when Breckinridge's army arrived in Lynchburg, many of his soldiers were barefoot. "General Breckinridge, with some troops, got here on Wednesday night, and we saw them passing out West Street, it was a most reassuring sight, and never were a lot of bronzed and dirty looking veterans, many of them barefoot, more heartily welcomed."[8]

In addition, the value of Confederate money had dwindled. This made it more difficult to requisition items like shoes in areas where the army moved. General Early was obtaining United States money from places along his route to prevent their destruction, which provided funds for the operation of his army.

There had been few battlefield casualties in the fighting at Lynchburg. Thus, even though General Early's forces controlled the field after General Hunter's pullout on the night of June 18, 1864, there was no ready source of shoes from the Union dead as had been the case on other battlefields of the war.

General Early's Army of the Valley stopped at Staunton on June 26, 1864, to reorganize and to be resupplied. Many men had fallen out of the ranks for lack of shoes. Early said, "Nearly, if not quite half of the company's officers and me were barefooted or nearly so, and a dispatch had been sent from Salem by courier and Lynchburg, by telegraph, to Richmond requesting shoes to be sent to Staunton but they had not arrived."[9] At that point, Early's army had been marching and in the field for almost two weeks. Many of the men still needed shoes. However, time was of the essence for Early to fulfill General Lee's orders, which he was determined to do. This lack of adequate shoes for his army affected his ability to proceed but did not slacken his pace. When General Early reached Winchester on July 2, 1864, from Staunton, which he had left on the 28th, they had still moved at a pace of almost 20 miles per day when they were on the move.

General Early had left a number of wagons at Staunton for the specific purpose of bringing up additional shoes for his army when they arrived from Richmond. These wagons were to follow his route and catch up with him while on the move. This was the best that could be done under the circumstances.[10]

The lack of shoes had caused many of the men to fall out and straggle on the march down the Valley. John O. Casler, a private in the 33rd Virginia, was an example of those soldiers who had been disabled from marching barefoot and who had been hospitalized as a result, being held at Winchester instead of making the march to Washington. The straggling was sufficiently severe that General Early was forced to detail some Louisiana troops to collect individuals who had fallen out or who were unable to continue and to maintain them at Winchester.[11] This took hundreds of men from Early's already reduced command to look after the hundreds who had broken ranks on the line of march, reducing the effective strength of Early's army. Many of these men would rejoin Early's forces when they returned to the Valley after his attack on Washington.

As Early's army marched out of Winchester on July 3, 1864, to Martinsburg and Harpers Ferry, the Union stores at those places contained a possible source of shoes. However, Major General Franz Sigel had been able to get off four train-loads of goods from Martinsburg before it was evacuated. As the Union supply depots were overrun, what was found was mainly foodstuffs. No major source of shoes was found.[12]

As the Confederate forces crossing the Potomac at Boteler's Ford and various other places between Harpers Ferry and Shepherdstown, they had to either remove and carry their shoes or else cross in relatively deep water getting their shoes wet. The latter course would make marching more difficult. John Worsham of the 21st Virginia Infantry described taking off his shoes and carrying them while his feet were getting cut on very sharp rocks on the Potomac River bottom.[13] At that point, Early's ill-shod army, which was trying to maintain a fast pace to timely move on Washington, was hampered to a degree by being barefoot, both in crossing the rock-strewn river and in marching on country roads thereafter.

As late as July 6, 1864, in Hagerstown, Maryland, General John McCausland's Confederate cavalry forces were still seeking shoes or boots as part of the items they were seeking to obtain from local establishments in that city.[14]

Meanwhile, wagons loaded with additional shoes for Early's army from Richmond were coming down the Valley and across the Potomac. They finally arrived as the divisions of Early's army were marching east of Frederick through the mountain passes toward that city. The shoes were then distributed to the men.[15]

The largest storehouses and depots for quartermaster's materials of all types were in Washington. Thus, the need for rapid movement to execute Lee's plan was enhanced by the need for some of the provisions and stores, including shoes, that would have been available to Early's army had it been able to take possession of Washington, even for a brief period.

As it was, the lack of adequate shoes for the army did not prevent Early's army from making good progress down the Valley after Hunter retreated into West Virginia and good progress on specific days subsequently. However, it clearly was somewhat of a factor contributing to Early's tarrying on the Upper Potomac, which was ultimately fatal to his attempt to take Washington.

CHAPTER 12

Grant Fails to Meet Early's Threat

The saving of the Union was and continued to be President Abraham Lincoln's priority in 1864. On March 8, 1864, Ulysses S. Grant, who had achieved major victories in the west at Fort Donelson, Vicksburg and Chattanooga, was called east to be awarded the rank of Lieutenant General. He was the first person to hold that rank since George Washington. General William Tecumseh Sherman succeeded Grant as commander in the west. General Henry Halleck became chief of staff.[1]

After coming east to Washington, Grant had gone to the White House to meet President Lincoln, who advanced to take his hand and expressed pleasure at seeing him.[2] Lincoln was pleased at the warm reception accorded Grant. He felt that the path to victory was wide enough for them to walk abreast.[3]

After the ceremony of Grant's commission as Lieutenant General, Grant and Lincoln talked in private. Lincoln explained that the procrastination of some prior commanders had caused him on occasion to issue military orders. He told Grant that all he wanted him to do was to take responsibility and to act. Lincoln would provide whatever assistance was needed.[4] Grant was quite modest and was quietly confident.[5] He had the confidence of Lincoln and the Congress as he assumed his duties. Lincoln believed he now had the general he needed to vigorously pursue the Confederates and save the Union. As Grant began his spring campaign, Lincoln wrote him expressing confidence in what he had done.

> ...I wish to express, in this way, my entire satisfaction with what you have done up to this time so far as I understand it. The particulars of your plans I neither know, or seek to know. You are vigilant and self-reliant; and, pleased with this; I ask not obtrude any restraints upon you. While I am anxious that any great disaster or the capture of our men in great numbers should be avoided, I know that these points are less likely to escape your attention than they would mine. If there is anything wanting which is in my power to give, do not fail to let me know it.[6]

Grant was to attack Lee, Sherman was to move through Georgia from the west and capture Atlanta, and Butler was to move against Richmond from the James. The movement into action of numerically superior Union forces was what Lincoln wanted.[7]

Grant undertook to advance toward Richmond through the Wilderness. The terrain gave Lee, fighting from the defensive, an enormous advantage. Grant pushed on, although taking terrible casualties, with bulldog tenacity.[8]

Grant wrote his wife on May 13, 1864, that the world had never seen so protracted and bloody a struggle.[9] Secretary of the Navy Gideon Welles found the anxiety from the battles difficult and said that it diverted the mind from mental activity.[10] Attorney General Bates found the carnage to have been unexampled.[11] In the fighting in the Wilderness alone, Grant lost an estimated 17,500 men. Lee lost less than half as many, 7,500, but still a staggering total. After Shiloh, Alexander McClue had been told by Lincoln he could not spare Grant because of fights.[12]

The anxiety and strain on President Lincoln was tremendous. Gideon Welles recorded that

Lieutenant General Ulysses S. Grant, commanding general (National Archives).

there were nights when he simply could not sleep.[13] At times Lincoln was overcome with sorrow at the tremendous loss of life. In a speech at the Great Central Sanitary Fair at Philadelphia on June 16, 1864, Lincoln said: "War, at the best, is terrible, and this war of ours, in its magnitude and in its duration, is one of the most terrible. It has destroyed property, and ruined homes; it has produced a national debt and taxation unprecedented.... It has carried mourning to almost every home, until it can almost be said that the 'heavens are hung in black.'"[14]

Schuyler Colfax, later Grant's vice president, visited Lincoln at the White House during the Battle of the Wilderness and found Lincoln's face to be the saddest he had ever seen. However, Lincoln spoke of Grant with confidence and hope.[15] Having experienced previous Union commanders who retreated after taking terrible losses at the hands of Lee, Lincoln kept faith in Grant's tenacity to persist in the face of such great adversity.

On May 11, 1864, Lieutenant General Ulysses S. Grant wrote Secretary of War Edwin M. Stanton, saying, "I propose to fight it out on this line if it takes all summer."[16] President Lincoln literally kissed reporter Henry Wing, who brought a verbal message from Grant that there would be no turning back.[17] And push on he did.

Grant fought Lee at Spottsylvania as he maneuvered south for almost two weeks. Again, Grant took substantial casualties. But, at the Mule Shoe Salient, Lee lost almost an entire division in men captured. The fighting was hard, bloody and intense. Grant's casualties of 26,441 killed, wounded and captured were again almost triple Lee's 9,030.[18]

Lee had slowed Grant down, but had not stopped him. Grant was fighting a battle of attrition, replacing losses which Lee could not. Grant again had pushed relentlessly south and engaged the Confederate forces in almost constant fighting, which sapped the strength of both sides. War weariness was gripping the North. The *New York Times* reported that men on both sides had to climb over piles of dead and dying men, in some places stacked 3 or 4 deep.[19] Lincoln realized that Grant had the type of dogged tenacity that wins.[20]

From Spottsylvania, Grant headed in the direction of Hanover Junction. This was the crucial place where the Richmond, Fredericksburg and Potomac Railroad, running from Washington to Richmond, crossed the Virginia Central, which went from Richmond to Charlottesville. Here Grant engaged Lee for several days of intensive fighting on the North Ana River. Grant's casualties, although much smaller, totaled 1,973. Lee's, again considerably lower, totaled 1,460.[21]

Grant again was blocked but not stopped by Lee on the North Ana. Lee had to keep fighting because he knew if Grant hemmed him in in Richmond and put Richmond and his army under siege, it was only a matter of time before Grant broke his supply lines and forced him to capitulate.[22]

The fighting continued at Cold Harbor in early June 1864. Grant always regretted that his last assault at Cold Harbor had ever been made.[23] His army's assaults against an extremely strong Confederate defensive position resulted in senseless carnage and drew to a close the bloodiest five weeks of the Civil War. Grant's losses at Cold Harbor were about 7,000. Lee's were 1,500.[24] The total for both sides for the Overland Campaign was 86,000 men.[25]

As Cold Harbor was going on, Secretary of the Navy Welles recorded that "the immense slaughter of our brave men chills and sickens us all."[26] Welles later would say that the Union troops had suffered much but had accomplished little.[27] However, Grant, in spite of the huge losses incurred by his army, was still popular and commanded some attention at the Republican Convention that had occurred in early June 1864. A radical delegation from Missouri, pledging to switch to Lincoln after the first ballot, was in favor of Grant.[28] A White House visitor had told Lincoln that nothing could defeat him except Grant taking Richmond and being nominated at the Democratic convention.[29]

Thus, in spite of horrific losses in a campaign that had led to a stalemate and had not ended the war or even put it close to a conclusion, Grant retained the confidence of Lincoln. Lincoln retained the confidence of his party. Although there were constant demands for peace, with the opposition Democrats touting peace as part of their proposed platform, the war continued to grind on. There was roughly a 5-month period between the Republican convention and the election. Lincoln' s prospects, although not altogether bright in June 1864, would be influenced by the outcome of Sherman's Atlanta Campaign and Grant's continued actions before Richmond.

Grant was determined to strike a bold blow against Lee that would force him to defend Richmond or face loss of his vital communications center at Petersburg. To do this, Grant undertook a brilliant and forceful maneuver. Without warning, Grant sent his army across the James River and in a movement toward Petersburg. On the morning of June 13, 1864, Lee found that the Union lines at Cold Harbor were empty.

The Union forces under General William "Baldy" Smith, General Winfield Scott Hancock and others were on their way to Petersburg, an important rail and communications center south of Richmond. Unfortunately for Grant, his brilliant maneuver was not adroitly executed. There were inordinate delays by both Smith and Hancock in executing their orders. Part of the problem was "Baldy" Smith in getting his artillery up. Smith's failure to vigorously attack on June 15 was a major failure that allowed the Confederates to successfully defend Petersburg and prolong the war.

Fortunately for Lee, Petersburg was ably defended by a relatively strong force under General Pierre Gustave Toustant Beauregard. Beauregard, along with Joseph E. Johnston, had led the Confederate army to victory at First Bull Run (Manassas). He had also successfully managed the defense of Charleston against Union attacks by land and by sea. He was able to timely notify Lee of Grant's change of position and hold the lines at Petersburg until the arrival of reinforcements.[30]

Grant, with a superior force, had undertaken a strategy that, with proper execution, should have resulted in Lee's loss of the vital communications and supply lines and could have cut short the war by a significant period. Such a dramatic result could have provided the battlefield victory so desperately needed after the long and bloody Overland Campaign, which ended at Cold Harbor. However, the brilliant result hoped for had been fumbled away by inept movements. Thus, Grant was forcing Lee into a stalemated siege which would ultimately be fatal to the Confederacy but in the short term maintained a status quo which was not encouraging to the populace of the war weary North.

However, Grant, in executing his daring strategy, had done something that had not yet been done by a commander in the east — removal of the primary fighting force from between Lee and Washington. In doing this, Grant had done something Halleck was very much against. The theory had been that the defenses of Washington and other places could be depleted of troops to be sent to Grant as long as Grant assured that Washington would be protected. Now Washington was not protected except for the army in the Shenandoah Valley under General David Hunter.[31] Hunter was to prove to be unwilling to follow Grant's orders, which would have provided substantial protection to Washington had his army moved to Charlottesville or Gordonsville as directed. Moreover, Hunter was so inept in the operation of his army as to move in his discretion to Lynchburg with inordinate delays and with inadequate munitions and supply lines.

As a result of the greatest intelligence failure of the Civil War, Hunter's ineptitude and disobedience of orders, Grant's unwillingness to control Hunter and ensure his orders were followed by either replacing him or taking necessary action, and Grant's unwillingness to credit intelligence he had that showed Early had been at Lynchburg and the Valley and not at Richmond, Grant unnecessarily opened up the potential for a Union assault on Washington — in an election year with everything at stake — which should have succeeded had Lee's plan been executed better and more timely.[32] Grant blundered badly, in part because Hunter blundered badly and Grant allowed him to do it. Grant was facing the most daring man he had ever faced on a battlefield. It almost changed everything.

It was not until August 1864, after Early's attack on Washington and aborted move toward Point Lookout had occurred, that Grant acted to address the issues that had allowed Lee's plans to unfold. Replacing Hunter, Albion Howe, Lew Wallace, Darius Couch and others, Grant opted for a unified command system, with Major General Philip H. Sheridan to assume overall command in the various jurisdictions. He was a man Grant could trust and would work with closely.[33]

Grant, having realized the massive failure of the intelligence system as it had previously operated, put in place a system where he, and not the battlefield commanders like Hunter, had immediate access to intelligence that was not delayed or filtered before he received it. In short, Grant took control of command and control operations that went a long way to assuring that the catastrophe that almost befell the Union before Washington in July would not reoccur.

However, the way the greatest intelligence failure of the Civil War unfolded, and Grant's incongruous, belated and inadequate response to it, was a major factor in making possible Lee's plan not only to take Washington but also to free the prisoners at Point Lookout.

General Grant responded slowly to Early's threat. In part this was due to his own remarkable operation moving his army south of the James. This movement was brilliant in conception and should have resulted in the fall of Petersburg, the Confederate's major rail center south of Richmond, which Lee's staff officer, Major Giles Cook, described this way: "The Federals lost their best chance to take Petersburg by storm on that June morning. W.F. Smith, their commander, had 16,000 troops under arms and thousands more upon the march. Beauregard's 5,000 could barely hold the fortifications. Smith lost the whole day, studying our position; getting his men ready. Finally at 6 o'clock, he was ready to open fire. Then he found his artillery chief had sent the gunner's horses to water. It took an hour to get them back. Precious hour! It saved Petersburg."[34]

It took Grant more than three weeks to realize that Early had left the Confederate defenses at Petersburg. Lieutenant Colonel Robert Stribling of the Confederate Army found it remarkable that an army commander could have lost sight of a whole corps or the opposing army for nearly a month.[35] The serious consequences of a Confederate occupation of Washington even for a brief time could have included recognition of the Confederacy by England and France. Grant seemed oblivious to the danger to Washington until it was almost too late.[36]

Hunter's departure from the Shenandoah Valley had left a Union intelligence vacuum.[37] Moreover, there was a telegraph link from Washington to Wilmington, Delaware, down the Eastern Shore of Maryland and across the Chesapeake Bay, ultimately ending up at City Point, Virginia, which involved lengthy delays in the transmission and receipt of messages.

Some information, however, had come in regarding Early. On June 18, 1864, Halleck had telegraphed Grant that the cavalry sent with dispatches for Hunter had found the Confederates in possession of Staunton and Lexington in his rear. They had been unable to reach him. This certainly suggested some type of Confederate force in the Valley. Hunter had replied to none of Halleck's contacts as of July 3.

Colonel George Sharpe of the Bureau of Information had written to General Andrew Humphreys, commander of the 2nd Corps of the Army of the Potomac, on June 20, 1864, that a prisoner from General Richard Anderson's 1st Corps of the Army of Northern Virginia stated that "Early's Corps" (part of Ewell's command) had left General Lee at Cold Harbor and had moved toward Lynchburg.[38] On June 21, 1864, five prisoners from A.P. Hill's corps corroborated this information, which was passed from Sharpe to Humphreys.

Major General Benjamin F. Butler telegraphed Grant on June 23, 1864, that "John Conroy 14th Va regt Hunton's brigade states that he saw a Richmond paper today & that it stated that Early now commanding Ewell's Corps had a fight yesterday with Maj Gen Hunter 12 miles from

(From left) Colonel George Sharpe, John C. Babcock, unidentified and John McEntee, Bureau of Military Information (Library of Congress).

Lynchburg & that Hunter was retreating & endeavoring to join Averell's forces." Grant had received correspondence from Union commanders in the Shenandoah Valley that Early commanded a force in their front. However, Early was not located until early July, when his troops were in Maryland.[39] General Hunter, in a report on June 28, 1864, had stated he withdrew in the face of a superior force constantly receiving reinforcements from Richmond. This also suggested that Early was gone. Grant telegraphed Halleck on June 28, 1864, "I wish you would put Gen Hunter in a good place to rest and as soon as possible start him for Charlottesville to destroy the Rail Road there effectively." Clearly, Grant did not fully appreciate the circumstances in that theater of operations.[40] On the 28th, Halleck telegraphed General David Hunter, directing him to telegraph Lieutenant General Grant about his operations. Hunter did not reply. Halleck also told Grant that the rail line west of Harpers Ferry had been attacked. Thus, Grant was being informed very directly that Hunter was not in a position to protect the main route from the Valley to the north.[41]

Captain John McEntee of the Bureau of Military Information had told Colonel Sharpe on June 28 that Hunter had engaged part of Ewell's Corps, commanded by Early, but that he thought Early was still at Richmond.[42] John Garrett, president of the Baltimore & Ohio Railroad, telegraphed the War Department on June 29 that Breckinridge and "Early's Corps" were moving up with a large number of men and expressed concern.[43] However, General Winfield Scott Hancock had telegraphed Brigadier General Seth Williams on July 1 that three deserters from

Hill's Corps said Ewell's Corps had arrived the day before.[44] Grant had not received information from Sigel in late June that Early was threatening him.[45] This provided conflicting information.

General Franz Sigel finally did telegraph Washington on July 2, 1864, that a large Confederate force was near Strasbourg. Charles A. Dana, assistant secretary of war, indicated, "In the first days of July we began to get inquiries at City point from Washington concerning the whereabouts of the Confederate generals Early and Ewell."[46] Grant replied to Halleck's assertion on July 1 in conflicting reports of Confederate forces in the Shenandoah Valley that Early's Corps had retreated to Richmond. Grant stated to Halleck on July 1, "Ewell's Corps has returned here." General Ulysses S. Grant still maintained that position on July 3, telling Halleck, "You can direct Sigel in answer to his dispatch of 10:30 A.M. of today better that I can. Early's corps is now here. There are no troops that now can be threatening Hunter's Dept, except the remnant of the force W.E. Jones had and possibly Breckinridge. If there is anything threatening any portion of his Department however you need not send him here."[47]

Brigadier General Max Weber at Harpers Ferry telegraphed William Prescott Smith, the transportation manager of the Baltimore & Ohio Railroad, that the Confederates had taken possession of Martinsburg, that Sigel was marching toward Harpers Ferry and that the Confederate cavalry under Ransom was moving to Williamsport.[48] Correspondence between Captain Max Woodhull and Smith of the Baltimore & Ohio on July 3, 1864, discussed the movement of hospital patients away from Frederick and apparent danger.[49] Halleck informed Grant on July 3 that Early and Breckinridge were reported moving down the Shenandoah Valley. Halleck had informed Grant that General Sigel reports that Early, Breckinridge and Jackson, with Mosby's guerillas, are said to be moving from Staunton down the Shenandoah Valley. "I ordered General Hunter up to the line of the [Baltimore & Ohio] railroad, but he has replied to none of my telegrams and has made no report of his operations or present condition. Sigel has been ordered to telegraph directly to him, to inform him of the condition of affairs, and to ask for instructions.... The three principal officers in the line of the road are Sigel, Stahel, and Max Weber. You, can, therefore, judge what probability there is of a good defense if the enemy should attack the line in force." Grant informed Major General George G. Meade that Sigel had telegraphed that Early, Breckinridge, Jackson and Mosby were reported moving down the Shenandoah Valley. He questioned whether it was certain Early had returned to his front. Meade has also informed Grant that no prisoners had been taken from Early's Corps.[50] The only information he had was from deserters who had returned from Lynchburg. Grant maintained his position that Early was still at Richmond.[51] Part of the problem was that Grant simply did not believe information he had that Early was gone.

On July 4, 1864, approximately three weeks after Early had left Petersburg, Grant started a significant search for intelligence as to the whereabouts of Early. Grant advised Halleck at 4:00 P.M. on July 4 that a deserter that morning reported that Ewell's Corps was in the Shenandoah Valley with the intention of going into Maryland and Washington. Grant told Halleck to hold all of the forces he could in Washington, Baltimore, Harpers Ferry and Cumberland.[52]

General Ethan Allen Hitchcock visited Halleck, Stanton and Lincoln to express his concern as to the dangers Early posed. A deserter also reported on July 4 Early had gone to Maryland with his entire corps. On the 5th, Meade became convinced that Early was gone.[53] On July 5, 1864, at 10:30 A.M., J. Donohoo of the Headquarters of the Middle District in Baltimore telegraphed Smith of the Baltimore & Ohio that the Confederates were now in Harpers Ferry.[54]

As of July 5, 1864, Grant still did not know definitively where Early was and was confused by conflicting reports about him.[55] This was in spite of Sigel's direct transmission that a large Confederate force was in the Valley and the president of the Baltimore & Ohio Railroad's reports of destruction of railroad property by "Early's Corps." Finally, as a precaution, on July 5 Grant did direct General Meade to send a good division and dismounted cavalry to Washington. Grant told Halleck at midnight on July 5, "Your dispatch of 12:30 P.M. recd. I have ordered to Washington the dismounted Cavalry & one Divn of Infantry which will be followed by the balance of the corps if necessary. We want now to crush out & destroy any force the enemy does send out. Force enough can be spared from here to do it I think now there is no doubt but Ewell's corps is coming from here."[56]

Meade sent Ricketts's 6th Corps division and all the dismounted troopers from the 2nd Cavalry Division via City Point.[57] Secretary of the Navy Gideon Welles in his diary for July 6, 1864, noted that military authorities did not seem to know whether a reported 30,000 Confederate troops were going to Washington.[58] However, on July 7, Grant telegraphed Halleck confirming that 3,000 dismounted cavalry and a total force of 9,000 had been sent to Washington.[59] The two remaining divisions of the 6th Corps were to follow and the 19th Corps was diverted to Washington while en route from New Orleans, arriving on the 11th. Halleck had already informed Grant,

> The line from Monocacy to Harper's Ferry has been cut, and the re-enforcements sent from here fell back to the Monocacy. General Howe has been sent with about 2,800 men to force his way to Harper's Ferry. We have nothing reliable in regard to the enemy's force. Some accounts, probably very exaggerated, state it to be between 20,000 and 30,000. If one-half that number we cannot meet it in the field until Hunter's troops arrive. As you are aware, we have almost nothing in Baltimore or Washington, except militia, and considerable alarm has been created by sending troops from these places to re-enforce Harper's Ferry. You probably have a large dismounted cavalry force, and I would advise that it be sent here immediately. It can be remounted by impressing horses in the part of Maryland likely to be overrun by the enemy. All the dismounted fragments here were armed as infantry and sent to Harper's Ferry.[60]

Thus, even though General Early had been quite tardy in getting his troops up from Martinsburg and across the Potomac and in motion from July 3 through July 6, it had not necessarily been fatal to the execution of Lee's plan to attack Washington and liberate the prisoners at Point Lookout, because Grant had not taken precautions to strengthen the defenses of Washington until July 5. Rickett's 6th Corps Division departed on July 6, 1864, and arrived in Baltimore on July 8 and at Monocacy Junction on July 9.

Grant's inaction, partially explicable by the lack of sufficient military intelligence information, had left the door of opportunity open to Early to seize Washington and move on to Point Lookout. Grant had failed to timely follow up on the information he had, suggesting Early had been at Lynchburg and then in the Valley from Hunter and Sigel. Having stripped Washington of its garrisons, Grant was slow to protect the capital when it was in danger. Grant admitted in his memoirs, "If Early had been but one day earlier he might have entered the capital before the arrival of reinforcements I had sent."[61]

Even though Point Lookout was 90 miles southeast of Washington, making Early's timetable very tight, he did not seize the initiative and engage in a footrace that could have gotten him to Wallace's 2,500 home guards and militia on the Monocacy before Ricketts arrived on July 9. Early was delayed by extorting money from the citizens of Hagerstown and Frederick not to burn the cities, by delays in moving his troops into Frederick due to the timid leadership of his cavalry under General Robert Ransom, and because of his failure to aggressively move his army to Frederick from the Potomac in the first place. Early compounded his initial tardiness by further delays which made it possible for a substantial Union force to oppose him on his way to Washington, which need not have been. Grant's lack of timely response could have enabled the taking of Washington at great cost to the Union cause, but ultimately did not.

There were huge amounts of military stores in Washington. The president was there. The potential military and political ramification of either burning the capital or having harm come to the president were incalculable. Grant had left that door open by his failure to timely act. Early, by his failure to seize the multiple opportunities open to him, closed that window of opportunity. Lee's bold endeavor, like Grant's for taking Petersburg, failed not in the brilliance of its conception but in the failure of its execution, difficult as it was to accomplish.

CHAPTER 13

Early Hindered by Lack of Cooperation with Mosby

The most frequent and constant threats to the defenses of Washington in 1864 before Early's raid were the attacks in the area made by Colonel John Singleton Mosby and his 43rd Battalion of Virginia Cavalry. Having Mosby's cooperation in attacking Washington was crucial to Early's success. Mosby had an enviable record in threatening those defenses and troop movements in the area based on years of knowledge and involvement.

Mosby started as a private in the 1st Virginia Cavalry under General W.E. "Grumble" Jones, later killed in the Battle of Piedmont. He was at First Bull Run (Manassas) and was commissioned a 1st lieutenant in February 1862. Mosby was a scout under General J.E.B. Stuart, riding around McClellan's army on the Peninsula in 1862. The Partisan Rangers Law was enacted in 1862 which allowed partisans to be regularly received into the service and to wear uniforms similar to the regular Confederate army uniform. These men were to be paid for arms and ammunition they secured from Union forces for the Confederate government. Mosby was mustered into the Confederate army and operated with the 43rd Virginia Battalion. This unit generally served in the area of Loudon County, Virginia, which became known as "Mosby's Confederacy."

Most of the time, Mosby's units operated in groups of 20 to 80 men. In 1863, his men captured Brigadier General Edwin H. Stoughton at Fairfax Court House.

In 1864, his attacks on General Hunter's wagon trains contributed greatly to his ammunition problems, which were a major factor in the outcome of the Lynchburg Campaign. Vexed by the effectiveness of these partisans, Lieutenant General Ulysses S. Grant in 1864 ordered Mosby and his men hung without trial when captured. Brigadier General George Armstrong Custer did execute six of Mosby's men captured at Front Royal in 1864. Mosby was wounded seven times in the Civil War. After the war, he and Grant became friends. Grant felt few southern officers could have successfully commanded a separate force in the rear of the Union armies without losing their entire force.[1]

However, when Early's army marched into the northern Shenandoah Valley in late June and early July of 1864, Early did not contact Mosby. Early had been informed on the way down the Valley by two commissary chiefs, Major Wells J. Hawks and Major John Harmon, that army resupply was problematic, with only some of the needed stores having arrived from Richmond and other locales. Another quartermaster, Hugh Schwartz, was told on July 2 that the Loudon County area lacked sufficient provisions for a large army.[2] Mosby ran into one of Early's commissary officers at Rectortown on July 2, 1864, and heard about the raid. On the evening of July 2, 1864, Captain George W. Booth of Bradley Johnson's command talked with Colonel John Singleton Mosby. Mosby agreed to help. On July 3, 250 cavalry gathered under Mosby at Upperville. He started for the Potomac and moved 10 miles west of Leesburg in Loudon County. He also had a 12-pounder howitzer. On the 4th of July he left camp to move west toward Union communications centers.[3]

Mosby took 250 men to break communications between Harpers Ferry and Washington in an attack at Point of Rocks on July 4, 1864.[4] Point of Rocks was on the Potomac River at a place where the C & O Canal and the Baltimore & Ohio Railroad pass through a gap in the Catoctin Mountains. Point of Rocks was defended for the Union by two companies of infantry and two companies of Loudon County rangers. Mosby drove off those troops, plundered their camps, forced a train back to Sandy Hook and disrupted rail and telegraph communications to Washington for two days.[5] The *National Intelligencer* of July 6, 1864, reported that a Mrs. Dixon of Point of Rocks had been killed by rebel fire while sitting in her doorway and that a pleasure boat carrying Treasury Department employees on an outing had been attacked and burned, with six of the seventeen employees being missing in that attack. On the evening of July 4, Mosby ordered a scouting party of the 43rd Virginia Battalion to recross the Potomac and cut the telegraph wires. Wat Bowie led the party, which included Jim Wiltshire, Charlie Dear, Stoney Mason, Bush Underwood, Jin Lander, Ned Gibon, Clay Adams and Monroe Henshell. A detachment of the 8th Illinois Cavalry was also attacked at the aqueduct at the mouth of the Monocacy River.

There had been a newspaper report that a group of Treasury Department employees had left Georgetown on a trip to Harpers Ferry by the canal boat *Flying Cloud*. The department personnel were at dinner on their return when the boat was fired on about 50 yards from the lock near Point of Rocks. The lock keeper was gone. The men on the boat jumped ashore. Four men of the party tried unsuccessfully to open the lock. The Confederate cavalry now had reached the tow path of the canal and fired on the men. The Treasury employees fled, and Mosby's men set fire to the canal boat after taking everything of value. Seven of the seventeen-person party were missing, including Captain Hobart of the canal boat.[6]

A Union force had left Washington on July 4, 1864, to reinforce Harpers Ferry. Mosby's Point of Rocks attack had prevented these men from reaching Harpers Ferry. They went back to Monocacy Junction and then to Monrovia until the track was cleared.

General Max Weber at Harpers Ferry and General Lew Wallace at Baltimore telegraphed Chief of Staff Henry Halleck that the Confederates had crossed the Potomac in force at Point of Rocks. Halleck had telegraphed Grant on July 5 that "Genl Howe has been sent there with about twenty-eight hundred men to force his way to Harper's Ferry."[7]

Halleck had sent 2,800 dismounted cavalry under General Albion Howe to force their way to Harpers Ferry. When Howe reached Point of Rocks, the Confederates were gone. Howe proceeded to Maryland Heights and Halleck ordered him to stay there.[8]

Lieutenant Colonel David Clendenin of the 8th Illinois Cavalry had been sent from Washington to Point of Rocks on a scouting mission on July 5, 1864. Mosby then skirmished with the 8th Illinois Cavalry, which had occupied Point of Rocks. After Mosby's departure, the 8th Illinois Cavalry moved north to the valleys west of Frederick and assisted General Lew Wallace in resisting Early's advance. Mosby did not prevent Clendenin's move nor did he participate in the cavalry battles west of Frederick on July 7 and 8. Mosby's disruptive attack was a factor in Halleck's actions, which took a substantial number of troops available to defend the city from Washington.

After the Point of Rocks attack, Mosby sent two of his men to Early, who was at Sharpsburg, to provide intelligence on enemy strength and convey Mosby's willingness to obey Early's orders. Early requested that Mosby support him by not only cutting rail and telegraph communications but reconnoitering toward Washington.[9] This was on July 6, 1864.[10]

Early claimed Mosby did not follow his instructions or provide him with information:

From Sharpsburg I had sent a message to Mosby, by one of his men, requesting him to cross the Potomac, below Harper's Ferry, cut the railroad and telegraph and endeavor to find out the condition of things in Washington, but he had not crossed the river, and I received no information from him.[11]

Henry Heaton, a guide and scout with Mosby and Lieutenant Beattie, claimed that on the morning of July 5, 1864, they took a dispatch from Mosby to Early informing him of what had been done and offering to cooperate with Early in any movement, reaching Early at Sharpsburg. They gave him all the information they had about the number and distribution of Union troops east of the Blue Ridge. They said that they returned with an oral message from Early that his purpose was to proceed to Washington after maneuvering forces from Maryland Heights.[12]

Mosby in his memoirs did not mention contact with Early after his men's initial contact with him. Mosby's men did little to help Early.[13] On July 6, 1864, Mosby, scouting near Aldie, Virginia, inflicted substantial casualties on the 13th New York Cavalry and the 2nd Massachusetts Cavalry in a fight at Mt. Zion Church. The Union losses were 14 dead, 37 wounded and 55 captured out of about 150 troopers engaged.[14] On July 11, 1864, the day Early was before Fort Stevens, Mosby appeared at Poolesville not far from Washington but did not find the Union 8th Illinois Cavalry there. Mosby camped for the night at Seneca with about 250 men.

Early had a substantial need for scouting, intelligence and cavalry assistance as he moved north into Maryland. After the Point of Rocks attack, Mosby's forces returned to Virginia. The Loudon rangers and Lieutenant Colonel David Clendenin's 8th Illinois Cavalry were able to provide stubborn resistance to the advance of the Confederate cavalry forces in the valleys west of Frederick. Mosby's men could have made a difference in scouting for Early's advance and helping clear the Union cavalry units that were resisting that advance. Mosby's men could have also helped seize the bridgeheads at the Monocacy River at a time they were lightly defended, which McCausland failed to do later. Moreover, Mosby had frequently attacked the defenses of Washington and would have had insights into their weaknesses and the troop strengths in the area. Early's main cavalry command under Bradley Johnson was taken from him for the Point Lookout raid. Ransom was an ineffective cavalry commander. Mosby could have provided invaluable assistance to Early but did not act.

Mosby dismissed Early as an "old fraud."[15] Mosby clearly had the ability to have been of substantial assistance to Early in gathering intelligence as to the condition of the defenses of Washington and their vulnerability to attack. He was also a formidable adversary to Union scouts and cavalry units and was capable of substantial disruption by his actions, as evidenced by the Point of Rocks attack. Why there was no follow through as a result of the meeting between Mosby's men and Early on July 6 is largely unexplained

COLONEL JOHN SINGLETON MOSBY COMMANDED THE 43RD VIRGINIA BATTALION (NATIONAL ARCHIVES).

either by Mosby or Early. Mosby's failure to provide information on the status of the defenses of Washington in combination with the Union's prevention of civilians from leaving Washington and hence providing information was a handicap to Early and apparently reinforced his hesitation to attack at Fort Stevens in the early afternoon of July 11, a hesitation fatal to the success of Early's mission.

CHAPTER 14

Washington's Defenses Depleted by Removal of Troops to Maryland Heights

After General David Hunter, later relieved by General Grant, fled into West Virginia with over 15,000 men in June 1864, leaving the road to Washington partially open, all that stood between General Early and Washington were the forces of General Franz Sigel near Martinsburg, West Virginia, and those of General Max Weber nearby, garrisoning Harpers Ferry.

Brigadier General Albion Howe, head of the Artillery Depot in Washington, had a large number of dismounted men in Washington at the beginning of July 1864. By July 2, General Sigel at Martinsburg and General Weber at Harpers Ferry had reported that numerous Confederate divisions were moving down the Valley toward them. General Henry Halleck in Washington was growing increasingly concerned. Halleck had very little confidence in Sigel and Weber and wanted to avoid a surrender like that of Colonel Dixon Miles's forces in the Antietam Campaign where Stonewall Jackson took over 10,000 Union prisoners. Late on July 3, 1864, Halleck decided to send Brigadier General Albion Howe with 2,800 men to help defend Harpers Ferry.[1]

Howe's men embarked by rail for Harpers Ferry in response to Halleck's order. Howe's directions had been to take three separate parts of his force by rail to Point of Rocks, Maryland. There he was to rendezvous with a cavalry unit and proceed to Harpers Ferry. If the rail line was destroyed or blocked, his force was to repair it. Howe was then to take a portion of his force back to Washington.[2]

The telegraph had been cut at Point of Rocks on July 4 by Colonel John Singleton Mosby's men, but had been repaired by W.W. Shock of the Baltimore & Ohio Railroad. How-

GENERAL HENRY HALLECK, UNION CHIEF OF STAFF (LIBRARY OF CONGRESS).

14. Washington's Defenses Depleted by Removal of Troops to Maryland Heights

ever, General Weber at Harpers Ferry had been able to telegraph John W. Garrett, president of the Baltimore & Ohio, at 10:48 A.M. on July 4, that 2,000 cavalry and a force of Confederate infantry were in sight. Weber said he would retreat, if pressed, to Maryland Heights, which was across the Potomac and commanded the city. This information was forwarded to Henry Halleck and Secretary of War Stanton. Garrett had told Stanton on July 3 that Early, Breckinridge and Imboden were north of Winchester with between 15,000 and 30,000 men and that the garrison at Harpers Ferry could not stop Early.[3]

At this point, all that was between Early and Washington were a few thousand militia and home guards under the command of General Lew Wallace in Baltimore. The force being sent to Harpers Ferry by rail was interrupted by Mosby's July 4 raid on Point of Rocks. On July 4, 1864, Wallace was concentrating his forces at Monocacy.[4]

Meanwhile on July 3 and 4, General Franz Sigel and General Max Weber had been able to accomplish a remarkable retreat with their garrison forces from Martinsburg and Harpers Ferry without substantial loss.[5] Sigel's command consisted of two veteran infantry regiments, the 23rd Illinois and the 10th West Virginia in Harris's brigade, four other regiments of infantry, about 1,000 dismounted cavalry and two battalions of the 5th New York Heavy Artillery.[6] Weber's

ARTILLERY PARK SIMILAR TO ONE COMMANDED BY HOWE IN WASHINGTON (LIBRARY OF CONGRESS).

small force numbered about 580 men, making the total force of somewhat over 5,000.[7] Weber had not communicated to Garrett or the War Department that he wanted or needed reinforcements. Neither had Sigel. They were in a nearly impregnable position.

On July 6, 1864, Brigadier General Albion Howe's relief force finally reached Harpers Ferry in the predawn hours. On the morning of July 6, Howe reported to Washington that his relief force had reinforced the Union armies already on Maryland Heights.[8]

At the time of Early's attack on Washington on July 11 and 12, 1864, General Alexander McD. McCook's forces commanding the city's northern defenses consisted of 7,886 men, 2,800 of whom were convalescents from hospitals in Price's Provisional Brigade and 1,800 of whom were civilian Quartermaster employees.[9] Yet, Halleck had chosen to put a more substantial part of his force defending Washington, about 2,800 men, at risk by sending them directly toward Early, who almost five times as many men. This force was a collection of national guard troops from Ohio, dismounted cavalry, and light artillery used as infantry.

Although the defenses of Washington with their over 800 guns had been almost completely stripped of veteran artillerists while some places, like the Washington end of Long Bridge, needed both artillerists and artillery, Halleck selected Brigadier General Albion Howe to go to Harpers Ferry. He chose to send out of Washington the general who on May 17, 1864, had submitted a report on the defenses of Washington and their composition, staffing and needs. He also had headed the artillery depot in Washington and thus was aware of what armaments were available at the time.[10] Howe was the person with the most immediate knowledge of the defenses of Washington, including their artillery capabilities and troop strength and weaknesses in the lines.

BRIG. GEN. ALBION HOWE, SENT TO HARPERS FERRY BY HALLECK (LIBRARY OF CONGRESS).

Thus Halleck was not only taking 2,800 men from the defenses but the man who knew the most about them and how to defend them. Why Halleck would choose to send a person with Howe's unique knowledge and experience when Washington itself was threatened with attack by General Early and calls were being made for militia troops from northern states for its defense is not readily explicable.

After commanding an artillery brigade in the Peninsular Campaign, Howe had been made a brigadier on June 11, 1862. He commanded an infantry brigade in the Maryland Campaign of 1862 and then served at Fredericksburg and Chancellorsville. In the fall of 1863, General Howe was placed in command of the Artillery Depot in Washington in an apparent move to remove him from infantry command.[11] In May 1864, Howe was assigned to inspect and report on the defenses of Washington, a task for which his artillery background qualified him. Thus, not only was Howe taken from a position in Washington for which he was uniquely suited, but was again put in an infantry command for which he was not.

Part of the force being sent was light artillery to be used as infantry. Brigadier General Howe had three batteries of artillery from Washington serving as infantry. Thus the already stripped artillery forces at Washington were being stripped further at a time when General John G. Barnard, chief engineer, was requesting Halleck to send experienced artillery forces back from Grant's army to Washington.[12]

The other forces in Howe's command were dismounted cavalry and Ohio militia. The 170th Ohio was commanded by Colonel Miles Sanders. Major General Christopher Augur, commanded of the 22nd Corps at Washington, was concerned about the need for artillerists and the protection of Washington. He ordered Battery L of the 1st Ohio Light Artillery under Captain Frank C. Gibbs and the 1st Maine Battery under Captain Albert Bradbury retained in Washington.[13] On July 7, 1864, President Lincoln issued Special Order 230 naming Brigadier General Albion Howe to replace Major General Franz Sigel.[14] Major General Julius Stahel would also be replaced. Sigel was directed to report to Major General David Hunter, who was still hundreds of miles away in West Virginia and had been out of communication with General Halleck. How General Sigel was to accomplish his order to report is unclear.

A telegram on the morning of July 8, 1864, to William Prescott Smith, transportation master of the Baltimore & Ohio Railroad, reflected that General Howe had previously arrived and had started for Sandy Hook near Harpers Ferry.[15] Howe had not been able to get all of the way to Harpers Ferry by rail and had had to march part of the way.[16] After arriving on July 6, 1864, Howe had sent a telegram from Harpers Ferry to Lieutenant Colonel David Clendenin telling him to go to Frederick and to find out about Confederate forces reported to be in the Boonesboro area west of South Mountain. Howe had also asked General Halleck for instructions. Halleck told him to try to effectuate a juncture with General Hunter and to try to reach Washington.[17]

How and where he was to meet up with Hunter, who had not been in effective communication with the War Department, is unclear. In fact, Hunter would not reach Harpers Ferry until after Early's attack on Washington and return to Virginia. Halleck was aware of concern that his sending Howe to Harpers Ferry had generated, telling Grant, "As you are aware, we have almost nothing in Baltimore and Washington, except militia, and considerable alarm has been created by sending troops from those places to re-inforce Harper's Ferry."[18]

While Lew Wallace was taking aggressive action to meet and delay Early, Howe did nothing to assist in that process, staying in Harpers Ferry until August, when he was relieved by Grant. Howe and Hunter together had forces totaling nearly 23,000 men in Early's rear as he marched on Washington. Neither threatened Early or blocked his retreat into Virginia after Early's attack on Washington and aborted move toward Point Lookout. Lee could not have asked for more. Although apparently unknown to Early, Halleck's actions had greatly enhanced his chances for successfully executing Lee's plan.

Early was not able to make the most of the situation. Rather than press on immediately toward Washington on July 3 and 4, he stayed in the area of Martinsburg and Harpers Ferry on those days. Sigel and Weber had been allowed to escape to Maryland Heights, which commanded Harpers Ferry. His relative inaction and dilatoriness from July 3 through 6 offset the blunders of Grant and Halleck on the Union side in not timely responding to Early's threat and in sending forces from Washington respectively. Early's slow movements on the Upper Potomac continued to be a substantial overriding factor in his failure to pierce the defenses of Washington and secure the release of the prisoners at Point Lookout.

CHAPTER 15

Seaborne Attack on Point Lookout in Conjunction with Early's Forces Called Off

During the winter of 1863, General Robert E. Lee had considered a Confederate military operation against the prison at Point Lookout, which housed a large number of men taken from the Army of Northern Virginia. Action was not taken at that time in large part due to circumstances in the field involving operations by the Union and Confederate armies.

There had been complaints in the spring of 1864 by the residents of the Northern Neck between the Potomac and the Rappahannock about the threat of a Union invasion. General Robert E. Lee wrote his son, General G.W. Custis Lee, on April 7, 1864, about an attack in the St. Mary's River in Maryland to thwart such an attack:

> I think the best thing we can do is to destroy the boats in the St. Mary's River.... I am confident that Col Wood, if he can procure the means, can accomplish it. I have sent down to procure accurate information about them if possible. Colonel Wood might do the same. I can furnish volunteers from the 9th Virginia Cavalry, who are acquainted with the shores of the Potomac, and who are now in the lower Rappahannock. Captain Fitzhugh of the 9th VA Cavalry, the officer who destroyed the enemy's steamers on Cherrystone Creek, on the Eastern Shore of Virginia, I have no doubt could join him with some of his men.[1]

An unidentified agent in Southern Maryland wrote Major Norris of the Confederate Signal Corps on June 9, 1864, advising the importance of a drive being made to capture or release the Confederate prisoners at Point Lookout or to undertake a raid on Washington. Due to a lack of troops in the area, the garrison at Point Lookout was inferred by the agent to be weak.[2]

After Early had been dispatched to Lynchburg and while he was marching in the Shenandoah Valley toward Winchester, General Lee on June 26, 1864, in a letter to Confederate president Jefferson Davis discussed his intention to free the Confederate prisoners at Point Lookout in conjunction with Early's attack on Washington. Lee suggested that Brigadier General Bradley T. Johnson lead the cavalry forces in the field for the attack on Point Lookout and that Colonel/Commander John Taylor Wood lead the naval part of the amphibious assault:

> Great benefit might be drawn from the release of our prisoners at Point Lookout if it can be accomplished. The number of men employed for this purpose would necessarily be small, as the whole would have to be transported secretly across the Potomac where it is very broad, the means of doing which must first be procured. I can devote to the purpose the whole of the Marylanders of this army, which would afford a sufficient number of men of excellent material and much experience, but I am at a loss where to find a proper leader. As he would command Maryland troops and operate upon Maryland soil it would be well that he should be a Marylander. Of those connected with this army I consider Col. Bradley T. Johnson the most suitable, he is bold & intelligent, ardent & true and yet I am unable to say whether he possesses all the requisite qualities. Everything in an expedition of the kind would depend upon the leader. I have understood that most of the garrison at Point Lookout was composed of Negroes. I should suppose that the commander of such troops would be poor &

feeble. A stubborn resistence, therefore, may not reasonably be expected. By taking a company of the MD. artillery, armed as infantry, the dismounted cavalry and their infantry organization, as many men would be supplied as transportation could be procured for. By throwing them suddenly on a beach with some concert of action among the prisoners, I think the guard might be overpowered, the prisoners liberated and organized, and marched immediately on the route to Washington. The artillery company could operate the guns captured at the Point. The dismounted cavalry with the released prisoners of that army could mount themselves on the march, and the infantry would form a respectable force. Such a body of men under an able leader, although they might not be able without assistance to capture Washington, could march around it and cross the Upper Potomac where fordable. I do not think they could cross the river in a body at any point below Washington, unless possibly at Alexandria. Provisions, &c, would have to be collected in the country through which they pass. The operations on the river must be confided to an able naval officer, who I know will be found in Colonel Wood. The subject is one worthy of consideration, and can only be matured by reflection. The sooner it is put in execution, the better, if deemed practicable.[3]

On June 27, 1864, Bradley T. Johnson was assigned by General Early to take command of the brigade of General W.E. "Grumble" Jones, who had been killed at the Battle of Piedmont.[4] Lee wrote Jefferson Davis on June 29, 1864, that if Early's movement could be united with the release of prisoners at Point Lookout, the advantages would be great:

> I think it is our policy to draw the attention of the enemy to his own territory. It may force Grant to attack me or weaken himself to attack. From either of these events, I anticipate good results; news of Johnson's success will help Early; libertation of Point Lookout would also be useful.[5]

General Robert E. Lee met with John Taylor Wood regarding the release of the prisoners.[6] Wood was part of an elite group of officers serving in the Confederate navy who had outstanding ability and had distinguished themselves in their service. He was the grandson of President Zachary Taylor and nephew of Confederate president Jefferson Davis. Wood was appointed a midshipman in the United States Navy in 1847 following a course at the Annapolis Naval School. He served on the USS *Brandywine* during the Mexican War and graduated second in his class at the Naval Academy in 1853. Wood received a commission as 1st lieutenant in the Confederate navy in October 1861.[7]

Wood had been an officer on the ironclad Virginia and was involved in her actions at Hampton Roads.[8] He held the rank of commander in the Confederate navy. In 1863, he had also been made an aide to President Jefferson Davis and was appointed a colonel in the Confederate army.[9]

JOHN TAYLOR WOOD, WHO WAS TO LEAD THE AMPHIBIOUS ASSAULT ON POINT LOOKOUT (NAVAL HISTORICAL CENTER).

Wood also had considerable experience as a raider and organizer of commando operations on the Chesapeake Bay and Potomac River during the war. On October 7, 1862, he had attacked the United States transport schooner *Frances Elmore*, loaded with hay, while anchored off Pope's Creek on the Maryland side of the Potomac River south of Washington.[10] Rowing out in small boats and using grappling hooks, the Confederates got onto the deck and overpowered the crew. The vessel was burned. Captain Smith, a mate and five deckhands were sent to Libby Prison in Richmond.[11] Subsequently, Wood sighted the *Alleganian* anchored off Gwynn Island in Matthews County north of Norfolk on the Chesapeake on the night of October 28, 1862. The ship was a Union merchant vessel carrying a load of guano from Baltimore to London. Wood and his men, armed with cutlasses and revolvers, took the ship without resistance. The ship was then set on fire. The captain, first mate and pilot were taken prisoner. Others of the crew were set adrift in small boats. The vessel was valued at $200,000.[12]

On August 22, 1863, John Taylor Wood had gone to the Chesapeake Bay and found two Union gunboats moored off Stingray Point in Middlesex County, Virginia. After boarding the USS *Satellite*, a wooden sidewheel steamer with a 32-pounder, a 12-pounder howitzer and a 40-man crew, and the screw steamer USS *Reliance* with a 32-pounder Parrott and 24-pounder howitzer and 40-man crew, Wood brought the captured ships up to Urbanna on the Rappahanock River where they were protected by Thomas Rosser's 5th Virginia Cavalry. Wood then set out on the *Satellite* and took the coal steamer *Golden Rod* off Gwynn Island and the schooners *Coquette* and *Two Brothers* in the Rappahanock.[13] Some of Rosser's sharpshooters went to sea briefly with Wood. They then conveyed 57 prisoners to Richmond.[14]

General Lee was utilizing an experienced naval officer in the Chesapeake theater. John Taylor Wood also had experience with coordinated land-sea operations. He led a naval expedition at New Bern, N.C., in coordination with Confederate infantry forces under Major General George Pickett, that resulted in the burning of the *Underwriter*, without a land attack ever having been made.[15]

Wood himself had been considering a plan to launch a surprise attack on the Union Prison Camp at Point Lookout. This plan was to take Confederate troops across the Potomac River for a raid on Point Lookout. On July 2, Wood delivered a letter from Jefferson Davis to General Lee about the plan and was to provide information on the release of the prisoners. Wood and Major General G.W. Custis Lee were given joint command of the land operation to free the prisoners at Point Lookout. General Robert E. Lee responded to Davis:

> "& to learn from him the arrangements to release the prisoners"; would trust Wood to lead the operations on land or sea; advises not communicating with prisoners beforehand nor advancing rescuers to the Potomac; would recommend sending Hoke with Wood, but does not want to lose Hoke's services; will alert Early; "No Corps has left Gen. Grant," although the 9th is rumored to have departed.[16]

The plan, discussed on the night of July 2, 1864, at Lee's headquarters near Petersburg, was for Wood to run the blockade at Wilmington, North Carolina, and come up the Chesapeake Bay. After running the blockade, Wood would go into the Chesapeake, disrupt the telegraphic cable between Fortress Monroe and Cherrystone Point, and then appear before Point Lookout. At dawn on July 12, 1864, Wood would have troops make a surprise waterborne attack as he beached at Point Lookout where the Potomac River meets the Chesapeake Bay in conjunction with a simultaneous assault by Bradley Johnson's cavalry force. Wood's amphibious force would be bringing arms to equip the Confederate prisoners. The prisoners and Johnson would then join Early's attack on Washington or otherwise pass to the north of Washington and cross the Upper Potomac into Virginia. There was to be no communication with the Confederate prisoners at Point Lookout about the plan.[17]

On July 2, Captain John Simms, commanding the Confederate Marine Battalion at Drewery's

Bluff, was ordered to send all available men to Wilmington, North Carolina. On July 3, 1864, 130 Confederate marines and 150 seamen left Richmond for Danville, Virginia. They were then to proceed to Greensboro, North Carolina, and Goldsboro, North Carolina, before arriving at Wilmington on July 6.[18]

John Taylor Wood received special orders from Jefferson Davis on July 4, 1864. General W.H.C. Whiting, the Confederate commander at Wilmington, North Carolina, was instructed to furnish Wood with two Parrott rifled guns to cover the amphibious landing at Point Lookout. Whiting was also ordered to cooperate in every way with Wood in organizing the mission. Wood was told by Davis to execute orders and to communicate with the general in charge of the district where he operated. He had discretion to modify orders as circumstances required.[19]

Brigadier General G.W. Custis Lee, Colonel/Commander John Taylor Wood, and Colonel Fleet Cox of the 40th Virginia Cavalry, familiar with the lower Potomac, met with Major General Fitzhugh Lee and his staff on the way to Wilmington, North Carolina, on July 5. On July 5, 1864, Wood departed Lee's headquarters for Wilmington, N.C., to set the plan in motion. He began to assemble a crew and select ships for the operation.[20]

Brigadier General G.W. Custis Lee was on President Jefferson Davis's staff as a military aide. He had been first in his class at West Point. Davis valued his service and opinions. Custis Lee was often sent to the front lines to evaluate defenses, take confidential messages and advise on the reorganization of the army. Earlier in 1864, he had provided able service in helping repel the Kilpatrick-Dahlgren raid on Richmond. Custis Lee had been one of the leaders in organizing the Point Lookout raid. He would later head a regiment at Sayler's Creek.[21]

While Wood was going to Wilmington on July 6, 1864, Captain Robert E. Lee, son of General Robert E. Lee, commander of the Army of Northern Virginia, had ridden to General Early's headquarters near Sharpsburg, Maryland, and given him orders which directed him to dispatch Brigadier General Bradley T. Johnson and his cavalry on a raid to free the Confederate prisoners at Point Lookout.[22] On the 12th, Johnson was to take the freed prisoners north toward Washington. It was not until the evening of July 8, 1864, that General Johnson was called to General Early's headquarters in Frederick, Maryland, and told about the Point Lookout mission he was to undertake the next day.[23]

John Taylor Wood was able to obtain the *Let-Her B* and the *Florie*, two extremely fast ships, for the mission. They had been seized by the Confederate government. The *Florie* had been commanded by Commander John Moffatt of the Confederate States Navy earlier in 1864. The *Let-Her B*, which had been on the Mersey in England in February 1864, was a powerful schooner capable of a speed of 17 to 19 knots. She had loaded in Hamilton, Bermuda, and cleared for Wilmington, North Carolina.[24]

Wood was also able to obtain a large amount of firearms. He was to have secured 20,000 muskets.[25] General G.W. Custis Lee advised Davis on July 8, 1864, that the promised arms had not come but were en route from Columbia, S.C. General Whiting in Wilmington had offered all the arms he had, but they were not of the desired caliber.[26]

The plan had become known to the Union, however. On July 7, Major General Benjamin F. Butler had advised the War Department of information from a deserter that part of Early's mission was to attack Point Lookout and release the prisoners. The Navy Department increased its patrols off Point Lookout on July 8 and July 9, 1864.[27]

President Davis told General Lee on July 8, 1864, that the expedition was spoken of on the street and questioned whether it should proceed.[28] John Taylor Wood wired Davis on July 9, 1864, of his readiness to proceed.

Col. Wood to Pres. Davis   Wilmington   July 9, 1864
  Will try to get out tonight am badly off for officers, but hope for the best. I request that you will not act on Williams case until I see you.

                                              J. Taylor Wood
                                              Confederate States Navy[29]

On July 10, 1864, Jefferson Davis replied to Wood suggesting calm consideration as to whether to proceed:

Col. J. Taylor Wood   Richmond, Va. July 10. 1864
Wilmington, N.C.
  Telegram of yesterday received. The object and destination of the expedition have somehow become so generally known that I fear your operations will meet with unexpected obstacles. General R.E. Lee has communicated with you and left your action to your discretion. I suggest calm consideration and full comparison of views with General G.W.C. Lee, and others with whom you may choose to advise.
                                              Jeff'n Davis[30]

Confederate prisoner of war Charles Hutt stated that 300 men were transferred from Point Lookout to Elmira, N.Y., on July 9, 1864.[31] It was being rumored in Richmond that prisoners at Point Lookout were being transferred to northern prisons.[32]

General W.H.C. Whiting had contacted Davis about knowledge of the mission on July 11.

JEFFERSON DAVIS, CONFEDERATE PRESIDENT (NATIONAL ARCHIVES).

Dispatch in cipher received 8 P.M. Forwarded by telegraph to Ft. Fisher. Still moonlight. No doubt will reach w. Sent Gen. R.E. Lee dispatch yesterday L telegraphed he would start tonight but gentleman from Charleston reported to me object was known there. Reported it immediately & said it was on the street. Sent this to Wood — Don't know what day will decide but will inform tonight- am satisfied nothing was known here until today when became general. Great delay caused by stopping of arms from Columbia.[33]

On July 10, 1864, General G.W. Custis Lee had sent a telegram to Davis indicating his belief that any attempt at that point would be fruitless. War Clerk John B. Jones had recorded that John Tyler had described the operation in a letter to General Sterling Price and also noted, "We have a rumor today of the success of a desperate expedition from Wilmington, N.C. to Point Lookout, Maryland, managed to liberate the prisoners of war (20,000) confined there and to arm them."[34]

On July 11, 1864, Davis contacted

GENERAL G.W. CUSTIS LEE IN GROUP INVOLVED IN PLANNING AND COMMANDING OF POINT LOOKOUT OPERATION (LIBRARY OF CONGRESS).

John Taylor Wood and General G.W. Custis Lee, telling them that the prisoners at Point Lookout were reported being transferred according to dispatches from Washington published in the *New York Herald* of July 8.[35]

Davis ordered the mission aborted although there were still about 15,000 prisoners left at Point Lookout.[36] Jefferson Davis may well have been misinformed by the newspaper information as to the actual number of men at Point Lookout.

Meanwhile, Wood was in the last stages of preparation to leave. It was a 390 knot run from Wilmington to Point Lookout, which would take about 24 hours through the Capes of the Chesapeake with the vessels he had. Wood had moved his forces to the mouth of the Cape Fear River to run the blockade when he found out that the mission had been called off. Davis feared the Union would concentrate its fleet at the mouth of the Chesapeake and destroy Wood.[37] Meanwhile Bradley Johnson's cavalry raid had resulted in the burning of bridges, the destruction of railroad property and the cutting of telegraph lines to the north near Baltimore. He had gotten beyond Washington on the road to Point Lookout when the mission was called off on July 12, 1864.[38]

In August 1864, John Taylor Wood commenced services with the CSS *Tallahassee* in his famous raids on Atlantic coast shipping wherein he captured 30 vessels in a cruise to Halifax, Nova Scotia.[39]

The tight time line, in part caused by Confederate delays, and the Union's obtaining news of the mission ultimately caused its demise. This audacious seaborne plan in the hands of a daring leader who knew the Chesapeake Bay well could have succeeded had Early not delayed so substantially — a problem compounded slightly by Bradley Johnson's own delays.

CHAPTER 16

Wallace Aggressively Contests Early's Move to Frederick

Major General Lew Wallace was in command of the Middle Department, 8th Corps, in Baltimore, Maryland, on July 5, 1864, when part of Early's Army of the Valley was just crossing the Potomac near Shepherdstown. Wallace had earned the enmity of Grant at Shiloh. where he took his division on the wrong road which effectively took him out of the battle on the crucial first day.

Wallace received information that a column of Confederate cavalry had been raiding in the border counties of Pennsylvania and were moving east in the Middletown Valley, suggesting that Washington or Baltimore were possible objectives. The terrible consequences of a possible entry into the national capital were on Wallace's mind. Earlier on July 3, Wallace and his aide, Lieutenant Colonel Samuel B. Lawrence, had learned from newspaper accounts that General Hunter was in West Virginia and would be no help.[1]

Wallace seized the initiative and immediately began gathering the limited troops available to him, which were the 3rd Maryland Regiment, Potomac Home Brigade, under Colonel Charles Gilpin, the 11th Maryland commanded by Colonel Landstreet, several companies of the 149th Ohio militia, three companies of the 144th Ohio militia under Colonel A.L. Brown, a few companies of the 1st Maryland, Potomac Home Brigade, and a 6-gun battery of Maryland light artillery under Captain Alexander, totaling about 2,300 men.[2] Wallace concentrated his troops on the Monocacy River.[3] He rejected a request by John Garrett, president of the Baltimore & Ohio Railroad, to take a position somewhere between Monocacy Junction and Harpers Ferry.[4]

MAJOR GENERAL LEW WALLACE VIGOROUSLY CONTESTED EARLY'S ADVANCE TO FREDERICK (LIBRARY OF CONGRESS).

16. Wallace Aggressively Contests Early's Move to Frederick

The Washington and Baltimore pikes, and the Baltimore & Ohio iron bridge at the Monocacy, which linked those two cities with Harpers Ferry, converged in a space of two miles there. The river covered the entire front of Wallace's position. There were few fords and there were commanding heights on the eastern bank of the Monocacy, where Wallace was positioned. Conversely, the ground on the other side of the river was level and almost without obstructions.[5]

On the night of July 4, 1864, the part of the 8th Illinois Cavalry in camp was ordered to ride from Washington to meet the threat of Colonel John Singleton Mosby and General Jubal A. Early to Frederick. Companies E and H were already at Muddy Branch, Maryland, up the Potomac from Washington. Companies B, C, I, K and M were in camp in Washington, where they had been mounting patrols, checking passes, preserving order and acting as provost guards. The troopers were under the command of Lieutenant Colonel David Clendenin.

Clendenin took his force about 20 miles from Washington on the night of the 4th up the Potomac River. His men went into camp about 1:00 A.M. on July 5, 1864, and left camp at 6:00 A.M. heading for Point of Rocks on the Potomac, where they hoped to intercept Mosby.[6]

James Williamson of Company A of Mosby's 43rd Virginia Battalion noted that his force of about 250 men had arrived at Point of Rocks on the morning of July 4, 1864, and had exchanged fire with two companies of Loudon Rangers cavalry under Captain Keyes and two companies of infantry. Shelling from the Confederate 12-pounder caused the Union forces to retreat along the tow path by the C & O Canal. Having torn the planking from a bridge over the canal, the Union forces maintained a fire from a small earthwork commanding the bridge before the cavalry retreated toward Frederick and the infantry moved into the mountains. The 43rd Virginia Battalion remained on the Virginia side of the Potomac on the 5th of July.[7]

On July 5, 1864, Clendenin's cavalry force entered Point of Rocks about noon. Colonel Mosby's forces fired on the Union troopers from the Virginia side of the river with two pieces of artillery. Clendenin then deployed his men dismounted and drove off Mosby's force. Mosby tried to cross at Nolan's Ford but was blocked by the men of the 8th Illinois Cavalry.[8]

After a small force of the 43rd Virginia Battalion crossed near the Monocacy and took some prisoners, Mosby's force moved toward Leesburg on the night of the 5th.[9]

On July 6, Companies K and C of the 8th Illinois Cavalry went up the Potomac to Sandy Hook and returned about 11:30 A.M. Clendenin got a telegram from Brigadier General Albion Howe directing him to go to Frederick, as the Confederates were reported at Boonesboro west of Frederick. Wallace also asked Clendenin to report to him. Clendenin took his entire force to Frederick. Mosby's force was riding in a different direction, engaging the 13th New York Cavalry and the 2nd Massachusetts Cavalry near Mt. Zion Church.[10]

Wallace joined Brigadier General Erastus Tyler, who had been preparing the defenses there, at the railroad bridge over the Monocacy on July 5. Confederate cavalry had seized Middletown and scouting parties were within three miles of Frederick. McCausland's cavalry was battling a unit of the 6th U.S. Cavalry on the outskirts of Hagerstown, from which horses, government property and railroad equipment had been previously removed to Carlisle and Harrisburg.[11] Wallace was the one person on July 5, 1864, who seemed aware that Early was coming. He was seeking to head him off on his own initiative, without direction from Halleck or Grant, who remained somewhat in the dark as to Early's intentions.

Meanwhile, Early was slowly getting some of his forces across the Potomac and was still skirmishing with Sigel's forces on Maryland Heights. Early and his staff took time to dine with the family of staff officer Henry Kyd Douglas. McCausland's cavalry was far in front of Early's main forces, which were still on the Upper Potomac.[12] Breckinridge's forces were still at Maryland Heights on the 6th.

While Early was still at Sharpsburg on July 6 talking to Captain R.E. Lee, son of General Robert E. Lee, commander of the Army of Northern Virginia, regarding the attack on Washington and the dispatch of Brigadier General Bradley T. Johnson on a raid near Baltimore and on to Point Lookout to liberate the Confederate prisoners there, Wallace was gaining additional intelligence information and further concentrating his forces to slow the progress of Early's advance units to create additional delays Early could not afford.[13] On the 6th a scouting party of about 75 men from the 12th Pennsylvania Cavalry, Means' Loudon Rangers, Cole's Cavalry and another independent unit went to Middletown, west of Frederick, and engaged Confederate pickets before returning to Frederick.[14] On the evening of July 6, 1864, and in the early morning of the 7th, Wallace's command numbered about 2,500 men.

Lieutenant Colonel David Cledennin of the 8th Illinois Cavalry, who had skirmished with Mosby at Point of Rocks on July 5, arrived at Frederick about 8:00 P.M. on July 6. He received orders to report personally to Major General Lew Wallace at Monocacy Junction.[15]

Wallace directed Clendenin to take the pike to Middletown until he located Confederate forces and ascertained their strength and composition.[16] Clendenin was to go northward into the Pleasant Valley west of Frederick and provided important scouting information on Early's advance to Wallace.[17]

Meanwhile, as Wallace was engaged in consolidating his forces and moving to find Early, on July 6, 1864, Brigadier General McCausland, leading the advance of Early's army, entered Hagerstown and spent precious time obtaining $20,000 from three banks to prevent the burning of the city. McCausland also obtained 120,000 bushels of oats, 400 cavalry saddles from supplies for the 5th U.S. Cavalry and numerous horses before moving on to the Boonesboro area and Catoctin Mountain. Early was also in touch with Colonel Mosby in a mostly unsuc-

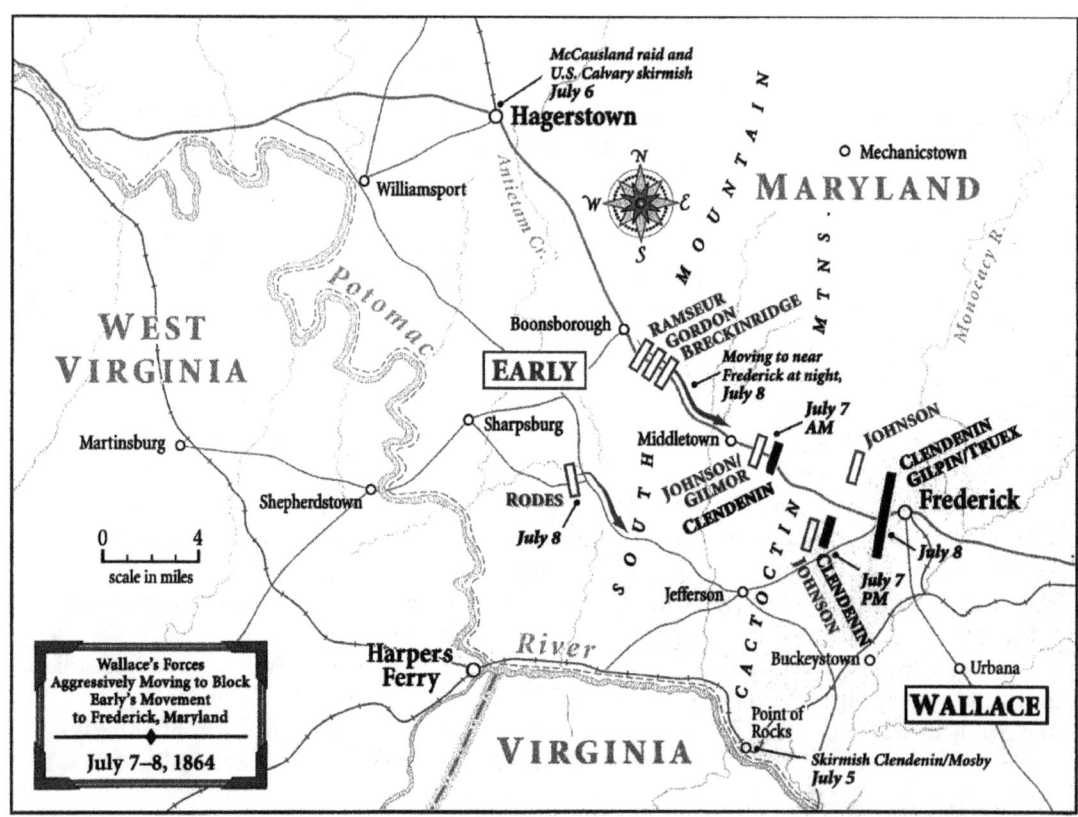

MAP OF ENGAGEMENTS WEST OF FREDERICK: POSITIONS OF FORCES (MAP BY DAVID DEIS).

cessful effort to gain cooperation from him.[18] Many of Early's troops were still on the Upper Potomac.

Clendenin, with a section of Alexander's light artillery battery, left Frederick on July 7, 1864, on the road to Middletown to slow the Confederate advance. The Union cavalry met an about equal Confederate cavalry force two miles west of Middletown. A detachment of the 8th Illinois Cavalry with artillery support engaged men of Johnson's brigade slowly falling back toward Frederick.[19]

With less than 750 men, Clendenin vigorously contested the movement of Bradley Johnson's Confederate cavalry division. Brigadier General Bradley T. Johnson was moving toward Frederick by way of Middletown. Gilmor with the 1st and 2nd Maryland Cavalry and a substantial force under Johnson's direction wanted to flank the Union troops, but General Robert Ransom, a former infantry officer in overall charge of the cavalry, initially denied the request, which delayed the Confederate advance.[20]

About 10:00 A.M. on July 7, Ransom had changed his mind and agreed to a flanking movement. Clendenin withdrew back to the summit of Catoctin Mountain. Ransom had feared that Union forces would be reinforced and wanted to wait until infantry support and artillery came up. Clendenin then further withdrew to the suburbs of Frederick.[21]

About 10:00 A.M. on the 7th, Clendenin advised Wallace that the Confederates were slowly pushing him back and would reach Frederick in about two hours unless Wallace intended to defend it. Clendenin continued to slowly retreat to Catoctin Mountain. There he placed the artillery into position and began to shell the Confederate skirmish line. After holding off Johnson's forces for five hours, the Confederate flank movement was taking effect. Clendenin withdrew to Frederick.[22]

Wallace sent Colonel Charles Gilpin and the 3rd Regiment, Potomac Home Brigade, 150 men from the 159th Ohio and one gun to reinforce Clendenin. Thus Gilpin and Clendenin had 150 men of the 159th Ohio mounted infantry, the Loudon County Rangers, as well as 300 men from the 8th Illinois Cavalry and Gilpin's regiment.[23] Gilpin deployed his men across the Hagerstown Pike about one-half mile west of Frederick's suburbs, to which line Clendenin fell back. About 4:00 P.M., the Confederates opened with three pieces of artillery on Hogan's Hill and Red Hill, and one of Johnson's guns was later dismounted. The lines were engaged and a little before dark, Gilpin charged the Confederates, who withdrew to Catoctin Mountain.[24] Ransom had decided to wait for Early's infantry to come up before pushing into Frederick. This added further delay to the Confederate advance. While his cavalry advance was being heavily contested by the Union cavalry forces west of Frederick, the Confederates withdrew to Catoctin Mountain for the night.

On July 7, 1864, Early's army was still en route to Frederick. Rode's Division was coming up from Shepherdstown. Breckinridge reached Rohrersville between the South and Catoctin mountain ranges. Ramseur's men were still around Sharpsburg. Mudwall Jackson's brigade of Ransom's cavalry division was engaged by Cole's Independent Cavalry near Antietam Creek with the Confederates being thrown back. A part of the Cole's cavalry detachment joined up with Wallace at Monocacy Junction, mainly operating behind Confederate lines as they advanced.[25] Ramseur's division was in charge of Early's trains and was coming up to Middletown. On the evening of July 7, an expected shipment of shoes arrived, and Early distributed them to his men.[26]

Wallace remained active. At around midnight on the night of the 7th, Brigadier General Erastus Tyler and Colonel Brown's command was sent to Frederick. Tyler had led a brigade of the 5th Corps that had been heavily engaged at Fredericksburg and Chancellorsville. He had substantial battlefield experience. Tyler, after having ascertained reinforcements were needed in Frederick, sent three companies of the 144th Ohio and seven companies of the 149th Ohio to Colonel Gilpin on the morning of July 8, along with some additional artillery. Samuel Miller of the 144th Ohio stated they started at midnight, marched 14 miles and were in a line of battle all day until 3:00 P.M., when they started to fall back about daylight on July 8. Cole's cavalry was also engaged in some minor skirmishes.[27]

The vanguard of 6th Corps men of Rickett's Division started arriving at Monocacy Junction. Wallace accompanied Colonel William Henry's 10th Vermont regiment of the 6th Corps to Frederick, where they joined the Union line and were engaged. Two men from the 10th Vermont, 1st Lieutenant George E. Davis of Company D and Corporal Alexander Scott of Company D, would be awarded the Congressional Medal of Honor for their heroic actions the next day at the Battle of the Monocacy. Lieutenant Colonel Catlin and the 11th Maryland were left to hold the railroad bridge over the Monocacy.[28] Meanwhile, on the morning of July 8, 1864, Brigadier General Erastus Tyler gave Lieutenant Colonel Clendenin orders to take his cavalry out of Frederick to find the position of the Confederate forces. One company of the 8th Illinois Cavalry went out on the Harpers Ferry Pike. Major Waite took Companies B and C of the 8th Illinois Cavalry and one gun of Alexander's battery out on the Middletown Pike. After driving back the skirmishers, Major Waite set up his artillery and opened up near Hagen's tavern, holding Gilmor and Johnson in check. Lieutenant Colonel Clendenin and his 8th Illinois Cavalry and one of Alexander's guns continued to skirmish with Bradley Johnson and Gilmor's men near Hagen's Tavern on the Hagerstown and Harpers Ferry roads for a significant period of time.

Captain Morris of Company M of the 8th Illinois Cavalry went out of Frederick on a road to the right of Major Waite's command. His force was attacked by a battalion of Confederate cavalry on the afternoon of the 8th. Captain Morris was killed and his unit fell back before a superior force.[29]

As Wallace was preparing to conduct a reconnaissance over Catoctin Mountain on the morning of July 8, he received a telegram from Sigel telling him the Confederates had left Maryland Heights and were marching up the Middletown Valley toward Boonesboro. Wallace decided to wait in Frederick.[30] He wanted to show Early that 6th Corps troops were there and to suggest a larger force than he had. Colonel William S. Truex of Rickett's 1st brigade march up and down in an effort to deceive Early concerning the 6th Corps presence there at Frederick.[31]

On the afternoon of July 8, Wallace received a telegram from General Albion Howe at Harpers Ferry directing him to join him there, but Wallace asked for his help in a concentrated action as the Confederates were marching toward Boonesboro.[32] At about 4:00 P.M. Wallace saw Early's divided force marching east. General Rodes was marching toward Jeffer-

LIEUTENANT COLONEL DAVID CLENDENIN, COMMANDER OF 8TH ILLINOIS CAVALRY IN ENGAGEMENTS NEAR FREDERICK (UNITED STATES ARMY MILITARY HISTORY INSTITUTE).

son on the Harpers Ferry Pike after having gone through Crampton's Gap in South Mountain. Ramseur, Gordon and Breckinridge were all moving to Middletown on the Hagerstown Road from Boonesboro.[33]

Wallace received a telegram from Lieutenant Colonel Catlin at Monocacy Junction that a heavy force of Confederates was moving toward Monocacy Junction on the Buckeystown Road, which threatened his line of retreat. Wallace stated that he had made up his mind to fight. He telegraphed Halleck that he was withdrawing immediately from Frederick city to put himself in a position to cover the road to Washington. Wallace withdrew through Frederick on the night of July 8 to the railroad bridge at Monocacy Junction.[34]

Lieutenant Colonel Clendenin's cavalry force was involved in covering the rear of the Union army retreating from Frederick on the night of July 8, 1864. His force left about 2:00 A.M. on the morning of the 9th. It moved down the Baltimore Pike, arriving at Monocacy Junction at daylight. He deployed his cavalry force on the Georgetown Pike, down the Monocacy and between the river and the Buckeystown Road.[35]

When Wallace arrived at Monocacy Junction, Ricketts was there. Truex's 1st brigade of 1,750 men consisted of the 106th New York under Captain E.M. Paine, the 151st New York under Colonel Emerson, the 14th New Jersey under Lieutenant Colonel L.K. Hall, the 10th Vermont under Colonel Henry and the 87th Pennsylvania under Lieutenant Colonel Stahle. The 1,600-man 2nd brigade under Colonel McClennan consisted of the 138th Pennsylvania, the 9th New York Heavy Artillery under Colonel Seward, the 126th Ohio under Lieutenant Colonel Ebright and the 110th Ohio under Lieutenant Colonel Binkley.[36]

At Early's headquarters at Middletown west of Frederick on July 8, two days after Early's meeting with Captain R.E. Lee at Sharpsburg, Early told Brigadier General Bradley Johnson of Lee's plan to free the Confederate prisoners at Point Lookout in conjunction with John Taylor Wood.[37] Johnson was to lead the endeavor and, after freeing the prisoners, was to meet up with Early at Bladensburg. Early asked Johnson to keep an eye on his flank at Frederick before moving off to cut the rail and telegraph lines south of Baltimore. The rendezvous at Point Lookout with Wood was scheduled for July 12. Johnson expressed the opinion to Early that the mission was impossible to accomplish.[38]

Early was also involved in trying to implement a plan to obtain $200,000 from four financial institutions in Frederick. This was to keep the city from being burned. This activity was not part of Lee's directions to Early.[39]

Early was scrambling to come up to Washington and had been slowed by aggressive resistance from Wallace's Union forces as well as by his time-consuming efforts to obtain money from the citizens of Hagerstown and Frederick. Early's men were also heavily involved with obtaining supplies. There was also a slow pace in getting up to Frederick from the Upper Potomac which took until the 8th even though Early got there on the 3rd. This had given Rickett's men time to get up from City Point and join Wallace. Early would be delayed a full day again on July 9 by the hard fight on the Monocacy, which would sap the strength of his army in terms of men, supplies and the wounded he would have to leave behind. Moreover, Early had not even told Johnson of the Point Lookout plan until two days after he himself was apprised of it. When time was of the essence, Early had hesitated.

On the other hand, Wallace had reacted quickly to Early's advance. He had sent Clendenin out west of Frederick to find out where Early was and to challenge the advance elements of his army. This had effectively kept Early from taking Frederick on the 7th and getting to the Monocacy ahead of Ricketts. The Union forces had been as aggressive as the Confederates had been cautious. The dilatoriness on the Upper Potomac had been compounded by the Confederate slowness in getting to Frederick and on toward Washington. Certainly if Early had been early rather than late in getting to the Monocacy, he would have faced 2,500 home guards and militia without the veteran 6th Corps troops. The result at the Monocacy clearly would have been different and probably at Washington as well. Wallace, in his autobiography, stated that Early had fooled away his time and mistakenly had not crossed the Potomac at Edward's Ferry near Harpers Ferry, which had cost him the opportunity to take Washington.[40]

CHAPTER 17

General Ransom Costs Early Time

General Jubal A. Early, in his long and meritorious service throughout the Civil War in the Army of Northern Virginia, had expressed on numerous occasions his relative disdain for the cavalry branch.[1] In the Valley Campaign of 1862 and the Seven Days Battles, Second Bull Run (Manassas), Antietam, Fredericksburg and Chancellorsville, many of the Confederate successes had been achieved by skillful infantry maneuver or Stonewall Jackson's genius, such as in his "foot cavalry" operations in the Valley, his marching behind Pope's lines to cut his communications and supplies, or his turning the Union left flank at Chancellorsville. It had been J.E.B. Stuart who had left Lee blind at Gettysburg by not providing him proper intelligence or following orders.[2]

When Early himself had been given independent command by General Robert E. Lee to pursue his plan to expel Hunter from the Shenandoah Valley and attack Washington and, later, Point Lookout, the assignment of an able and experienced cavalry officer to command the force of cavalry assembled was apparently not a priority.

Wade Hampton was an extraordinarily able cavalry officer. He was ordered by Lee to pursue Sheridan as he moved from Richmond, leading to the important and clearcut Confederate victory at Trevilian Station which made Lee's gamble possible. Hampton was there, as were his able brigade commanders such as Thomas Rosser and Lunsford Lomax. Fitzhugh Lee was also there. His brigadiers were similarly able. These men were not sent to lead in Early's cavalry command.

However, Early was assigned a very capable and daring cavalry officer who had served with Stonewall Jackson and whom Wade Hampton was planning to use to launch his own attack on Washington. This man had been instrumental in thwarting the Kilpatrick-Dahlgren raid on Richmond and had been engaged both at Trevilian Station and in many previous cavalry engagements around Richmond.[3] He was the man Lee wanted to lead the raid to Point Lookout and to cut the rail and communications links between Washington, Baltimore and the North.[4] However, Johnson was not given the overall command of Early's cavalry — even though he was one of the most able and daring of the officers in Early's cavalry command.

Rather, the command of Early's cavalry was given to Major General Robert Ransom. Ransom was a former infantry officer and was little distinguished as a cavalry officer. At the time he was called to command the cavalry of the Western Department of Virginia, which included Lynchburg, he was in command of a force operating at Deep Bottom near Richmond. The cavalry in his command lacked discipline and leadership.[5] It does not appear that General Early had any input as to who would command his cavalry operation. In fact, Early had reason to be concerned about the cavalry forces that had become part of his army. Before the Battle of Piedmont, Brigadier General John C. Vaughn had brought up a small force of less than 1,000 men from southwestern Virginia, who were from a variety of Virginia and Tennessee units. At the Battle of Piedmont, Vaughn had sat idly by as the Union forces exploited a gap between his lines and those of "Grumble" Jones, leading to Jones's death and the defeat of the Confederate forces.[6] Another Confederate cavalry officer present, Brigadier General John D. Imboden, along with Vaughn watched the onslaught against Jones's forces without engaging a large part of the Confederate forces present.[7]

As Major General David Hunter was moving down the Valley, Imboden had remained at Waynesboro and gathered his forces. His performance in this respect had been reasonable.

Brigadier General John McCausland, with his own force of about 1,500 men, had succeeded in conducting a skillful operation in falling back before Hunter and obstructing his progress between Lexington and Lynchburg, although he had been criticized for his conduct at Lexington in putting the city and its civilians unnecessarily at risk. He otherwise had performed well in destroying bridges and slowing Hunter's advance — drawing praise from Early in his *Autobiographical Sketches*.[8]

At Lynchburg itself, the actions of the Confederate cavalry were mixed. On the afternoon and evening of June 16, 1864, McCausland had been engaged with Averell moving toward New London, about 10 miles southwest of Lynchburg, contesting the Union advance. This task he had accomplished, delaying the Union advance and then falling back during the night about 6 miles to the Quaker Meeting House on the Salem Pike.[9] McCausland then had been sent north to the Forest Road, where he disputed the advance of the Union cavalry under Brigadier General Alfred Duffie for much of the next two days, forcing him to fight dismounted in the woods on either side of the road and delaying his movement toward Lynchburg.[10]

When Imboden's forces had retreated in the face of the larger forces of Crook and Averell on the afternoon of the 17th near the Quaker Meeting House, Early had called up the infantry under Ramseur to form the left wing of a defensive line that extended north in a curved line up Salem Pike to the Forest Road. Even though Imboden had done what was asked of him, Early had cast aspersions on the cavalry, noting that the infantry coming up were no "buttermilk rangers."[11]

Although to this point the Confederate cavalry at Lynchburg had vigorously contested Hunter's advance and battled Averell's and Duffie's forces, their conduct at the conclusion of the battle and in following up the retreating Hunter had not been optimal.

Imboden had been on the Confederate left and had moved off on the road north to Campbell Court House away from the retreating Union army. By the time Imboden had become aware of the Union retreat and had gotten back, his force had not been able to get to Liberty before the retreating Union troops. McCausland, who had so ably contested Hunter's advance and Duffie on the Forest Road, took the wrong road and was unable to reach Liberty before Hunter's fleeing army.[12] Thus, Early's cavalry had failed to properly contest the Union withdrawal, to Early's chagrin.

The cavalry subsequently pursued Hunter's army with only limited success. Averell's rearguard actions, although resulting in some losses, contained the Confederate pursuit. The felling of trees to obstruct the Confederate movements, as well as night marches and other tactics, operated to keep the pursuing Confederate cavalry from cutting off Hunter.[13]

However, due to the negligence of Brigadier General Alfred Duffie in not protecting a key road crossing at Hanging Rock, the Confederate cavalry had been able to disable a large number of Union guns and wagons and to take a number of prisoners. Advancing Union infantry forces were able to force McCauland's cavalry back and limit the results he was able to achieve. Duffie had much more seriously compromised Hunter's advance on Lynchburg and abetted Early's by his failure to destroy the Tye River Bridge and interrupt rail traffic on the Orange & Alexandria Railroad between Charlottesville and Lynchburg in his raid from Lexington. Also, his failure to return until the night of the 13th had further slowed Hunter's already delayed move toward Lynchburg.[14]

After Hunter left the theater of military operations and fled to West Virginia, Early moved down the Valley to Staunton and reorganized his army. Even though Major General Ransom had not engaged in field command at Lynchburg and had limited experience with cavalry operations, he was continued in command of the Cavalry Division.[15]

One brigade was under the command of William L. "Mudwall" Jackson, a second cousin of Stonewall Jackson, who had served with Jackson in the Valley Campaign of 1862, the Seven Days, Cedar Mountain, Second Bull Run (Manassas), Antietam and Fredericksburg. He had also served under General Albert Jenkins.[16]

John McCausland, not "Mudwall" Jackson, had taken over for Jenkins after his death at Cloyd's Mountain in May 1864. His field service in the Lynchburg Campaign had been relatively distinguished. He was also assigned to command a cavalry brigade in Early's army.[17]

The third brigade was led by Brigadier General Bradley T. Johnson. Johnson brought some troops of the Maryland Line with him when he jointed Early but basically took over the brigade of General William "Grumble" Jones, who had been killed at the Battle of Piedmont.[18] Johnson had a good record and was highly thought of by both Wade Hampton and Robert E. Lee. He was to capably lead the raid around Baltimore toward Point Lookout and to cover Early's retreat from Washington.

Thus, unlike the battle-tested Confederate cavalry divisions of Wade Hampton and Fitzhugh Lee, who had been able to meet and defeat the Union forces they had encountered throughout the war to that point, the forces of Early were a polyglot group of diverse forces with mixed records in command as well as in prior field performance with a relatively untested leader.

The first cavalry operation to cost Early significant time in the execution of Lee's gamble was at Leetown on July 3, 1864. Brigadier General Bradley Johnson's cavalry forces in advance of Ramseur and Rodes's infantry divisions leaving Winchester were held up and thrown back by the entrenched forces of Colonel James A. Mulligan for about five hours.[19] This impeded Early's ability to more timely get to Martinsburg and Harpers Ferry and prevent General Sigel and General Weber from escaping to Maryland Heights.

Subsequently, Brigadier General Imboden had limited success in the implementation of orders to destroy some railroad lines and property in the area of Martinsburg on July 3. General Early said Imboden had partially destroyed the bridge over the South Branch of the Potomac but did not dislodge the guard from the blockhouse. General Early felt little was accomplished. McCausland had accomplished a lot at Back Creek and his movements to Martinsburg.[20]

However, the critical failure that compounded the lost time Early had spent tarrying on the Upper Potomac before Harpers Ferry and Maryland Heights had occurred on July 7, 1864.

Brigadier General Bradley Johnson was from Frederick, was familiar with the country and was leading the Confederate advance from Catoctin Mountain to Frederick. His advance was being contested primarily by units of the 8th Illinois Cavalry under Lieutenant Colonel David Clendenin with elements of Alexander's battery of the Baltimore Light Artillery.[21]

On the morning of the 7th, Johnson wanted to flank Clendenin's smaller force and to move quickly to Frederick. Major General Ransom was concerned that this might expose the Confederate forces in a way to put them in danger, and he overruled Johnson. For a matter of hours the Confederate advance on Frederick was stalled several miles west of the city. The Union forces under Brigadier General Erastus Tyler were able to reinforce Clendenin with troops and artillery. With these additional forces in place, the Union forces were able to contain the Confederate advance — keeping the Confederates out of Frederick on July 7.[22]

As a result of this delay, instead of probably controlling Frederick on July 7 and moving on Monocacy and Washington on July 8, a full day earlier than otherwise occurred, Early's forces accomplished this a day later. Johnson was the man in the field with the best call as to what was needed and how to accomplish it. Time was of the essence. Ransom had no reasonable tactical reasons for the delay, which he later countermanded hours too late. His actions were timid and costly.

This one crucial failure in cavalry command itself may have cost Early the time needed to enter Washington at a time it was weakly defended. Moreover, if Early had been able to move on Monocacy on the 8th of July rather than the 9th, the Union army would not have been in proper position — Ricketts was still coming up. Landstreet's 11th Maryland was all that really controlled the Monocacy bridges during much of July 8.[23] Part of Wallace's forces were at Frederick and would have had to reposition themselves at Monocacy. Instead of having artillery in the field to be used to its best advantage and waiting for Early, Wallace might have been put into a position of having to scramble to make a defense had Early been able to come up earlier.

Early might have had time to properly survey the battlefield, which he did not on the 9th.[24] He might have flanked Wallace using the Buckeystown Road or moved on toward Washington, whichever made tactical sense under the circumstances.

Although Johnson's raid around Baltimore and on toward Point Lookout was in many respects brilliant, it, too, was too late. The day lost by Ransom might have been enough to pull off the Point Lookout part of the operation, even without John Taylor Wood. As it was, Johnson was on the road to Upper Marlboro when called back.[25] With a 24-hour head start, Johnson could have probably accomplished his mission. Early would also have been much more likely to have been in a position to have timely made an assault on the defenses of Washington. Some of the convalescents and other troops put in the line before the 6th and 19th Corps troops arrived would not have even been available on July 10 — making the defenses of Washington even weaker than they were when Early arrived on the 11th.[26] Ransom's crucial failure in cavalry command on July 7 cost Early dearly as well as Lee in the execution of his plan.

CHAPTER 18

Hunter and Howe Fail to Move to Threaten Early

After the Confederate assault on Major General David Hunter's wagons and artillery at Hanging Rock on June 21, 1864, Hunter's army began an arduous retreat through West Virginia. Private William Stark recorded that on the road to New Castle on June 22, 1864, a barrel of flour had been found. The woman who owned it claimed the family would starve without. The Union soldiers claimed the same and took it. Meanwhile, the Union force had to ford the same stream, 30 yards wide and knee deep, 17 times that day. The army's movement across West Virginia was difficult.[1]

On June 22, 1864, General Hunter's chief of staff, Colonel David Hunter Strother, proposed a plan to burn the baggage and kill the cattle they had, giving everyone three days' rations. Strother wanted Hunter's army to move to Fincastle, then Buchanon. From there, the army would move across the Shenandoah Valley to Charlottesville, near their bases. General George Crook opposed the move, which would have put Hunter in Early's rear.[2] Major General Hunter decided to keep the army moving west through West Virginia to Sweet Springs and White Sulphur Springs.[3]

Hunter's army moved twenty miles on June 22 to Sweet Springs. At this point, General Hunter realized his army was not being pursued by Early's forces. Hunter simply believed that Early had returned to Lee's army, but did not know where he was. Guerrillas had attacked the wagon train sent from Liberty.[4]

On June 24, 1864, Strother had suggested to Hunter that the army should go north to New Creek in a valley parallel to the Shenandoah Valley. The Valley of the South Branch of the Potomac had roads, supplies and forage. This route would take Hunter's army from Warm Springs to Franklin and Moorfield. This would place Hunter's army near Winchester and in a position to assist should Early attack Sigel. However, General Crook again disapproved of Strother's plan, instead advocating a movement through the Kanawha Valley to Charleston, West Virginia. Crook believed there to be large supplies at Gauley and Meadow Bluff, only three days' march, and very large supplies at Charleston.[5] Hunter again agreed with Crook, primarily on the basis that there were supplies available at Meadow Bluff and Gauley.[6] Meanwhile, Hunter's army had continued to move through mountainous country under difficult conditions, where hundreds of exhausted and fatigued men fell out on the line of march.[7]

Neither Henry Halleck nor General Ulysses S. Grant knew of Hunter's whereabouts or plans until June 28, 1864, although Grant was aware of a newspaper report about Hunter of June 25. Halleck had earlier contacted Grant on June 19, 1864, expressing doubt that General Stahel could resupply Hunter and the opinion that Hunter should either go to West Virginia or return to Grant's army. Grant replied on June 21, suggesting verbal orders to Hunter to either go to West Virginia or join Grant before Richmond.[8]

Hunter's forces moved on the afternoon of the 24th for White Sulphur Springs, traveling through narrow gorges which were traversed without interference from Confederate troops or guerrillas. Some of Hunter's men found sour bran there which was full of worms; they baked and ate it anyway. The men marched all night toward Lewisburg. Hundreds and possibly thousands straggled. Many had worn out their shoes and were barefoot.[9]

On June 26, 1864, Brigadier General Crook recommended that Hunter and his staff move ahead of the army to Charleston. At that point, Hunter's forces were about 20 miles from Gauley. Hunter ordered his forces to remain at Gauley for two days to obtain necessary rations and allow stragglers to rejoin the force. Hunter was ill and remained at Gauley with his army.

Hunter and his staff met up with trains with 70,000 rations moving east to meet his army, which was at Gauley. On June 23, 1864, Hunter got news from Grant as to occurrences through June 22, discussing the situation at Petersburg. Hunter himself reported to Washington that he had retreated due to an ammunition shortage and his belief he was facing superior numbers of Confederate forces who could easily be reinforced from Richmond.[10]

General Hunter's message to Washington had not reached Halleck by July 3. He sent a message to Grant on that date telling him he had ordered Hunter up to the line of the Baltimore & Ohio Railroad, but that Hunter had not responded to any of Halleck's telegrams and had made no report of his operations or present condition.[11]

Obviously, General Hunter was not aware of or concerned about Early's threat or timely moving back into the theater of military operations. Nor was he apparently concerned about the fact that he had left no force in the Valley to prevent Early's movement north therein. Grant seemed to be similarly unconcerned about Hunter's movements and had agreed with Halleck about the alternative of going to West Virginia after Hunter had retreated from Lynchburg. Rather than moving as vigorously as possible to Charleston on the path that he had chosen and then moving by boat and by rail up to the Baltimore & Ohio Railroad at Cumberland, Maryland, Hunter had rested his army for three days. One of his brigade commanders, Colonel Rutherford B. Hayes, wrote, "While we have suffered a great deal from want of food and sleep, we have lost very few men, and are generally in the best of health."[12]

On June 30, 1864, the army moved toward Charleston with General Hunter being in an ambulance, before Hunter and his staff embarked on a steamer for 10 miles along the Kanawha River to Charleston. Having already rested his army for three days at Gauley, Hunter proceeded to rest them again at Charleston. This was in spite of the fact that Hunter had received news on July 1 that the Confederates were demonstrating in the Shenandoah Valley and moving toward Martinsburg. Strother thought that the Confederate force could be nothing more than cavalry.[13]

Hunter was reorganizing and refitting his army. He was also gathering steamers to transport his army to Parkersburg. There he planned to embark his troops on the Baltimore & Ohio Railroad.[14]

While Hunter was resting himself and his army for three days each at Gauley and Charleston, West Virginia, at a time he knew that there was no one in the Shenandoah Valley to face Early, Early was moving down the Valley with alacrity toward Martinsburg and the Potomac. Hunter had already rejected two suggestions from his chief of staff, Colonel David Hunter Strother, that would keep him closer to Early. One option would have put him in Charlottesville; the other would have put him in the Valley of the South Branch of the Potomac from which movement to Martinsburg would have been reasonably feasible. Thus, not only had Hunter lost a lot of time, which appeared to be the hallmark of his movements; also, he had remained out of touch with both Grant and the War Department in Washington. When he did send a message, long-delayed in being received, in late June 1864, it did not paint an accurate picture of what had occurred.

At this point an army of over 18,000 men was not making any appreciable effort to get up to the railroad and move east to deal with Early's army. On July 3, 1864, Colonel Strother had reported hearing from Grant that Early was coming back from Lynchburg and was in his front at Richmond. That same day some of Hunter's men boarded the steamer *Jonas Powell* to move up the river to Parkersburg.[15] After Halleck had telegraphed Grant that he had had no reports from Hunter, Grant had seemed to assume that Hunter would be able to handle the situation. Grant told Halleck on July 4, 1864, that Hunter should be able to meet the Confederate threat.

Private William Stark reported that the 34th Massachusetts had a hard march of 25 miles on July 2 and another 6 miles on July 3 to Pyatt, West Virginia, where they stayed all day. The regiment was still in camp on July 4. It was not until 4:00 P.M. that the men went on board the steamboat that was to transport them north.[16] Thus, the better part of two additional days had been spent in camp—making almost eight days delayed on returning to the Potomac.

The boat carrying General Hunter was underway earlier on the 4th of July, however, and reached Parkersburg about 6:00 P.M. There Major General David Hunter was advised that Major General Franz Sigel had been driven from Martinsburg by a large force of Confederates under General Ewell. Hunter's chief of staff assumed it to have been merely a cavalry raid.[17]

The War Department had been out of contact with Hunter for an extended period. On the night of July 4, 1864, General Franz Sigel and General Max Weber had moved to Maryland Heights, leaving Harpers Ferry in the hands of Early's Confederate army. Secretary of War Edwin Stanton sent an ascerbic telegram to Hunter on July 5:

> The rebels for two days back have been operating against Martinsburg, Harper's Ferry, and other points in the line of the Baltimore railroad. These points being in your department you are expected to take promptly such measures as may be proper to meet the emergency. This Department has for some time been without any information as to where your forces are and how employed. You will please report to the Adjutant-general the position of your forces, and acknowledge the receipt of this telegram.[18]

Hunter replied to Stanton on July 5, 1864, that he was gathering his straggling troops in Parkersburg and would push on to Martinsburg as soon as he could. Halleck advised Hunter by telegram that he was still in command of all Union forces opposing Early's army that went to Maryland. Earlier Hunter's wife told Welles that Hunter had gotten off safely.[19] Hunter at that point was approximately 270 miles west of Martinsburg. However, he was on the rail line and was in his position to move his troops more expeditiously than if a march back were required.

Having been at Parkersburg since the 4th, Hunter realized the criticism he was under for having let Early go down the Valley unopposed and not having come back to defend the Upper Potomac.[20] Brigadier General Jeremiah Sullivan's infantry division was embarked on trains at Parkersburg on the morning of July 6. Sigel telegraphed Hunter on July 6, 1864, that Confederate forces were in front of him at Harpers Ferry. Stanton telegraphed Hunter to move his whole force eastward as fast as possible as Sigel reported that Confederate forces had been crossing the Potomac at Antietam ford for the past 40 hours.[21]

While Sullivan's forces had been dispatched, General Hunter remained at Parkersburg on July 7 at a time Early's lead cavalry elements under Brigadier General Bradley T. Johnson were moving on Frederick. On July 7, 1864, an editorial appeared in the *Parkersburg Gazette* critical of Hunter and the expedition.

Hunter became enraged and ordered editor James E. Wharton arrested and imprisoned. Hunter also ordered that Wharton's newspaper be destroyed and his offices closed. Hunter was particularly concerned with wording he claimed gave aid and comfort to the Confederates." We were sorry to see so much suffering among them. Men are completely worn out, and many of the driven had died of starvation.... The suffering of the soldiers in their movement from Lynchburg to Charleston was terrible, and they half require rest and surgical care."[22] The editor was released after a few days' imprisonment.[23]

On the night of July 7, 1864, General Hunter finally left Parkersburg en route to Cumberland. At this time Early was moving through the passes of the Catoctin Mountains on Frederick. At 10:00 A.M. on July 9, 1864, General Hunter arrived in Cumberland, Maryland—almost a hundred miles from Frederick, beyond which Early's army had passed.

Over time, the War Department had come to realize that Hunter was not moving up to engage Early as they had contemplated. After having heard from John Garrett, president of the Baltimore & Ohio Railroad, on July 3 about the movement of large Confederate forces in the Valley, Secretary of War Edwin Stanton had wired Garrett that Hunter had been under orders three days before to move his forces up to threatened points and that Brigadier General Jeremiah Sullivan's cavalry should already have been up.[24]

Having left on July 6, Brigadier General Jeremiah Sullivan's infantry brigade did not reach Martinsburg until July 10. Although these men could have been moved east by rail to get to the rear of Early's army, they were not. Hunter himself remained in Cumberland from July 9 through July 14-the period of the Battle of the Monocacy and Early's attack on Fort Stevens—ostensibly moving forward troops still coming in from the west.[25] Hunter had been advised of Early's attack on Washington. At the time the national capital was being threatened, General Hunter continued an inept and dilatory response—not even putting himself in a position to challenge Early's return to Virginia.

Assistant Secretary of War Charles Dana had come to Washington to act as an observer for Grant. Dana recommended that General David Hunter be immediately relieved, describing him, in Stanton's words, as more incompetent than Sigel. He also stressed the need for a unity of command:

EDWIN STANTON, LINCOLN'S SECRETARY OF WAR (NATIONAL ARCHIVES).

Nothing can possibly be done toward pursuing or cutting off the enemy for want of a commander. General Augur commands the defenses of Washington, with A. McD. McCook and a lot of brigadier-generals under him, but he is not allowed to go outside—. Wright commands his own corps—. General Gillmore has been assigned to the temporary command of those troops of the Nineteenth Corps in the city of Washington. General Ord to command the Eighth Corps and all other troops in the Middle Department, leaving Wallace in command of the City alone. But there's no one head to the whole, and it seems indispensible that you should at once appoint one.—Hunter will be the ranking officer if he ever gets up, but he will not do; Indeed, the Secy of War directs me to tell you in his judgment Hunter, ought instantly to be relieved, having proven himself far more incompetent that even Sigel.[26]

On July 11, 1864, General Henry Halleck had ordered General Hunter to join with Brigadier General Albion Howe to move on Washington.[27] Grant on July 12 named General Horatio G.

Wright to head the forces pursuing Early. On the evening of July 13, 1864, Halleck telegraphed Hunter that Wright with over 12,000 men was following Early on his retreat from Washington, and asked Hunter to join in the pursuit.[28]

Hunter had lost track of Brigadier General Jeremiah Sullivan, who had left Martinsburg. Hunter was making inquiries by wire to Captain Thomas McCann in Martinsburg as to where General Wright was and where General Early was. Hunter went himself to Martinsburg, arriving on the morning of July 14. He then left by horseback for Harpers Ferry to join up with Brigadier General Albion Howe. He was accompanied by Duffie's brigade of cavalry.[29]

Howe had done nothing either to assist Wallace at the Monocacy or to come up from Harpers Ferry to get in Early's rear and aid in the defense of Washington. When Early's army

GIDEON WELLES, LINCOLN'S SECRETARY OF THE NAVY AND CRITIC OF THE DEFENSE TO EARLY'S RAID (NATIONAL ARCHIVES).

had left the area of Maryland Heights on July 7, 1864, moving east, General Howe had been in a position to threaten his lines of communications and harass him from the rear. Sigel's Reserve Division on Maryland Heights, Weber's garrison forces from Harpers Ferry and Howe's 2,800 men from the defenses of Washington had taken very minor losses in Early's demonstration before Maryland Heights. Thus, Howe had a relatively strong force to use to assist Wallace or menace Early's rear, which he did not use.

On July 8, 1864, Major General Julius Stahel with the Union cavalry from Harpers Ferry was ordered to leave Maryland Heights and follow the Confederate forces though Pleasant Valley to Boonesboro. Stahel disobeyed orders and spent the night in Pleasant Valley. On July 15, 1864, Major General Stahel was relieved of duty in the Department of West Virginia.[30]

Major General Lew Wallace recorded a conversation between himself and Brigadier General James B. Ricketts upon Rickett's arrival at Monocacy Junction concerning Halleck's actions and Howe's inaction, stating in part:

> "But Halleck, what is he doing?"
> "Defending Harper's Ferry."
> Ricketts looked at me curiously, and said, "I don't understand you."
> "Instead of strengthening me here, he has sent batteries and thousands of men to the old Ferry, and they are on Maryland Heights now, of no more account in the defense of Washington than so many stones. I have been here three days, and he has not so much as wired me a word of intelligence respecting the enemy, or in the way of encouragement."

Then I told Ricketts of the invitation I had received to go to Harper's Ferry and join the useless army on Maryland Heights.

"What. And give Early a clear road to Washington! Never-never! We'll stay here. Give me your orders."[31]

When Hunter got to Harpers Ferry on July 15, 1864, he got a telegram from Halleck telling him to put his troops under the command of Brigadier General George Crook and to send them to join Major General Horatio G. Wright. He was also to join Wright and put himself under Wright's orders.[32] Hunter was given the choice of joining Wright in a subordinate position or retaining command of the Department of West Virginia, with troop command responsibilities being under General George Crook.[33] General Hunter felt insulted and asked Secretary of War Edmund Stanton to be relieved of command. Wright had advised Halleck on July 14 that he had been unable to get any intelligence from General Hunter's command.[34] Hunter then contacted Secretary of War Stanton:

> I have the honor to express to you my sincere regret that His Excellency the President should have seen fit, in a telegram from General Halleck on yesterday's date, to have so far censured my conduct as to place before me the alternatives, either of turning over my command of troops in the field to one of my brigadiers or volunteering to serve under a junior of my own rank; the difficulties in the latter alternative being increased by the too obvious inference from General Halleck's words, that my abandoning my command to the subordinate in question would be preferred. I am further censured by the President, through General Halleck, for not having made sufficiently frequent reports to Washington of the condition of affairs in my department.[35]

Hunter directly telegraphed President Abraham Lincoln asking to be relieved of command because he was being scapegoated for the blunders of others.

> I again most earnestly request to be relieved from the command of this department. Your order, conveyed through General Halleck, has entirely destroyed my usefulness. When an officer is selected as a scapegoat to cover up the blunders of others, the best interests of the country require that he should at once be relieved of command.[36]

Incredibly, Hunter then told General Grant that he had been unaware that he had anything to do with the defense of Washington:

> I was not informed that I had anything to do with the defense of Washington, and supposed General Halleck had made ample provision for this purpose. I hope, general, you will do me the justice to say that I have done my whole duty, and I beg that you will give me a command of some type.[37]

Grant supported Hunter in a message to Assistant Secretary of War Charles Dana, stating he failed to see Hunter had not acted with great promptness and success.

On July 15, 1864, the day Hunter was asking to be relieved of command, Lieutenant General Ulysses S. Grant sent directions to Halleck:

> It would seem from dispatches just received from Mr. Dana, Assistant Secretary of War, that the enemy are leaving Maryland. If so, Hunter should follow him as rapidly as the jaded condition of his men will admit. The Sixth and Nineteenth Corps should be got here without any delay, so that they may be used before the return of the troops sent to the Valley by the enemy. Hunter moving up the Valley will either hold a large force of the enemy or he will be enabled to reach Gordonsville & Charlottesville. The utter destruction of the road between these two place will be of immense value to us.[38]

The unwieldy command situation in the Union army facing Early continued. Halleck told Hunter on July 17, 1864, that Grant wanted him to pursue Early all the way to Charlottesville. He was explicitly told that if he had to retreat, he was to keep the Confederate forces in his front. Hunter was also to protect the crossings of the Potomac and Washington and was not to fall back to West Virginia to save his army. If Hunter could not cut the railroads at Charlottesville, he was to go south in the Valley, destroying as much provision as possible and making it so crows flying over the Valley would have to carry their own provender with them.[39]

Grant told Halleck on July 18 that Hunter should always stay between the Confederate forces and Washington. He was not to be drawn into an unequal fight south of the Potomac.[40] Hunter was at department headquarters at Monocacy Junction.[41] The Confederates under Breckinridge achieved success at Snicker's Ferry on July 18 and at Kernstown on the 24 when Crook was defeated. McCausland went north with a force of 4,000 troopers on July 30 and burned Chambersburg, Pennsylvania, at Early's direction when demands were not complied with.[42]

Hunter received a telegram from President Abraham Lincoln on July 22, 1864, asking if he had been able to take care of the Confederates when they turned their back on him when they found that General Wright had left, to which Hunter replied in the negative.[43] Hunter sent a second message to Lincoln on the 22nd asking if he should chase Early in the Shenandoah as Grant had directed or establish blocking positions in the Blue Ridge gaps to protect Washington.[44]

On July 27, Secretary of War Edwin Stanton at the direction of the president placed all military operations in the Department of Washington, the Department of the Susquehanna, the Department of West Virginia and the Middle Department in Halleck's hands.[45] Halleck advised Grant that while Hunter was collecting forces at Harpers Ferry, Confederate forces crossed the Potomac on the 29th and moved into Chambersburg, destroying the city.[46]

Hunter had not gotten himself in the theater of operations to protect Washington; he had not meaningfully assisted in dealing with Early's threat after Early's retreat from Washington on July 13, 1864. He had not followed Grant's orders to move on Charlottesville — a repeat of the earlier order in June 1864 that he did not follow.

After Chambersburg, Grant solved the command problem himself. On the 31st of July, 1864, he called Major General Philip H. Sheridan to headquarters at City Point and offered him a unified command, telling Halleck that unless Hunter was in the field in person, Sheridan should be put in command of all troops in the field.[47] Grant went directly to Monocacy without stopping at Washington. Grant stated:

> I found General Hunter's army encamped there, scattered over all the fields along the bank of the Monocacy with many hundreds of cars and locomotives, belonging to the Baltimore and Ohio Railroad, which he had taken the precaution to bring back and collect at this point. I asked the general where the enemy was. He replied that he did not know. He said the fact was, that he was so embarrassed with orders from Washington moving him first to the right and then to the left that he had lost all trace of the enemy.[48]

Grant wanted to put Sheridan in the field with Hunter at headquarters performing administrative duties. Hunter wished to be relieved entirely and was.[49] Grant wanted the Union army to move into the Valley at once. From Harpers Ferry the army was to find if the Confederates were north of the Potomac and, if so, attack. If found south of the Potomac, then the army was to push south taking all forage, provisions and stock needed and destroying the rest. Grant wanted to wage total war. Grant wanted prompt and active movements against the Confederate forces and for Sheridan to always keep them in his sight.[50]

The split command of Augur, Couch, Ord, and Hunter with separate field commands under Wright and Crook was replaced with a unified command under Sheridan. The aggressive Shenandoah Valley Campaign of late summer and fall 1864 followed.

CHAPTER 19

Confederates Fail to Secure Bridge at Monocacy Junction

General Robert E. Lee's daring plan to attack Washington and Point Lookout with a relatively small force depended upon speed and adroitness in strategy and logistics to achieve the tactical advantage under changing circumstances in enemy territory. Stonewall Jackson talked about and practiced mystifying, misleading and surprising the enemy to achieve victory.[1] Lieutenant General Jubal A. Early and Major General Lew Wallace both understood the tactical significance of Monocacy Junction where, in a space of approximately two miles, the Baltimore Pike, the Georgetown Pike and the Baltimore & Ohio Railroad all crossed the Monocacy River.[2]

On July 8, 1864, Early had directed Brigadier General John McCausland to take his cavalry force to capture the railroad bridge at Monocacy Junction. Once having seized it, McCausland was to go downstream and operate on the left flank of the Union forces. He also was to cut the telegraph wires between Harpers Ferry and Baltimore. Early described the movement he wanted as follows: "McCausland was ordered to move to the right, and the next day cut the telegraph and the railroad between Maryland Heights and Washington and Baltimore—cross the Monocacy, and occupy the railroad bridge, at the junction near Frederick."[3]

Early was not in a position to move McCausland's cavalry brigade in an earlier and more timely fashion on Monocacy when it was lightly defended on July 8, in part because McCausland's force had been delayed by its movement to Hagerstown on July 6, where they spent much of the day extorting money from financial institutions to prevent the burning of the city, and by slowness in getting up to and around Frederick.[4] Had McCausland been able to get to the Monocacy on July 8, the Confederates could possibly have denied the Union forces the strong defensive position they used so effectively at the Battle of the Monocacy on July 9, 1864. Moreover, the Confederate cavalry would have been in the rear of Lieutenant Colonel Clendenin's cavalry force, Colonel Gilpin's Maryland regiment, Truex's brigade of Rickett's division, and Tyler's forces then at Frederick, which moved to Monocacy on the night of July 8. McCausland would potentially have been in a position to damage the railroad and seriously disrupt the flow of Brigadier General James Rickett's troops coming up from Grant's army by rail from Baltimore.

That is not to say that McCausland's mission, if it could have been undertaken earlier, would have been easy. Wallace had come up from Baltimore and had begun to concentrate his forces at the Monocacy by July 5.[5] The 11th Maryland, under Colonel Charles Landstreet, had just mustered in on July 3, 1864, and had just come up to Monocacy, as had Alexander's Baltimore Battery of Light Artillery and companies of Colonel Root's forces from Annapolis. Wallace had refused a contingent of 300 stragglers from Sigel's army who wound up at Frederick, sending them to Annapolis to guard the Parole Camp and getting local forces in return. A hundred men from the 159th Ohio commanded by Captain Edward H. Leib of the 5th U.S. Cavalry and a detachment of the 5th U.S. Cavalry commanded by Captain H.S. Allen also came to joint Wallace's army at Monocacy Junction.[6]

Lieutenant Joseph Lane of Company C of the 22nd Pennsylvania Cavalry, who had brought a wagon train from Monocacy to Frederick, was brought into Wallace's command along with several of his men. There were seven companies of the 149th Ohio and three companies of the 159th Ohio as well under Colonel A.L. Brown. Colonel Charles Gilpin commanded the 3rd Maryland Potomac Home Brigade. Wallace also had four companies of the 1st Maryland Potomac Home Brigade. There were men from the 144th Ohio at Monocacy as well as the 10th Vermont commanded by Colonel William Henry. Other units of Truex's brigade of Ricketts's command had left Baltimore at 12:50 A.M. and 3:20 A.M. respectively on July 8th and arrived at Monocacy Junction before dawn.

BRIG. GEN. JOHN MCCAUSLAND LED CAVALRY BRIGADE AT FREDERICK AND MONOCACY (LIBRARY OF CONGRESS).

However, most of those troops were not at Monocacy on July 8. Brigadier General Tyler with Colonel Gilpin's 3rd Maryland and Leib's 159th Ohio with three more guns from Alexander's battery had been sent to Frederick on July 7 by Wallace as reinforcement to stem the advance of the Confederate cavalry moving on Frederick. On the 8th, men from the 10th Vermont, 144th Ohio, 149th Ohio and other units were sent to Frederick to reinforce Tyler.[7]

On July 8, 1864, Lieutenant Colonel Catlin with men from the 11th Maryland was left at the railroad bridge crossing the Monocacy. Thus, the bridgehead was vulnerable, although there would be more troops arriving from Rickett's command.[8]

However, Early's order to Brigadier General McCausland was not issued until the afternoon of the 8th, contemplating a movement on the 9th when it would be too late. Thus, the Confederate commander's idea was tactically important but too late to be effectively implemented.

This was due in part to the time McCausland had spent in Hagerstown, northwest of Frederick about 26 miles, in a raid to extort money from the banks in the city to prevent its being burned. On July 5, 1864, Early had sent McCausland there with orders to ransom the city for $200,000. The advance units under Lieutenant George Shearer of Company H of the 1st Maryland Cavalry fought with a part of a company of the 6th U.S. Cavalry under Lieutenant Hancock T. McLean, who had come from Carlise Barracks, Pennsylvania, to resist the Confederate incursions in the area.[9]

McCausland's whole force entered Hagerstown on the 6th. Due to a missed decimal point, McCausland asked for $20,000 from local financial institutions to be raised within three hours.

The Washington County Bank of Williamsport paid $5,000. The Hagerstown Savings Bank contributed $5,000, and the Hagerstown Bank put in $10,000.

McCausland also sought stockpiles of government property. These included hats, boots and other items. Some clothing was supplied by business establishments, including 99 pairs of boots and 123 pairs of shoes.[10]

The whole operation took most of the day on July 6. It was not until dusk that he moved off in the direction of Boonesboro. He first moved to Funkstown and then to Boonesboro.[11] Boonesboro was about 9 miles southeast of Hagerstown on the road to Frederick. It was about 17 miles from Frederick by the main road.

However, McCausland was in a very difficult position to go around Frederick. He went to Boonesboro on the 7th. He kept moving in a counter–clockwise direction about 25 miles mainly south to Jefferson where he bivouacked with this command on the night of the 8th.[12] This route was not on the main roads and had to cross the Catoctin Mountains.

However, men from the rest of Early's cavalry command had been within several miles of Frederick on July 7 and were within relatively easy striking distance of Monocacy Junction on July 8. Early's best chance to timely attack the railroad bridgehead on July 8 would have been with men from Johnson's or possibly "Mudwall" Jackson's brigade. Choosing McCausland's brigade for the assignment would necessarily delay the operation.

There was a window of opportunity on July 8 when Monocacy Junction was defended by recent recruits while Wallace, Tyler and their forces defended Frederick and impeded the progress of the Confederate advance. The Confederates were unable to seize it.

McCausland did attempt to effectuate his orders. He left Jefferson on the morning of July 9. His force was guided by a local resident to the toll gate on the top of Catoctin Mountain. From there, his force move until they reached the Point of Rocks Road. McCausland took that road, moving toward Frederick. He split his command, moving toward Frederick on parallel roads. The command reunited on the Buckeystown Road. He then became engaged with Company B of the 8th Illinois Cavalry under Lieutenant George Corbit.[13] He was with Confederate forces on the west side of the Monocacy River at 9:00 A.M. on July 9. He was requested by staff officers to find a ford over the river, which he did. Ultimately his forces would lead the initial attack on the Union positions across the river.

Early's desire to seize the railroad bridge over the Monocacy was reasonable and strategically important. He gave an untimely order to a cavalry officer in the most difficult position to accomplish it in a timely manner. Had the mission been undertaken differently, the results could have been different and affected the outcome of the rest of the campaign.

CHAPTER 20

Early Delayed by Battle of the Monocacy

The Battle of the Monocacy on July 9, 1864, is widely considered as the battle that saved Washington by giving General Horatio G. Wright's 6th Corps troops and General Quincy Gillmore's 19th Corps troops additional time to get to Washington for the relief of the city, closing off Early's opportunity to take and burn the city and potentially capture or kill President Lincoln.[1] Glenn Worthington put it this way:

> It seems indisputable that had it not been for the stubborn battle fought at the Monocacy on July 9, 1864, by the Union troops under Gen. Lew Wallace, whereby Early's march on Washington was delayed fully 24 hours, Early would have captured that city on July 11th. That 24 hours gave barely enough time for reinforcements from City Point to arrive. If Early could have reached Fort Stevens on the 10th, he would have had time to rest his men overnight and make a vigorous assault on the city the next morning. Indeed, the works were still but feebly manned on the 11th, [and] he might have gone in on the 10th had he reached the city that day. It is shown by the records that the miscellaneous troops gathered hastily together in the city for its defense were not brought even into the semblance of an organization until the afternoon of the 11th, and that they were sent that same afternoon, a heterogenous assemblage, to the fortifications and even outside, without even the slightest training as a body of fighting men to defend the city.[2]

However, the Battle of the Monocacy, which delayed Early's attack a full day and caused him substantial casualties, might well have been avoided, as the Confederates were in a position to simply march around Wallace's strong defensive line protected by a river that was difficult to cross and by heights from behind that river. As Benjamin F. Cooling in *Jubal Early's Raid on Washington* succinctly put it, "Certainly the Confederates missed a superb opportunity to avoid a bloody confrontation, outmaneuver Wallace, and get back on schedule for the march to the capital. The Buckeystown route eluded Jubal Early as he watched his cavalry clatter up and begin to seek a way across the river closer to the covered bridge and junction."[3] Lew Wallace was pleased at the delay of Early getting up to the battlefield: "I felt a thrill of gratification. Four hours gained! Four hours, and Early was still in Frederick, not one step nearer his great prize. Think when the dawn covered the steeples of the town from the envelope of the night! Should I give notice to the authorities in Washington, and to General Grant at City Point, of what was going on? Not yet — I said to myself — not yet."[4] Early was not getting any citizen information, as General Ricketts had been ordered to permit no persons through the Union lines without a pass from headquarters.[5]

Part of the problem Early faced on the morning of July 9, 1864, was that Brigadier General Bradley T. Johnson, who was from Frederick and was familiar with the area, was being dispatched on that morning on his raid to free the prisoners at Point Lookout after having made sure Early's left flank was covered.[6] Another was that Brigadier General John McCausland, who had been ordered on July 9, 1864, to secure the Monocacy crossing before securing Frederick,

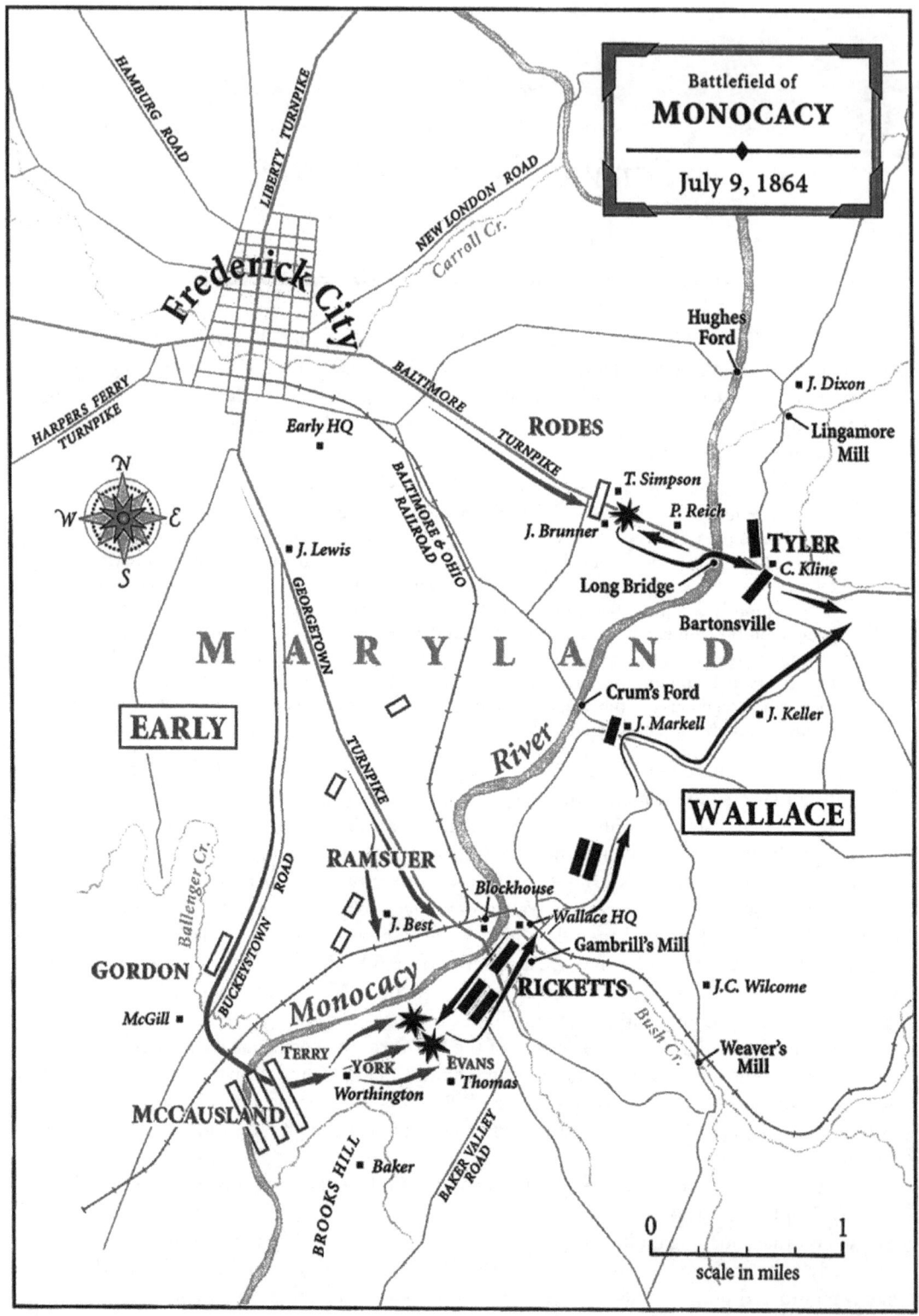

MAP OF BATTLEFIELD OF MONOCACY SHOWING DISPOSITION OF FORCES (MAP BY DAVID DEIS).

had not done so.[7] Another problem was that Early was not up with his troops but spent part of the morning in the city of Frederick. Early had established a temporary headquarters at the Robert Hammond house at Second and Market Streets in Frederick. On the morning of July 9, 1864, he was still in Frederick seeking a ransom of $200, 000 from the town plus 20,000 pounds of bacon, 6,000 pounds of sugar, 3,000 pounds of coffee, and salt.[8] At 8:00 A.M., Early had drafted a note at the Hammond House asking for $200,000 to spare the city.

Early's staff involved in the negotiating for the money included Major W.J. Hawks, commissary chief, Major John A. Harmon, quartermaster, Dr. Hunter McGuire, chief surgeon, and Lieutenant Colonel William Allan, ordinance chief. An impasse occurred all morning. Early rode forward by late morning to see how the advance at the Monocacy was progressing.[9] Ultimately, that afternoon, $64,000 was obtained from the Frederick Town Savings Institution, $44,000 from the Central Bank, $33,000 from the Frederick County Bank, $31,000 from the Franklin Savings Bank and $28,000 from the Farmers and Mechanics Bank.[10]

Meanwhile, Brigadier General Robert D. Lilley's brigade of Stephen D. Ramseur's Division went east of Frederick on the National Road early in the morning on July 9 and threw out skirmishers.[11] All of Early's three divisions which had left Frederick on the morning of July 9 had soon encountered forward Union positions and were engaged. Early considered options to a costly assault on Union bridgeheads at Monocacy Junction and found an attack on the Union left flank to provide the only real option for success.[12]

On the morning of July 9, 1864, battle lines were set along the Monocacy River. Wallace's right wing was under the command of Brigadier General Erastus Tyler, a battle-hardened veteran officer. Under his command were the 3rd Maryland Potomac Home Brigade, the 1st Maryland Potomac Home Brigade, the 11th Maryland, the 144th Ohio National Guard, the 149th Ohio National Guard, a detachment of the 159th Ohio National Guard, companies of the 8th Illinois Cavalry and three guns of Alexander's Baltimore Light Artillery. Colonel A.L. Brown with the 149th Ohio and other troops under his command were posted at the Stone Bridge, over which the Baltimore Pike crossed the Monocacy River. The holding of this bridge was crucial to the protection of Wallace's right flank as well as to his line of retreat to Baltimore.

Colonel Gilpin, with three companies of the 3rd Maryland Potomac Home Brigade, was in line at Crum's Ford between the Stone Bridge and the railroad. Colonel Landstreet and the 11th Maryland was at the railroad bridge in reserve along with other companies of the 3rd Maryland Potomac Home Brigade.

Major General Lew Wallace, in command of the Union forces at Monocacy, anticipated that the left of his line would be the main point for the Confederate attack. There he placed his most experienced troops from the 6th Corps under General James B. Ricketts across the pike to Washington and covering the wooden bridge across the Monocacy River. Here were posted the 106th New York, the 151st New York, the 14th New Jersey, the 10th Vermont and the 87th Pennsylvania of Colonel W.S. Truex's brigade. Also there were the 138th Pennsylvania, the 9th New York Heavy Artillery, the 126th Ohio, the 122nd Ohio and the 110th Ohio of Colonel McClennan's brigade. A third brigade of Ricketts's command stayed at Monrovia and did not come up for the battle. Lieutenant Colonel David Clendenin and the 8th Illinois Cavalry covered the lower fords south of Ricketts's forces.

Captain Braun's detachment of the 1st Maryland Home Brigade was on the western bank of the Monocacy serving as skirmishers on about a three-quarter-mile line. There was also a 24-pounder howitzer in a blockhouse guarding the railroad and the bridges.

Early only focused on the direct route south to Washington and did not focus on any maneuvers using the Buckeystown Road. That morning five companies of the 8th Illinois Cavalry cavalry were all that was guarding the Buckeystown-Urbanna axis around Monocacy Junction, which Early did not meaningfully consider.[13]

At around 8:00 A.M., the Confederates set up a skirmish line and put their guns into action. About 9:00 A.M., the Confederate forces began to move rapidly to the left in an effort to flank Brigadier General Ricketts's position. The Confederates also attacked at the Stone Bridge, where Colonel A.L. Brown was posted. Brown, with determined resistance, was able to hold his line with great difficulty.

Ricketts, seeing the Confederate movements, moved his lines to the left to the river bank. There his forces were subjected to an enfilading fire from the Confederate guns. Wallace sent Ricketts two additional guns. Wallace was also forced to put most of his reserves into the line. The wooden bridge and blockhouse were burned and the forces defending them were recalled.

It was not until late morning that a ford was located and McCausland moved to cross the Monocacy River. He effectuated a dismounted cavalry charge against Union positions beyond that was repulsed with substantial losses. Early said he was examining the situation to his right, where the Buckeystown Road was located, when McCausland solved the problem for him by attacking.[14]

Early then ordered Major General John C. Breckinridge's force to assist McCausland and pursue the attack. Early also ordered General John B. Gordon to move forward and attack the Union left to drive their forces from a position covering the Monocacy crossings and to allow Ramseur to cross on the road to Washington. Ramseur skirmished with the forces in his front while Gordon pursued the assault on Ricketts's position.

Early then brought 40 guns to bear effectively in support of McCausland and Gordon.[15] The major Confederate attack was not able to be made until the afternoon of the 9th with Gordon's Division.[16]

The fighting was fierce during the battle. Confederate general John B. Gordon, whose division did the heaviest fighting, described the Battle of the Monocacy as short, decisive and bloody:

MAJOR GENERAL JOHN B. GORDON LED A MAJOR CONFEDERATE ASSAULT AT MONOCACY (LIBRARY OF CONGRESS).

> With an able commander in my front, and his compact ranks so well placed as to rake every foot of the field with their fire, with the certainty of having my lines broken and tangled by fences and grain stacks at every rod of the advance, it is not difficult to understand the responsibility of hazarding battle without supporting Confederate infantry in reach. The nerve of the best-trained and bravest troops is sorely taxed, even under the most favorable condi-

BRIG. GEN. CLEMENT EVANS, WOUNDED AT MONOCACY (LIBRARY OF CONGRESS).

BRIG. GEN. ERASTUS TYLER COMMANDED THE UNION RIGHT AT MONOCACY (UNITED STATES ARMY MILITARY HISTORY INSTITUTE).

tions, when assaulting an enemy well-posted and pouring an incessant well-directed fire into their advancing ranks. To how much severer test of nerve were my troops to be subjected in this attempt to charge where conditions forced them while under fire to break into column, halt and reform, and make another start, only to be broken again by immovable stacks, all over the field. I know, however, that if any troops in the world could win victory against such adverse conditions, those high-mettled Southern boys would achieve it there. En echelon by brigades from the right the movement began. As we reached the first line of strong and high fencing and my men began to climb over it, they were met by a tempest of bullets, and many of the brave fellows fell at the first volley. But over they climbed or tumbled, and rushed forward, some of them halting to break down gaps in the fence, so that the mounted officers might ride through. Then came the grain stacks. Around them and between them they pressed on, with no possibility of maintaining orderly alignments or returning effective fire. Deadly missiles from Wallace's ranks were cutting down the line and company officers, with their words of cheer to the men but half spoken. It was one of those fights where success depends largely on the prowess of the individual soldier....

The Union lines stood firmly in this second position, bravely defending the railroad and highway to Washington.

Between the two hostile lines there was a narrow ravine down which ran a small stream of water. In this ravine the fighting was desperate and at close quarters. To and fro the battle swayed across the little stream. The dead and wounded of both sides mingling their blood in its waters. Nearly one-half of my men and a large number of Federals fell there. Many of my officers went down, and Gen. Clement A. Evans, the trusted leader of my largest brigade, was severely wounded....

Wallace's army, after the most stubborn resistance and with heavy loss, was driven from the railroad and the pike in the direction of Baltimore. The Confederate victory was won at fearful cost and by practically a single division, but it was complete, and the way to Washington was opened for Early's march.[17]

Brigadier General Zebulon York called Monocacy the bloodiest and fiercest encounter in which he had ever been involved.[18] T.E. Morrow of the 8th Louisiana of York's brigade said his unit lost more in numbers of men at the Monocacy than in any other battle except Sharpsburg.[19]

BRIG. GEN. JAMES B. RICKETTS COMMANDED THE UNION LEFT AT MONOCACY (UNITED STATES ARMY MILITARY HISTORY INSTITUTE).

BRIG. GEN. ZEBULON YORK, A CONFEDERATE BRIGADIER ENGAGED IN HEAVY FIGHTING AT MONOCACY (LIBRARY OF CONGRESS).

Terry's brigade had come to the assistance of Gordon at a crucial time. James A. Hutcheson of Terry's brigade reported 59 killed and wounded of 153 men in the fight. However, Captain Robert E. Park of the 12th Alabama reported that Brigadier General Cullen Battle's brigade was not actively engaged at the Monocacy. This was the case with a substantial part of the Confederate forces. For instance, Echol's brigade was guarding the trains and was not brought up until after the battle was concluded. Most of the fighting had been done by only one division.[20]

In the late afternoon, Wallace had seen the Confederate movement to take the field unfolding: "And presently the slouch-hatted skirmishers began firing. Then, as at a signal, the battle broke from its leash. All the guns on the other side of the river awoke, reminding me of sleeping dogs responding to a kennel-cry. And again, drowning the cackle of the more distant skirmishers, and the yelping, they searched the low places and the high everywhere behind, over and in front of Ricketts."[21]

About 4:00 P.M., Wallace ordered Ricketts to make preparations to move his men back from their lines to the Baltimore Pike to his north. Brigadier General Erastus Tyler's reserves had been sent to Colonel A.L. Brown, holding the Stone Bridge. Wallace ordered the Stone Bridge to be held at all costs. Tyler held it until after 5:00 P.M. when Wallace's main force was moving on the Baltimore Pike toward New Market. Attacks in his rear caused Brown's men to scatter into the woods. Tyler and Brown were able to avoid capture. A substantial part of Wallace's losses, a total of 1,054 men, were reported missing or captured. This was as a result of the pressure of Early's forces after the retreat had been undertaken.[22]

However, the Union troops at the Monocacy did fight. Colonel Allen Brown of the 149th Ohio 100-days regiment was ordered to fight to the last extremity by Wallace between 4:00 P.M. and 5:00 P.M. on July 9. He was able to retreat and get many of his men off the field by 6 P.M.[23] His unit lost over 130 men, holding Early as long as possible.[24]

Grant in his memoirs categorically stated that the delay caused by Wallace was crucial in protecting Washington.[25]

The Confederate army of General Jubal Early passed to the south side of the Monocacy on the night of July 9, 1864.[26] Certainly the stubborn resistance and hard fought battle had cost Early dearly in terms of time and men. There were 408 Confederate dead buried in Frederick even though Early claimed to have lost only 700 men. Those were the casualties in Gordon's brigade alone.[27] Also, 405 Confederate soldiers were left in hospitals, not being able to be moved.[28]

It is difficult to know if a flanking maneuver, marching around the Union's strong defensive position on the Monocacy, could have placed Early far closer to Washington on July 9. There would have been a substantial Union force in his rear, including the 1,000 of Ricketts's men at Monrovia who never made it to the battlefield. At any rate, considering the large amount of time lost prior to the 9th on the way to the Monocacy, the day lost on the Monocacy on the 9th was time that Early could not afford to lose in his quest to capture Washington and free the prisoners at Point Lookout.

Occupying Washington, dispersing the United States Government and destroying the Archives could have been completed in a single day's possession of the city or less.[29] Early had achieved command of Ewell's old corps because he was considered a resourceful officer.[30] After the Monocacy, Early did move on toward Washington and tried to achieve his objectives in spite of the obstacles.

CHAPTER 21

Johnson-Gilmor Raid Toward Baltimore and Point Lookout

During the winter of 1863–64, General Robert E. Lee had considered a plan to free Confederate prisoners at Point Lookout, which had been precluded by military threats by the Union army in Virginia.[1] Bradley Johnson had also proposed to General Wade Hampton a plan to take 200 well-mounted men across the Potomac to capture President Lincoln at the Soldier's Home in Washington where he spent his summer evenings guarded by only a small detachment of cavalry. Johnson had been with Stonewall Jackson in his 1862 Valley Campaign. He had also commanded a brigade at Second Bull Run (Manassas).[2] However, in late June 1864, Lee was in correspondence with Confederate president Jefferson Davis concerning a coordinated land-sea assault at Point Lookout. General John B. Gordon, a division commander under Early, stated:

> The second object (the release of our prisoners confined at Point Lookout) had to be abandoned at a somewhat earlier date because of the inability to perfect needful antecedent arrangements. Some days prior to our crossing the Potomac into Maryland — General Lee wrote twice to President Davis (June 26th and 29th) touching on the possibility of effecting this release. It was General Lee's opinion that it would not require a large force to accomplish this object.— He said to the President "I have understood that most of the garrison at Point Lookout is composed of Negroes.... A stubborn resistance, therefore, may not reasonably be expected." He was ready to devote to the enterprise the courage and dash of all Marylanders in his army. The greatest difficulty, he thought, was to find a suitable leader, as success in such a venture depended largely on the brains and pluck of the man who guided it. He asked the President if such a leader could be found; his own opinion was that General Bradley T. Johnson of Maryland was the best man in his acquaintance for the special work.[3]

Lee thought that Johnson could move easily through secessionist-sympathizing southern Maryland, living off the country. However, his route would be through Baltimore, and Baltimore was getting prepared. While General Early was en route from Lynchburg down the Shenandoah Valley, General Schenk, in control of the defenses of Baltimore, prohibited the sale of arms and ammunition without a military permit. Persons needed passes to go outside the city of Baltimore. The sum of $400,000 was appropriated for the defense of the city. About 1,000 black men worked on the fortifications.

On July 6, 1864, after serious delays on the Upper Potomac, Early was near Sharpsburg, Maryland. He was visited at his headquarters by Captain Robert E. Lee, son of the Commander of the Army of Northern Virginia, with orders from General Lee to dispatch Brigadier General Johnson to cut railroad and telegraph communications north from Baltimore and to proceed to Point Lookout, about 90 miles southeast of Washington, to coordinate with an amphibious assault to be made by John Taylor Wood.[4] Early himself described the matter as follows:

> On the 6th I received a letter from General Lee by special courier, informing me that, on the 12th, an effort would be made to release the prisoners at Point Lookout, and directing me to take steps to

unite them with my command, if the attempt was successful; but I was not informed of the manner in which the attempt would be made — General Lee stating that he was not, himself, advised of the particulars.[5]

Even though Early was almost 200 miles from Point Lookout at that time, with a short time frame in which to operate, he did not give the order to Brigadier General Johnson about the expedition he was to lead until two days later on the evening of July 8, 1864, which considerably narrowed the window of opportunity for Johnson.

That evening Johnson received the long-anticipated orders from Early directing him to march around Baltimore, burn the bridge on the railroads leading northward, and cut the telegraph wires. In circling the city he was to break up communications between Baltimore and Washington before moving on and attacking Point Lookout on July 12. Col John Taylor Wood, with marines and sailors, was to launch a coordinated assault from the water. Johnson was then to march fifteen-thousand odd newly freed prisoners to Bladensburg, where Early would be waiting, and cross the Potomac. If Early proceeded to capture Washington, he could arm the men from the capital's arsenals. The trek was 250 miles long and had to be made in three days and nights. Johnson told Early that he did not believe the condition of his horses would allow such an undertaking in the time allotted. Early ordered him to make the effort.[6]

Johnson told Early that the scheme gave him "four days, not ninety six hours to campaign nearly three hundred miles, not counting time lost to destroy bridges and railroads, but that [he] would do what was possible for men to do." Essentially, Johnson had too much to do and too little time to do it to accomplish the goal of freeing the prisoners at Point Lookout. First, he had to screen Early's advance on the Monocacy before undertaking the mission. As soon as Johnson was certain that Early's army was protected at Monocacy, he was to strike off toward Baltimore.[7] He had not only to destroy rail and telegraph communications between Washington, Baltimore and the North but also to procure transportation, including mounts for the prisoners he was seeking to release. The two-day delay in getting the orders and being able to start on the raid in light of all else that had to be done did not leave sufficient time for the execution of the plan.

The problem was that Union forces still held Frederick on June 8, 1864, and Johnson was involved in attacking them. The failure to seize Frederick on the 7th had delayed Early's duty to move on both Monocacy Junction and Point Lookout.

Had Johnson been given the Point Lookout orders earlier and been able to timely attack Frederick on the 7th, he could have more timely sought to undertake the Point Lookout raid and could have potentially played havoc with the railroads carrying Rickett's 6th Corps veterans to Wallace on the Monocacy on July 8, which troops were critical to Wallace's delaying Early on his move toward Washington. Regardless, Johnson's force achieved remarkable success before being recalled from its mission on the way to Point Lookout. As it was, even with all of the difficulties involved in preparing for the operation, Johnson's cavalry raid around Baltimore in conjunction with Colonel Harry Gilmor was one of the most spectacular of the war.

Early on the morning of July 9, 1864, Johnson, with his brigade of cavalry and a battery of horse artillery, moved north of Frederick. Johnson described his cavalry command as being about 800 half-armed and badly disciplined mountaineers from southwestern Virginia. These men were brave, fearless and undisciplined, unwilling to be controlled by orders. Regardless, these men were determined and capable.

Johnson's orders were to strike the railroads from Baltimore to Harrisburg and Philadelphia. He was also to cut the rail lines between Baltimore and Washington and to burn the bridge over the Gunpowder River before moving on to Point Lookout.[8]

His brigade quickly moved to Liberty, New Windsor and Westminster toward Reisterstown.[9] All the good and serviceable horses in that part of Maryland were hurried away to places of safety, particularly in the New Windsor area, where the Confederates spent the night of July 9, 1864.[10]

Colonel Harry Gilmor was to take his cavalry force, numbering about 175 men from the 1st and 2nd Maryland Cavalry, to Westminster and Cockeysville near Baltimore and attack the North Central Railroad. Johnson at New Windsor ordered Gilmor to take 20 men on fresh horses and cut the telegraph wires at Westminster on July 9, 1864.[11] There were about 150 Union soldiers at Westminster, which Gilmor proceeded to drive off toward Baltimore. Within a short period, he had seized the town, posted pickets, and cut the telegraph. Gilmor described the event as follows:

> It was near sunset where we approached and there learned there were one hundred and fifty men in the town.
> Trusting to their supposing we were well backed, we drew sabers, closed up the column, and charged through the town at a fast gallop, with horses well in hand, and on the look-out for ambuscade in the cross streets. A few blue-coats were to be seen and the boys gave them an awful yell when they saw them, which brought everyone to the doors and windows, and when a handkerchief was waived by a fair hand the yelling was louder than ever. The foe took two or three rapid looks, fired two or three shots, and then made for Baltimore.
> The telegraph was seized, the wires cut, and the town picketed in less than fifteen minutes, and I shook hands with my friends, lots of whom I have there.[12]

On July 10, 1864, Gilmor with about 175 men from the 1st and 2nd Maryland Cavalry was again detached from the main body of Johnson's troopers and ordered to raid the Philadelphia, Wilmington & Baltimore Railroad and fire the Gunpowder River bridge.[13]

Gilmor took possession of the railroad at Cockeysville on July 10, 1864, burned a bridge over the Gunpowder River and established pickets within fifteen miles of Baltimore. He destroyed another bridge over the Gunpowder in the direction of Towsontown as well. Gilmor said:

> I had also sent a flag of truce to the drawbridge where two hundred infantry and the gunboat Juniata, sat to protect it, demanding a surrender, and was about ordering some sharpshooters to push them a little, when the second train of twelve passenger-cars came up and was easily captured. The engineer of this also escaped, but I took the engine in hand, ran it up to the station, and unloaded it in the manner of the first (allowing each passenger to have his baggage).... While the train was being unloaded I kept up a good head of steam on the engine, and, when everything was clear, ordered Captain Baily [sic] to move up his sharpshooters, and try to drive the infantry out of the bridge. He soon reported that they had fled to the gun-boat, and setting the train on fire, I backed the whole flaming mass down on the bridge, catching some of the infantry a little way from shore upon the structure, and compelling them to jump into the water. The train was running slowly, and stopped right on the draw, where it burned and fell through communicating the fire and destroying the most important part of the bridge.[14]

Brigadier General Johnson burned the rest of the railroad bridges on July 10. His forces occupied Towsontown, Westminster and Reisterstown and tore up the North Central track at Cockeysville.[15] This action was part of Johnson's tripartite strategy of cutting communications links with Washington, Baltimore and the North, cutting rail links and moving to free the prisoners at Point Lookout.

The *Baltimore Sun* of July 11, 1864, reported what was occurring on July 10, covering both Johnson's and Gilmor's actions:

> Yesterday A.M. a force of Confederate cavalry moved around Westminster and Union Bridge on the Western Maryland Railroad. They continued their advance and during the day reached the Relay House of the North Central Railroad. They destroyed the bridge over the Gunpowder River, the bridge just above Cockeysville. Cavalry roved the entire section.[16]

The USS *Juniata* under Ensign William J. Herring and Company F of the 159th Ohio militia under Lieutenant Robert Price failed to protect the Gunpowder River bridge at Magnolia

Station.[17] Colonel Gilmor planned to enter Baltimore on the 11th either by Charles Street or Falls Road and leave by the Franklin Turnpike. He found that a large force of Union militia had barricaded the streets in Baltimore and were waiting for him. At daylight on July 11, 1864, Gilmor and his forces cut the Bel Air and Harford roads and cut the telegraph. After losing Sergeant Fields to a fatal wound by a Union-sympathizing civilian, Gilmor moved on toward the railroad bridge where the Philadelphia, Wilmington & Baltimore Railroad crossed the Gunpowder River and captured Union major general William Franklin, who was on the train. Franklin, however, was able to escape.[18]

On July 11, 1864, Johnson's cavalry brigade went from Cockeysville through the Greenspring Valley to near Baltimore City. Johnson's troopers damaged the Baltimore & Ohio Railroad and telegraph wires near Woodstock.[19] A detachment of the 1st Maryland Cavalry under Lieutenant Blackstone on July 11, 1864, burned Maryland governor Augustus Bradford's summer home in retaliation for the burning of former Virginia governor John Letcher's home in Lexington, Virginia, in June 1864 by Union general David Hunter.[20] Baltimore was threatened.

COLONEL HARRY GILMOR, A CONFEDERATE RAIDER LEADING PART OF THE ATTACK ON BALTIMORE AREA (LIBRARY OF CONGRESS).

However, in spite of the difficult time consideration, both Johnson and Gilmor had spent time during the raid visiting with friends, which had somewhat delayed their progress. That night Johnson rested his command for a few hours at the home of John N. Carroll.[21] He used the Rossborough Inn near the Maryland Agricultural Station as a headquarters.

The plan called for Johnson to be at Point Lookout, more than sixty miles distant, on the morning of July 12. Johnson was a day behind the schedule needed to get to Point Lookout. He had previously passed Beltsville, damaging the railroad there before heading his forces for Upper Marlboro. Johnson drove off a large force of Union cavalry at Beltsville and destroyed the railroad and telegraph lines. Several hundred mules were also captured to serve as mounts for the prisoners from Point Lookout.[22] Seven railroad cars and other government property were burned by the Confederates. They also burned twelve gondolas and eleven ballast cars and cut down the telegraph poles.

About midnight on the 11th, Confederate scouts reported to Johnson that 6th and 19th Corps veterans were en route to Washington. Johnson sent an officer and five men to report the news to Early. Going toward Point Lookout, Johnson was on the road to Upper Marlboro when a scout from Early reached him and directed him to abandon his effort and rejoin Early's main force.

Johnson described the events this way:

> It was now the morning of Tuesday, the 12th. I was due that night at Point Lookout, the extreme southeast point of Maryland, in St. Mary's County. It was physically impossible for men to make the ride in the time designated. I determined, however, to come as near as possible. I sent an officer with a detachment to ride at speed through the country, impressing fresh horses all the way, and to inform

Railroad bridge over Gunpowder River (circa 1869), destroyed in Gilmor's raid (Library of Congress).

the people along the route that I was coming. They were unanimously my friends, and I requested them to have their horses on the roadside so I could exchange my broken-down animals for their fresh ones, and thus borrow them for the occasion. During the proceeding day I had been taking horses by flankers on each side of my column and kept a supply of fresh ones at the rear of each regiment. As soon as a man's horse broke down he fell on a fresh horse, left his old one and resumed his place. By this means I was enabled to march at a trot which with a cavalry column is impossible for any length of time without breaking down horses, and broken-down horses speedily break down men. With fresh horses, however, I hoped to make a rapid march and get to Point Lookout early on the morning of the 13th. After returning from the pursuit of Wilson's cavalry, I turned the head of the column to Upper Marlboro and had proceeded only a short time when I was overtaken by a courier from General Early. He brought me orders to report at once to the headquarters at Silver Springs, on the Seventh Street Road. I moved down the Washington Road to the Agricultural College and thence along the line of the Federal pickets, marching all night, occasionally driving in a picket and expecting at any moment to be fired upon from with [sic] works, within range of which I was moving. I reported to General Early after midnight and found the whole army in retreat.[23]

Johnson later learned that information about the plan was in the Richmond newspapers, eliminating the element of surprise. On July 10, 1864, Colonel/Commander John Taylor Wood had moved down the Cape Fear River from Wilmington carrying several field pieces, thousands of weapons and a detachment of Confederate marines under General G.W. Custis Lee. The expedition was called off on the 11th by Confederate president Jefferson Davis, as word had gotten out of the expedition.

Meanwhile Gilmor proceeded with further actions in the Baltimore area before rejoining Johnson's command at Poolesville. Johnson was extensively involved in rearguard actions at Rockville, protecting the Confederate army as it withdrew from Washington.[24]

> At sunrise we were all in the saddle, moving toward Rockville, where I expected to join General Early, Captain O — acting as our pilot, for he knew the country thoroughly. Toward evening we learned that Early had fallen back to Poolesville, and that the enemy had possession of Rockville. This obliged us to take a direct course through Montgomery County for Poolesville, marching all night without halting.[25]

After all the damage that had been caused and with Union forces alerted, Johnson still managed to take his command across the whole northeast front of Washington's defenses unscathed to reach Early's army.[26]

Johnson's daring and well-executed raid raised havoc in the area around Baltimore. The disruption of rail and telegraph communications between Washington and Baltimore was substantial. So were the disruptions between Baltimore and the North. The Point Lookout aspect of Lee's plan could have succeeded under more favorable circumstances. With earlier communication of it to Johnson and an earlier start, it could have succeeded even without the amphibious assault by John Taylor Wood and General G.W. Custis Lee.

CHAPTER 22

Wallace's Retreat to Baltimore Aids Early's Advance on Washington

Brigadier General Martin Hardin, who was instrumental in protecting the northern defenses of Washington against Early's attack, noted that it was anticipated that Lew Wallace, if defeated, would fall back toward Washington to strengthen the defenses there.

> It was expected that Wallace would, if defeated, retreat in the direction of Washington, so that the remnant of his army could then be used to strengthen the garrison of that city. When, on the morning of the 10th, the authorities in Washington heard that Wallace had not only been defeated, but that he had retreated in the direction of Baltimore, and had left the roads to Washington clear for Early, they became, to put it mildly, somewhat alarmed.[1]

Wallace had ordered a retreat toward Baltimore after the Battle of the Monocacy on the evening of July 9, 1864.[2] When Major General Lew Wallace was forced to retreat from the battlefield at the Monocacy, Lieutenant Colonel David Clendenin with three companies of the 8th Illinois Cavalry fell back through Urbanna. The 1,000-man 17th Virginia Cavalry was hotly pursuing them. However, the Confederate force lost their battle flag and standard bearer in the fight. The 8th Illinois skirmished in small squads in effectively covering the movement of Wallace's army from the field. Clendenin was able to join General Wallace's forces at New Market. From that time until they arrived at Baltimore, the 8th Illinois Cavalry operated as a rear guard during the day and picketed in front of the troops at night. Screened by Lieutenant Colonel David Clendennin's 8th Illinois Cavalry as well as members of the 159th Ohio mounted infantry and Sixth Corp Veterans from the 67th Pennsylvania, 5th Maryland and 122nd Ohio who did not get to the Battle of the Monocacy, Wallace retreated through New Market, Mount Airy and Cookesville, on the National Road to Ellicott's Mills toward Baltimore. He got to a point about 12 miles from New Market on the night of July 9, 1864.

John Garrett, president of the Baltimore and Ohio Railroad, had dispatched three additional locomotives and ninety empty rail cars to Ellicott's Mills to assist in getting the troops and wounded of Wallace's army off the battlefield. In his first action report after the battle, Wallace conceded he had failed in his objective at the Monocacy to block the road to Washington.[3]

When Major General Lew Wallace retreated north from the Monocacy battlefield to the Baltimore Pike and moved off to the east, he had not received indication from Early's movements that he was going to be marching toward Baltimore or would be threatening that city. Rather, the clear line of march for Early's army was going toward Washington, about 35 miles away. Even if Wallace's army was not in a position to engage Early after the hard fight at the Monocacy on July 9, Wallace could have posed a considerable danger to Early's communications, supply line and rear guard. Had he suggested that option to General Henry Halleck rather than defending the city he moved to defend, Baltimore, by de facto having moved to do that before Halleck's orders confirmed it, Halleck's response might have been different.

22. Wallace's Retreat to Baltimore Aids Early's Advance on Washington

In the aftermath of Monocacy, it was not at all clear that the defenses of Washington would be able to withstand an attack by Early's veteran force. Wallace has received substantial credit for saving Washington at Monocacy. It came close to not having been, with Early's getting to Washington hours before the 6th and 19th Corps troops arrived.

Neither Halleck nor Wallace have explained why Wallace's force was not expected to continue to defend the national capital after Monocacy. In fact, Brigadier General Martin Hardin has written of the surprise in Washington that Wallace had moved off to Baltimore rather than to Washington. One of Ricketts's brigades was at Monrovia — to the consternation of Ricketts. Wallace reported that these troops joined his retreating army at New Market. So, there were fresh troops that could have been used.[4] Regardless, there was a fully open path for Early to move on Washington.

Wallace's anticipation of the Confederates' attempting to cut him off at New Market proved unfounded, as he discussed in his report:

> To have at my column off at New Market, the rebels had only to move their cavalry round my right by way of Urbanna and Monrovia; suspecting such was his plan, I used the utmost expedition to pass the command beyond that point. The danger proved imaginary. The reinforcement, for which I waited so anxiously the last two hours of the engagement, reaching Monrovia in good time to have joined me, halted there — a singular proceeding for which no explanation has yet been forwarded to me....
>
> The three regiments in Monrovia joined me at New Market, and afterward served a good purpose in covering the right of the weary column, which bivouacked for the night about twelve miles from the battlefield.[5]

Wallace, in his report to Colonel E.D. Townsend, assistant adjutant general, stated categorically that it was his intention to march from the Monocacy directly to Baltimore apparently from the outset and well before Halleck's order much later that night. Why he chose initially not to move off to defend Washington is unexplained, as Early stayed by the Monocacy battlefield the night of the 9th and Wallace was on the march. So he would have had a head start.

> My intention upon leaving the battlefield was to march directly to Baltimore, which by the concentration at Monocacy, had been left almost defenseless. Had this purpose been carried out, they would have reached the city on the evening of the 10th in time to have driven off the marauders who, under Johnson, had moved from Frederick City and taken position in the vicinity of Cockeysville. Such a result would very probably have saved the bridges on the Philadelphia railroad. But under an order received *en route* to Ellicott's Mills, directing me to "rally my forces and make every effort to retard the enemy's march on Baltimore," I thought it my duty to halt Rickett's division with cavalry and a battery at the Mills, that being the first point on the pike at which it was possible to resupply the men with rations and ammunition.[6]

Chief of Staff Henry Halleck received a message from Wallace about 11:40 P.M. on the night of July 9, 1864, advising him of the defeat at the Monocacy and his retreat toward Baltimore.[7] Wallace halted by Brigadier General James B. Ricketts's brigade at Ellicott's Mills on the night of the 9th, where they could receive rations and be resupplied with ammunition. They were still in a position to have moved toward Washington and into Early's rear on the 10th had Wallace sought to do so. He did not. Thus, when it became certain that Early was moving to Washington, Wallace ordered Ricketts to proceed to Baltimore. The rest of Wallace's forces did as well. Alexander's Battery of the Baltimore Light Artillery moved to Baltimore on the morning of July 10, 1864, for ammunition and supplies. Captain Edward H. Leib of the 5th U.S. Cavalry, after helping to cover the rear of the retreating Union forces and skirmishing with Confederate cavalry, went to Baltimore on July 11 and was ordered to go to Camp Carroll. The 1st Maryland Potomac Home Brigade companies G, C, G, H and K went to Fort Worthington in Baltimore on July 10.[8] This was after Halleck had advised Wallace to retard the enemy's march toward Baltimore when it was evident that there was no enemy march toward Baltimore.[9]

Nor was Brigadier General Bradley T. Johnson's raid around Baltimore the claimed basis for the move of Wallace's army. Wallace's cavalry was not sent to deal with Johnson and Gilmor but was used to protect the rear of Wallace's army when there was no Confederate pursuit except initial pursuit from the battlefield on the night of the 9th. Early was getting his supplies and wagons across the Monocacy on the night of the 9th and did not pursue Wallace — suggesting he was heading for Washington.

Wallace was not directed to himself move toward Washington or to dispatch Ricketts's division there or even Colonel J.F. Stanton's brigade, which was not involved in the fighting. Wallace still had a formidable force that he could either have moved toward Washington parallel to Early or have put in a position to attack his rear. He did neither. Nor did he promptly proceed to Baltimore to protect it against Johnson because of Halleck's order. Wallace's actions in not falling back toward Washington and further delaying Early certainly opened the way for Early to attack Washington.

Wallace was supplanted as commander of the Middle Department and the 8th Corps by General Orders 228 by General E.O.C. Ord. This was done on July 11, 1864.[10]

Although Halleck had told Wallace to retard the Confederate march on Baltimore, it was only done after Wallace had moved his army in that direction. Falling back on the road to Washington would have exposed Wallace to substantial losses, but it also would have aided substantially in the defense of the city, which was Wallace's objective. Wallace's failure to retreat toward Washington, before communications from Halleck, gave Early one last opportunity to seize Washington under Lee's daring initiative.

CHAPTER 23

Hot Weather Slows Early's Move on Washington

The 2nd Corps in 1864 as it marched under Early was not the same as the troops that had served under Stonewall Jackson in his Valley Campaign of 1862. In the Overland Campaign of May and early June of 1864, generals Leroy Stafford, J.M. Jones, George Doles and Junius Daniel had been killed and generals R.D. Johnston, Harry Thompson Hays, J.A. Walker and John Pegram had been seriously wounded.[1]

Harry Thompson Hays's Louisiana brigade, now commanded by Colonel W.R. Peck, contained fragments of the 5th Louisiana, 6th Louisiana, 7th Louisiana, 8th Louisiana and 9th Louisiana regiments. Leroy Stafford's old brigade, now under command of Colonel Waggoner, consisted of fragments of the 1st Louisiana, 2nd Louisiana, 10th Louisiana, 14th Louisiana and 15th Louisiana.[2]

Stonewall Jackson's 1st brigade or the "Stonewall" brigade contained the 2nd Virginia, 4th Virginia, 5th Virginia, 27th Virginia and 33rd Virginia. Jones's old brigade, now under the command of Colonel R.H. Dugan, was composed of the 21st Virginia, 25th Virginia, 42nd Virginia, 44th Virginia, 48th Virginia and 50th Virginia.[3] Brigadier General Clement A. Evans's Georgia Brigade in Gordon's Division was made up of fragments of seven regiments. Thus, going into the long march to Washington and ultimately Point Lookout, the forces under Early in 1864 were a mere shadow of what they had been before the hard fights in between, including the recent five-week Overland Campaign culminating with Cold Harbor.[4] The hot weather would further tax these troops.

These men had been through almost five weeks of unremitting, hard fighting at the Wilderness, Spottsylvania, the North Ana and Cold Harbor. The commander of Jackson's old division, Edward "Allegheny" Johnson, was captured at the Mule Shoe Salient at Spottsylvania as were several thousand of his men.[5] Thus Early was not leading fresh troops in the execution of Lee's plan but men who had been under the stress of battle for a very long time under difficult circumstances.

At the time of Early's march on Washington and Point Lookout in July 1864, Washington was suffering one of the longest spells of hot weather in its history. There were 47 straight days without rain. Each day of July 1864 before Early's appearance before Fort Stevens, the temperature had been in the 90s.[6]

After they had left Gaines Mill, Early's troops had marched 80 miles to Charlottesville from June 13 through June 16.[7] Early's men then fought in the Battle of Lynchburg on June 17 and 18, 1864.[8] Thereafter, Early's troops chased Hunter's retreating forces for several days of hard pursuit before marching north. Colonel David Hunter Strother, General David Hunter's chief of staff, recorded in his diary on June 16, 1864, as the Union troops were approaching Lynchburg, that the day was very hot. Early's men should have experienced similar conditions.[9] Early put it this way:

My command had march[ed] sixty miles in three days pursuit, over very rough roads, and that part of it from the Army of Northern Virginia had had no rest since leaving Gaines Mill.[10]

As Early's troops were marching down the Shenandoah Valley, Grant, Meade, and Lee at Richmond had all mentioned the heat as being a major reason that there was little military activity in that theater then. Grant had told Meade that while the excessive heat continued he would try to give his troops what rest he could.[11]

At Staunton, in late June, it was reported that there had not been any rain in 23 days.[12] The night in Washington was reported to be warm on June 29 as the heat wave continued.[13] Again, the march from Winchester to Leetown of over 20 miles on July 3 was described by Ramseur's men as oppressively hot.[14] Ramseur had been unable to provide assistance to Bradley Johnson's cavalry, which had been held up for hours at Leetown by Colonel James Mulligan. Obviously, the heat was a contributing factor.[15] The weather was hot and dry. Early did not push his men as they went into Maryland.

On July 6, 1864, Early was in an orchard at Sharpsburg, where he was stated to have been mapping his future plans on a hot afternoon.[16] July 7 was reported as a hot day in Frederick.[17] As Captain Robert Park of the 12th Alabama of Rodes's Division noted in his diary for July 8, as he was on the march toward Frederick, "the Sun was very hot indeed to-day, and marching very uncomfortable."[18] Early's army camped at Monocacy on the 9th after the battle and tried to sleep in spite of the heat.

John Worsham of the 21st Virginia found July 10, as Early's army was marching from the Monocacy toward Rockville and Washington, to have been terribly hot. There was a great deal of straggling among the men. Heat prostration felled hundreds.[19] The weekend of July 9 and 10 was described to be one of severe summer heat and high humidity.[20] On July 11, 1864, Lieutenant General Jubal A. Early stated, "The previous day had been very warm, and the roads were exceedingly dusty, as there had been no rain for several weeks. The heat during the nights had been very oppressive. This day was an exceedingly hot one, and there was no air stirring. While marching, our men were enveloped in a suffocating cloud of dust, and many of them fell by the way from exhaustion. Our progress was therefore very much impeded, but I pushed on as rapidly as possible."[21] The thermometer was in the mid–90s, debilitating both Union and Confederate forces.[22] The temperature was 94° F at the W.H. Farquhar Farm near Sandy Spring, Maryland.[23]

Early estimated that he had only about a third of his force available at Fort Stevens at noon on July 11:

> Of those remaining a very large number were greatly exhausted by the last two days marching, some having fallen by sunstroke, and I was satisfied, when we arrived in front of the fortifications, that not more than one-third of my force could have been called into action.[24]

Thus the exceedingly hot and humid weather had seriously affected the fighting ability of Early's men trying to get up to Washington while it was still lightly defended. This compounded the problems of the previous delays on the Upper Potomac and before Frederick, which had already cost Early significant time in the execution of Lee's gamble.

The eminent Civil War historian Benjamin Franklin Cooling, in *Jubal Early's Raid on Washington: 1864*, stated, "Given their condition by the hot July of 1864, perhaps the presence of their beloved Jackson might not have made much difference, despite the lackluster performance of their opponents."[25]

Certainly it can be argued that Jackson's presence would have made a difference. Regardless, the heat was definitely a factor affecting Early's army from the time it left Gaines Mill until it arrived before Washington. In spite of the difficult circumstances, Early's army had come a long way, fighting at Leetown, Maryland Heights, in the area west of Frederick and on the Monocacy.

However, the almost three days lost at Martinsburg, Harpers Ferry and west of Frederick magnified the problem of the weather as he struggled to get to Washington. In the end, the heat was one of many factors that caused Lee's gamble to fail under the circumstances of its execution.

CHAPTER 24

Early Loses Opportunity to Enter Washington at Fort Stevens

After the Battle of the Monocacy on July 9, 1864, Jubal Early's soldiers moved out at dawn on July 10. Brigadier General John McCausland's cavalry led the advance of the mile-long column of Early's army, traveling in 90-degree-plus heat and raising enormous clouds of dust. Major William Fry of the 16th Pennsylvania Cavalry had gathered about 500 horsemen from various units at the Giesboro Depot in Washington and had gone out to Rockville northwest of Washington to check on Early's advance, where he was joined by a squad of the 8th Illinois Cavalry. Fry engaged McCausland's large cavalry force along the Rockville Pike, being gradually pushed back through Rockville. Fry's two lines were broken and he retired from his final stand on Viers Mill Road about a mile south of Rockville in the face of Confederate artillery.[1]

The concern in Washington posed by this troop movement was substantial. Halleck had telegraphed Grant, "What you say about getting into Early's rear is perfectly correct, but unfortunately we have no forces here for the field. All such forces were sent to you long ago. What we have here are raw militia, invalids, convalescents from the hospitals, a few dismounted batteries, and the dismounted and disorganized cavalry sent up from the James River. With these we expect to defend our immense depots of stores and the line of entrenchments around the city; but what can we do with such forces in the field against a column of 20,000 veterans? One-half of the men cannot march at all. The only men fit for the field was Ricketts's division, which has been defeated and badly cut up under Wallace."[2]

At about 4:00 P.M. on July 10, 1864, Fry sent a message to Major General Christopher Augur, commanding the 22nd Corps at Washington, warning him to strongly guard the forts in the Tennallytown area. McCausland proceeded down the Georgetown Pike and River Road approaching Tennallytown, where the 100-pounder rifled cannon at Forts Reno and Bayard opened up. McCausland reported to Early that the hilltop fortifications near Tennallytown were impregnable.

Early himself spend the night of July 10 at Gaithersburg and passed through Rockville on the morning of the 11th. After receiving McCausland's report, Early avoided Tennallytown and marched eastward onto Viers Mill Road and later the Seventh Street Road toward Silver Spring — adding considerable distance, 10 to 12 miles, to the route to reach Washington. His lead division arrived at Fort Stevens in the center of the Union northern defenses about noon on July 11, although skirmishing had begun along the Seventh Street Road around 11:00 A.M.

On the morning of July 11, 1864, the oppressive heat and dust from the march caused a substantial number of men from Early's force to fall out. John Worsham of the 21st Virginia described Gordon's division as stretched out like skirmishers due to the oppressive conditions. Isaac Bradwell of the 31st Georgia noted that shelling by badly trained and frightened militia occurred when they were several miles from Washington. Bradwell found little opposition, but Early only wanted to make a demonstration and did not order an assault on the works.

Some Confederate troops on the march as they approached over a mile from Fort Stevens straggled at the Silver Spring mansion of Francis Preston Blair, Sr. There they found two hogsheads of rum, which they dug up in the front yard, where Blair's son-in-law, Admiral Samuel Phillips Lee, had hidden them. The mansion was ransacked as was the nearby Falklands mansion of Postmaster General Montgomery Blair, until guards were ordered placed by general officers who later arrived.

Picket posts had been established in advance of the Union lines at Fort Stevens, which were manned by men of the 150th Ohio, a national guard regiment made up of men from Oberlin College. A command post under Sergeant George R. Fackler was set up on the Seventh Street Road. A three-man post was set up in front of Fort Stevens where the Piney Branch Road left the Seventh Street Road. Another post had been set up on a hill about a mile in front of Fort Stevens.

The Confederate advance of men in General Robert Rodes's division drove in the Union pickets. The 62nd Virginia Mounted Infantry of Smith's Brigade under Colonel George Smith approached Fort Stevens in column and then moved out to the right and left to probe the defenses of Fort Stevens. Sharpshooters took up positions in the Carberry and Rives farmhouses nearby.

I.G. Bradwell of the 31st Georgia described the situation as Gordon's division came up next to Rodes's men in front of Fort Stevens on July 11: "To our astonishment and regret, when we were formed for battle the order to advance did not come. We expected to move forward immediately and drive the few frightened defenders out of the works, enter the city, capture Lincoln, and demand of him peace and more humane treatment for the helpless prisoners in the hands of the government. General Gordon ordered up a battery of twenty pound rifled funs to approach the works and reply to the heavy guns where were firing so awkwardly. The artillery men took position about five hundred yards from the enemy and began a very accurate fire."[3]

FORT STEVENS, FOCAL POINT OF EARLY'S ATTACK (NATIONAL ARCHIVES).

The garrison at Fort Stevens on the morning of July 11, 1864, when the Confederates arrived, consisted of 209 men from the 150th Ohio National Guard, the 13th Michigan Battery under Captain Charles DuPont, and the 25th New York Cavalry. In addition there were 500 or 600 men in the rifle pits, many of whom were inexperienced. Early himself recognized that the defenses were feebly manned.[4]

Brigadier General Martin Hardin, the courageous one-armed commander of a critical part of the northern defenses of Washington facing Early, noted there were 23 hours for Early to attack between the time of McCausland's advance on Fort Reno and the arrival of the first troops of the 6th Corps at Fort Stevens around 3:00 P.M. on July 11. He did not do so.

> The official reports of the officers in immediate command at the time show that the Rebel advance arrived in front of Fort Reno at 4 P.M. on Sunday (the 10th), and that the advance of the Sixth Corps arrived in the rear of Fort Stevens after 3 P.M. on Monday (the 11th). Thus there were, at least, twenty-three hours of opportunity thrown away by the Confederate commander.[5]

Confederate cavalryman John N. Opie felt a rebel yell and a charge could have taken Washington when the Confederate forces arrived. He also thought that General Early was about the only one in the army that thought such an attack was not possible to accomplish.[6]

Lieutenant General Jubal A. Early described what Rodes's men had found before them in front of Fort Stevens:

> Rodes' skirmishers were thrown to the front, driving those of the enemy to the cover of the works, and we proceeded to examine the fortifications to ascertain if it was practicable to carry them by

BRIG. GEN. HARDIN'S HEADQUARTERS, NORTHERN DEFENSES OF WASHINGTON (LIBRARY OF CONGRESS).

assault. They were exceedingly strong, and consisted of what appeared to be enclosed forts of heavy artillery, with tiers of lower works in front of each pierced for an enormous number of guns, the whole being connected by curtains with ditches in front and strengthened by palisades and abattis. The timber had been filled with cannon all around and left on the ground, making a formidable obstacle, and every possible approach was raked by artillery. On the right was Rock Creek running through a deep ravine which had been made impassable by the felling of timber on each side, and beyond were woods and the Georgetown Pike which had been reported to be the strongest of all. On the left, as far as the eye could reach, the works appeared to be of the same impregnable character.[7]

Early also felt that the marching and the hard fighting had broken down many of the men of his command. He had estimated that only a third of the men in his force could have been put into action in front of Fort Stevens.[8]

Early's assessment of the feasibility of an attack on the 11th when his forces came up before Fort Stevens was shared by some of the officers of his command. Major Henry Kyd Douglas of the "Stonewall" Brigade noted, "It has been said that if Early had moved more rapidly and assaulted at once (presuming, I suppose, that his men were all centaurs) he might have gone into Washington. I do not believe it. If he had I am sure he would never have gotten out again. In fact, I am satisfied neither he nor any officer with him expected to take Washington."[9]

Brigadier General Armistead Long, Early's chief of artillery, found "The want of appreciation is entirely due to the erroneous opinion that the city of Washington should have been taken; but this may be passed over as one of the absurdities of the public criticism of the conduct of the war."[9] He credited Early with marching over 400 miles in a month, dispatching two Union armies and creating an important diversion.

About 600 dismounted cavalrymen under Major George Briggs of the 7th Michigan Cavalry joined the men in the rifle pits about 1:30 P.M. on the 11th. These men were able to drive back the Confederates to a line about 1,100 yards from Fort Stevens.

The concern in Washington at the Confederates' approach had been described by L.E. Chittenden, registrar of the Treasury. He had breakfasted the morning of July 11, 1864, at Willard's Hotel in the company of three army officers, including an officer of the Veteran Reserves. At the invitation of that officer, Chittenden had left Fifteenth Street opposite the Treasury and had proceeded through Georgetown to Tennallytown. The officer of the Veteran Reserves had thought that Early would have attacked that morning. Chittenden could see the Confederate approach from Tennallytown. Upon returning to the Treasury, he found the treasurer, his cashier and four principal clerks filling empty canvas mail sacks with Treasury notes and other securities. The men were working hard. A small steamboat had been secured by the treasurer to carry off the money and securities as needed.[10] Assistant Secretary of the Navy Fox had also ordered a steamboat be readied in case the speedy removal of the president became necessary. Because of earlier delays and dilatoriness, the window of opportunity on July 11 was roughly from noon to 3:00 P.M. This was crucial because President Lincoln was a spectator at Fort Stevens and was subject to being killed or captured, according to his personal secretary. President Lincoln had left the fort on the 11th before Wright's 6th Corps veterans got there.[11] Also, that window of opportunity provided enough time to raise havoc in the city and seriously damage the Union politically.

New York correspondent Sylvanus Cadwallader wondered at Early's inaction. He stated that the Union line could have been carried at any point with the loss of perhaps 100 men.[12] Major General John B. Gordon, one of Early's division commanders, said as well that the Union works could have easily been entered:

> It has been claimed that at the time we reached these outer works they were fully manned by troops. This is a mistake. I myself rode to a point on those breastworks at which there was no force whatsoever. The unprotected space was broad enough for the easy passage of Early's army without

RUINED HOUSE NEAR FORT STEVENS IN BATTLEFIELD AREA (LIBRARY OF CONGRESS).

resistance It is true that, as we approached, Rodes' division had driven in some skirmishers, and during the day (July 11th) another small affair had occurred on the Seventh Street road, but all the Federals encountered on this approach could not have manned any considerable portion of the defenses.[13]

Brigadier General McCausland, who was at Fort Reno on July 10, also claimed that Early was dilatory in bringing up his army and making the attack when there was opportunity to do so. Early himself had ridden forward and glimpsed the works and determined that they were not fully manned: "I rode ahead of the infantry, and arrived in sight of Fort Stevens on the road a short time after noon, when I discovered that the works were but feebly manned."[14]

Early's troops merely probed the skirmish line, getting within 110 yards of Fort Stevens with a brisk exchange of fire. At Nearby Fort Lincoln, Admiral Goldsborough commanded Navy Yard men in the lines.[15] The troops of Robert Rodes's division drove in the Union skirmishers but found the works exceedingly strong with reconnaissance consuming the balance of July 11.[16] Henry E. Alvord, a soldier on the weak skirmish line facing Early, felt Washington was absolutely at his mercy for a period of time and that taking the city even for more than a day would have had tremendous adverse consequences for the Union:

> On Sunday, July 10th, I rejoined my regiment and being on that thin and weak skirmish line of Union cavalry, stretching across the Seventh Street Road to Tennallytown and beyond,—seing the overpowering force of the enemy in front—knowing that no veteran reinforcements of consequence had arrived, and that there was little but raw militia and a demoralized populace in our rear,—I felt then,—as I do still,—that for the greater part of two days the city of Washington was absolutely at the mercy of the Confederates. It is manifest that Early could not have held the city for more than a day, and that he might have lost a large part of his command, this he well understood, for he was fully informed of the situation. But occupation for that brief period of time would have accomplished much. There can be little doubt that had the attacking party been led by a bolder and more vigorous general,—such an [sic] one as "Stonewall" Jackson, Job [sic] Pickett or "Jeb" Stuart,—President Lincoln and his cabinet would have been forced to leave the Capital, the Federal buildings and archives would have been destroyed, as well as enormous depots of military stores, and considering the critical political condition of the country at that time, who can tell what would have been the effect upon the destiny of the Nation? But Jubal Early made no earnest attack.[17]

REAR ADMIRAL LOUIS GOLDBOROUGH COMMANDED MEN FROM THE NAVY IN LINE AT FORT LINCOLN (LIBRARY OF CONGRESS).

Another Union soldier, Francis C. Adams, stated: "Washington was in danger, and Washington might have been captured with little trouble had the enemy sent the right man to command his troops."[18] Adams went on to say that the Confederates could have entered the city and enforced its surrender but that General Early was not the man for that enterprise. Washington was at his mercy, but he did not know it. Even if he had known, Adams felt he lacked the ability to seize the opportunity.[19] Brigadier General Martin Hardin, who was a brigade commander in the defense of Washington under Major General Alexander McD. McCook, also felt that the Confederate commander had contributed to the unsuccessful outcome for his forces: "At this late day one trembles at the thought of the position in which our little force was placed, and the responsibility which devolved upon it. I thank the God of battles that He was not on this occasion, 'on the side of the heavies battalions,' and that a 'Stonewall Jackson' was not in command of the splendid Army that faced us."[20]

Registrar of the Treasury L.E. Chittenden also concluded that Washington could have been attacked on the morning of July 11, 1864:

> He passed the night of the 10th within five miles of Washington. Presumptively, he could have attacked next morning, when a considerable of his force was at Silver Spring and above Georgetown, within two miles of the defences. His own statement of the positions of his force on the 11th is very indefinite. The first detachment of the Sixth Corps did not reach the defences until after four in the

afternoon. Had he made the attack on the morning of the 11th, he would have found the city in the condition supposed by General Lee when the campaign was projected. The Confederate army would have met with no resistance except from raw and undisciplined forces, which, in the opinion of General Grant, and it was supposed of General Lee also, would have been altogether inadequate to its defence. Its capture and possession for a day would have been disastrous for the cause of the Union. Early would have seized money in the Treasury, the archives of the departments, the immense supplies of clothing, arms, and ammunition in store; he would have compelled General Grant to raise the siege of Richmond; he would have destroyed uncounted millions in value of property, and he would have had the same opportunity to retreat of which he availed himself the next day.

But with his veterans behind the defences, he would have had no occasion to retreat. The released prisoners at Point Lookout in two days would have added 20,000 to the strength of his army. The Confederates in Maryland would have swarmed to his assistance, and he could certainly have held the capital long enough to give great Britain the excuse she so much desired, to recognize the Confederacy and break the blockage. After the danger had passed, when its magnitude became apparent, there was but one opinion among the friends of the Union. It was that we had escaped a loss of prestige and property, compared with which previous disasters would have been trifling, and probably a blow fatally destructive to the Union cause.[21]

Major General Alexander McD. McCook, commanding at Fort Stevens on July 11, noted that the Confederates on retiring had taken possession of a house on the right of the Seventh Street Road to Silver Spring which afforded excellent cover and was on an elevated piece of ground. There they posted sharpshooters as well as at a house on the left of that road. About thirty Union skirmishers were hit by sharpshooters on the afternoon of the 11th.

Assistant Secretary of War Charles Dana criticized General McCook for allowing the Confederate sharpshooters to pick off men at the embrasures of Fort Stevens.[22]

General Horatio G. Wright's advance of his 6th Corps troops arrived at Fort Stevens around 3 P.M. on July 11, 1864. A portion of the 19th Corps veterans also arrived on the afternoon of July 11.[23] Gillmore was assigned to command part of the northeast defenses of Washington. The arrival of the veteran troops sealed off Early's opportunity to take and burn Washington. After the 6th and 19th Corps reinforcements arrived, Early was in no position to make an attack on the 12th. He then withdrew.

General Hardin, who performed a major role in the defense of Washington, felt that there were

MAJOR GENERAL ALEXANDER McD. McCOOK, COMMANDING AT FORT STEVENS (LIBRARY OF CONGRESS).

a number of factors, other than Early's dilatoriness and failure to make a determined attack, which contributed to the success of the defense. One key factor was the preventing of citizens from leaving Washington who could have provided Early with intelligence on the state of Washington's defenses. Others included the prompt formation and firm defense of the picket lines, putting up a bold front by the garrison and the firing of the guns of the forts freely as well and the prompt arrival of the 6th and 19th corps. "The causes of the successful defence (outside of Early's dilatoriness and his failure to make a determined attack) were: the forbidding of citizens to pass outside the lines; the prompt formation of a picket line, and the firm defence of the same; the formidable character and appearance of the fortifications, with the bold front put on by the little garrisons (the men were required to appear first in one part, then in another in the works, firing the large guns freely at every collection of the enemy); the extraordinary vigilance of the garrison, especially along East Branch; and, finally the opportune arrival of the Sixth and Nineteenth Corps."[24]

MAJOR GENERAL HORATIO G. WRIGHT COMMANDED THE 6TH CORPS AT FORT STEVENS (LIBRARY OF CONGRESS).

Early was an able officer who had come to the gates of Washington against all odds. His friend, John Warwick Daniel, had said, "The March of Early from Cold Harbor to Charlottesville, Lynchburg, Salem, Staunton, Winchester, across the Potomac and Monocacy, and through the South Mountain passes to Washington and back to Virginia between the 13th of June and 14th of July, a distance of 510 miles, an average of sixteen miles a day, is for length and rapidity, without parallel in our own or any modern war."[25]

The chance to enter Washington and change the course of the war would never come again. As when he was with Ewell at Gettysburg, he failed to act unequivocally. Had he been able to throw even the one-third of his forces he conceded were available to him at the defenses at Fort Stevens around noon on the 11th, the questions would no longer linger.

General Lee had been anxiously awaiting word from Early about the capture of Washington, according to Edward Pollard in *Lee and His Lieutenants*. He was disappointed in the failure of his lieutenant, Early, to fulfill his expectations, although views differ on that.

Early's retreat and the Valley Campaign of the fall of 1864 to follow would ultimately cause the diminution of Early's army to a mere skeleton force at Waynesboro. On March 30, 1865, he would be relieved of command.

Although the great opportunity had been missed in July 1864, General Lee persisted in his belief that Washington remained vulnerable to attack. In early August 1864, Lee responded to Grant's naming General Philip H. Sheridan to command the Union forces in the Shenandoah Valley by sending Major General Richard H. Anderson, with an independent command, to Culpepper. Anderson arrived in Culpepper on August 12 with Kershaw's division and a battalion of artillery. He was soon joined by Fitzhugh Lee's cavalry division. Anderson was directed by Lee to use whatever enterprise was available to injure the Union forces.[26] Although he ostensibly was to be of support to Early, which he was, he was still only 50 miles from Washington. Anderson had discretion to mount a threat there if he deemed it advisable. Anderson's recall to Richmond in the fall of 1864 closed this offensive option.

CHAPTER 25

Veteran Reserve Troops and Convalescing Officers Help Defend Washington

Wounded and convalescing officers in Washington at the time of Early's attack substantially assisted in the city's defense. Brigadier General Martin Hardin, who had sustained his fourth war wound on the North Ana and had already lost his arm, was recuperating in Washington at the time of Early's invasion of Maryland and attack on Washington. Hardin had served in the Peninsular Campaign, the Seven Days Battles, Groveton, Second Bull Run, Mine Run and the North Ana. He lost his arm after having been ambushed near Catlett's Station in the Bristoe and Mine Run campaigns and was wounded again on the North Ana. His father, Major General John J. Hardin, had been killed in action at Buena Vista in the Mexican War.[1]

On July 9, 1864, Hardin was named under Special Order 168 to head Haskin's brigade of the 22nd Corps—manning the defenses of Washington north of the Potomac.[2] Early was fighting on the Monocacy on July 9 and would be heading right for those northern defenses. The wounded and convalescing Hardin, a capable officer of undoubted courage, had the responsibility to hold the northern defensive line with a patchwork force.

Major General Alexander McD. McCook on July 11, 1864, at 12:30 A.M. telegraphed an order that Hardin was to command the line from Fort Sumner to Fort DeRussy.[3] Hardin was placed in a sector deemed crucial—where the road from Frederick passed to Tennallytown, a likely area of attack.[4] "He initially had one company of U.S. artillerists, five or six companies of light artillery and four companies of the 151st Ohio national guard to hold that sector."[5]

Also convalescing in Washington at the time of Early's attack was Colonel J.M. Warner of the 1st Vermont Heavy Artillery, who commanded the artillery companies under Hardin. Warner brought men up from river batteries and placed them in weak spots in the line between Forts Sumner and Reno on the northwest perimeter of the defenses of Washington.[6]

In addition to wounded and convalescing officers joining the ranks to defend the city in major command roles, there were many wounded men who did the same as part of Veteran Reserve regiments. The Invalid Corps, the forerunner of the Veteran Reserve Corps, had been formed by General Order 105 of the War Department dated April 28, 1863, to make good use of soldiers rendered unfit for active duty because of wounds or disease. Under General Order No. 105, the Invalid Corps was established to secure troops from the officers and enlisted men in the field who were unfit for duty on account of their wounds or disability incurred in the line of duty. Pursuant to Circular 13 of May 25, 1863, the acting assistant provost marshal of each state was directed to form a recruiting rendezvous in the immediate vicinity of headquarters for the recruitment of honorably discharged soldiers desiring to return for three years service or until the end of the war. Under Circular 14 of April 27, 1864, these veteran reserve troops were to be credited against the quota for their state. The Invalid Corps became the Veteran Reserve Corps under General Order 111 of March 18, 1864.[7] The men who were still able to hold a musket, perform guard duty or do some marching were made part of the 1st Battalion. Those who could not were part of the 2nd Battalion.

Seven Veteran Reserve regiments were involved in the defense of Washington when Early threatened the city in July 1864. Those were the 1st, 6th, 9th, 12th, 19th, 22nd and 24th Veteran Reserve regiments.[8] The 10th Veteran Reserve regiment was sent by rail to aid in the defense of Baltimore on July 10, 1864, one day before General Early's arrival in front of Fort Stevens and the northern defenses of Washington. Another regiment, the 18th Veteran Reserve regiment was sent from Washington to nearby Laurel, Maryland, to protect the Baltimore & Ohio Railroad coming from Annapolis to Washington.

The 1st Veteran Reserve Regiment had been organized at Washington, D.C., on October 10, 1863. The regiment had been formed by combining ten companies of the 1st Battalion of men who could carry a gun and engage in combat, being the 17th, 34th, 97th, 103rd, 113th, 114th, 142nd, 144th, 148th and 151st companies. These men had been involved in duties at the prisoner of war camp at Elmira, New York. They were also involved in the discharging of regiments at Rochester, New York, before returning to Washington. The men who served in the regiment during Early's attack remained in the defenses of Washington before being mustered out in the fall of 1865. These men dressed in the distinctive Veteran Reserve uniform.

Lieutenant John Worsham of the 21st Virginia in Rodes's Division in the forefront of Early's troops on July 11, 1864 thought the Veteran Reserve troops he saw were town or city militia, as the men looked like they were wearing linen dusters.[9] The men were actually wearing a regular uniform consisting of a forage cap, sky blue trousers, and a sky blue jersey with dark blue trimming like the jackets of the U.S. Cavalry.

Indeed, the men of the 1st Veteran Reserve Regiment as well as the other veteran reserve forces fighting in the defenses of Washington were anything but raw militia. Alfred Bellard of the 1st Veteran

BRIG. GEN. MARTIN HARDIN, CONVALESCING BRIGADIER, COMMANDED IN NORTHERN DEFENSES (UNITED STATES ARMY MILITARY HISTORY INSTITUTE).

Reserve Regiment had been in the 5th New Jersey and had been wounded in the leg at Chancellorsville in May 1863.

Private Bellard described the action involving the 1st Veteran Reserve Regiment at the time of Early's attack:

> On Sunday the 10th orders came to move, so with 35 rounds of blue pills {minie balls} in our cartridge boxes, and our knapsacks on our backs, we left camp at seven o'clock P.M. and forming the brigade on Pen. Ave. we marched through Georgetown and Tennallytown with our band playing and our colors flying. The streets being thronged with people to see us off. Reaching Fort Reno soon after, we halted, and the brigade was deployed out as skirmishers(about 3 feet between each man) in the rifle pits. Orders were given to keep awake and have an eye on the supposed rebels in front. We remained there all night, but as for being awake, I for one did not, for I had several cat naps during the night. Had the rebs made an attack on us that night, nothing could have saved it, as there was not troops around the city but our brigade, and we were supposed to be unfit for active service.[10]

The 1st Veteran Reserve Regiment was involved in action on July 12. Alfred Bellard described what occurred:

> Bellard's regiment went out on the skirmish line, as the rebels were now on our front, and the artillery had got to work. By this time the 6th and 19th corps from the army had arrived and went into action at Fort Stevens. Our line was on a range of hills that surrounded the city and was well fortified with earthwork forts, and with siege guns, the entire chain of forts connected by rifle pits. In the afternoon our Rgt. was ordered to relieve the 6th on the skirmish line. Advancing to the edge of the hill, we were deployed out as skirmishers with our company on the extreme left.... After we had scrambled over lots of brushwood, we finally reached our position on the crest of the hill, and saw the rebel skirmishers posted on an range of hills in front of us, but out of range so far as we were concerned, as we were armed with smooth bore muskets, while the rebels had long range rifles.[11]

The 6th Veteran Reserve Regiment was led in the defenses of Washington by Lieutenant Colonel F.S. Palmer. This regiment had also been organized on October 10, 1863, in Washington by consolidating ten companies of the 1st Battalion. Palmer had seen service with the 2nd Pennsylvania Heavy Artillery. He had been wounded at Chapin's Farm before the forming of the Veteran Reserves.[12] The colonel of the 6th Veteran Reserve Regiment was Moses Wiswell, who had previously been with the 28th New Jersey. During Early's attack, Wiswell was serving in a military government post in Washington and did not have line responsibilities.[13]

Another of the Veteran Reserve regiments to serve in the defenses of Washington during the time of Early's attack was the 9th Veteran Reserve Regiment.[14] It also had been organized at Washington in October 1863 by the consolidation of ten companies of the 1st Battalion to form the regiment.[15]

The regiment was commanded by Colonel George W. Gile. Gile had enlisted in the 38th Pennsylvania Volunteers as a major in 1861. He took over command of the regiment when the commanding officer was mortally wounded at Second Bull Run (Manassas). Gile was promoted to lieutenant colonel on September 1, 1862, to take over the regiment. He was severely wounded at Antietam sixteen days later and was discharged in March 1863 due to war wounds. He then entered the 9th Veteran Reserve and during the time of Early's attack exercised overall command of the veteran reserve forces in Washington. On May 5, 1865, Gile was brevetted a brigadier general.[16]

On July 10, 1864, the regiment was ordered to march on a moment's notice after Wallace's defeat at the Monocacy. The 9th Veteran Reserve Regiment was put into action in the lines at Fort Stevens.[17]

The 12th Veteran Reserve Regiment replaced a heavy artillery regiment in the defenses of Washington on May 12, 1864. The regiment was put in the line to the right of Fort Stevens running toward Fort Totten and was involved in meeting Early's advance.[18] Colonel Farnesworth

Troops of Ninth Veteran Reserve Regiment served in northern defenses of Washington (Library of Congress).

commanded the Regiment. First Lieutenant Robert Roberts, mustered in from the 4th New Jersey, served a regimental officer and the regiment's quartermaster.[19] The regiment was formed in Albany, New York, in October 1863. It served in action near Fort Stevens.[20]

The 19th Veteran Reserve Regiment had been raised on January 12, 1864, at Washington, D.C., by the consolidation of ten companies of the 1st Battalion. The regiment was commanded by Colonel O.V. Dayton, who was brevetted a brigadier general.[21]

The 24th Veteran Reserve Regiment was commanded by Major James W.H. Stickney, who had originally been a major in the 3rd New Jersey.[22] The regiment had been organized in February 1864 at Washington.[23]

An additional regiment, the 18th Veteran Reserve Regiment, had been sent from Washington to nearby Laurel, Maryland, to guard the railroad. The 18th had been organized in May 1864 in Washington and was led by Lieutenant Colonel Charles F. Johnson.[24] Johnson had served in the 81st Pennsylvania in the Army of the Potomac's 1st Brigade and had participated in the Seven Days Battles. At Charles City Crossroads leading his men against Stonewall Jackson's troops, he was shot four times.[25] The regiment had seen been sent to Port Royal, Virginia, on May 24, 1864, to guard prisoners and supplies. Johnson was named to head a 1,500-man provisional brigade there. After Wade Hampton had defeated Sheridan at Trevilian Station, he attacked White House Landing. Johnson's brigade, including the Veteran Reserves, had been in the rifle pits and participated in the defense.[26]

After having returned to Washington, the unit was transferred on July 10, 1864, to Laurel Station on the Baltimore & Ohio Railroad. Six companies of the 18th were guarding from Annapolis Junction to Washington.[27]

The six veteran reserve regiments were under the command of General Alexander McD. McCook. Convalescents under Lieutenant Henry Turner also helped garrison Fort Stevens.[28] Men of the 9th Veteran Reserve Regiment served in the rifle pits to the left of Fort Stevens toward Fort DeRussy as of 7:00 A.M. on the 11th. Men of the 12th Veteran Reserve Regiment served to the right toward Fort Totten.[29]

The Veteran Reserve forces available for the defense of Washington were reduced while Early was en route to Washington. General Christopher Augur on July 10, 1864, ordered the 10th Veteran Reserve Regiment stationed at the Soldier's Home to take the train to Baltimore to help defend that city, thus depleting further the already reduced defense forces taken by Grant for the Army of the Potomac and the Army of the James, operating before Richmond and Howe's force sent by Halleck to Harpers Ferry on July 8.[30] Considering that the defenses of Washington were undermanned significantly, the loss of even a regiment such as the 10th Veteran Reserve was significant.

The Veteran Reserve regiments of the brigade commanded by Colonel George Gile were heavily involved the defense of Washington through the three days of Early's attack. The 9th Veteran Reserve Regiment contained approximately 350 men led by Lieutenant Colonel R.E. Johnston. The regiment left Camp Fry about 4:00 P.M. on July 10, 1864, and reported to Major General Alexander McD. McCook at Crystal Spring, Maryland. At about 8:00 P.M. they bivouacked for the night.[31]

The rest of Gile's brigade of veteran reserves was ordered to report to General McCook without delay and arrived at Tennallytown at about 11:15 A.M. on the 10th of July. The 22nd regiment under Colonel Rutherford was placed in the rifle pits in front of Fort Sumner. The 6th Veteran Reserve Regiment under Lieutenant Colonel F.S. Palmer was placed in the rifle pits to the left of Fort Reno in front of Tennallytown with its right on the Rockville Pike. The 1st Veteran Reserve Regiment under Lieutenant Colonel Trotter was placed in the rifle pits to the right of Fort Reno. The 19th Veteran Reserve Regiment under Colonel O.V. Dayton and the 24th Veteran Reserve Regiment under Major J.W. Stickney massed in column directly to the rear of Fort Reno.[32]

The 9th Veteran Reserve Regiment formed a line of battle from 1:00 A.M. on July 10 to 7:00 A.M. on July 11. They then were ordered into the rifle pits to the right of Fort Stevens.[33] These men served there with the 2nd Vermont and the 3rd Vermont of the 6th Corps, who arrived on the afternoon of the 11th. Men of the 12th Veteran Reserve Regiment under Colonel Farnsworth were on the line to the right of Fort Stevens going toward Fort Totten. They served along with civilian employees of the Quartermaster General, the 2nd District of Columbia.[34]

The 24th Veteran Reserve Brigade was moved from Fort Reno to Fort Mansfield on July 11, 1864. One company of the 19th Veteran Reserve Regiment was taken from the rear of Fort Reno and move out on picket duty on the Rockville Pike. They were attacked by Confederate forces and suffered two wounded. The 19th Veteran Reserve Regiment was placed in rifle pits connecting Battery Smead and Fort DeRussy. At 2:30 P.M. on July 11, 1864, the 1st Veteran Reserve Regiment was sent to rifle pits to the left of Battery Smead.

The 6th Veteran Reserve Regiment was sent to rifle pits to the right of Fort DeRussy.[35] West of Rock Creek there was heavy skirmishing. Sharpshooters and other Confederate forces were trying to get by the abattis in the Rock Creek Valley, and their fire took a toll on men in the Fort Kearay and Battery Smead.[36] The 22nd Veteran Reserve Regiment moved from Fort Sumner to Fort Kearny. They then took pressure off the rifle pits in front of the fort.[37]

At 4:00 P.M. on July 11, 1864, the 9th Veteran Reserve Regiment was ordered to advance as skirmishers outside Fort Stevens and relieve the 25th New York Cavalry (dismounted). After a brief engagement in when they lost one killed and 11 wounded according to Colonel Gile, they advanced the skirmish line until seven companies were relieved by 6th Corps troops. Three companies stayed on the skirmish line.[38]

The skirmish action was heavy, with the Confederates getting within 110 yards of Fort Stevens by 1:00 P.M. on July 11. After concentrated cannon fire from Fort DeRussy on the west and Forts Slocum and Totten on the east as well as from Fort Stevens along with the heavy skirmishing, Early hesitated to attack.[39] By doing so, he lost his opportunity to break through the lightly defended Union lines on the afternoon of July 11, 1864.

Early in 1881 stated that the deployment of dismounted troopers, cavalry and others in the rifle pits along with artillery fire had defeated the Confederate hopes of getting possession of the works by surprise.[40]

The expected Confederate attack to breach the Union line did not come. The president was in Fort Stevens on the afternoon of July 11. Had a concentrated attack been made and the president captured, his political fortunes, the leadership of the war effort and the ability to carry out Grant's war of attrition against Lee may well have turned out differently.

After 5:00 P.M., three companies of the 19th Veteran Reserve Regiment, one company of the 6th and one company of the 1st were deployed as skirmishers in front of the flanks of Fort DeRussy and Battery Smead. They advanced the line 1500 yards. At 5:00 P.M., the 24th Regiment was brought over to Fort Reno from Fort Mansfield. They occupied the rifle pits in front of the fort. When the Confederates were seen reinforcing their lines about 7:30 P.M. on July 11, 1864, Colonel Gile sent the 6th Veteran Reserve Regiment to strengthen the skirmish line in the center. Six companies of the 22nd Veteran Reserve Regiment were set out on the left of the line. This skirmish line extended from the Rockville Pike on the left to about 2,000 yards beyond Rock Creek on the right.[41] It had been slightly adjusted to reflect the shift in position of the main body of the Confederates.

Colonel Price's Provisional Brigade was organized from hospital, convalescent and distribution camps of the Department of Washington. This unit of 2,800 men was the largest force under the command of Major General McCook in the northern defenses of Washington and was held in reserve in the rear of Fort Slocum near Fort Stevens.[42] A detachment was in the trenches between Fort Stevens and Fort Totten. It was one of three brigades under the command of Brevet Major General Montgomery Meigs.

At 3:00 A.M. on the morning of July 12, 1864, Colonel Gile's entire Veteran Reserve Brigade was under arms. Gile ordered Lieutenant Colonel F.S. Palmer, commanding the 6th Veteran Reserve Regiment on the right of the skirmish line, to advance that line and take possession of a hill about a quarter mile out occupied by Confederate sharpshooters. In the face of considerable Confederate resistance, the hill was taken at the cost of one wounded. Six companies of the 22nd Veteran Reserve Regiment and three companies of the 19th left the center of the line and moved forward. The left of the line was then taken two miles forward of the defensive works.[43]

At 7:00 A.M., the 24th Veteran Reserve Regiment was moved from Fort Sumner to Fort Kearny. At 1:00 P.M. on July 12, 1864, the companies of the 6th Veteran Reserve Regiment on the skirmish line were replaced by the men of the 1st Veteran Reserve Regiment. In response to an order to send one regiment to Fort Reno, Colonel Gile sent the 6th Veteran Reserve Regiment, which had just been relieved of picket duty and had been under fire. When the 6th Veteran Reserve Regiment got to Fort Reno, it furnished three commissioned officers and 82 enlisted men for picket duty, with the rest of the regiment occupying rifle pits from the left of Fort Reno to the left of the Rockville Pike. At 5:00 P.M., the 1st Veteran Reserve Regiment was relieved by the 25th New York Cavalry and occupied the rifle pits formerly occupied by the 6th regiment.[44]

About 5:00 P.M. on July 12, 1864, Company H of the 6th Veteran Reserve Regiment under Captain Clark was involved in trying to take a barn Confederate sharpshooters had been using to fire on Union skirmishers in front of Fort DeRussy and to ascertain if the Confederates were placing some artillery by the building. Clark confronted a contingent of about 200 Confederates and withdrew after ascertaining that artillery was not being placed there. Clark and four members of Company H were wounded. According to General Martin Hardin, the determined effort to hold the picket line showed the Confederates that they would have to make a desperate effort in order to take the position at Fort DeRussy. Colonel Gile and the men of the Veteran Reserve Corps were commended by General Hardin for their actions.[45]

About 7:30 P.M. a force was sent forward to test the line on Colonel Gile's right. After a skirmish, the Confederates withdrew. The men of the Veteran Reserve Brigade remained under arms from midnight on July 12 until 5:00 A.M. on July 13. At that time a commissioned officer and 10 enlisted men were sent to ascertain the whereabouts of the Confederates. They found the Confederates had withdrawn their picket line and had retreated during the night.

After Gile had reported to headquarters about 7:30 A.M. on July 13, he sent six companies of the 6th Veteran Reserve Regiment to support Colonel Lowell's Massachusetts cavalry, who were engaging the Confederates about six miles away on the Rockville Pike. At 12:30 P.M., all troops in the brigade then on the skirmish line, except the 9th Veteran Reserve Regiment, took their positions in the rifle pits. At 2:00 P.M., the 6th Veteran Reserve Regiment returned to Fort Reno.[46] In response to an order from General DeRussy at 8:40 P.M. on July 13 to report to Arlington, Virginia, without delay, Colonel Gile brought his men except the 9th Veteran Reserve Regiment, to Arlington by 2:00 P.M. on July 14.

The Veteran Reserves had performed commendably as part of the successful Union defense of Washington. They were a definite factor in Early's hesitancy and inability to take and burn the city when he had a chance.

COLONEL O.V. DAYTON COMMANDED THE 19TH VETERAN RESERVE REGIMENT IN DEFENSES OF WASHINGTON (LIBRARY OF CONGRESS).

CHAPTER 26

Quartermaster Employees Serve in Washington's Defense

One of the most remarkable, versatile and capable officers in the Union army was Quartermaster General Montgomery Meigs, who was made a brigadier general and quartermaster general by President Lincoln on May 15, 1861.[1] The connections between Montgomery Meigs and General Robert E. Lee were remarkable. Both were born in the South — Lee in Westmoreland County, Virginia, along the Potomac River and Meigs in Augusta, Georgia. Both Lee and Meigs had attended West Point, and both had distinguished academic records, finishing high in their classes. Both were engineering officers. In 1837, Meigs went with Lee to survey the Mississippi River from Iowa to St. Louis. Part of their work involved developing a plan to make the Des Moines Rapids and the Rock River Rapids navigable for shipping. Also, the harbor at St. Louis was silting up. The flow of the river needed to be altered to keep the harbor at St. Louis open and viable. All of those engineering projects on which Lee and Meigs cooperated in 1837 were successful. Ultimately, Meigs and his son, John, a Union officer killed in 1864, would both be buried at Arlington National Cemetery — property seized from the Lee family under Meigs's auspices.[2]

In the days prior to the outbreak of the Civil War, Meigs had been asked by Secretary of State Seward to develop a plan, which would be presented to President Lincoln, for relieving and holding Fort Pickens on Santa Rosa Island in Pensacola harbor. In cooperation with Admiral David Dixon Porter, an expedition was undertaken to accomplish this, initially without the knowledge of the secretary of war or the secretary of Navy.

Meigs, who also worked on the U.S. Capitol and the Washington Aqueduct, applied his organizational genius to the massive task of supplying and equipping the Union army in the years that followed.[3] As quartermaster general, Meigs had fed, clothed, housed and transported more than a million men. He was also responsible for disbursing more than a billion dollars from the United States Treasury, $431 million in the last year of the war alone, a large sum for the time. His remarkable service as quartermaster general also included command of Grant's supply bases at Fredericksburg and Belle Plain in 1864, personal supervision of the supply of Sherman's army at Savannah in January 1865, and the reopening of Sherman's supply line in March and April 1865.[4]

Meigs was also a man President Lincoln turned to for advice. When General George B. McClellan, the commander of the Army of the Potomac, became ill in 1862, he refused to tell Lincoln about his plans for engaging the Confederate forces. Lincoln asked Meigs what to do. Meigs suggested that the commander-in-chief consult with McClellan's division commanders. McClellan quickly returned to health and addressed the issues.[5]

Meigs' distinction was widely recognized. Future presidential candidate James G. Blaine said of him, "Perhaps in the military history of the world there was never so large an amount of money disbursed upon the order of a single man ... accurately vouched and accounted for to the last penny."[6]

Meigs also had organized male workers in the Quartermasters Corp in Washington into military units for over a year by 1864.[7] The men had engaged in drills, although the arms issued had been recalled. However, the organization in Washington and Alexandria had not been kept up except for Chief Quartermaster Lieutenant Colonel Greene of the Military Department of Washington.

Although the drilling ceased before the time of Early's attack, Meigs was able to react quickly to the crisis at hand: the lack of adequate troops for the defense of Washington in 1864.[8] On July 9, 1864, after talking to Secretary of War Stanton, Meigs directed the clerks of the Quartermaster General's Office as well as the clerks and workers employed by the offices of the Quartermaster's Department in Washington and Alexandria, Virginia, to be organized and armed.[9]

Meigs was aware Early was at the Monocacy engaging the Union forces under Lew Wallace and Ricketts on July 9.[10] Montgomery Meigs well understood the depleted troop strength status in the defenses of Washington and the threat to the city Early posed. Late on the evening of July 9, Meigs reported to Chief of Staff Halleck under orders from Secretary

QUARTERMASTER GENERAL (BVT. MAJOR GENERAL) MONTGOMERY MEIGS LED QUARTERMASTER EMPLOYEES AS LINE OFFICERS NEAR FORT STEVENS (LIBRARY OF CONGRESS).

of War Stanton to provide full services such as would not unduly interfere with his duties as quartermaster general.[11] General Halleck directed Meigs to provide for the relief of troops guarding quartermaster stores and some public buildings by clerks and other operatives of the Quartermaster's Department. A battalion of 250 clerks from the Quartermaster General's Office performed those duties.[12]

On Sunday, July 10, 1864, and Monday, July 11, 1864, arms were procured from the arsenal for the quartermaster's men who did not have them. Brevet Major General Montgomery Meigs had offered the services of the quartermaster's men to General Augur, commanding the Department of Washington.

On Monday, July 11, Augur directed that Meigs and his men report to Major General Alexander McD. McCook as Early was reported to be approaching Washington via the 7th Street Road to Fort Stevens.[13] Leaving in the city a large portion of wagon-master teamsters and others to assist the 6th and 19th Corps men with transportation, Meigs went with 1,500 to 2,000 men under command of Brigadier General D.H. Rucker and reported to McCook at Fort Stevens on the evening of July 11, 1864. His fully armed and equipped men were put in the line forthwith.

Major General McCook directed Brevet Major General Meigs to march his men to Fort Slocum to be advised by Colonel Haskins, who was directing the forts on the right. A staff officer pointed out a mile-long line of rifle pits where Meigs's men were to be posted. They spent

UNFINISHED CAPITOL: MEIGS ASSISTED ON THE PROJECT (NATIONAL ARCHIVES).

the night of July 11 and morning of July 12 there under arms. On the morning of July 12, General Meigs received orders from General McCook to assume command of the troops from the entrenchments from Fort Stevens to Fort Totten. He had command of a two-mile line with 5,000 men and light artillery.

General Meigs organized his troops into a division of three brigades. The 1st brigade, under Brigadier General D.H. Rucker, consisted of quartermaster's men from the depot of Washington with a detachment from Colonel Price's Provisional Brigade. These men occupied the entrenchments on the right between Fort Stevens and Fort Totten. The 2nd brigade was commanded by Brigadier General Paine. It consisted of the 12th Veteran Reserve Regiment, the 2nd District of Columbia and three companies of quartermaster's men from the depot of Washington. They occupied the entrenchments on the left between Fort Stevens and Fort Slocum. The 3rd brigade was commanded by Colonel Francis Price of the 7th New Jersey, who was succeeded in command by Colonel Farnesworth of the 12th Veteran Reserves and later by Colonel Alexander of the 2nd District of Columbia.[14]

Price's Provisional Brigade was organized from the hospital, convalescent and distribution camps of the Department of Washington. It was held in reserve and bivouacked in the rear of Fort Slocum. On July 12, 1864, Meigs's division including the quartermaster's men consisted of 4,914 men supported by light artillery.

Three companies of quartermaster's men from the depot of Washington were engaged in a skirmish in front of Fort Stevens on July 12, 1864. Under Lieutenant Colonel E.M. Green, chief quartermaster of the Department of Washington, they were with men under Brigadier General Paine. John Rynders of Company B was wounded, and a former member of the Quartermaster Department who accompanied Company B as a volunteer was killed. Captain Robert E. Park of the 12th Alabama reported, "Some of the enemy seen behind their breastworks, were dressed in citizen's clothes and a few had on linen coats. I suppose those were 'Home Guards' comprised of Treasury, Postoffice and the Department clerks."[15]

Two regiments of the Provisional Brigade relieved the 12th Veteran Reserve Regiment and the 2nd District Columbia in the trenches about 4:00 P.M. on July 12, 1864. About 9:00 P.M. these regiments were placed in reserve and ordered by General McCook to Fort Saratoga to report to General Gillmore of the 19th Corps. They remained near Fort Thayer on the 13th. On the 14th, they were returned to General Meigs's command. General Meigs was up early on the 14th.

> I was up at 2 o'clock, my men were all under arms, and I rode to Fort Stevens and took position on the parapet to watch the breaking day. The gray dawn spread over the landscape widely extended in sight. An occasional shot from a suspicious pick and low of a cow or bray of a mule also broke the stillness of the morning, and at last the sun rose and all remained quiet. Cavalry were sent out, who reported the rebel positions abandoned.[16]

During this period about 400 quartermaster's men from the Department of Washington in five companies were on picket duty in Alexandria, Virginia, at the request of Brigadier General Slough. Other companies drilled and were held in reserve. The employees of Captain J.G.C. Lee, assistant quartermaster of Alexandria, were also organized and on duty.

On July 14, 1864, the quartermaster's men were relieved of duty in the trenches as General Early had retired from the area. General Meigs turned over command of his division to Brigadier General Paine on that date. General Order No. 2 of July 14, 1864, from the headquarters of Meigs's division, signed by Brevet Major General Montgomery Meigs relieved the quartermaster's men of their duties in the trenches and ordered Rucker to march the quartermaster civilians to Washington to return to their regular duties. They were to keep up their military organization and drill.[17]

Later McCook commended Meigs for his willing and untiring discharge of duty. On July 16, 1864, Meigs directed that the organization of the clerks, workmen and laborers be kept up and a certain time should be devoted to drill at regular periods. There were to be occasional battalion-sized drills. Necessary equipment for the drills was to be placed in the armories. Officers were to have letters of appointment from the quartermaster general with non-commissioned officers being assigned according to army regulations. Lieutenant colonels and colonels were to be selected from officers on duty at the depot with other officers from various designated groups. Each company would have a captain, one first lieutenant, five sergeants, five corporals and one hundred privates.

Each regiment was to have a colonel, lieutenant colonel, one major and one adjutant, one quartermaster and one commissary of subsistence. All quartermaster employees should wear a department badge, and those who took the field in defense of Washington would wear a special badge. Organization of the companies and regiments was entrusted to Captain E.E. Camp, assistant quartermaster, to be assisted by Captain Charles Tompkins. Camp was authorized to issue all orders necessary to carry out Meigs's instructions.[18] Meigs and his men had not only performed admirably on little notice in the defense of Washington but would be ready to do so again if necessary.

The service of the quartermaster's men was important in the defense of Washington. However, it is important that these 1,500 men were not in the lines and were not available at noon on July 11 near the time Early arrived. Nor were the 2,800 convalescents in Price's Provisional Brigade. Both forces became available after the 6th and 19th Corps troops arrived. Thus, almost half of the forces McCook had under his command would not have been in the defenses had Early attacked when he arrived before Fort Stevens. Thus, the contributions of Meigs and the quartermaster's employees are significant but were belated in terms of the crucial time for the defense of Washington when the city was most at risk.

CHAPTER 27

Lack of Intelligence on Washington Defenses Handicaps Early

The Confederates had maintained significant espionage operations in Washington since the commencement of the Civil War. Rose Greenhow's intelligence information had greatly assisted the Confederates at First Bull Run (Manassas).[1] Confederate clandestine operations across the Potomac into Washington were conducted in a favorable environment because many persons in southern Maryland and the District of Columbia were sympathetic to the Confederacy After First Bull Run, E. Porter Alexander, General Beauregard's chief of artillery and a signal officer, sent E. Pliney Bryan, a private in the Confederate army, to a spot on the Maryland side of the Potomac about 15 miles below Alexandria. Messages and newspaper accounts sent by courier were then transmitted to the Confederates across the river by signal. The system was disrupted in the spring of 1862 with Bryan's arrest.[2]

Also, on April 20, 1861, Major William Barton of the Virginia militia in Fredericksburg telegraphed Governor Letcher about a line being established to Baltimore from opposite Aquia Creek. A secret line involving the Confederate Signal Corps evolved on the lower Potomac.[3]

The Confederate espionage network was under the personal direction of Confederate president Jefferson Davis and others. James M. Seddon, Confederate secretary of war, was in charge of the War Department Secret Service and the Signal Corps. Confederate secretary of state Judah P. Benjamin was in charge of the State Department Secret Service. Other were involved through scouting and the interrogation of prisoners.[4]

Captain William Norris became head of espionage operations for the Confederate Signal Corps and the Confederate Secret Service Bureau in July 1862. Norris believed that one of his group's main duties was to take over management and supplying of secret lines of communication across the Potomac. Lieutenant Charles Cawood was placed in charge of a permanent station across the Potomac from a Maryland farm of Confederate sympathizer Thomas Jones, about 40 miles south of Washington. Jones was involved in the pickup and delivery of packets of information, including information from Northern newspapers.[5]

Norris also utilized a doctor's line composed of physicians sympathetic to the Confederacy. Doctors moved about freely in their practices. They were often able to secure a great deal of information on their person or in their medical bags.[6] Dr. Cornelius Boyle of Alexandria and Baltimore dentist A.J. Volck were two of those involved.[7]

Norris made a proposal to Seddon, the Confederate secretary of war, on September 13, 1862, concerning an established system of rapid communication with operatives in Maryland and the North.

> The verbal suggestion recently made respecting regular and rapid communication with Maryland and the north are [sic] received. Employing eight couriers and seven seamen, I propose to furnish the Government daily with communications from our friends in Washington, Baltimore, &c.&c. and also northern journals and perhaps with dispatches from the army.

Assistant Quartermaster General Charles Thomas (left foreground) and staff assisted in defense of Washington (Library of Congress).

Even should the present line be interrupted, it might be judicious to multiply the chances of transmitting army intelligence, and should our forces advance at once through the route through lower Maryland would for some time be the most safe, direct and available.

Trusty messengers and the Federal mail will be the agents relied upon across the Potomac. Mr. Maddox, now raising a regiment of cavalry in Maryland, has with great spirit and self devotion volunteered to execute this part of the duty. His means of obtaining intelligence from men of judgment and position in Washington are peculiarly great, also his facilities for forwarding dispatches. In this connection I beg to suggest for consideration of the President, a proposition to station a reliable officer in Quebec his duty to convert into cipher, and in the reverse, and to forward all dispatches of the President to and from our agents and ministers abroad.

I believe that this could be accomplished with but little delay beyond that of regular mail time and with no possibility of discovery.

The details of the several plans have been fully matured, and only await your approval to be put into immediate operation.[8]

A plan for two lines of communication across the Potomac was soon approved. One line went across the Potomac into southern Maryland; one went down the James to Fortress Monroe near Norfolk.[9]

On the Virginia side of the Potomac, Lieutenant Cawood operated a signal camp at Mathias Point across from Port Tobacco, Maryland. A second camp was located near Oak Grove, Virginia, in Westmoreland County, run by Sergeant Harry Bogden in 1864–1865.[10]

Benjamin Stringfellow, along with E. Pliny Bryan, had established an organization in Alexandria, Virginia, which remained in place throughout the Civil War.[11] Thomas Nelson Conrad was another Confederate spy operating in Washington and after mid–1864 out of Eagle's Nest about 35 miles south on the Lower Potomac. He was a chaplain with the 3rd Virginia Cavalry. Conrad had organized an espionage ring that operated out of the home of Thomas Green, a Washington lawyer who represented Virginia in claims against the United States government arising from the Revolutionary War and War of 1812.[12] He also ran an information line from Maryland Point across to Acquia Creek.[13]

In 1862, Thomas Nelson Conrad had been able to obtain General George B. McClellan's order of battle during his Peninsular Campaign. He was also able to place double agent Edward North with Colonel Lafayette C. Baker in the U.S. War Department's Secret Service. Being warned in 1863 that Baker was after him, Conrad went south of Washington on the lower Potomac where he assisted couriers in the passage and transmission of information.[14] His operations later involved the unsuccessful November 1864 plot to kidnap President Lincoln on the way to the Soldier's Home.[15] The reports from 1863 and 1864 by Lieutenant Colonel Charles Venable of General Lee's staff reflect a substantial amount of reasonably accurate information still coming to the Confederate government through Conrad.[16]

The fact that there were many Confederate spies and rebel sympathizers in Washington was well known to the Union command facing Early's advance on Washington. General Lee, however, in writing to Davis about the plan to move on Washington and later Point Lookout, in effect stated that those places were not strongly defended.[17] Moreover, the Northern newspapers were a constant source of information about a whole variety of subjects from which troops strength information could be at least deduced. Although some information had obviously been obtained about the status of the defenses of Washington before or during Grant's Overland Campaign, Early did not claim to have any present information about troop strength in Washington and the vulnerability of the defenses immediately before his arrival.[18] Thus the Union tightening of civilian ingress and egress into Washington obviously had some effect in diminishing the intelligence available to Early. Also, there was an apparent failure of Confederate espionage networks to get him this information.

After the Battle of the Monocacy on July 10, 1864, when Early was marching toward Washington, Brigadier General Martin Hardin, who commanded a portion of the northern defenses of Washington, noted that orders were issued to stop every citizen trying to leave Washington or go outside the city: "As there were numerous Rebel sympathizers, orders were issued, Sunday night (10th) to the division to stop every citizen who attempted to pass from the city to the surrounding country."[19] Hardin concluded that "the causes of the successful defence (outside of Early's dilatoriness and failure to make a determined attack) were ... the forbidding of citizens to pass outside the lines."[20] Thus, a ready source of intelligence for Early was kept from him.

The experience of Treasury Department official Lucius Chittenden documented the great difficulty of a citizen to even get to Fort Stevens under the pass system in effect, much less to get outside the lines on July 12, 1864. After procuring a pass from Secretary of War Edwin Stanton, Chittenden went driving out on the Seventh St. Road, where he passed a large number of the 6th Corps troops on the march. He and his companion were stopped by a Union soldier who checked their identification. There was firing from Confederate soldiers and there were not a lot of citizens passing there. Ultimately, Chittenden and his companion had to take cover to protect themselves from the firing around them before they were able to get to Fort Stevens.[21]

General Early remarked about the lack of information from sources in Washington that the city was undefended as he appeared with his army in front of Fort Stevens on July 11, 1864:

Patrolling Potomac at Aqueduct Bridge: civilian ingress and egress controlled (Library of Congress).

"If we had any friends in Washington, none of them came out to give us information, and this satisfied me that the place was not undefended."[22] Early himself supported General Hardin's claim that the prevention of citizens from going outside the lines had been a significant factor in deterring Early's attack on Fort Stevens on the afternoon of July 11, 1864.

However, Nelson A. Fitts of Co. B of the 9th New York Heavy Artillery, who was a prisoner marching along with the Confederate forces, stated that numerous local inhabitants came out on the morning of July 11, 1864, to give the Confederates information on troop disposition in Washington "Sunday morning, July 10, on the left of New Market, while retreating, I was taken prisoner by a squad of the Twentieth Virginia Cavalry, and was taken to headquarters of that regiment and marched with them to Silver Spring, on the Seventh-street road, getting there on Monday the 11th about 3 P.M. The cavalry joined the rest of the command between Rockville and the Seventh-street road, and I passed the entire length of it, saw their troops and artillery. I also observed some of the inhabitants that gave them information in regard to the forces in Washington, and I would point out the places and men if I were to go back on the same road."[23]

Alexander Hunter, a Virginia soldier, claimed that a stream of people had met the Confederate skirmishers and told them that there were only government clerks in the trenches and advocated entry into Washington.[24]

While some corroborating information concerning troop strength and disposition certainly got to the Confederates, it does not appear to have gotten up the chain of command to be made known to General Early by the time of his arrival at Fort Stevens. However, both Early and Gordon by observation saw that the works were but feebly defended; Gordon stating, "I myself rode to a point on those breastworks at which there was no force whatever."[25] However, the lack of information to the contrary led Early, as he stated, to believe they were defended.[26]

CHAPTER 28

Actions at the Blair Mansions a Minor Factor in Early's Failure to Enter Washington

During the first week of July 1864, General Jubal Early's forces were moving from Winchester, at the head of the Shenandoah Valley, across the Potomac into western Maryland. There were rumors of the movement of a Confederate force toward Washington. Elizabeth Blair Lee cautioned her father, Francis Preston Blair, Sr., about the danger to his home, Silver Spring, and her brother Montgomery's Falklands due to the Confederate advance toward Washington.[1] Elizabeth was married to Admiral Samuel Phillips Lee, a Union naval officer who was related to General Robert E. Lee.[2] Francis Preston Blair, Sr., and his son, Montgomery, Lincoln's postmaster general, were gone to Pennsylvania.[3] Elizabeth's mother refused her request to take the family silver and other valuable property to the Blair House on Pennsylvania Avenue in Washington.[4]

After defeating Major General Lew Wallace in the Battle of the Monocacy on July 9, 1864, General Early rested on the battlefield preparing to move on toward Washington. On the morning of July 10, 1864, the Confederate forces began their advance on an unencumbered path to Washington, Lew Wallace and his army having moved off toward Baltimore.[5]

Early's army moved from Monocacy Junction about 20 miles to Rockville on July 10, 1864. The weather was extremely hot. The Confederate forces on their march were choked by enormous clouds of dust. The order of battle had General Robert Rodes in the van followed by Gordon's division, Ramseur, and Echols, with artillery being interspersed throughout between them.[6] Early's army, while on the march, engaged in some undisciplined conduct which included the seizure and destruction of civilian property.[7]

Silver Spring and Falklands, near the Sev-

MONTGOMERY BLAIR, LINCOLN'S POSTMASTER GENERAL (MASSACHUSETTS COMMANDERY OF THE MILITARY ORDER OF THE LOYAL LEGION AND THE UNITED STATES ARMY MILITARY HISTORY INSTITUTE).

enth Street Road in Montgomery County, Maryland, were each about a mile from Fort Stevens, which was just inside Washington, anchoring its northern defenses. These mansions were still over 10 miles from the Confederate forces marching on Washington on July 10. If Early's army had moved directly to Washington by the Georgetown Pike, which was the most direct route from Rockville, the Confederate army could have bypassed the Blair mansions. Early's army straggled badly on the 10th.[8] The 20 miles they marched was about all Early could get from his men at this point. They had had a lengthy and difficult battle on the 9th. Some of the men were marching wounded.

Advance units of Brigadier General John McCausland's cavalry brigade clashed with units sent out from Washington under Lieutenant Fry on the 10th. McCausland's men, who pushed back the Union cavalry force to Tennallytown near Fort Reno, were trying to determine what lay ahead for Early on the Georgetown Pike.[9]

Early's army got underway early on the 11th. McCausland's cavalry force moved to Tennallytown, which was protected by Fort Reno.[10] Near there the River Road and the Georgetown Pike entered Washington. The east-west Military Road connected the area by Fort Reno with forts to the east. Fort Reno was protected by heavy guns.

Brigadier General John McCausland's cavalry force did not attempt to attack Fort Reno or to enter Tennallytown on the morning of July 11, 1864. Rather, based primarily on visual observation, McCausland concluded that the fortifications protecting Washington in this northwest sector were impregnable and not vulnerable to attack. He reported his observations back to Early and suggested that he might want to consider a more easterly route that would be somewhat longer.[11]

Early's men moved to Washington on the Seventh Street Road. Major General Robert Rodes's men, with General Early with them in the advance, moved by the Blair mansions to Fort Stevens, which Early noted around noon was feebly defended. Some of the Confederate force continued to straggle in the heat, denying Early a fully effective force when he reached Fort Stevens.[12]

Confederate troops, on reaching the Falklands mansion near the Seventh Street Road, undertook the wholesale destruction of the building. Falklands was an elegant country estate. Lincoln had played with the Blair grandchildren there. It had a second floor library with curved bookshelves full of bound volumes of Shakespeare and Sir Walter Scott. This had been the scene of a meeting of Lincoln's cabinet in 1863.[13] The house was ransacked. Books were taken from the bookcases. China was broken. Linens were torn up. The doors were battered in.[14] The time spent on this destruction of property contributed to some extent to the delay in the Confederates having an adequate force at Fort Stevens to timely make an attack.

Montgomery Blair, the owner of Falklands, was from an important and influential family connected with the Union.[15] He had invited Abraham and Mary Todd Lincoln to stay at the Blair House on Pennsylvania Avenue near the White House before Lincoln's inauguration.[16] President Lincoln made Blair's son, Montgomery, his postmaster general. Montgomery Blair was from the border state of Maryland and had advocated war as had his father.[17]

Montgomery Blair, a postal reformer, had discussed the imposition of the blockade in Lincoln's cabinet.[18] Lincoln ultimately imposed the blockade, which became an important deterrent to the ability of the Confederacy to wage war. Contrary to most in the cabinet, Montgomery had joined Secretary of State Seward in favoring the return of Confederate emissaries Mason and Slidell in the Trent Affair.[19] In a stroke of political genius, Lincoln in turning the men over to England had in effect forced England to recognize a position held since before the War of 1812 concerning the seizure of contraband while avoiding a war that would be damaging to the Union.[20]

Montgomery Blair was a West Point graduate and was considered a man of great intelligence and sound judgment. Lincoln had considered him as a replacement for Simon Cameron as secretary of war, a post which ultimately went to Edwin M. Stanton.[21] Blair was also very loyal to Lincoln. He went with him to Gettysburg for the Gettysburg Address.[22]

Thus, Blair was a well-known supporter of Lincoln. He was a cabinet member. The Union troops under General David Hunter in Lexington, Virginia, had burned the home of ex-governor John Letcher as well as buildings on the grounds of the Virginia Military Institute that had been the homes of private individuals associated with the Confederate cause.[23]

Brigadier General Bradley T. Johnson in his raid around Baltimore and movement toward Point Lookout burned the home of Governor Bradford of Maryland in retaliation for Hunter's actions. Later, Brigadier General McCausland with Johnson would burn Chambersburg, Pennsylvania, for failing to pay a ransom for the city. Thus, the ransacking and destruction of Montgomery Blair's home while he and his family were away was not entirely unexpected.

At this point on the 11th, Blair's Falklands mansion was only ransacked. It would subsequently be burned as the Confederates withdrew from the city and left the area.[24]

Across the Seventh Street Road was the family mansion of Francis Preston Blair, Sr., Montgomery's father as well as the father of Union general Frank Blair, and later to be an emissary from Lincoln to Jefferson Davis to discuss peace. Union soldiers entered the premises. They scattered papers. Documents and books were thrown about. After going through the bedrooms and wine cellar, the lawn was strewn with items of furniture and clothing. Some of the soldiers dressed up in items of personal attire and ran around the lawn. According to a family legend by a descendant of Francis Preston Blair, Sr., and Samuel Phillips Lee, Confederate soldiers dug up the front yard at Silver Spring. They found and took some silver as well as two hogsheads of whiskey which had been obtained by General Robert E. Lee's cousin and Francis Preston Blair's son-in-law, Rear Admiral Samuel Phillips Lee. The family silver that Elizabeth Blair Lee had sought to protect was taken.[25]

GENERAL FRANK BLAIR WAS INVOLVED IN EFFORTS TO GET MCCLELLAN TO WITHDRAW AS AN OPPONENT TO LINCOLN IN THE ELECTION (MASSACHUSETTS COMMANDERY OF THE MILITARY ORDER OF THE LOYAL LEGION AND THE UNITED STATES ARMY MILITARY HISTORY INSTITUTE).

Confederate soldiers had engaged in undisciplined destruction of property that was fully outside their purpose to enter and take Washington, which was within their grasp or nearly so. This diversion of troops for nonmilitary purposes operated to unnecessarily delay Early in getting his army up and in a position to attack.

The destruction at Silver Spring ended when Early and Breckinridge arrived there. Breckinridge, a relative of

SILVER SPRING, HOME OF FRANCIS PRESTON BLAIR SR., RANSACKED BY CONFEDERATE TROOPS (LIBRARY OF CONGRESS).

Blair's, was very upset by the pillaging that had gone on: "Cursing the marauding soldiers, Breckinridge made them return the stolen items. He retrieved the scattered papers and documents and sent them away for safekeeping. He asked Early to station a guard on the grounds to preserve the trees, grapery, shrubs, horses and crops."[26]

Breckinridge had visited with the Blairs when he was vice president of the United States and had a particular fondness for the family. He had explained to Early that years before in a difficult part of his life Francis Preston Blair, Sr., had taken him in and had been kind to him.[27] Breckinridge was insistent that there be no further destruction. A neighbor later told Francis Preston Blair, Sr., that Breckinridge had treated Silver Spring with more concern than if it had belonged to Jefferson Davis.[28]

Captain Robert Park of the 12th Alabama of Gordon's Division was bivouacked near Silver Spring. He reported that it was under guard and was not being disturbed.[29]

Early made Silver Spring his headquarters for the night of July 11, 1864.[30] That evening Early and his division commanders, Gordon, Rodes, Ramseur and Breckinridge, all agreed that an attack on what were extremely strong fortifications now defended by veteran troops from Grant's army would be unwise.[31] The Confederates undertook to withdraw.

What occurred to cause the burning of Montgomery Blair's Falklands estate is not entirely clear. Elizabeth Blair Lee had written her husband that Falklands had been "torched."[32] Early stated, "On the night of the 13th, the house of Postmaster General Blair near Silver Spring was burned, and it was assumed by the enemy that it was burned by my orders. I had nothing to do with it and do not yet know how the burning occurred."[33] Even though there had been substantial shelling destroying numerous houses in the area, this shelling was not reported by Confederate officers at the Silver Spring mansion to have caused the destruction of Falklands. It has generally been assumed that soldiers of the retreating Confederate army set fire to the building. Upon his return a furious Montgomery Blair lambasted Washington officials, particularly Henry Halleck, for not having done more to protect the city.[34]

Doris Kearns Goodwin notes that "the time the Confederates lost during the Battle of the Monocacy and the frolic at Silver Spring allowed Washington to mobilize its defenses."[35] Certainly there was some loss of time and diversion of military personnel from the movement to Washington. However, in the larger picture of factors that affected Lee's gamble, this was relatively minor. Certainly Rodes was not prepared to attack in force at noon on July 11, and this situation may have contributed somewhat. More significant was the straggling through the ranks that had occurred that day as well as the oppressive heat that made marching difficult. The episodes at the Blair mansions were part of a larger picture of events that made the execution of Lee's plan fail. What could have changed the course of the war did not.

CHAPTER 29

McCook's Force Outside Fort Stevens Deters Early's Assault

On July 11, 1864, the Union defenses at Fort Stevens were under command of Major General Alexander McD. McCook. McCook had seven brothers and five first cousins fight in the Civil War. His brothers Daniel McCook, Jr., Edwin S. McCook and Robert L. McCook and first cousins Anson G. McCook and Edward M. McCook were all Union generals.[1] Alexander McD. McCook graduated from West Point in 1852. He had been fighting Utes and Apaches in the West from 1853 to 1857, fighting in the Battle of Sawatchee Pass, at the Arkansas River and in the Gila River Expedition.[2] After participating in First Bull Run (Manassas) as a colonel in the 1st Ohio, McCook became a brigadier general. On the second day at Shiloh, he repulsed Beauregard's counterattack. At Perryville on October 8, 1862, McCook's division took the brunt of the Confederate assault and suffered substantial casualties. At Stone's River in December 1862, McCook's division was also heavily engaged and held the field. He was made a major general in the summer of 1862.[3] He had been court martialed and exonerated for his conduct at Chickamauga and was in Washington in July 1864 on his way back to his home in Dayton, Ohio, when called to command at Fort Stevens.[4]

> Reporting in person at the War Department on the Morning of July 10, I was directed to report to Maj. Gen. H.W. Halleck, U.S. Army, who assigned me to duty in the Department of Washington to command a reserve camp to be located on or near Piney Branch Creek, about midway between Washington and Fort Stevens on the north. In company with Lieut. Col. B.S. Alexander, U.S. Engineers, I at once proceeded to examine the ground for the camp, also to make a hasty examination of the fortifications on the north of Washington. Returning at 6:00 P.M., and receiving my final instructions from Maj. Gen. C. C. Augur, commanding department, I proceeded to Piney Branch where the Second Regiment District of Columbia Volunteers, Colonel Alexander, and the Ninth Regiment Veteran Reserve Corps, Lieutenant-Colonel Johnston, Captain Gibbs (Ohio) battery, and Captain Bradbury's (Maine) battery had already reported.
>
> Monday morning discovered the fact that the only troops on the north of Washington were small garrisons in the forts, small detachments of cavalry in the front, and the troops above-mentioned. Hearing of the near approach of the enemy, the idea of a reserve corps was at once abandoned and every man was brought forward and posted in the rifle pits to the best advantage, and as a strong skirmish line as prudent was established. During the morning several additional regiments of Veteran Reserve corps and several detachments of dismounted cavalry reported for duty. They were posted in the rifle pits on either side of the main road leading to Silver Spring. Captain Berry of the Eighth Illinois Cavalry, being stationed with his company on the road leading from Silver Spring to Leesborough, dispatched a courier at 10:00 A.M. on the 11th, informing me that the enemy was advancing in force on the road with infantry, artillery and cavalry. At 12 A.M. a strong line of enemy's skirmishers came into view, advancing upon our position. The picket line at this moment was composed of 100 days men of One hundred and fiftieth Ohio, and portion of the Twenty-Fifth New York Cavalry (dismounted). Being satisfied that they would not contend favorably with the enemy's line, they were ordered to fall back slowly, fighting, until they reached the rifle-pits. Fire was then opened at proper

points upon our line, and the enemy was held in check until the dismounted of the Second Division of the Cavalry Corps, Army of the Potomac, 600 strong, commanded by Maj. George G. Briggs, Seventh Michigan, Cavalry, were made ready to go out, drive the enemy back and reestablish our picket line. This was handsomely done about 1:30 P.M., the enemy's skirmishers being forced back, and our line well established at 1100 yards in front of the works. The enemy not developing any force other than their skirmish line.[5]

Hearing of the approach of the Confederates near Washington on July 11, McCook directed that men be brought forward and posted in the rifle-pits to the best advantage. A strong skirmish line was also established. During the morning of the 11th several additional regiments of the Veteran Reserve Corps and detachments of dismounted cavalry arrived, and McCook posted them in rifle pits on either side of the Seventh Street Road. The Union men were a combative foe supported by fortress artillery.[6] One hundred five artillerists, found by Quartermaster General Meigs in Price's Provisional Brigade, taken from the Washington hospitals, were used to man batteries at Fort Stevens.[7]

At noon, when the Confederates attacked the 100-days' men of the 150th Ohio and dismounted troopers of the 25th N.Y. Cavalry, they fell back to the rifle pits.[8] At this time, McCook only had 209 men inside Fort Stevens after their arrival,[9] he sent Major George Biggs and 600 dismounted troopers of the 2nd Division of the Army of the Potomac's Cavalry Corps to drive back the Confederates and reestablish the picket line. About 1:30 P.M. on July 11, the picket line was reestablished about 1100 yards in front of the fort. The situation remained this way until 3:00 P.M., when Major General Horatio G. Wright and the advance of the 6th Corps veterans arrived.[10]

John Henry Cramer, in his work *Lincoln Under Enemy Fire*, discussing the battle at Fort Stevens in meticulous detail, described General Alexander McD. McCook as follows: "Moreover, the Union soldiers were in the hands of a capable leader; for, on the morning of July 11th, the fighting Ohioan, General Alexander McCook, had been placed in the command of the defense of the Capital. Assisting were Major General Quincy Gillmore, leader of the stouthearted Nineteenth Corps, Quartermaster General Montgomery C. Meigs, and Brigadier General Martin Hardin. Fear gripped neither the generals nor the men; grimly they looked on the Confederates and prepared for an expected assault."[11]

Brigadier General Martin D. Hardin, who commanded part of the line under McCook, called him "a gallant officer who never did himself more credit than on this occasion."[12]

McCook's somewhat unorthodox strategy of putting most of his forces outside of the defenses, rather than inside, and carrying on a forceful engagement with the enemy outside the works had operated to stall a major assault on the early afternoon of July 11, 1864, until help could arrive, making a major assault no longer practicable.

Benjamin Franklin Cooling in *Monocacy: The Battle That Saved Washington* stated that the Confederate skirmish line had found a combative foe, fully supported by fortress artillery, once the combat moved to within fifty to one hundred and fifty yards of the fort.[13] Brigadier General Martin Hardin described McCook's prompt formation and maintenance of the picket line as being one of the significant factors in the successful defense of Washington against Early's assault.[14] McCook's tactic of putting most of his force on the skirmish line and maintaining rapid fire was unusual military practice but operated to give the impression of strength and greater numbers.[15]

On July 16, 1864, Special Order 175 relieved Major General Alexander McD. McCook from duty in the Department of Washington. He was order to report in person to the adjutant general of the United States Army.[16]

McCook went on after the Civil War to be a long-time aide-de-camp to commander-in-chief of the army William T. Sherman in 1875. Later he headed the infantry and cavalry school at Fort Leavenworth, Kansas.[17] Having been a major general in the volunteers, he achieved that same rank in the regular army after the Civil War.[18]

CHAPTER 30

Convalescing Union Troops Help Defend Washington

As Early approached Washington, the need for Union troops to man the defenses was acute. Convalescents were being utilized. On July 9, 1864, Halleck had telegraphed Major General George Cadwalader at Philadelphia to send all convalescents from the hospitals there capable of defending Washington's forts and rifle pits. General McCook's report of his troop strength in the northern defenses of Washington reflected 7,886 men.[1] Of these 2,800 were convalescents in Price's Provisional Brigade, taken from almost every hospital in Washington and every regiment in the Army of the Potomac.[2] What is more important is that these men were not available to General McCook at Fort Stevens at noon on July 11, 1864, when Early arrived before the fort.[3] They only came up later that evening.[4]

COLONEL FRANCIS PRICE OF THE 7TH NEW JERSEY HEADED PRICE'S PROVISIONAL BRIGADE OF CONVALESCENTS (JOHN W. KUHL COLLECTION AT THE UNITED STATES ARMY MILITARY HISTORY INSTITUTE).

In June 1864, there were 19 military hospitals in Washington, Georgetown and Alexandria.[5] Surgeon D.W. Hliss of the U.S. Volunteers headed the Armory Square Hospital at Seventh Street between C and D streets, further toward the downtown from Fort Stevens on the Seventh Street Road where the fighting took place. Carver Hospital, another major medical facility, was located at the terminus of the city railroad on Fourteenth Street. A.F. Stelden of the U.S. Volunteers was the chief surgeon in charge. West of the terminus of the city railroad on Fourteenth Street was Columbian Hospital. Surgeon T.R. Crosby of the U.S. Volunteers headed the medical staff. At the corner of Fourteenth Street and Massachusetts Avenue was DeMarres Hospital, under the command of surgeon J.S. Hildreth. Douglas Hospital, at New Jersey Avenue and I Street, had Assistant Surgeon William Thomson of the U.S. Army in charge.[6]

ARMORY SQUARE HOSPITAL, SOURCE OF CONVALESCENT SOLDIERS FOR DEFENSE OF WASHINGTON (LIBRARY OF CONGRESS).

Some other hospitals were Emory Hospital, Harewood Hospital on Seventh Street, and Judiciary Square Hospital at 5th and E streets, where Assistant Surgeon Alex Ingram of the U.S. Army was in charge. There were also hospitals outside of the city, including the Finley Hospital north of the city and Fairfax Seminary Hospital near Alexandria, Virginia.[7]

Elizabeth Bacon Custer, wife of Union general George Armstrong Custer, described Washington at this time as being grim. Daily the trains, boats and wagons brought large numbers of dying and wounded Union troops to Washington. In some ways the city was like one large hospital. She visited Mount Pleasant Hospital to help comfort the wounded, appalled at the number of men who had lost a limb.[8]

Lincoln Hospital, one mile east of the Capitol, was headed by Assistant Surgeon J.C. McKee of the U.S. Army. Mount Pleasant Hospital on Fourteenth Street was headed by Assistant Surgeon C.A. McCall of the U.S. Army. Seminary Hospital was at the corner of Washington and Gay Streets in Georgetown and was headed by Surgeon H.W. Ducalet of the U.S. Volunteers.

Stanton Hospital was at New Jersey Avenue and I Street and was headed by Surgeon J.A. Liddell of the U.S. Volunteers. Assistant Surgeon P. Glennan, U.S. Army, was in charge of Stone Hospital on Fourteenth Street. St. Elizabeth's Hospital was used as an insane asylum and was headed by Acting Surgeon C.H. Nichols of the U.S. Army. The 1st Division General Hospital was located in Alexandria, Virginia.[9]

Poet Walt Whitman, who assisted in Washington hospitals during the Civil War, later described the plight of wounded men he attended during their suffering and often death. There were tens of thousands of men suffering from battlefield wounds as well as from malaria, smallpox and other diseases.[10]

Colonel Francis Price of the 7th New Jersey, wounded at Gettysburg and later brevetted a brigadier general, had collected from Washington area hospitals a force of about 2,800 men from practically every unit of the Army of the Potomac and had formed them into a provisional brigade.[11] At about 10:00 P.M. on July 11, 1864, they were put in reserve in the rear of Fort Slocum.[12] This position was decided upon, according to McCook, because "information received led men to believe that the enemy would demonstrate further to our right."[13] From this group 105 artillerists were utilized in the batteries at Fort Stevens.[14]

General Wright of the 6th Corps had arrived about 3:00 P.M. on July 11 with the advance of his men.[15] On July 12, 1864, General McCook had 7,886 men under his command of which 2,800 were the men from the hospitals in the Provisional Brigade.[16]

General Henry Halleck, chief of staff, had written on July 10, 1864, "What we have here are raw militia, invalids and convalescents from the hospitals, a few dismounted batteries, and the dismounted and disorganized cavalry sent up from the James River."[17]

The convalescents had not been organized and brought into line by noon on July 11, 1864, just as the quartermaster employees had not. Had Early attacked shortly after noon on July 11, even these men would not have been available.

Chapter 31

Lincoln Under Fire at Fort Stevens

James C. Cannon of the 150th Ohio recalled President Lincoln's arriving at Fort Stevens about noon on July 11, 1864, escorted by the Black Horse Cavalry, with the president passing quickly from cannon to cannon within the fort. "About noon the Black Horse cavalry escort of the President, dashed up to our postern. Lincoln hastily left the barouche, entered the fort, and passing from gun to gun, looked out upon the field it covered." According to George T. Stevens of the 77th New York, a 6th Corps veteran, President Lincoln was at the 6th Street Wharf in Washington at 2:00 P.M. on July 11, 1864. He was chatting with the troops and taking a bite out of a piece of hardtack.[1] Thus Lincoln would have been at Fort Stevens at the time Early had arrived before it. The president was at risk of being in the fort when it was subject to being overrun had Lieutenant General Jubal A. Early attacked before the 6th Corps forces arrived at either 3:00 P.M. or 4:00 P.M.[2]

At some point on July 11, Lincoln also would have been under enemy fire.[3] He thus would have been subject to being shot by a Confederate sharpshooter as about 30 Union troops would be on July 11 and 12.[3]

Although the fort was relatively secure from Confederate assault after the arrival of General Wright's 6th Corps forces, it was not secure from the marksmanship of the Confederate sharpshooters until General Wheaton's assault at the end of July 12 and the destruction by cannon fire of houses providing cover for sharpshooters.[4] General McCook's failure to more quickly address the problem of Confederate sharpshooters was the subject of severe criticism from Assistant Secretary of War Charles Dana, who was at Fort Stevens.[5]

On July 12, 1864, Confederate sharpshooters were still at the Carberry House west of the Seventh Street Road and at the Reeves House about ¼ mile east of the Seventh Street Road—both about 1000 yards north of Fort Stevens in the defenses of Washington.[6] These sharpshooters were pouring a steady fire on the Union troops stationed at Fort Stevens.[7] A soldier at the fort, David T. Bull, described the firing of the sharpshooters at figures on the parapet and the wounding of a doctor near President Lincoln in a letter to his wife two days after the incident: "There was a large force of them gathered around a house in front of the Fort and there was a sharp shooter get up in the top of the house and thought he would kill some of our men that was on the parapet. Old Abe and his wife was in the Fort at the time and Old Abe and his doctor was standing up on the parapet and that sharp shooter that I spoke of shot the doctor through the left thigh."[8]

Another soldier, Peter H. Kaiser, saw Lincoln from a short distance when a man was wounded near the president. "In the midst of the battle, I saw standing on the parapet a few rods from the gun to which I was assigned, a tall man wearing a stovepipe hat and long coat, who was watching the progress of the fighting with the closest interest, wholly unmindful of the danger in which he stood. Many eyes were turned in his direction, and upon inquiry I learned that the man was President Lincoln. General Wright in command of the 6th Corps stood near him with a field glass, viewing the contest, when a bullet wounded a soldier nearby."[9] Lincoln's stovepipe made his figure possibly seven feet tall.[10] Lucius Chittenden said:

> Leaving the ditch, my pass carried me into the fort, where, to my surprise, I found the President, Secretary Stanton, and other civilians. A young colonel of artillery, who appeared to be the officer of the day, was in great distress because the President would expose himself, and paid little attention to his warnings. He was satisfied the Confederates recognized him, for they were firing at him very hotly, and a soldier near him had just fallen with a broken thigh. He asked my advice, for he said the President was in great danger.
>
> "What would you do with me under like circumstances?" I asked.
>
> "I would civilly ask you to take a position where you were not exposed."
>
> "And if I refused to obey?"
>
> "I would send a sergeant and a file of men and make you obey."
>
> "Then treat the President as you would me or any civilian."[11]

Presidential secretary John Hay, in his diary of July 12, 1864, stated: "The President again made a tour of the fortifications; was again under fire at Fort Stevens, a man was shot at his side."[12]

General Horatio G. Wright, commanding the 6th Corps, recounted the incident where a surgeon was shot next to the president at Fort Stevens, where Lincoln was forcibly directed to seek cover:

PRESIDENT ABRAHAM LINCOLN WAS IN DANGER AT FORT STEVENS (NATIONAL ARCHIVES).

> He took his position by my side on the parapet, and all my entreaties failed to move him, although in addition to the stray shots that were passing over, the spot was a favorite mark for sharpshooters.
>
> When the surgeon was shot and after I had cleared the parapet of everyone else, he maintained his ground until I told him I should have to remove him forcibly. The absurdity of the idea of sending off the President under guard seemed to amuse him, but in consideration of my earnestness in the matter, he agreed to compromise by sitting behind the parapet instead of standing upon it."[13]

George T. Stevens of the 6th Corps recalled: "While the battle was in progress, President Lincoln stood upon the parapet of the fort watching, with eager interest, the scene before him. Bullets came whistling around, and once severely wounded a surgeon who stood within three feet of the President. Mrs. Lincoln entreated him to leave the fort, but he refused; he, however, accepted the advice of General Wright to descend from the parapet and watch the battle from a less exposed position."[14]

Oliver Wendell Holmes, Jr., later a justice on the United States Supreme Court, also claimed to have told the president to get down in circumstances where bullets were flying near the him.[15]

RUINED HOUSE NEAR WHERE SHARPSHOOTERS WERE FIRING IN THE AREA OF FORT STEVENS (LIBRARY OF CONGRESS).

The wounded surgeon was C.V. Crawford of the 102nd Pennsylvania, who suffered a serious thigh wound.[16] Whether General Wright, Captain Oliver Wendell Holmes, Jr., or someone else directed him to get down is disputed.[17] What is not disputed is that President Lincoln could have easily have been killed or wounded standing in an exposed position under enemy fire.

Moreover, as substantiated by John Hay in his diary and by Colonel William Griffith, President Lincoln had been at Fort Stevens both on July 11, 1864, and July 12, 1864.[18] Thus Lincoln not only barely avoided being shot on the 12th, but was in the fort on July 11 when it was subject to Confederate attack.

Thus there was an element of chance involved. Obviously, even if Early had not taken and burned Washington, but had succeeded in injuring or killing the president, the political chaos would have been enormous and the course of the war put into question. Lee's bold plan, even with the notable failures in its execution, had still put Early close enough to potentially cripple the Union cause either by a timely attack on July 11 or a sharpshooter's near miss on the 12.

CHAPTER 32

Foreign Recognition of the Confederacy and Lincoln's Problematic Reelection

In the spring and summer of 1864, Grant was fighting a war of attrition against Lee. At the Wilderness, Spottsylvania, the North Ana and Cold Harbor, the Union forces suffered terrible losses accompanied by substantial but lesser losses by Lee's army — 86,000 men in all over a period of seven weeks.[1] Sherman was moving inexorably toward Atlanta in a bloody campaign that was still inconclusive in July 1864. After three years of war, squeezed by General Winfield Scott's Anaconda plan, the Confederacy faced a foe with eight times the draftable manpower, six times the financial resources and an overwhelming superiority in commercial, maritime and naval power.[2] In civil wars from the 17th century on, there was a striking correlation between foreign intervention and insurgent victories in those wars.[3] Foreign intervention was crucial to the survival of the Confederacy. A major military success was necessary to abet that process. At Antietam in 1862 and Gettysburg in 1863, Lee had invaded the North only to be turned back. In July 1864, through Early's army, he was back a third time during a period of war weariness and political uncertainty in the North. Although, taking and burning Washington, even for a short time, and returning the equivalent of a corps of veterans to Lee's army was fraught with great difficulty, if successful Lee's plan could change everything.

The French and British governments had been contemplating intervention in the American Civil War since 1861.[4] Intervention had been seriously contemplated when Confederate emissaries Mason and Slidell were seized on the high seas in the Trent Affair.[5] However, the capture of New Orleans, Nashville and Memphis along with Union military victories at Fort Donelson, Pea Ridge, and Shiloh plus the initial success of McClellan's Peninsular Campaign between February and May 1862 caused the pressure for intervention to lessen.[6]

Lee's stunning successes in the Seven Days Battles, at Second Bull Run (Manassas) and in his invasion of Maryland in September 1862, coupled with Confederate successes in Kentucky and Tennessee, had moved intervention closer. At that time, Lord Russell, the British foreign secretary, favored recognition of the Confederacy.[7] The semi-official newspaper in Paris urged Northern leaders to accept mediation in the summer of 1862. The French Minister in Washington approached Secretary of State William Seward about mediation after Pope's defeat at Second Bull Run. Seward remained unalterably opposed to mediation, saying there could be no compromise. In Seward's view, peace would only come when the Confederates laid down their arms.[8]

British Prime Minister Palmerston and Chancellor of the Exchequer William Gladstone both talked of Confederate independence in the fall of 1862 after the Union defeat at Second Bull Run. Although there was substantial support for mediation, the outcome of the subsequent battlefield engagement was viewed by Palmerston as a basis for determining their future course of action.[9] There would be a pause in September 1862 and a reevaluation of the issue of mediation. A cabinet meeting was proposed relating to negotiations on the basis of separation.[10] The

French Emperor, Napoleon III, wanted recognition for the Confederacy as well by the summer of 1862, but only if the British extended recognition.[11]

Lee well understood that foreign intervention was important for independence and that his invasion of the North, if successful, might lead to foreign intervention. He felt that a defensive strategy could not prevail against a stronger opponent. Aggressive military operations were necessary to achieve battlefield victories that could lead to independence.[12] However, the Confederate invasion of the North was turned back at Antietam on September 17, 1862. The result at Antietam frustrated the Confederate hope for recognition and intervention.[13]

The defeat at Perryville on October 8, 1862, checked the Confederate advance in the west. Moreover, George Cornwall Lewis, British secretary for war, whose opinions were highly respected, said in a memorandum issued in October 1862 that British intervention would be a mistake. The Confederacy had not sufficiently established itself on the battlefield in his opinion. Also, it would be difficult to reinforce Canada during the winter.[14] Lewis again raised substantial questions in November 1862 about the difficulties European powers would have in sending armies and fleets across the ocean , how their wooden vessels would do against Union ironclads and how the peace process would be handled by multiple powers. Ultimately, Lewis's views prevailed. Palmerston advised Lord Russell that the Confederate defeats had ended any chance of successful mediation and recommitted Britain to the role of observer.[15] The French Emperor had asked the British to consider a proposal for a six months' armistice during which the Union blockade would be lifted and peace negotiations would begin. This proposal was rejected by the British cabinet.[16]

Countervailing the support of the Confederacy by England and France was the Union's support by Russia. President Lincoln, after Fort Sumter and shortly after the outbreak of hostilities, made forging a strategic alliance with Russia his top foreign policy priority. This was a masterstroke of political and diplomatic genius. The Czar had freed the serfs in 1861.[17] Russian support for the Union and what would happen in Europe if war broke out were extremely important considerations for England and France in this period after the Crimean War.[18]

Moreover, President Lincoln subsequently issued the Emancipation Proclamation, committing the Union to the abolition of slavery at least in the border states, delaying the prospect of intervention by the British.[19] Palmerston, among others and the British press ridiculed the Emancipation Proclamation.[20]

In Britain, public opinion was divided, with the upper classes generally favoring the recognition of the Confederacy and the middle and lower classes opposing it.[21] Slavery had been abolished in the British Empire, and there was a strong movement in the country against slavery.[22]

Lincoln had named Cassius Marcellus Clay, Henry Clay's nephew, to be ambassador to Russia in May 1861.[23] In the Trent Affair controversy, Foreign Minister Gorchakov undertook a policy of impartiality, as Russia was standing firmly behind the Union.[24] This entente or friendship was widely publicized.[25]

After being recalled as ambassador as a result of political intrigues in June 1863, Clay returned to Washington and gave President Lincoln information on the European political situation, warning that European governments were prepared to intervene and possibly recognize the independence of the Confederacy. Russia strongly supported the Union.[26] This would be important In terms of emancipation and opposing the recognition of the Confederacy.

Lincoln continued to support Russia and took action on emancipation. Russia had also contacted the French emperor about his proposal for an armistice and lifting the blockade. The British ambassador to Russia advised Foreign Secretary Lord Russell that the Russians had rejected the proposal.[27] This was when, in October 1862, the British cabinet determined to be onlookers until the war took a more decided turn and backed away from mediation.[28]

Russia refused to join England and France in their efforts at mediation and to secure an armistice between the Union and the Confederacy. Gorchakov told Russell on November 7, 1862, that Russia refused to participate in an armistice which would prejudice future peacekeeping efforts.[29]

Napoleon III continued his efforts to obtain peace talks into January and later in 1863 while his Mexican intervention was ongoing. A note was sent to the State Department urging negotiations with the Confederates.[30] Horace Greeley, editor of the New York *Tribune*, became involved with and met personally with the French minister to the United States. Secretary of State William Seward condemned Greeley's actions and advised the French minister that negotiations would not be undertaken.[31]

The French diplomatic relationship with the Confederacy was tied up with his involvement in Mexico. In May 1862, French troops had been defeated at Puebla. Napoleon III sent a larger army under General Forey who invested Puebla in January 1863 and captured it in May 1863, Mexico City was also taken in June 1863.[32] When France had entered Mexico, Secretary of State Seward had an understanding of no permanent aggrandizement in the Western Hemisphere.[33] The Union regarded France and Mexico as belligerents and avoided intervention.

In the fall of 1863, Archduke Maximilian accepted the Mexican throne. French foreign minister Drouyn de Lhuys sought to maintain strict neutrality in the Civil War to avoid a conflict with the Union over Mexico.[34] Seward saw France as too preoccupied in Mexico to intervene in the Civil War. France saw the Union as too tied down in its own struggle to intervene in Mexico.[35]

Confederate victories at Fredicksburg and Chancellorsville presaged another Confederate invasion of the North in the summer of 1863, which culminated at Gettysburg. Again, as at Anietam, intervention by Britain and France and possibly other European powers was hanging in the balance. If Lee achieved victory, it feared it might inevitably lead England and France to recognize the independence of the Confederacy. Even after Gettysburg, Britain and France were still deliberating intervention on the side of the South. However, England distanced itself somewhat from the Confederate cause as a neutral. Ships being built at the Laird shipyard in Liverpool were seized and towed out of the port and anchored offshore. They were later sold to the Royal Navy on May 20, 1864, becoming the *Scorpion* and the *Wivern*.[36]

Russia was determined to avoid a repetition of the Crimean War, when her fleets were bottled up in the Baltic and Black seas. Based on intelligence that the outbreak of war by Britain and France was imminent, Russia sent her fleets to both coasts of the United States simultaneously in September 1863.[37] Thus, if France and Britain intervened, it could provoke a global conflict.

The Russian fleets stayed in American waters for seven months. In December 1863, the Atlantic fleet went from New York to Washington. During the winter of 1863–1864, Admiral Popov advised California governmental authorities that in the event of a British or Confederate naval attack on the West Coast, his ships would clear for action and would assist in repelling any attempt against the security of the places there.[38]

The Palmerston government maintained its position in 1863 and in 1864 that it would not intervene until the Confederacy had demonstrated to the Union on the battlefield that subjugation of the South was impossible.[39] Intervention meant war with the Union. The Union army and navy had grown substantially in strength. Russia supported the Union and was hostile to England, increasing the global dimensions of the potential conflict.[40]

The British were taking some actions to distance themselves from belligerent acts hostile to the Union. The steamer *Pimpero*, under construction on the Clyde River in Glasgow, was repossessed in April 1864 by its owners, who agreed not to use it for warlike purposes. Another ship under construction in the Thomson yard in Glasgow was sold in 1864 as the British would not permit is use by the Confederacy.[41]

With the problem of the Laird rams resolved, there were no serious diplomatic controversies for the United States and England in 1864. The British ministry remained against recognition. There were no startling military successes by the Confederates sufficient to rally pro-Southern support and create a renewed opening for recognition.[42] Although there were numerous pro-Confederate associations in England, because of the issue of slavery, there was no substantial movement that could force recognition.[43]

France in late 1863 had been preoccupied with Maximilian's accession to the Mexican throne and with the likelihood of war with Russia over Poland; this deterred progress in France's recognition of the Confederacy.[44] By the spring of 1864, the consolidation of the Mexican Empire had become the primary concern of Napoleon III.[45] The lack of sympathy for the Confederate cause at the time by Napoleon III was confirmed by Commissioner Slidell to President Davis.[46]

Moreover, ships secretly constructed in France for the Confederacy in 1863 were held up in 1864. In February 1864, the French government declared that the ships could not leave port. In July 1864, the ships were declared for sale, and they were sold a month later to Denmark and Prussia.[47]

The semiofficial French press gave the impression that the defensive war being fought by the Confederacy on its own soil could last a long time, until the Union sued for peace. Almost everyone in France interested in the conflict recognized that a great deal depended on the election of 1864.[48]

A factor that the French were constantly monitoring was the success of military campaigns. In the summer of 1864 at the time of Early's march toward Washington, Grant's campaign before Richmond and Sherman's toward Atlanta were viewed as indecisive.[49]

Although French and British actions in 1864 were closing the door on recognition, that door had not fully been closed. There was considerable public sentiment in both countries favorable to the Confederate cause, albeit tempered by the slavery issue. Had Jubal Early been able to burn Washington, capture or injure President Lincoln or force him to flee the capital, the door to European recognition might well have been reopened. Further, had such events occurred, Lincoln's reelection, already in some jeopardy, might well have been placed in further doubt. The circumstances that affected the outcome of the attack on Washington and Point Lookout, although now confined to a footnote in the saga of the Civil War, might well have dramatically altered the course of history.

In a very real sense, Early's raid on Washington and Point Lookout in July 1864 may have been the Confed-

WILLIAM SEWARD, LINCOLN'S SECRETARY OF STATE (UNITED STATES ARMY MILITARY HISTORY INSTITUTE).

eracy's last best hope to influence the 1864 election and invite European intervention. It is not clear that Early fully understood what was at stake in Lee's intention to turn the tables on Grant and the Union and how it could have played out on the world stage. Civil War veteran George Haven Putnam said:

> He [Early] could fairly have expected to have captured the President, while he certainly would have secured the money supplies of the Treasury and could probably have destroyed munitions of all kinds in the armories of the army warehouses. At this time Louis Napoleon was still pressing upon England the policy of recognizing the establishment of the Southern Confederacy. The news that, more than three years after the beginning of the war, a Confederate force had been able to penetrate into the lines of the National Capital would certainly have been used as a text or argument for the contention that the Confederacy was fairly established and the success of the North was impossible.[50]

While European intervention was at stake in Early's attack on Washington, the reelection of President Lincoln was also in issue. Lincoln's reelection was very much in doubt in the spring and summer of 1864. Lincoln himself expressed the concern that he could not be reelected. Henry C. Raymond, head of the Republican National Party, said, "The tide is setting strongly against us."[51] Although the strong 78 percent army vote for Lincoln and the positive support garnered by the fall of Atlanta was reflected in a strong showing by Lincoln in the November 1864 election, in July 1864 that outcome was far less certain.[52] It would have been even more so if Early had taken Washington even for a little while.

Since early 1863, Horace Greeley, editor of the New York *Tribune*, had been working to find an alternative presidential candidate to Abraham Lincoln. Greeley was very much opposed to Lincoln's renomination, In 1863, Greeley had talked to General William Rosecrans about a possible presidential bid.[53] Rosecrans was not interested. His disastrous defeat at Chickamauga late in 1863 ended any thoughts of his opposing Lincoln. Greeley then sought to support Grant, Sherman or Butler.[54]

Early in 1864 the Chicago *Tribune* and *Harper's Weekly* came out in support of the President's reelection.[55]

During the latter part of 1863 and into 1864, Salmon P. Chase, secretary of the treasury in Lincoln's cabinet, had been working with people opposed to Lincoln to gain support for his own presidential bid. In February 1864, the Pomeroy Committee circulated a document to leading Republicans espousing the candidacy of Salmon P. Chase, a member of Lincoln' cabinet. A major proposition of this undertaking was that Lincoln's reelection chances were practically impossible. After exposure, Chase's presidential bid was withdrawn in March 1864.[56]

Lincoln's political problems persisted. The Augusta (Georgia) *Constitutionalist* of January 22, 1864, stated that the presidential election would be shaped and determined by the results of the war. Lincoln's strategy was to get endorsements for his reelection at the state level.[58] Lincoln was pushing for an autumn convention as winning the war would take longer. Ultimately, a convention was scheduled for the National Union Party, as the Republicans were called, for Baltimore on June 7, 1864.[59]

Montgomery Blair had gone to see McClellan to try to persuade him to take Henry Halleck's position. In May 1864, Frank Blair wrote S.L.M. Barlow, national chairman of the Democratic Party, stating it would be in the best interest of the country in McClellan did not run.[60] The elder Blair went to New York to meet with Barlow. Barlow took his communication to McClellan, who met with Blair but refused to agree to his proposal.[61]

Clearly there was significant concern in Lincoln' s cabinet about his reelection prospects.

Montgomery Blair's father, Francis, followed up on this proposal by returning to Washington and telling Lincoln what had happened. Lincoln expressed neither approval nor disapproval.[62]

Lincoln struggled in 1863 and 1864 to bring radical Republicans in line. Prominent abolitionists particularly felt that Lincoln had not done enough to further their cause.[63] John C. Fremont was the first Republican presidential candidate in 1856. In 1864, a group of abolitionists and radicals supported him for president. The main centers of anti–Lincoln sentiment were among the Germans in St. Louis and New York. In early May 1864, there was a movement toward a convention to nominate Fremont for president. Among those involved were abolitionist Wendell Phillips and Elizabeth Cady Stanton. The radical republicans met in a separate convention in May 1864 before the national Republican convention.[64]

On May 31, 1864, a convention was held in Chapin Hall in Cleveland by a party called Radical Democracy. Fremont was nominated for president and John Cochrane of New York for vice president. The party's planks included that the Union be preserved, that the rebellion be suppressed by force of arms without compromise, that the United States constitution be amended to prohibit reestablishment of slavery and to secure for all persons equality under the law. Additionally, the party sought to reaffirm the Monroe Doctrine and opposed the establishment of any anti-republican government on the continent. Reconstruction was to be in the province of Congress. There would be a direct vote for president and one-term presidency. Confiscation of rebel lands was also proposed.[65]

Manton Marble, editor of the New York *World*, called these actions a flank movement. Henry Raymond of the New York *Times* felt that Radical Democracy was a party of "ultra patriots, soreheads and cranks."[66] Lincoln supporters were concerned that the Radicals could take enough votes from Lincoln in several large states to throw them to the Democrats.

Powerful newspaper editors strongly opposed Lincoln. These men included James Gordon Bennett, editor of the New York *Herald*, and Manton Marble, editor of the New York *World*.[67] Certainly the taking and burning of Washington, even briefly, by Confederate General Early in July 1864 would have exposed Lincoln's reelection efforts to stringent criticism in the press.

President Lincoln also had experienced considerable congressional opposition in early 1864 in the areas of patronage and reconstruction. A major political battle involved the Radical Republican attempts to have Congress control reconstruction, which in part involved a forcing of transformation on Southern society — although Republicans had much common ground. The Wade-Davis bill would have taken control from the Executive Branch. Lincoln did not sign the bill, executing a pocket veto. Wade and Davis stated that the president's pocket veto indicated a persistent though unavowed purpose by Lincoln to defeat the will of the people through executive perversion of the Constitution.[68] Thus there was a substantial split in the Republican party with which he had to deal, which affected the reelection equation.

One way Lincoln sought to address the problems of splits in the party was trying to get a major political figure from that faction on his presidential ticket. General Benjamin Butler, although of very limited military ability, had become popular in the North for his tough handling of the Confederate populace of New Orleans and its environs in Louisiana after its capture. An emissary from Lincoln approached Butler about running for vice president on the ticket with Lincoln.[69] This would have helped relieve political opposition to Lincoln. Butler refused, believing the vice presidency not to be politically advantageous enough, having an eye on the presidency.[70] Lincoln's approach to Butler suggested his own concern about his reelection chances.

Opposition to Lincoln was being fomented by the Confederacy itself. Confederate president Jefferson Davis knew that while Lincoln was in power the war would be prosecuted vigorously. Nor would there be any compromise on Confederate independence.[71]

In the spring of 1864, Davis sought to turn popular Sentiment against Lincoln in favor of peace. He believed election of a Peace Democrat in 1864 or a Democrat with a peace plank in his platform was in the interest of the Confederacy.[72] Davis sent two commissioners to Canada carrying substantial assets in drafts in gold to incite Northern discontent. Jacob Thompson and

32. Foreign Recognition of the Confederacy and Lincoln's Problematic Reelection

Clement C. Clay successfully went to Canada. Plans were developed for a raid of Camp Douglas in Chicago during the Democratic convention and a raid to free Confederate prisoners on Johnson's Island.[73]

Thompson was also in contact with Clement Vallandigham, head of the Sons of Liberty, an organization claiming numerous adherents in the Midwest, which was active in supporting peace efforts.[74]

The Republican convention, called the National Union Convention, was held in Baltimore in early June 1864. Although the war was not going well, Lincoln was nominated for reelection with the military governor of Tennessee being nominated for vice president.[75] However, nomination for reelection did not necessarily mean success at the polls.

War weariness was affecting the country. The failure of Grant and Sherman to achieve decisive victories was amassing large numbers of casualties operated to undermine morale in the populace.[76] The 17,000 lost in the Wilderness were followed by the 23,361 at Spottsylvania, the 7,000 at Cold Harbor and the 1,973 at the North Ana.[77] Hunter's operations before Lynchburg and in the Shenandoah Valley had gone badly. He and his army had retreated to West Virginia and Ohio. Before Hunter had taken over, Sigel had been defeated at New Market.

Navy secretary Welles on June 2, 1864, noted that the immense slaughter in Grant's army chilled and saddened him. He further noted in his diary of June 11, 1864, that there was little from the army that was decisive or satisfactory but bodies by the hundreds were being brought daily to Washington.[78]

The New York *World* of July 12, 1864, at the time of Early's attack on Washington questioned who would revive the positive response that had come at the beginning of Grant's campaign.[79] General Bedford Forrest had threatened Sherman's lengthy supply lines, defeating a Union force at Brice's Crossroads. It was not until Forrest was defeated at Tupelo on July 14, 1864, that Sherman's supply line was secured.[80] Republican George Templeton Strong said that Grant's movements had been destined to cause mourning . He feared the blood and cost of the summer's campaign had taken its toll.[81]

Lincoln's call for 500,000 more men did not promise to be popular.[82] The president and his advisors were discouraged and frustrated by the events of the war and the public reaction to the president's call for additional troops. Lincoln did not believe it was possible for him to be reelected.[83]

Early's appearance in Maryland in July 1864 and his march toward Washington raised alarm in the North and concern about the northern commanders, including Grant.[84] There had been a call to the governors of several states for additional troops. Neither Grant nor anyone in Washington appeared to have a clear picture of what was going on.[85]

Lincoln's secretary of the navy, Gideon Welles, was harshly critical of Grant both before and immediately after Early's attack on Washington. In his diary of July 11, 1864, he stated:

> The truth is the forts around Washington have been vacated and the troops sent to General Grant, who was promised reinforcements to take Richmond. Be he has been in the vicinity more than a month, resting apparently, after his bloody march, but has affected nothing since his arrival on the James, nor displayed any strategy, while Lee has sent a force threatening the National Capital, and we are without a force for its defense. Citizens are volunteering, and employees in the navy yard are required to man the fortifications left destitute.[86]

Immediately after Early's withdrawal from outside the defenses of Washington, Welles expressed similar dissatisfaction: "While daily reinforced, Grant could push on to a given point, but he seems destitute of strategy or skill, while Lee exhibits tact. This raid, which might have taken Washington and which for several days cut off communications with the north, was devised by Lee while beleaguered at Richmond, and, though failing to do as much as might have been accomplished, has effected a good deal."[87]

The New York *World* of July 12, 1864, described Grant's stalemated campaign as a national humiliation.[88]

Copperhead and other opposition to the war and the demand for peace were substantial.[89] Efforts to establish a Northwest Confederacy were being undertaken by secret organizations like the Sons of Liberty.[90] This helped discredit opposition to the war. Shortly after Early's attack, peace negotiations would be undertaken at Niagara Falls and Richmond.[91] Although Lincoln sought to discredit the peace initiative by sending Horace Greeley to Canada and attaching a condition of abandoning slavery the Confederacy could not accept, that does not mean that the peace process could have been sidestepped had Early taken Washington. The Democrats were talking of running General George B. McClellan for president and were considering a peace plank.[92]

There could hardly have been a worse time for Washington to fall to a Confederate army. The Union was particularly vulnerable internally at this time. Foreign intervention was dependent on a decisive Confederate victory. Early's capture of Washington, even for a brief period, could have been such a victory. The timing for Lee's initiative was optimal. Circumstances made victory possible. However, ultimately Lee's plan failed in its execution and as a result of unexpected and remarkable Union actions to thwart it.

The stalemate at Petersburg continued in the summer of 1864. The disaster at the Crater at Petersburg on June 30, 1864, was more negative news in that military theater.[93]

Atlanta fell in September 1864.[94] It was in the west in September and October of 1864 that Lincoln's presidential election prospects improved, as it now appeared that the war would be won by the Union. Lee was besieged in Petersburg and Richmond, which made the end only a matter of time.[95] However the taking and burning of Washington in July 1864 would have overshadowed everything in the political, diplomatic and military theaters. Lee's plan should have changed everything, but did not.

CHAPTER 33

Epilogue: Early Reconsidered

Lieutenant General Jubal Anderson Early is not generally remembered as being a consistently outstanding line officer in some of the most difficult campaigns in which the Army of Northern Virginia was engaged. Most of these engagements were against much greater troop strengths and often against great odds. For instance, Lee left Early with a force of 10,000 men to face Sedgwick with 3 to 4 times that number at Fredericksburg in the Chancellorsville Campaign, in which Early effectively neutralized a substantial part of Hooker's force.[1]

His troops were part of the forces at Antietam that Lee so skillfully maneuvered to hold at bay a numerically superior force. Previously, at Fredericksburg, Early's forces had been part of the Confederate Army that devastated Burnside's frontal assaults on a very strong defensive position.[2] After being wounded early in the Peninsular Campaign of 1862, Early had returned to help in Lee's movement to chase McClellan to Harrison's Landing and to relieve Richmond.[3] Early was consistently effective in the Overland Campaign from the Wilderness to Cold Harbor.[4] When Lee's lieutenants are considered in historical perspective, Early's name is often obscured by those of others.[5] Yet, in terms of tactical skill, daring, audacity and intelligence, Early was clearly one of Lee's most skillful general officers.

Early was considered one of the most profane officers in the Confederate army — not just the Army of Northern Virginia. His oath-taking, cussing and verbal epithets were legendary.[6] Although often fondly called "Old Jube" and "Jubilee" by the men who fought for him, he was still regarded as cantankerous and surly.[7]

Further, he had often sour relations with subordinate officers who generally did not hold him in great affection. General John B. Gordon, who served under him for an extended period, had difficult relations with Early, as did most of the subordinate general officers in his command.[8] Early simply did not seek their opinions in military matters generally. Nor did he often follow their suggestions when they were proffered.[9]

When Lee considered Early to temporarily replace Longstreet, who had been wounded in the Wilderness, he was persuaded not to do so on the basis that Longstreet's officers and men would not desire to serve under Early.[10]

His disdain of cavalry officers and their input and service was also well known.[11] Early was, in short, a tough, hard-bitten, mostly effective military man who was smart, aggressive and bold. He was Lee's "Bad Old Man."[12]

Early is perhaps most remembered for his 1864 Valley Campaign against Major General Philip H. Sheridan. This was a campaign in which some of Early's most distinguished division commanders were killed in action: Major General Robert Rodes and Major General Stephen D. Ramseur.[13] It was a campaign that ultimately led to Early's being relieved of command by General Robert E. Lee at Waynesboro, when all Early had left was a skeleton force.[14]

Early's fall 1864 Valley Campaign was hallmarked by defeat. He had been defeated at the Third Battle of Winchester, where he faced a superior Union force, fought courageously, but was ultimately overwhelmed by numbers and driven from the field.[15] A few days later, making a stand at Fisher's Hill, the undermanned Confederates under Early were routed by a flanking maneuver.[16] Again at Tom's Brook, Early was defeated.

Early is perhaps most remembered for the Battle of Cedar Creek, where his forces delivered a devastating blow to a large Union force only to have defeat snatched from the jaws of victory when Early did not press his advantage.[17] Sheridan, riding from Winchester, was able to rally his troops and reclaim the field in what proved to be a major Union victory.

In essence, Early, in independent command with a limited force against a well-supplied and aggressive Union force, was consistently bested. Moreover, Sheridan was laying waste to the Valley, destroying the breadbasket of the Confederacy.[18]

Somewhat lost in the memory of the occurrences in the Valley in the fall of 1864 were some of the remarkable accomplishments on Early's part prior to that. His withdrawal from Washington on July 13, 1864, and rapid movement to Leesburg and across the Potomac River without effective Union pursuit or response caused Assistant Secretary of War Charles Dana to call it an "egregious blunder."[19] Secretary of the Navy Welles felt that the entire Lincoln administration appeared contemptible in the failure to effectively pursue Early.[20]

Early not only successfully crossed the Potomac into Virginia, but also defeated separately Union forces which had pursued him. After defeating a Union force at Cool Spring on July 18, 1864, Early inflicted a substantial defeat on General George Crook at Second Kernstown a few days later.[21] This was followed by the burning of Chambersburg, Pennsylvania.[22] Obscured in those successes against a non-unified command were the later, above-mentioned losses against a unified command under Sheridan. Except for some brief assistance by General Richard Anderson, Early had been on his own, trying to hold numerically superior forces a bay with a small army—which proved beyond his capacity to accomplish in the waning days of the Confederacy.

Early's raid, or his attack on Washington, has generally been regarded as a diversion to relieve pressure on Lee's army from Grant's forces in Richmond that got to the gates of Washington and fell back again.[23] Early with his little army had been held up on the Monocacy and was late.[24] Thus, the Battle of Fort Stevens, with its limited scope and casualties, along with the aborted Point Lookout raid, became a footnote in history.

However, fairly or unfairly, General Jubal A. Early will be remembered for his role on the first day at Gettysburg in not taking Cemetery Hill and in executing Lee's gamble to take Washington and Point Lookout in such a manner as not to succeed when success and changing the whole course of the war was possible.

At Gettysburg, General Robert E. Lee had given General Richard Ewell discretionary orders to take Cemetery Hill at the conclusion of the first day, which he expected to be executed. Ewell, in his discretion, did not make the attack.[25] Early, who was an aggressive battlefield commander and who had a substantial influence over Ewell, demurred to his decision and did not boldly push him to make the attack — which was clearly warranted and should have been made.[26] Thus, Early's omission has been widely viewed as affecting a major turning point in the Civil War adversely for the Confederacy.

Further, Early has been widely regarded on his movement to Washington as having fulfilled Lee's wishes for the operation.[27] Although Early accomplished some remarkable things, he clearly lost the opportunity Lee had envisioned and presented to him to take Washington, albeit briefly, free the prisoners at Point Lookout and change the course of the Civil War.

Lee's plan involved two phases. The first involved getting Early's Second Corps up to Lynchburg in time to relieve the city and protect Lee's endangered supply and communications lines with Richmond.[28] This Early did by aggressively moving his army by land to Charlottesville with hard marching after a vigorous and demanding participation in the long Wilderness Campaign through Cold Harbor. He further got his men from Charlottesville to Lynchburg by rail.[29] Through skillful conduct in managing the battlefield, he was able to defeat General David Hunter.[30] This in substantial part had been made possible by delays and blunders by Hunter and his refusal to follow Grant's orders.[31] The whole operation to relieve Lynchburg, in turn, had been made possible by Wade Hampton's stunning defeat of Sheridan at Trevilian Station.[32] Early was thus able to chase Hunter, who was low on supplies and ammunition, to West Virginia—out of the theater of operations.[33]

Due to Early's actions and a series of fortuitous circumstances, General Lee had been put in a position of turning the tables on Grant in an election year and taking Washington—while returning a corps-sized force to Lee's army. This would have been a stunning result which could have changed everything. Due to the war's greatest intelligence failure, this result remained possible because Grant did not know where Early was nor credit reports which would have caused him to act expeditiously to protect the nation's capital.[34]

Early had the drive, the intelligence and the daring to follow Lee's original plan to move north. Having accomplished his first phase objectives as well as he could have imagined, Early then moved to execute the second phase of Lee's plan which, if successful, would have put Early's name at the forefront of Confederate military leaders for audacity, daring and accomplishment.

Early moved his forces down the Valley with alacrity, reorganizing and resupplying while on the move, reaching Winchester by July 2.[35] However, it was there that a series of decisions and events occurred that fatally affected the full and timely execution of Lee's gamble. Early, based on some claims of Mosby's men about the limited availability of supplies for a large army, elected not to take the shortest route to Washington which had been authorized by Lee.[36] Instead, he opted for a longer route which put him on a collision course with Union forces at Leetown, Martinsburg and Harpers Ferry that he would otherwise have been able to avoid.

Then, after being held up for 5 hours at Leetown by the courageous stand of Union forces under Colonel James A. Mulligan, Early proceeded to allow Franz Sigel's Reserve Division at Martinsburg and Max Weber's garrison force at Harpers Ferry to escape to Maryland Heights, covering the direct route to Washington.[37]

After permitting his men to loot captured Union stores and liquor and feast for the better part of two days, Early remained in the area of Harpers Ferry until July 6, even though Sigel and Weber were in an almost impregnable position and he was going to take the same route toward Frederick later that he could have taken earlier.[38]

Union General Lew Wallace submitted that Early could still have crossed the Potomac at Edward's Ferry, moved down the Potomac and taken Washington.[39] Early did not do so. Rather, he tarried on the Upper Potomac for several days, losing time he did not have to lose.

These delays were compounded by another delay at Cacoctin Mountain caused by General Ransom's countermanding the orders of Bradley Johnson to flank the Union forces and move into Frederick on July 7, which would have changed the whole disposition and timetable for the Monocacy battle.[40] Moreover, Early himself was absorbed in extorting money from the citizens of Frederick not to burn the city. This delayed his getting to the battlefield, and cost him the ability to survey the field, possibly taking away the option of using the Buckeystown Road around the Union position or of altering the tactics involving McCausland's assault, which was already underway.[41]

As it was, the Battle of the Monocacy was a bloody, lengthy, costly fight undertaken primarily by only one division of Early's army. Although a victory, it delayed Early further by another day in his move to Washington.[42]

Lee was sufficiently confident of the potential success of his plan that the included the attack on Point Lookout in verbal orders communicated to Early on July 6.[43] Even though time was of the essence, Early did not communicate the Point Lookout raid orders to General Bradley

Johnson, who was going to lead it as well as cut rail and communications links between Washington, Baltimore and the North until July 8.[44]

The cumulative delays made the difficult move to free the prisoners at Point Lookout even more difficult. Johnson's raid was to operate in conjunction with an amphibious operation under Colonel/Commander John Taylor Wood from Wilmington, North Carolina.[45] This part of the plan had been devised by General Robert E. Lee and Confederate president Jefferson Davis while Early was on the march.[46] This phase of the operation was called off at the last minute due, in substantial part, to perceived leaks of news of the operation.[47]

Moreover, Early still got to Fort Stevens when it was viewed by him to be feebly manned on July 11, 1864, but did not attack due to concerns about sufficient forces being up and the strength of the fortifications.[48]

In the end, Lee's bold plan, brilliant in conception, failed in its execution as well as through the actions of unlikely Union commanders in acting to retard Early's movements. Early could and should have been remembered as an aggressive and intelligent general officer who executed Lee's plan to turn the tables on Grant and who changed everything. However, as he had done at Gettysburg, he hesitated and did not forcefully act sufficiently enough when time was of the essence and the course of the war hung in the balance.

After the Civil War, General Jubal A. Early was one of the foremost exponents of the Lost Cause. Although a very fine writer and able presenter of that point of view, he did not really assess his own crucial role in how that cause was lost in the midst of valiant efforts to make it even possible. In the end, too much time was unnecessarily spent along the way to Washington. Although Early had many of the attributes of Stonewall Jackson, he was not Jackson and did not achieve the same results. What could have changed everything did not.

Chapter Notes

Chapter 1

1. Paul F. Mottelay and Copeland T. Campbell, *The Soldier in Our Civil War*, vol. 2 (New York: Stanley Bradley, 1880), 285.
2. Benjamin F. Cooling, *Monocacy: The Battle That Saved Washington* (Shippensberg, PA: White Mane, 1984), 9–15.
3. William B. Feis, "A Union Military Intelligence Failure: Jubal Early's Raid, June 12 — July 14, 1864," *Civil War History*, vol. 36, no. 3 (Kent, OH: Kent State University Press, Sept. 1990), 209–211.

Chapter 2

1. Douglas Southall Freeman, *R.E. Lee: A Biography*, 4 vols. (New York: Charles Scribner's Sons, 1934–1935), vol. 2, 92; E.P. Alexander, *Military Memoirs of a Confederate* (New York: Charles Scribner's Sons, 1907), 111; Emory Speer, *Lincoln, Lee, Grant and Other Biographical Addresses* (New York and Washington: Neale Publishing, 1909), 47; Thomas L. Connelly, *The Marble Man: Robert E. Lee and His Image in American Society* (New York: Alfred A. Knopf, 1977), 198.
2. Edward Porter Alexander, *Fighting for the Confederacy: The Personal Recollections of General Edward Porter Alexander*, ed. Gary W. Gallagher (Chapel Hill, NC: University of North Carolina Press, 1989), 91–92; Freeman, *R.E. Lee*, vol. 2, 88; Speer.
3. Connelly 197; Freeman, *R.E. Lee*, vol. 2: 88; Philip Alexander Bruce, *Robert E. Lee* (Philadelphia, PA: George W. Jacobs, 1907), 220.
4. Connelly 197; Charles S. Venable, "General Lee in the Wilderness Campaign," in *Battles and Leaders of the Civil War*, Robert Underwood Johnson and Clarence Clough Buell, eds. (New York: Thomas Yoseloff, 1956), 241–242.
5. Freeman, *R.E. Lee*, 1:237–246.
6. Freeman 1:247–248.
7. Freeman 1:250, 252.
8. Freeman 1:254–256; A.L. Long, *Memoirs of Robert E. Lee* (New York, Philadelphia and Washington: J.M. Stoddard, 1876), 54; George Cantor, *Confederate Generals: Life Portraits* (Dallas, TX: Taylor Trade Publishing, 2000), 5.
9. Freeman, *R.E. Lee*, 1:256–258.
10. Freeman 1:257–258.
11. Freeman 1:260–264; A.L. Long 56.
12. Freeman 1:263–266; A.L. Long 57.
13. Freeman 1:268.
14. Freeman 1:269–271.
15. Freeman 1:271–272; A.L. Long 58.
16. Freeman 1:274–278; A.L. Long 66.
17. Alexander, *Military Memoirs*, 111.
18. J. William Jones, *Personal Reminiscences, Anecdotes and Letters of Gen. Robert E. Lee* (New York: D. Appleton and Company, 1874), 3–4.
19. J.W. Jones, *Personal Reminiscences*, 4–5.
20. J.W. Jones 5–6.
21. J.W. Jones 7.
22. J.W. Jones 7–8.
23. Patricia L. Faust, ed., *Historical Times Illustrated Encyclopedia of the Civil War* (New York: Harper Perennial, 1986), 667.
24. Faust 667.
25. Edward A. Pollard, *Lee and His Lieutenants* (New York: E.B. Treat, 1867), 137.
26. Alan T. Nolan, *Lee Considered: General Robert E. Lee and Civil War History* (Chapel Hill, NC: University of North Carolina Press, 2001), 77.
27. Nolan 102; John D. McKenzie, *Uncertain Glory, Lee's Generalship Re-examined* (New York: Hippocrene Books, 1997), 81.
28. Connelly 206–208.
29. Bruce 155–156; Faust 94.
30. Faust 94; 120–122.
31. Bruce 159–163; Faust 94.
32. Faust 328–329; Bruce 164–165.
33. Faust 92–93; Alexander, *Military Memoirs*, 199–201.
34. Jones 10–12.
35. J.W. Jones, *Personal Reminiscences*, 11–13; Faust 129–130.
36. Bruce 173.
37. Joseph L. Harsh, *Confederate Tide Rising: Robert E. Lee and the Making of Southern Strategy, 1861–1862* (Kent, OH: Kent State University Press, 1998), 59–60.
38. James M. McPherson, "No Peace Without Victory, 1861–1865" (presidential address at 118th annual meeting of the American Historical Association, Washington, DC, January 3, 2003), 2.
39. Peter S. Carmichael, ed., *Audacity Personified: The Generalship of Robert E. Lee* (Baton Rouge, LA: Louisiana State University Press, 2004), 9.
40. Faust 19.
41. Faust 20.
42. J.W. Jones, *Personal Reminiscences*, 15–16.
43. Faust 19–20; Freeman, *R.E. Lee*, 2:408–409.
44. Freeman 2:409–410.
45. Nolan 97; Alexander, *Fighting for the Confederacy*, 145–146; Carmichael 9; Harsh 59; Gary W. Gallagher, *Lee and His Generals in War and in Memory* (Baton Rouge, LA: Louisiana State University Press, 1998), 36–37.
46. Bruce 198–199; Faust 288–289.
47. J.W. Jones, *Personal Reminiscences*, 24–25.
48. James M. McPherson, *Battle Cry of Freedom: The Civil War Era* (New York: Oxford University Press, 1988), 572.
49. Faust 128; Alexander, *Military Memoirs*, 324–326.
50. Gary W. Gallagher, *Lee and His Army in Confederate History*

(Chapel Hill, NC: University of North Carolina Press, 2001), 224; J.W. Jones, *Personal Reminiscences*, 26.
51. Faust 126, 128.
52. Faust 126, 128; Bruce 209–210.
53. Faust 128–129; Robert R. Reich, "Lee at Chancellorsville" (Lincoln NE: University of Nebraska Press, 1996), 392–393.
54. J.W. Jones, *Personal Reminiscences*, 27.
55. Faust 129; Gallagher, *Lee and His Army*, 239–240.
56. Walter H. Taylor, *Four Years with Lee* (Bloomington, IN: University of Indiana Press, 1962), 83.
57. Freeman, *R.E. Lee*, 3:19.
58. Freeman 3:18–19.
59. Michael Palmer, *Lee Moves North: Robert E. Lee on the Offensive* (New York: John Wiley and Sons, 1998), 63–64, 83, 86–87; Edward H. Bonekemper III, *How Robert E. Lee Lost the Civil War* (Fredericksburg, VA: Sergeant Kirkland's Press, 1997), 125.
60. Nolan 100–101; Faust 23, 39, 300.
61. Nolan 100–101; Grady McWhiney and Perry D. Jamieson, *Attack and Die: Civil War Military Tactics and the Southern Heritage* (Tuscaloosa, AL: University of Alabama Press, 1982), 164.
62. Faust 827.
63. Faust 150, 516.
64. A.L. Long 348–349.
65. John B. Gordon, *Reminiscences of the Civil War* (New York: Charles Scribner's Sons, 1903), 273.
66. Noah Andre Trudeau, *Bloody Roads South: The Wilderness to Cold Harbor, May–June, 1864* (Baton Rouge, LA: Louisiana State University Press, 1989), 6.
67. Nolan 101.
68. Carmichael 26, 59, 64; Alexander, *Fighting for the Confederacy*, 348.
69. Lynda Lasswell Crist, ed., *The Papers of Jefferson Davis*, vol. 10 (Baton Rouge, LA: Louisiana State University Press, 1999), 10:246, 10:335.
70. Crist 10:486 n. 5; Pollard 137.
71. Crist 10:462, 10:466, 10:468 n. 4.
72. Pollard 137.
73. Martin D. Hardin, "The Defense of Washington Against Early's Attack in July 1864," In *Military Essays and Recollections*, Military Order of the Loyal Legion of the United States (MOLLUS), vol. 2 (Chicago, IL: A.C. McClurg, 1894), 135.
74. Gallagher, *Lee and His Army*, 212.

Chapter 3

1. W.W. Goldsborough, *The Maryland Line in the Confederate Army, 1861–1865* (Port Washington, NY: Kennekat Press, 1972), 203.
2. William H. Tidwell with James O. Hall and David Winfred Gaddy, *Come Retribution: The Confederate Secret Service and the Assassination of President Lincoln* (Jackson, MS: University of Mississippi Press, 1988), 19.
3. Goldsborough 203.
4. Goldsborough 203, Tidwell 236.
5. Bradley T. Johnson, "My Ride Around Baltimore in Eighteen Hundred and Sixty-Four," *Southern Historical Society Papers* vol. 30 (1902): 215–216, incorporating article from *Journal of the United States Cavalry Association* 2 (1889): 251; Eric Wittenberg, *Glory Enough for All: Sheridan's Second Raid and the Battle of Trevilian Station* (Washington, DC: Brassy's, 2001), 221; Robert Driver, Jr., *First and Second Maryland Cavalry, C.S.A.* (Charlottesville, VA: Rockbridge Publishing, 1999), 84.
6. Driver 70–71; Goldsborough 244.
7. Benjamin F. Butler, *Private and Official Correspondence of Gen. Benjamin F. Butler*, 5 vols. (Norwood, MA: Plimpton Press, 1917), 3:373–374; Francis Heitman, *Historical Register and Dictionary of the United States Army, 1789–1903* (Washington, DC: US Government Printing Office, 1903), 1052; Samuel F. Bates, *Martial Deeds of Pennsylvania* (Philadelphia, PA: T.H. Davis, 1876), 777–780; Lafayette C. Baker, *The United States Secret Service in the Late War* (St. Louis, MO: J.H. Chambers, 1889), 176–177.
8. Tidwell 241–242; J. William Jones, "The Kilpatrick-Dahlgren Raid Against Richmond," In *Southern Historical Society Papers*, vol. 30 (Richmond, VA: Virginia Historical Society, 1889), 516; Statement of Lieutenant Bartley, *Detroit Free Press*, March 11, 1882.
9. Goldsborough 188–189.
10. Goldsborough 188.
11. Driver 72.
12. Robert C. Black, *The Railroads of the Confederacy* (Chapel Hill, NC: University of North Carolina Press, 1952), 282; Goldsborough 189.
13. Goldsborough 191.
14. Goldsborough 189; J.W. Jones, "Kilpatrick-Dahlgren Raid," 518–519; Driver 72.
15. Tidwell 243; Goldsborough 189–192.
16. Goldsborough 191; Driver 72.
17. Goldsborough 191–192.
18. Goldsborough 190–191.
19. United States War Department, *The War of the Rebellion: A Compilation of the Official Records of the Union and Confederate Armies*. 4 series, 129 volumes (Washington, DC: Government Printing Office, 1880–1900), series 1, vol. 30, part 1, pp. 200–202 (hereafter "US War Dept."); Goldsborough 193.
20. Tidwell 243.
21. Goldsborough 193–194; James O. Hall, "The Dahlgren Papers," *Civil War Times Illustrated*, November 1983, 30–39; J.W. Jones, "Kilpatrick-Dahlgren Raid," 519–520, 530–535.
22. Goldsborough 195, 197, 203; Driver 74.
23. Goldsborough 195–197.
24. Goldsborough 197.
25. Driver 75–76; Goldsborough 198.
26. Goldsborough 198–200.
27. B. Johnson 215; Wittenberg, *Glory Enough*, 282 n. 71.
28. Driver 71; Wittenberg 212.
29. Goldsborough 203; Wittenberg 244–245; Henry Clay Mettan, "Civil War Memories of First Maryland Cavalry, C.S.A.," *Maryland Historical Magazine* 58 (1963): 154.
30. Driver 86; J.W. Jones, "Kilpatrick-Dahlgren Raid," 216.
31. Goldsborough 203.
32. Driver 86; Faust 396.
33. Driver 86–87; Thomas Nelson Conrad, *A Confederate Spy* (New York: J.S. Ogilvie, 1892), 19.
34. Conrad 20–21.
35. Ibid. 292.
36. Ibid. 363.
37. Ibid. 291.
38. Tidwell 442–443.

Chapter 4

1. J. H. Kidd, *Personal Recollections of a Cavalryman* (Iona, MI: Sentinel Printing, 1908), 342.
2. Wittenberg, *Glory Enough*, 23; US War Dept., ser. 1, vol. 36, part 1, p. 795.
3. Philip H. Sheridan, *Personal Memoirs of P.H. Sheridan*, vol. 1 (New York: Charles L. Webster, 1888), 415.
4. Sheridan 417–418.
5. US War Dept., ser. I, vol. 37, part 1, p. 598; Wittenberg, *Glory Enough*, 23.
6. Edward Longacre, *The Life and Wars of James H. Wilson* (Mechanicsburg, PA: Stackpole Books, 2000), 132.

7. Roger S. Keller, ed., *Col. Thomas L. Rosser: Riding with Rosser* (Shippensburg, PA: Burd Street Press, 1997), 38.
8. Wittenberg 23–24.
9. Wittenberg 76.
10. Wittenberg 332–333.
11. Matthew C. Butler, "The Cavalry Fight at Trevilian Station," in *Battles and Leaders of the Civil War*, ed. Johnson and Buell, 4:237.
12. Theo. F. Rodenbough, "Sheridan's Trevilian Raid," in *Battles and Leaders of the Civil War*, ed. Johnson and Buell, 4:233.
13. Wittenberg, *Glory Enough*, 25, 34, n. 64.
14. Rodenbough 233; Kidd 345.
15. Thomas Nelson Conrad, *The Rebel Scout: A Thrilling History of Scouting Life in the Southern Army* (Washington, DC: National, 1904), 110–111; Wittenberg, *Glory Enough*, 42–43.
16. Wittenberg, *Glory Enough*, 43.
17. M.C. Butler 237.
18. Wittenberg 53–56; US War Dept., ser. I, vol. 36, part 1, p. 796.
19. Wittenberg 56.
20. Kidd 346.
21. M.C. Butler 237; Wittenberg 71.
22. Kidd 347.
23. M.C. Butler 237; Faust 763.
24. Rodenbough 233–234; Kidd 349–355.
25. Kidd 360; Rodenbough 234.
26. George W. Booth, *A Maryland Boy in Lee's Army: Personal Reminiscences of a Maryland Soldier in the War Between the States* (Baltimore, MD: Press of Fleet, McGinley, 1898) 120; Driver 84.
27. Wittenberg, *Glory Enough*, 337.
28. Booth 120; Wittenberg 155, 160, 337–339.
29. Wittenberg 176, 177, 204.
30. Wittenberg 176.
31. Rodenbough 234; Wittenberg 176.
32. Wittenberg 176.
33. Rodenbough 234; Wittenberg 177.
34. Wittenberg 184; Asa B. Isham, *Historical Sketch of the Seventh Michigan Volunteer Cavalry* (New York: Town Topics, 1893), 60.
35. Kidd 363.
36. Wittenberg 184–185; Isham 60.
37. Wittenberg 189–191.
38. Wittenberg 192–193; Isham 60–61.
39. M.C. Butler 239; Rodenbough 234; Wittenberg 194.
40. Wittenberg 216–221.
41. Wittenberg 218–245.
42. Thomas T. Mumford, "A Confederate Cavalry Officer's Views on 'American Practice and Foreign Theory,'" *Journal of the United States Cavalry Association* 41 (1891): 202, quoted in Wittenberg 312.
43. Wittenberg 220; Sheridan 415.
44. Wittenberg 220.
45. Eric J. Wittenberg, *Little Phil: A Reassessment of the Civil War Legacy of General Philip H. Sheridan* (Dulles, VA: Brassey's, 2002), 37.

Chapter 5

1. Jack Lepa, *The Shenandoah Valley Campaign of 1864* (Jefferson, NC: McFarland, 2004), 33–45.
2. John D. Imboden, "The Battle of New Market, Va., May 15, 1864," in *Battles and Leaders of the Civil War*, ed. Johnson and Buell, 4:485.
3. Ulysses S. Grant, *Memoirs of Ulysses S. Grant*, 2 vols. (New York: Charles Webster, 1885), 2:238; US War Dept., ser. I, vol. 37, part 1, pp. 485, 492.
4. Edward A. Miller, Jr., *Lincoln's Abolitionist General: A Biography of General David Hunter* (Columbia, SC: University of South Carolina Press, 1997), 3, 37–42, 50–51, 71.
5. Faust 376.
6. "Sigel in the Shenandoah Valley in 1864," in *Battles and Leaders of the Civil War*, ed. Johnson and Buell, 4:491.
7. Cecil D. Eby, Jr., *A Virginia Yankee in the Civil War: The Diaries of David Hunter Strother* (Chapel Hill, NC: University of North Carolina Press, 1961), 231–232; Sanford A. Kellogg, *The Shenandoah Valley and Virginia 1861–1865: A War Sketch* (New York and Washington: The Neale Publishing Company, 1903), 164–165; Charles FitzSimons, "The Hunter Raid," in *Military Essays and Recollections* (MOLLUS) 04 (Chicago, IL: Cozzens and Beach, 1907), 392.
8. US War Dept., ser. I, vol. 37, part 1, p. 507; E. Miller 168.
9. Richard Duncan, *Lee's Endangered Left* (Baton Rouge, LA: Louisiana State University Press, 1998), 143; Feis, *Union Military Intelligence Failure*, 212–213.
10. Duncan 143–144; US War Dept., ser. I, vol. 37, part 1, p. 500.
11. E. Miller 168; US War Dept., ser. I, vol. 37, part 1, pp. 516–517; Lepa 48.
12. US War Dept., ser. I, vol. 37, part 1, p. 525.
13. Faust 711.
14. H.A. DuPont, *The Campaign of 1864 in the Valley of Virginia and the Expedition to Lynchburg* (New York: J.J. Little, 1925), 37–38.
15. E. Miller 170; Lepa 48.
16. DuPont, 49; US War Dept., ser. I, vol. 37, part 1, p. 528.
17. Strother 235–236; E. Miller 171; James Hunter Stevenson, *Boots and Saddles: A History of the First Volunteer Cavalry of the War Know as the First New York (Lincoln) Cavalry* (Harrisburg, PA: Patriot, 1879), 278.
18. US War Dept., ser. I, vol. 37, part 1, pp. 535–536.
19. Strother 235; US War Dept., ser. I, vol. 37, part 1, p. 525; Frank E. Vandiver, *Jubal's Raid: General Early's Famous Attack on Washington* (Gaithersburg, MD: Old Soldier Books, 1988), 36.
20. E. Miller 173.
21. US War Dept., ser. I, vol. 37, part 1, p. 749; Lepa 49.
22. Faust 535; Grant 1:512–575.
23. Harold R. Woodward, Jr., *Defender of the Valley: John Daniel Imboden, C.S.A.* (Berryville, VA: Rockbridge, 1996), 120–121; Imboden 4:485.
24. US War Dept., ser. I, vol. 37, part 1, p. 749; Spencer C. Tucker, *Brigadier General John Imboden: Confederate Commander in the Shenandoah* (Lexington, KY: University Press of Kentucky, 2003), 227; Woodward 119.
25. Marshall Moore Brice, *Conquest of a Valley* (Charlottesville, VA: University of Virginia Press, 1965), 25–26, 29, 33, 37; Vandiver 36; E. Miller 173–174.
26. Brice 26; Thomas Francis Wildes, *Record of the One Hundred and Sixteenth Ohio Volunteer Infantry in the War of the Rebellion* (Sandusky, OH: I.F. Mack and Bros., 1874), 89.
27. E. Miller 169–170.
28. Strother 236; Brice 64.
29. E. Miller 173.
30. Lepa 50.
31. Strother 239.
32. E. Miller 173; Strother 239–240 (quote); US War Dept., ser. I, vol. 37, part 1, pp. 555–556; Richard B. Kleese, *Shenandoah County in the Civil War: The Turbulent Years* (Lynchburg, VA: H.E. Howard, 1992), 67–68.
33. Brice 26–27, 29, 35; Tucker 235.
34. Strother 240–241; E. Miller 175; Imboden 4:485.
35. Brice 33, 37; Lepa 51.

36. F. Ray Sibley, Jr., *The Confederate Order of Battle*, vol. 1: *The Army of Northern Virginia* (Shippensburg, PA: White Mane, 1996), 83; Cooling, *Monocacy*, 248; Imboden 4:485.
37. Frank Moore, ed., *The Rebellion Record: A Diary of American Events* (New York: Van Nostrand, 1868), 11:486.
38. Brice 34–35; Woodward 120–121; Imboden 4:485.
39. Lepa 52; Brice 39.
40. Lepa 53.
41. Strother 242; Brice 43.
42. Strother 243; Woodward 125.
43. E. Miller 185; Woodward 125–126.
44. Lepa 54.
45. George Case Setchell, " A Sergeant's View of the Battle of Piedmont," *Civil War Times Illustrated* 2 (May 1963): 44.
46. William C. Walker, *History of the Eighteenth Regiment Connecticut Volunteers* (Norwalk, CT: published by the committee, 1885), 231–234; Lepa 54.
47. Strother 244; Lepa 54–55.
48. Milton W. Humphries, *A History of the Lynchburg Campaign* (Charlottesville, VA: Michie, 1921), 42; Brice 73.
49. Thomas J. Reed, *Tibbitts Boys—A History of the 21st New York Cavalry* (Lanham, MD: University Press of America, 1997), 130–133; Brice 73; E. Miller 186.
50. Brice 71, 73–74; Lepa 56.
51. US War Dept., ser. I, vol. 37, part 1, p. 118.
52. Lepa 56; Brice 75.
53. Brice 74; E. Miller 187; Robert H. Krick, "The Cause of All My Disaster: Jubal A. Early and the Undisciplined Valley Cavalry," in *The Struggles for the Shenandoah: Essays on the 1864 Valley Campaign*, ed. Gary Gallagher (Kent, OH: Kent State University Press, 1991), 87.
54. Brice 79–80; Lepa 58.
55. John Newton Opie, *A Rebel Cavalryman with Lee, Stuart and Jackson* (Chicago, IL: W.B. Conkey, 1899), 221.
56. US War Dept., ser. I, vol. 37, part 1, p. 95.
57. Lepa 56–57; C.J. Rawling, *History of the First Regiment of Virginia Infantry* (Philadelphia, PA: J.B. Lippincott, 1897), 173–174.
58. Scott Patchan, *The Forgotten Fury: The Battle of Piedmont, Va.* (Fredericksburg: Sgt. Kirkland's Museum and Historical Society, 1996), 224–225.
59. Duncan 247; Imboden 4:486.
60. Strother 245.
61. E. Miller 188.
62. US War Dept., ser. I, vol. 37, part 1, p. 153; Lepa 60.
63. Strother 246.
64. US War Dept., ser. I, vol. 37, part 1, p. 598; E. Miller 185.
65. Grant 1:592; FitzSimons 394; Strother 248; E. Miller 189.
66. Strother 248–249.
67. Strother 250–252.
68. Edward H. Phillips, "The Shenandoah Valley in 1864: An Episode in the History of Warfare" (Charleston, SC: The Citadel, The Military College of South Carolina, May 1985), 11; Kellogg 165.
69. Strother 250; Warner, *Generals in Blue*, 103.
70. Strother 250.
71. Strother 250–251.
72. Faust 578.
73. George Morris and Susan Foutz, *Lynchburg in the Civil War* (Lynchburg, VA: H.E. Howard, 1984), 36.
74. Opie 222; Charles Triplett O'Ferrall, *Forty Years in Active Service* (New York and Washington: The Neale Publishing Co., 1904), 101.
75. Woodward 129.
76. Brice 89, 99, 106, 115; Mark Boatner III, *The Civil War Dictionary* (New York: David McKay, 1959), 433.
77. Crist 10:451.
78. Crist 10:451.
79. Freeman, *R.E. Lee*, 3:368.
80. Charles C. Osborne, *Jubal: The Life and Times of General Jubal A. Early, C.S.A., Defender of the Lost Cause* (Chapel Hill, NC: Algonquin Books, 1992), 240–241; Crist 10:456.
81. Crist 10:457.
82. Jeffrey D. Wert, *From Winchester to Cedar Creek: The Shenandoah Campaign of 1864* (Carlisle, PA: South Mountain Press, 1987) 7; Crist 10:468 n. 4.
83. FitzSimons 399.
84. Lepa 64.
85. Wittenberg, *Little Phil*, 220; Lepa 65.
86. E. Miller 192; Strothe 252.
87. US War Dept., ser. I, vol. 37, part 1, p. 96; E. Miller 192.
88. Strother 252.
89. Brice 115.
90. Ibid.
91. Grant 1:592.
92. E. Miller 197; Brice 115; Strother 252.
93. Brice 117–118.
94. Brice 118.
95. Morris and Foutz 39–40; Brice 118–119.
96. J. Addison Waddell, *Annals of Augusta County* (Staunton, VA: C. Russell Caldwell, 1902), 492; Morris and Foutz 39; Charles M. Blackford, "The Campaign and Battle of Lynchburg," *Southern Historical Society Papers*, vol. 30 (Richmond, VA: William Ellis Jones, 1901), 284–285.
97. Brice 118–119; Blackford 284–285.
98. Brice 118–119; George Crook, *General George Crook: His Autobiography*, ed. Martin F. Schmitt (reprint, Norman, OK: University of Oklahoma Press, 1946), 119; Strother 253.
99. US War Dept., ser. I, vol. 37, part 1, p. 96.
100. Strother 252; E. Miller 192.
101. Strother 252–253; Jennings C. Wise, *Military History of the Virginia Military Institute* (Lynchburg, VA: J.P. Bell, 1915), 354.
102. E. Miller 192.
103. G. Crook 116–117; Strother 253.
104. E. Miller 193.
105. Strother 253.
106. Strother 254.
107. Strother 254–255.
108. Strother 255.
109. US War Dept., ser. I, vol. 37, part 1, p. 97; E. Miller 194.
110. Strother 257; E. Miller 195.
111. G. Crook 117.
112. Rutherford B. Hayes, *Diary and Letters of Rutherford Birchard Hayes, nineteenth president of the United States*. 6 vols., ed. Charles Richard Williams (Columbus, OH: State Archeological and Historical Society, 1922), 4:473–474.
113. DuPont 69.
114. US War Dept., ser. I, vol. 37, part 1, p. 607; Lepa 64.
115. Strother 256.
116. Ibid.; William Server Lincoln, *Life with the 34th Massachusetts Infantry in the War of the Rebellion* (Worcester, MA: Press of Noyes, Snow and Co., 1879), 306.
117. E. Miller 197.
118. Strother 257.
119. Ulysses S. Grant, "General Grant and the Wilderness Campaign," in *Battles and Leaders of the Civil War*, ed. Johnson and Buell, B4:151.

Chapter 6

1. Freeman, *R.E. Lee*, 3:401; Crist 10:462, 10:468 n. 4.
2. US War Dept., ser. I, vol. 36, part 3, p. 897; Freeman 3:401.
3. US War Dept., ser. I, vol. 37, part 1, p. 346.
4. Bruce Catton, *Civil War* (New York: Fairfax Press, 1984), 209, 213; Chittenden 422; Crist 10:486.
5. William B. Feis, *Grant's Secret Service* (Lincoln and London:

University of Nebraska Press, 2002), 217.
6. Osborne 14.
7. Osborne 16.
8. Millard Kessler Bushong, *Old Jube: A Biography of General Jubal A. Early* (Boyce, VA: Carr, 1955), 22–24; Warner, *Generals in Gray* (Baton Rouge, LA: Louisiana State University Press, 1959), 79.
9. Faust 233.
10. Cantor 130.
11. Faust 233.
12. Charles R. Bowery, Jr., *Lee and Grant: Profiles in Leadership from the Battlefields of Virginia* (New York: Amacom, 2005), 124; Sorrel 238–239.
13. Robert Stiles, *Four Years Under Marse Robert* (New York and Washington: The Neale Publishing Co., 1903), 189.
14. Bushong 180–181; Early, *Autobiographical Sketch*, 372.
15. Douglas Southall Freeman, *Lee's Lieutenants: A Study in Command*, 4 vols. (New York: Charles Scribner's Sons, 1942–1946), 3:524.
16. Bushong 187.
17. Crist 10:468 fn4.
18. Henry Kyd Douglas, *I Rode with Stonewall* (Chapel Hill, NC: University of North Carolina Press, 1940), 33; Osborne 23.
19. Crist 10:468 n.4; Early 371.
20. Crist 10:468 Fn 4.
21. US War Dept., ser. 1, vol. 37, part 1, p. 346.
22. Jeffrey D. Wert, "Jubal A. Early and the Confederate Leadership," in *Struggle for the Shenandoah: Essays on the Valley Campaign of 1864*, ed. Gary Gallagher (Kent, OH: Kent State University Press, 1991), 19–23.
23. Early, *Autobiographical Sketch*, 371.
24. Crist 10:462; US War Dept., ser. I, vol. 51, part 2, p. 1006.
25. Early, *Autobiographical Sketch*, 371–372.
26. Early, *Autobiographical Sketch*, 381; Bushong 188.
27. Bushong 158; Osborne 251.
28. Osborne 252.
29. Early, *Autobiographical Sketch*, 372; Lepa 69.
30. Bruce 111, 117; Sibley 83; Morris and Foutz 38, 42; Crist 10:451; Lee to Davis, June 6, 1864 in Robert Edward Lee, *Lee's Dispatches: Unpublished Letters of General Robert E. Lee C.S.A. to Jefferson Davis and the War Department of the Confederate States of America, 1862–1865*, ed. Douglas S. Freeman (New York: G.P. Putnam Sons, 1915), cited in Crist 10:451; Early, *Autobiographical Sketch*, 373–374; Blackford 307.
31. Morris and Fautz 40.
32. US War Dept., ser. I, vol. 37, part 2, pp. 627–628, 631; E. Miller 197.
33. Strother 257.
34. Strother 257–258.
35. Strother 257.
36. Feis, *Military Intelligence Failure*, 218.
37. Feis 215.
38. Lepa 67.
39. Bushong 186; E. Miller 198; Strother 259.
40. Strother 258; E. Miller 197.
41. Strother 261.
42. Lepa 68.
43. US War Dept., ser. I, vol. 37, part 1, pp. 98–99; Osborne 257; Warner, *Generals in Blue*, 487–488; E. Miller 199.
44. Early, *Autobiographical Sketch*, 379.
45. Ibid.
46. Ibid., 375.
47. Charles H. Porter, "Operations of Generals Sigel and Hunter in the Shenandoah Valley, May and June, 1864," *Papers of the Military Historical Society of Massachusetts*, by the Society (Boston, MA: 1907), 6:81–82.
48. Early, *Autobiographical Sketch*, 373.
49. US War Dept., ser. I, vol. 37, part 1, pp. 762–763; Early, *Autobiographical Sketch*, 373; Morris and Foutz 42.
50. Lepa 69; Brian Thomsen, ed., *Commanding Voices of Blue and Gray* (New York: Tom Doherty Associates, 2002), 301–303.
51. US War Dept., ser. I, vol. 37, part 1, p. 763.
52. Early, *Autobiographical Sketch*, 373.
53. US War Dept., ser. I, vol. 37, part 1, p. 763; Lepa 69.
54. Jubal A. Early, *A Memoir of the Last Year of the War of Independence in the Confederate States of America* (New Orleans, LA: Blalock, 1867), 36; Early, *Autobiographical Sketch*, 372.
55. Osborne 254; Morris and Foutz 43; Lepa 70.
56. Bushong 188; Osborne 254.
57. Duncan, *Lee's Endangered Left*, 269.
58. John H. Worsham, *One of "Jackson's Foot Cavalry": His Experience and What He Saw, 1861–1865* (New York: The Neale Publishing Company, 1912), 229; Lepa 70.
59. Morris and Foutz 43; Imboden 4:486.
60. Strother 262.
61. Early, *Autobiographical Sketch*, 374; Morris and Foutz 43; E. Miller 197; Blackford 288.
62. Strother 263.
63. Ibid., 263.
64. Ibid.
65. US War Dept., ser. I, vol. 37, part 1, p. 99; E. Miller 200.
66. US War Dept., ser. I, vol. 37, part 1, p. 99; E. Miller 200; Osborne 257.
67. Strother 264.
68. Early, *Autobiographical Sketch*, 373; Osborne 255; John O. Casler, *Four Years in the Stonewall Brigade* (Dayton, OH: Morningside, 1971), 225.
69. Early, *Autobiographical Sketch*, 373; Faust 78.
70. Lepa 71–78; Early, *Autobiographical Sketch*, 374.
71. Early, *Autobiographical Sketch*, 374; Bushong 189; Lepa 70–71.
72. Imboden 4:486; Early, *Autobiographical Sketch*, 374.
73. Edward M. Daniel, *Speeches and Orations of John Warwick Daniel* (Lynchburg, VA: J.P. Bell, 1911), 541.
74. Morris and Foutz 44.
75. Imboden 4:486; Faust 378–379.
76. US War Dept., ser. I, vol. 37, part 1, p. 141.
77. John C. Bonnell, *Sabres in the Shenandoah: The 21st New York Cavalry, 1863–1866* (Shippensburg, PA: Burd Street Press, 1996), 87.
78. Major General David Hunter, "The Opposing Forces in the Lynchburg Expedition—The Union Army," in *Battles and Leaders*, ed. Johnson and Buell, 4:492; B. Franklin Cooling, *Jubal Early's Raid on Washington in 1864* (Baltimore, MD: Nautical and Aviation Publishing Co., 1989), 265–267.
79. Hayes 3:474.
80. William H. Armstrong, *Major McKinley: William McKinley and the Civil War* (Kent, OH, and London: Kent State University Press, 2000), 5.
81. Hunter, "Opposing Forces," 4:492; Cooling, *Jubal Early's Raid*, 265–267.
82. Lepa 71; Early, *Memoir*, 37–38.
83. US War Dept., ser. I, vol. 37, part 1, p. 99; Lepa 71.
84. Strother 265.
85. US War Dept., ser. I, vol. 37, part 1, p. 42.
86. US War Dept., ser. I, vol. 37, part 1, p. 650; Blackford 307.
87. E. Miller 201; Strother 265.
88. Early, *Autobiographical Sketch*, 375; Moore 11:531.
89. Strother 265.
90. DuPont 78.
91. Strother 265–266; Blackford 292.
92. US War Dept., ser. I, vol. 37, part 1, p. 148; E. Miller 202.

93. US War Dept., ser. I, vol. 37, part 1, p. 142; Woodward 138.
94. Morris and Foutz 47; Moore 11:531.
95. Morris and Foutz 47; Warner, *Generals in Gray*, 263.
96. Early, *Autobiographical Sketch*, 375–376.
97. Strother 266.
98. US War Dept., ser. I, vol. 37, part 1, p. 100.
99. DuPont 83; Moore 11:487.
100. Lepa 77.
101. Osborne 258.
102. Early, *Autobiographical Sketch*, 376.
103. US War Dept., ser. I, vol. 37, part 1, p. 143; Lepa 78.
104. Lepa 77.
105. William B. Stark, "The Great Skeddadle," *Atlantic Monthly*, July 1938, 86.
106. Early, *Autobiographical Sketch*, 376; Gordon 300.
107. Kellogg 176.
108. Tucker 260.
109. Early, *Autobiographical Sketch*, 379.
110. Stark 87.
111. US War Dept., ser. I, vol. 37, part 1, p. 160.
112. Early, *Autobiographical Sketch*, 376.
113. Strother 267–268.
114. Lepa 80; Strother 268–269.
115. Strother 269.
116. Stark 88.
117. John Y. Simon, ed., *The Papers of Ulysses S. Grant*, vol. 11, June 1– August 15, 1864 (Carbondale and Edwardsville, IL: Southern Illinois University Press, 1982), 101–102.
118. Strother 269; Lee, *Recollections and Letters*, 217.
119. US War Dept., ser. I, vol. 37, part 1, pp. 101–102; E. Miller 213.
120. Early, *Autobiographical Sketch*, 378.
121. Early, *Autobiographical Sketch*, 380–382.
122. Lee, *Recollections and Letters*, 217; Early 380.
123. Crist 10:484.
124. Ibid.
125. Ibid.
126. Strother 271.
127. Strother 272–275.
128. Stark 121–122.
129. E. Miller 215, 219, 221.
130. Freeman, *Lee's Lieutenants*, 3:524.
131. Bushong 187.
132. Jubal A. Early, "Early's March on Washington in 1864," in *Battles and Leaders*, ed. Johnson and Buell, 4:493.
133. Early, *Autobiographical Sketch*, 380.
134. Ibid., 380–382; Casler 225–228; Laura Virginia Hall, *Four Violent Years in the Shenandoah Valley, 1861–1865* (Strasburg, VA: Shenandoah Publishing House, 1968), 378–380; Cooling, *Monocacy*, 11; Moore 11:597.
135. Feis 220.
136. Ibid., 221.
137. Early, *Autobiographical Sketch*, 382–383.
138. Simon 11:262.

Chapter 7

1. National Park Service, "Jubal Early's Raid on Washington DC/Battle of Fort Stevens," in *Historic Resource Study*, part 1, chapter 7, p. 2; Early 371.
2. Early 380; Crist 10:487 n. 5; General A.L. Long, "General Early's Valley Campaign," in *Southern Historical Society Papers*, vol. 30 (Richmond, VA: Virginia Historical Society, 1877), 112.
3. Early 382; Benjamin Franklin Cooling, *Jubal Early's Raid on Washington: 1864* (Baltimore, MD: Nautical and Aviation Publishing Co., 1989), 24; Joseph Judge, *Season of Fire: The Confederate Strike on Washington* (Berryville, VA: Rockbridge, 1994), 116.
4. Early, "Early's March on Washington in 1864," 4:493; Early, *Autobiographical Sketch*, 382–383; Judge 116.
5. Cooling, *Jubal Early's Raid*, 25.
6. Early, *Autobiographical Sketch*, 371.
7. William B. Feis, "Neutralizing the Valley: The Role of Military Intelligence in the Defeat of Jubal Early's Army of the Valley, 1864–1865," in *Civil War History*, vol. 39, no. 3 (Kent, OH: Kent State University Press, 1993), 200–201; Feis, "Union Military Intelligence Failure," 209.
8. H.E. Matheny, *Major-General Thomas Maley Harris* (Parsons, WV: McClain, 1963), 87.
9. Cooling, *Jubal Early's Raid*, 267.
10. Ibid., 269–270.
11. Cooling, *Monocacy*, 13.
12. Ibid.
13. Early, *Autobiographical Sketch*, 383.
14. Cooling, *Jubal Early's Raid*, 187.
15. Early, *Autobiographical Sketch*, 383; Brian M. Thomsen, ed., *Commanding Voices of Blue and Gray* (New York: Tom Doherty Associates, 2002), 310.
16. Cooling, *Monocacy*, 13
17. Lew Wallace, *An Autobiography* (New York: Harper and Brothers, 1898), 754.

Chapter 8

1. National Park Service, Appendix E: "General Reports about the Defenses," in *The Civil War Defenses of Washington: A Historic Resource Study*, part 1, 22–35; US War Dept., ser. I, vol. 26, part 2, pp. 883–897; Benjamin Franklin Cooling and Walter B. Owen, *Mr. Lincoln's Forts: A Guide to the Civil War Defenses of Washington* (Shippensburg, PA: White Mane, 1984), 137–148.
2. John G. Barnard, *A Report on the Defenses of Washington to the Chief of Engineers*. US Army Corps of Engineers, Corps of Engineers, Professional Paper No. 20 (Washington, DC: The Government Printing Office, 1871), 496.
3. National Park Service, "Maintenance of the Defenses," 6:4; Cooling and Owen 103–148.
4. Boatner 578, 621.
5. National Park Service, app. E, 33.
6. National Archives, extract of military map of NE Virginia showing forts and roads and Civil War defenses of Washington, 1865, drawer 171, sheet 91; National Park Service, app. E, 33–34.
7. National Park Service, app. E, 24.
8. National Park Service, app. E, 23.
9. National Park Service, app. E, 25–28, US War Dept., ser. I, vol. 26, part 2, pp. 886–890.
10. General John G. Barnard to General S.P. Heinzelman, March 31, 1863, quoting report of Commission order by Secretary of War to report on defenses of Washington; US War Dept., ser. I, vol. 25, part 2, pp. 177–180; National Park Service, app. E, 15.
11. National Park Service, app. E, 22.
12. Barnard, *Report on the Defenses*, 84; National Park Service, app. E, 32–33.
13. National Park Service, app. E, 29–30.
14. George W. Ward, *History of the Second Pennsylvania Heavy Artillery (112th Regiment Pennsylvania Volunteers) from 1861–1866* (Philadelphia, PA: G.W. Ward, 1904), 75.
15. Edgar S. Dudley, "A Reminiscence of Washington and Early's Attack in 1864," in *Sketches of Civil War*

History (MOLLUS, Vol. 1; reprint, Wilmington, NC: Broadfoot, 1991), 115.

16. National Park Service, app. E, 30.

17. Horace J. Shaw and Charles House, *First Maine Heavy Artillery: A Regimental History* (Portland, ME: Charles House, 1903), 109; Whitelaw Reid, *Ohio in the War: Her Statesmen, Her Generals, and Soldiers* (Cincinnati, OH: Wilstack and Baldwin, 1868), 2:682; William Offutt, *Bethesda: A Social History of the Area Through World War Two* (Bethesda, MD: McNaughton, 1985), 38.

18. John M. Wilson, *The Defenses of Washington, 1861–1865* (Washington, DC: Military Order of the Loyal Legion of the United States, Dec. 1901), no. 38, 262.

19. Cooling and Owen 147; Edward W. Emerson, *Life and Letters of Charles Russell Lowell* (Columbia, SC: University of South Carolina Press, 2005), 321; Hardin 132–133; Cooling, *Jubal Early's Raid*, 120; National Park Service, app. H, 22–24.

20. Janet B. Hewett, ed., *Supplement to the Official Records of the Union and Confederate Armies*, part II, vol. 41, ser. 53 (Wilmington, NC: Broadfoot) 677, 682; J.G. Barnard to H.W. Halleck, July 9, 1864; US War Dept., ser. I, vol. 37, part 2, p. 140.

21. Cooling and Owen 143.

22. National Park Service, app. E, 31; Margaret Leech, *Reveille in Washington, 1860–1865* (New York: Harper and Bros., 1941), 337; Cooling and Owen 151.

23. Cooling and Owen 101–103.

24. Ibid., 151–152.

25. National Park Service, app. E, 31; Cooling, *Jubal Early's Raid*, 99–100; Reid 2:677, 682.

26. Cooling and Owen 156.

27. Revised United States Army Regulations of 1861 with Appendix Containing the Changes and Laws Affecting Army Regulations and Articles of War to June, 1863, Care of Fortifications, Art. IX, No. 42, (Washington, D.C.: US Government Printing Office, 1863).

28. National Park Service, app. E, 32.

29. J. Leeke, ed., *A Hundred Days to Richmond: Ohio's "Hundred Days" Men in the Civil War* (Bloomington and Indianapolis, Indiana: Indiana University Press, 1999), 129–137.

30. Cooling and Owens 167.

31. Ibid.

32. National Park Service, app. E, 32–33; Reid 2:681.

33. Cooling and Owen 167.

34. National Park Service 7:8.

35. Cooling and Owen 167.

36. J.M. Wilson 270.

37. National Park Service, app. E, 32.

38. National Park Service, app. E, 33; Reid 2:681.

39. Frederick H. Dyer, *A Compendium of the War of the Rebellion* (Des Moines, IA: Dyer Publishing, 1868), s.v. "First Vermont Heavy Artillery."

40. National Park Service, app. E, 33.

41. Reid 2:681.

42. National Park Service, app. E, 33–34.

43. Cooling, *Jubal Early's Raid*, 95.

44. US War Dept., ser. I, vol. 37, part 2, p. 140.

45. US War Dept., ser. I, vol. 37, part 2, p. 83; National Park Service, app. H, 1; Faust 40.

46. National Park Service, app. E, 27–28.

47. Hewett 677–682.

48. National Park Service, app. E, 28–29.

49. Dudley Landon Vail, *The County Regiment: A sketch of the Second Connecticut Volunteer Heavy Artillery* (Litchfield County University Club, 1908), 25, 46.

50. Reid 2:665.

51. National Park Service, app. E, 29; Official Souvenir and Program of Monument First Connecticut Heavy Artillery and Dedicatory Exercises (Hartford, CT: R.S. Peck, 1902), 60, 69, 81.

52. National Park Service, app. E, 27.

53. E.B. Bennett, "First Connecticut Heavy Artillery," *Historical Sketch and Present Addresses of Members*, (Hartford, CT: Star Print Co., 1889), 12–13; Reid 2:696.

54. National Park Service, app. E, 26.

55. Alfred Seelye Roe and Charles Nutt, *History of the First Regiment of Heavy Artillery, Massachusetts Volunteers* (Worcester and Boston: Commonwealth Press, 1917), 148–150; National Park Service, app. E, 26.

56. Frederick Phisterer, *New York in the War of the Rebellion* (Albany, NY: J.P. Lyon, 1912), s.v. "2nd New York Heavy Artillery."

57. Ibid.

58. National Park Service, app. E, 25.

59. Hewett 731; Phisterer, "2nd New York Heavy Artillery."

60. Cooling, *Jubal Early's Raid*, 260–262.

61. Shaw and House 109.

62. Vandiver 142.

63. Warner, *Generals in Blue*, 12; Cooling, *Jubal Early's Raid*, 97.

64. Hewett 749.

65. Cooling, *Jubal Early's Raid*, 99.

66. Ibid., 96.

67. Hardin 128; Cooling, *Jubal Early's Raid*, 100.

68. Cooling, *Jubal Early's Raid*, 99–100.

69. Judge 225.

70. Cooling, *Jubal Early's Raid*, 100–101.

71. Vandiver 143.

72. Judge 225; Leech 336; National Park Service, app. H, 27–28.

73. National Park Service, app. H, 28; Reid 2:681.

74. Lepa 106; Leech 335.

75. Cooling, *Jubal Early's Raid*, 115; William E. Doster, *Lincoln and Episodes of the Civil War* (New York: G.P. Putnam Sons, 1915), 252; Leech 341.

76. Dyer, s.v. "2nd District of Columbia"; National Park Service app. H, 25.

77. Charles H. Dana, *Recollections of the Civil War* (New York: D. Appleton, 1892), 232; Curt Anders, *Henry Halleck's War: A Fresh Look at Lincoln's controversial General-in-chief* (Carmel, IN: Guild Press of Indiana, 1999), 590.

78. Rear Admiral S.P. Lee to Gideon Wells, July 14, 1864 in National Park Service, app. H, 10.

79. Anders 590.

80. US War Dept., ser. I, vol. 37, part 1, pp. 234–235.

Chapter 9

1. Crist 10:487, 10:492–493; Magnus S. Thompson, "Plan to Release Our Men at Point Lookout," *Confederate Veteran* 20 (Feb. 1912): 69–70.

2. Early, *Autobiographical Sketch*, 385; Lee, *Recollections and Letters*, 131–132; Cooling, *Jubal Early's Raid*, 39.

3. Edwin W. Beitzell, *Point Lookout Prison Camp for Confederates* (Leonardtown, MD: Saint Mary's County Historical Society, 1991), 19–20.

4. Lonnie R. Speer, *Portals to Hell: Military Prisons in the Civil War* (Lincoln, NE: University of Nebraska Press, 1997), 148; Thomas McAnear, descendant of Pvt. Francis Oswalt, to author, January 25, 2007; Warner, *Generals in Gray*, 237–238.

5. Beitzell 20; J. Michael Martinez, *Life and Death in Civil War Prisons* (Nashville, TN: Rutledge Hill, 2004), 44.

6. Richard A. Blando, "A View of Point Lookout Prison Camp for Confederates," *Magazine of History* 8.1 (Fall 1993): 30; Beitzell 20, 176, 182; Charles W. Sanders, Jr. *While in the Hands of the Enemy: Military Prisons of the Civil War* (Baton Rouge, LA: Louisiana State University Press, 2005), 173.
7. US War Dept., ser. II, vol. 6, part 1, pp. 140–141.
8. A.W. Bartlett, *History of the 12th Regiment N.H. Volunteers* (Concord, NH: Ira Cross, 1887), 145–146; E.M. Colvin, "A Visit to Point Lookout Prison," *Confederate Veteran* 22 (December 1914): 544; Beitzell 116.
9. Sanders 173.
10. Beitzell 20; Heitman 2:508, 534.
11. Glenn H. Worthington, *Fighting for Time: The Battle That Saved Washington and Mayhap the Union* (Frederick, MD: Frederick County Historical Society, 1932), 21–23; Beitzell 20.
12. Martin A. Haynes, *History of the Second Regiment New Hampshire Volunteer Infantry, in the War of the Rebellion* (Manchester NH: C.F. Livingston, 1865), 155–161.
13. Dyer, s.v. "Twelfth New Hampshire Regiment."
14. Mike Drake and Mark Travis, *My Brave Boys: To War with Colonel Cross and the Fighting Fifth* (Hanover and London: University Press of New England, 2001), 135–138, 176, 242, 260.
15. Beitzell 41; Anthony M. Keiley, *In Vinculis, or the Prisoner of War* (New York: Bleilock, 1866), 58.
16. Beitzell 54, 105.
17. Ibid., 53.
18. Beitzell 20; Faust 588; Francis H. Casstevens, *Out of the Mouth of Hell, Civil War Prisons and Escapes* (Jefferson, NC, and London: McFarland, 2005), 163.
19. Beitzell 41.
20. Blando 33; Beitzell 41.
21. Beitzell 40–41.
22. Jane Turner Censer, ed., *The Papers of Frederick Law Olmstead*, vol. 4, *Defending the Union: The Civil War and the U.S. Sanitary Commission 1861–1863* (Baltimore, MD: Johns Hopkins University Press, 1986), 4:684; Beitzell 176.
23. US War Dept., ser. II, vol. 6, part 1, pp. 764–767; Beitzell 23.
24. Casstevens 163; E.M. Colvin, "Prison Experience at Point Lookout," *Confederate Veteran* 15 (September 1907): 400.
25. Bartlett 169.
26. Bartlett Yancey Malone, "Whipt 'Em Everytime: The Diary of Bartlett Yancey Malone (Jackson, TN: McCowat-Mercer, 1960), 98.
27. George H. Allen, *Forty-Six Months with the Fourth Rhode Island Volunteers* (Providence, RI: J.A. and R.A. Reid, 1887), 256, 257, 270.
28. Edward Longacre, *A Regiment of Slaves: The Fourth United States Colored Regiment, 1863–1866* (Mechanicsburg, PA: Stackpole Books, 2003), 65–67, 116–127.
29. Bartlett 159; Crist 10:488.
30. Reid 2:668.
31. Dyer, s.v. "29th U.S. Colored."
32. Massachusetts Adjutant General's Office, *Soldiers, Sailors and Marines in the Civil War*, vol. 6 (Norwood, MA: The Norwood Press, 1932), s.v. "5th Massachusetts Colored Cavalry"; Simon 11:119–121.
33. Beitzell 23:181; Official Register of the Volunteer Forces, US Army, Part VIII, Veteran Reserve Corps, US Colored Troops, Adjutant General's Office, Washington, DC: July 15, 1867.
34. Crist 10:488.
35. Beitzell 54.
36. Crist 10:485.
37. Beitzell 41; Malone 104.
38. Crist 10:510–516.

Chapter 10

1. Worthington 7.
2. Cooling, *Jubal Early's Raid*, 42, 249.
3. Early, *Autobiographical Sketch*, 383, 386; Robert E. Park, "The Twelfth Alabama Infantry, Confederate States Army," Southern Historical Society Papers (Richmond, VA: Virginia Historical Society, 1905) 33: 377.
4. John E. Olson, *21st Virginia Cavalry* (Lynchburg, VA: H. E. Howard, 1989), 23: Worthington 13; Faust 688.
5. Olson 23–24; Early, *Autobiographical Sketch*, 383; Faust 455–456.
6. Matheny 86–87.
7. Matheny 84.
8. Faust 435–436.
9. Matheny 84–87.
10. Bushong 195.
11. US War Dept., ser. I, vol. 37, part 1, pp. 175–176; Josephus Junior, *The Annals of Harper's Ferry, West Virginia* (printed at the Offices of the Beckley Union, 1872) 83; Matheny 88; C. Armour Newcomer, *Cole's Cavalry; or, Three Years in the Saddle in the Shenandoah Valley* (Freeport, NY: Books for Libraries, 1970), 127–128.
12. Bushong 195; Judge 127–128; Samuel Clarke Farrar, *The 22nd Pennsylvania Cavalry* (Pittsburg, PA: New Werner Co., 1911), 257–263.
13. Early, *Autobiographical Sketch*, 384.
14. Olson 24; Stephen D. Engle, *Yankee Dutchman: The Life of Franz Sigel* (Fayetteville, AK: University of Arkansas Press, 1993), 204–205.
15. Engle 205.
16. Cooling, *Jubal Early's Raid*, 26; Engle 204–205; US War Dept., ser. I, vol. 37, part 1, pp. 175–176.
17. Reid 2:664, 690, 691.
18. Leeke 111; Judge 128–130; Cooling, *Jubal Early's Raid*, 26.
19. Cooling, *Monocacy*, 14; US War Dept., ser. I, vol. 37, part 1, pp. 176.
20. Thomas McCurdy Vincent, "Early's March to Washington," in *Washington During War Time: A Series of Papers Showing the Military, Political and Social Phases During 1861–1865*, official souvenir of the thirty-sixth annual encampment of the Grand Army of the Republic, collected and edited by Marcus Benjamin under the direction of the Committee on Literature for the Encampment (Washington, DC: National Tribune Co., n.d.), 51.
21. Feis, *Grant's Secret Service*, 230.
22. Worsham 149.
23. Cooling, *Jubal Early's Raid*, 28–29.
24. Benjamin Franklin Cooling, *Symbol, Sword and Shield: Defending Washington During the Civil War* (Shippensburg, PA: White Mane, 1991), 188.
25. Early, *Autobiographical Sketch*, 383.
26. Jeffrey C. Weaver, *22nd Virginia Cavalry* (Lynchburg, VA: H.E. Howard, [missing year]), 31; Reid 2:664.
27. Festus P. Summers, *The Baltimore and Ohio in the Civil War* (New York: G.P. Putnam's Sons, 1939), 124.
28. James Earl Brown, "Life of Brigadier General John McCausland," *West Virginia History* 4.4 (July 1943): 239–293; Michael J. Pauley, *Unreconstructed Rebel: The Life of General John McCausland, C.S.A.* (Charleston, WV: Pictorial Histories, 1993), 48.
29. Tucker 263–264; US War Dept. ser. I, vol. 37, part 1, pp. 186, 190.
30. Matheny 88.
31. Moore 2:153; James R. Swisher, "Following Old Jube: Richmond to Washington," *Confederate Veteran* 5 (2000): 21.
32. Cooling 41; Crist 10:496.

33. Worsham 154; Vandiver 81.
34. Early, *Autobiographical Sketch*, 384.
35. Engle 205; Judge 133.
36. Lee C. Drickamer and Karen D. Drickamer, eds., *Fort Lyons to Harper's Ferry; On the Border of North and South with "Ramblin' Jour": The Letters and Newspaper Dispatches of Charles H. Moulton (34th Mass. Volunteer Infantry)* (Shippensburg, PA: White Mane, 1987), 192–193.
37. Bushong 195.
38. Wilhelm Kaufman, *The Germans in the American Civil War* (Carlisle, PA: John Kallmann, 1999); Warner, *Generals in Blue*, 545–546; US War Dept. ser. I, vol. 37, part 1, p. 185.
39. Matheny 89.
40. Engle 205; Daniel Carroll Toomey, *The Civil War in Maryland* (Baltimore, MD: Toomey Press, 1983) 101.
41. Early, *Autobiographical Sketch*, 384.
42. Engle 206; Judge 140.
43. Leeke 110–111; Worthington 14.
44. Judge 128.
45. Judge 141; James R. Swisher, *Warrior in Gray: General Robert Rodes of Lee's Army* (Shippensburg, PA: White Mane, 2000), 202.
46. Park 377.
47. Judge 141.
48. George E. Lester, "War Record of the Tom Cobb Infantry," in *This They Remembered*, United Daughters of the Confederacy, eds., Olgethorpe County Chapter 1292, (Washington, GA: Washington Publishing Co., 1965), 104–105; Cooling, *Jubal Early's Raid*, 28–29; Judge 141.
49. Kellogg 178.
50. Matheny 89–90; US War Dept., ser. I, vol. 37, part 1, pp. 176–177.
51. Cooling, *Jubal Early's Raid*, 27; Lepa 90.
52. US War Dept., ser. I, vol. 37, part 2, p. 592.
53. Early, *Autobiographical Sketch*, 384; Swisher, *Warrior in Grey*, 22; Bushong 196.
54. Feis, "Union Military Intelligence Failure," 223.
55. Judge 143; Richard L. Armstrong, *25th Virginia Infantry and 9th Battalion Virginia Infantry* (Lynchburg, VA: H.E. Howard, 1990), 80.
56. Worthington 262.
57. Cooling, *Jubal Early's Raid*, 37; Early, *Autobiographical Sketch*, 384.
58. Early, *Autobiographical Sketch*, 384.
59. Worsham 232–234; Vandiver 87, 98; Judge 143.
60. Faust 613.
61. Early, *Autobiographical Sketch*, 384; Cooling, *Monocacy*, 30.
62. Judge 146.
63. Douglas 293; Cooling, *Jubal Early's Raid*, 40.
64. Judge 145–146; Matheny 90; Cooling, *Jubal Early's Raid*, 41–42.
65. Irving McKee, "Ben Hur" Wallace: The Life of General Lew Wallace (Berkeley and Los Angeles, CA: The University of California Press, 1947), 71.
66. Wallace 704.
67. Wallace 706.
68. Cooling, *Jubal Early's Raid*, 269.
69. Worthington 258.
70. Wallace 707.
71. McKee 71.
72. US War Dept., ser. I, vol. 37, part 2, pp. 16–17; Lepa 87; Judge 129.
73. Cooling, *Monocacy*, 31, 38.
74. Feis, "Union Military Intelligence Failure," 222.
75. Wallace 711.
76. Cooling, *Symbol, Sword and Shield*, 191.
77. George E. Pond, *The Shenandoah Valley in 1864* (reprint, Wilmington, NC: Broadfoot, 1989), 174.
78. Wallace 707–708.
79. Worthington 53.
80. Judge 139; Vandiver 99–100.
81. Judge 137, 144–145; Bain 98–99.
82. Feis, *Grant's Secret Service*, 223; Judge 146.
83. Early, *Autobiographical Sketch*, 384.
84. US War Dept., ser. I, vol. 37, part 1, pp. 180–183.
85. Judge 150.
86. Matheny 90.
87. Cooling, *Jubal Early's Raid*, 39.
88. Cooling, *Jubal Early's Raid*, 42; Judge 151–152.
89. Judge 151–152.
90. Lee, *Recollections and Letters*, 131.
91. Royce Gordon Shingleton, *John Taylor Wood: Sea Ghost of the Confederacy* (Athens, GA: University of Georgia Press, 1979), 116.
92. Worthington 33.

Chapter 11

1. Judge 116; Early, *Autobiographical Sketch*, 371, 380–381; Cooling, *Jubal Early's Raid*, 17.
2. Faust 265, 358; Brice 19.
3. Richard D. Goff, *Confederate Supply* (Durham, NC: Duke University Press, 1969), 16, 20, 26.
4. Ibid., 118.
5. Report of Commissary General L.B. Northrup to Confederate Secretary of War John C. Breckinridge of February 9, 1865, published as "Resources of the Confederacy," *Southern Historical Society Papers* (Richmond, VA: Virginia Historical Society, 1905), 2:85–105, 2:113–128.
6. Thomas L. Livermore, *Numbers and Losses in the Civil War 1861–64* (Bloomington, IN: Kessinger Publishing, 2006), 2–3.
7. Goff 72; Black 177.
8. Cooling, *Jubal Early's Raid*, 42; Blackford 309.
9. Cooling, *Jubal Early's Raid*, 16; Early, *Autobiographical Sketch*, 381–382.
10. Early, *Autobiographical Sketch*, 382.
11. Cooling, *Jubal Early's Raid*, 16, 40; Casler 226–228.
12. Cooling, *Monocacy*, 14.
13. Worsham 233–234.
14. Cooling, *Jubal Early's Raid*, 42.
15. Early, *Autobiographical Sketch*, 385.

Chapter 12

1. Jean Edward Smith, *Grant* (New York: Simon and Schuster, 2001), 284, 286, 293–294; Faust 320; Bruce Catton, *Grant Takes Command*, (Boston: Little, Brown & Co., 1969), 129–132; William Tecumseh Sherman, *Memoirs of General T. Sherman* (New York: Library of America, 1990), 463.
2. Horace Porter, *Campaigning with Grant* (New York: Century, 1899), 18–19; Doris Kearns Goodwin, *Team of Rivals: The Political Genius of Abraham Lincoln* (New York: Simon & Schuster, 2005), 614–615; Shelby Foote, *Civil War* (New York: Random House, 1974), 6.
3. Porter 20.
4. Grant 370; Goodwin 617; Catton 143.
5. William McFeely, *Grant* (London: W.W. Norton, 1982), 152; Sherman 259.
6. John Hay, *Inside Lincoln's White House: The Complete Civil War Diary of John Hay*, ed. Michael Burlingame and John R. Turner Ettlinger (Carbondale, IL: Southern Illinois University Press, 1999), 192; Abraham Lincoln to U.S. Grant April 30, 1864, Abraham Lincoln, *Collected Works of Abraham Lincoln*, ed. Roy Basler (New Brunswick, NJ: Rutgers University Press, 1953), 8:324.
7. Michael Korda, *Ulysses S.

Grant: The Unlikely Hero (New York: Harper Collins, 2004), 97; Hay 193; Goodwin 618.
   8. E.M. Law, "From the Wilderness to Cold Harbor," in *Battles and Leaders of the Civil War*, ed. Johnson and Buell, 4:122; Faust 825.
   9. William B. Feis, *Grant's Secret Service: The Intelligence War from Belmont to Appomattox*, (Lincoln, NE: University of Nebraska Press, 2002), 268; Ulysses S. Grant to Julia Dent Grant, May 13, 1864, in *The Papers of Ulysses S. Grant*, ed. John Y. Simon (Carbondale and Edwardsville, IL: Southern Illinois University Press, 1982), 444; Alexander McClure, *Lincoln and Men of Wartimes*, (Lincoln, NE: University of Nebraska Press, 1997), 193–194.
   10. Gideon Welles, *Diary*, 2:33 (entry for May 17, 1864).
   11. Edward Bates, *The Diary of Edward Bates, 1859–1866* (New York: Da Capo, 1971), entry for May 14, 1864, 366.
   12. Faust 827; McClure 193–194.
   13. Welles 25 (entry for May 7, 1864).
   14. Lincoln, *Collected Works*, 7:394–395 (speech at Great Central Sanitary Fair, Philadelphia, PA, June 16, 1864).
   15. Doris Kearns Goodwin, *Team of Rivals: The Political Genius of Abraham Lincoln* (New York, London, Toronto and Sydney: Simon and Schuster, 2005). 620.
   16. Simon 10:422 (Ulysses S. Grant to Edwin M. Stanton, May 11, 1864).
   17. Henry E. Wing, *When Lincoln Kissed Me: A Story of the Wilderness Campaign* (New York: Eaton and Mains, 1913), 12–13.
   18. Mottelay and Campbell 2:406.
   19. *New York Times*, May 15, 1864.
   20. Hay 195.
   21. Mottelay and Campbell 2:407.
   22. Grant 2:462.
   23. Grant 1:588.
   24. Faust 150.
   25. Trudeau 341 (Table of Casualties).
   26. Welles 44 (entry for June 2, 1864).
   27. Ibid., 54–55 (entry for June 20, 1864).
   28. John C. Waugh, *Reelecting Lincoln* (New York: Crown, 1997), 192, 195, 196.
   29. *New York Times*, June 13, 1864.
   30. Faust 51.
   31. Worthington 13–14.
   32. Feis, "Union Military Intelligence Failure," 209–225.
   33. Feis, *Grant's Secret Service*, 241–242.
   34. James C. Young, *Marse Robert, Knight of the Confederacy* (New York: Rae D. Hinckle, 1929), 284.
   35. Robert M. Stribling, *Gettysburg Campaign and the Campaigns of 1864 and 1865 in Virginia* (Petersburg, VA: Franklin Press, 1905), 169.
   36. Frank Abial Flower, *Edwin McMasters Stanton: The Autocrat of Rebellion, Emancipation and Reconstruction* (Akron, OH: Soalfield, 1905), 389.
   37. Feis, *Grant's Secret Service*, 228.
   38. Cooling, *Jubal Early's Raid*, 32; Feis 220.
   39. Simon 11:113.
   40. Cooling, *Monocacy*, 19; Feis, "Neutralizing the Valley," 200–201.
   41. Simon 11:143.
   42. Feis, "Union Military Intelligence Failure," 220.
   43. Ibid., 221.
   44. Ibid., 221.
   45. Simon 11:131–153.
   46. Dana 22; Feis, "Union Military Intelligence Failure," 222.
   47. Simon 11:166.
   48. William E. Bain, ed., *B & O in the Civil War: From the Papers of William Prescott Smith* (Denver, CO: Sage Books, 1966), 11, 90.
   49. Bain 93.
   50. Anders 577; Simon 11:166–167.
   51. Cooling, *Monocacy*, 15.
   52. Feis, *Grant's Secret Service*, 231; Simon 11:169.
   53. Simon 11:153; Feis, "Union Military Intelligence Failure," 223.
   54. Bain 101–102; Anders 578.
   55. Feis, "Union Military Intelligence Failure," 223.
   56. Feis 223; Simon 11:170.
   57. Cooling, *Jubal Early's Raid*, 38; Cooling, *Monocacy*, 23.
   58. Welles 2:68 (entry for July 6, 1864).
   59. Anders 581.
   60. Anders 578; Simon 11:170.
   61. Grant 2:306.

Chapter 13

   1. National Park Service, "Maintenance of the Defenses," in *Historic Resource Study*, part 1, chapter 7, p. 1; Faust 514, 561.
   2. James Ramage, *Gray Ghost* (Lexington, KY: University Press of Kentucky, 1999), 155; Cooling, *Jubal Early's Raid*, 17; Cooling, *Monocacy*, 13.
   3. Ramage 161; Paul Ashdown and Edward Caudell, *The Mosby Myth* (Wilmington, DE: Scholarly Resources, 2002), 79; Jeffrey D. Wert, *Mosby's Rangers* (New York: Simon and Schuster, 1990), 171–173.
   4. Ashdown and Caudell 79; John D. Munson, *Reminiscences of a Mosby Guerilla* (New York: Moffet, Yard and Company, 1906), 93, 94, 99.
   5. Ramage 155–156; Kevin H. Seipel, *The Life and Times of John Singleton Mosby* (New York: St. Martin's Press, 1983), 116.
   6. Joan M. Dixon, "The Civil War Years, July 1, 1863–December 31, 1865," in *National Intelligencer Newspaper Abstracts*, Special Edition, vol. 2 (Bowie, MD: Heritage Books, 2001), 218; Ramage 15; Seipel 116; Munson 99; Judge 135.
   7. Anders 581.
   8. Ramage 157; Cooling, *Jubal Early's Raid*, 38.
   9. Ramage 161; Cooling, *Monocacy*, 43; Ashdown and Caudell 80.
   10. Ashdown and Caudell 80.
   11. Early, *Autobiographical Sketch*, 391.
   12. Major John Scott, *Partisan Life with Col. John S. Mosby* (New York: Harper and Brothers, 1867), 492; Ramage 161.
   13. John S. Mosby, *Memoirs of John Singleton Mosby* (Norwood, MA: Little, Brown, 1917), 275–276; Ashdown 80.
   14. Ramage 160–161; Ashdown and Caudell 80; Seipel 117; Virgil Carrington Jones, *Ranger Mosby* (McLean, VA: EPM, 1987), 189; Ramage 162.
   15. Ashdown and Caudell 80; Ramage 162; Jones 325; Ashdown 80.

Chapter 14

   1. Cooling, *Monocacy*, 21.
   2. Bain 98–99; Cooling, *Monocacy*, 57–58.
   3. Judge 139; Munson 99; Cooling, *Monocacy*, 46; Cooling, *Jubal Early's Raid*, 35.
   4. Ramage 63, 81, 104.
   5. Judge 141; Cooling, *Jubal Early's Raid*, 37.
   6. Matheny 89–90; Cooling, *Jubal Early's Raid*, 25.
   7. Cooling, *Jubal Early's Raid*, 25.
   8. Cooling, *Monocacy*, 57.
   9. National Park Service, app. H, 8–9.
   10. Leech 331, 333; National Park Service, app. E, 22–35.
   11. Warner, *Generals in Blue*, 239.

12. Cooling, *Monocacy*, 43, 57, 74; US War Dept., sec. 1, vol. 37, part 2, p. 140.
13. Ibid., 58.
14. Ibid., 74.
15. Bain 115.
16. Judge 129.
17. Cooling, *Monocacy*, 66; Cooling, *Jubal Early's Raid*, 96.
18. Simon 11:170.

Chapter 15

1. Thompson 69–70; Tidwell 145.
2. Tidwell 145.
3. Crist 110:492.
4. Early, *Autobiographical Sketch*, 381.
5. Crist 10:493.
6. Crist 10:496.
7. Raimondo Luraghi, *A History of the Confederate Navy* (Annapolis, MD: Naval Institute Press, 1996), 348; Shingleton 3–4.
8. John Bell, *Confederate Seadog: John Taylor Wood in War and Exile* (Jefferson, NC: McFarland, 2002), 71.
9. Bell 26; Faust 840–841; Shingleton 111.
10. Shingleton 64–69.
11. Shingleton 64–65; Luraghi 301.
12. Shingleton 68–69; Luraghi 301; Thomas J. Scharf, *A History of the Confederate States Navy from Its Organization to the Surrender of Its Last Vessel* (York: Rogers and Sherwood, 1957), 719.
13. Shingleton 85–87; Robert M. Browning, Jr., *From Cape Charles to Cape Fear: The North Atlantic Blockading Squadron During the Civil War* (Tuscaloosa and London: University of Alabama Press, 1993), 127.
14. Millard Kessler Bushong and Dean McKoin Bushong, *Fightin' Tom Rosser, C.S.A.* (Shippensburg, PA: Beidel Printing House, 1983), 58.
15. Browning 98–99; Luraghi 306–307.
16. Crist 10:496.
17. Shingleton 116–117.
18. R.E. Lee, *Lee's Dispatches: Unpublished Letters of General Robert E. Lee C.S.A. to Jefferson Davis and War Department of the Confederate States of America*, ed. Douglas Southall Freeman and Grady McWhiney (New York: Putnam, 1957), 269–271; Ralph W. Donnelly, *History of the Confederate States Marine Corps* (Wilmington, NC: privately printed, 1976), 78.
19. Crist 10:497, 10:502.
20. Tidwell 147; Donnelly 79.
21. Faust 429.
22. Cooling, *Jubal Early's Raid*, 39.
23. Ibid., 40, 158.
24. Donnelly 79; Catherine Lynch Deichmann, *Rogues and Runners: Bermuda and the American Civil War* (Hamilton, Bermuda: Bermuda National Trust, 2003), 48; *The Scanner* 7.6 (March 1975), Toronto Marine Historical Society.
25. Cooling, *Jubal Early's Raid*, 173.
26. Crist 10:510.
27. Cooling, *Jubal Early's Raid*, 173; Beitzell 53.
28. Crist 10:509.
29. Ibid., 10:510.
30. Ibid; US War Dept., ser. I, vol. 40, part 3, p. 761.
31. Beitzell 77.
32. J.B. Jones, *A Rebel War Clerk's Diary at the Confederate State Capital*, vol. 2 (Philadelphia, PA: B. Lippincott, 1866), 2:248.
33. Crist 10:512.
34. Crist 10:515; J.B. Jones 2:246.
35. Crist 10:514.
36. Cooling, *Jubal Early's Raid*, 173.
37. Crist 10:510, 10:515.
38. Cooling, *Jubal Early's Raid*, 173; Beitzell 52–53.
39. Shingleton 128–138.

Chapter 16

1. Moore 2:614; Faust 799; Judge 130.
2. Cooling, *Monocacy*, 39.
3. Moore 2:614.
4. Cooling, *Monocacy*, 38.
5. Moore 2:614.
6. Abner Hard, *History of the Eighth Cavalry Regiment, Illinois Volunteers, During the Great Rebellion* (Aurora, IL: 1868), 295.
7. James J. Williamson, *Mosby's Rangers: A Record of the Operations of the Forty-Third Battalion Virginia Cavalry from Its Organization to Surrender* (New York: Ralph B. Runyan, 1876), 185–187.
8. Hard 295–296.
9. Williamson 186.
10. Hard 296; Williamson 187–188; Moore 2:620–621.
11. Cooling, *Monocacy*, 28, 40; Richard R. Duncan, "Maryland's Reaction to Early's Raid," in *Maryland Historical Magazine* 64.3 (Fall 1969): 250; Toomey 102.
12. Cooling, *Jubal Early's Raid*, 27; Early, *Autobiographical Sketch*, 384; Judge 149.
13. Vandiver 92–94; Robert E. Lee, Jr.; 131; Early, *Autobiographical Sketch*, 385.
14. Toomey 103; Judge 154; Newcomer 129.
15. Hard 295–296; Moore 2:614; Judge 154.
16. Moore 2:614.
17. Cooling, *Jubal Early's Raid*, 43; Moore 2:614.
18. Cooling, *Monocacy*, 28; Ramage 161.
19. Moore 2:614; Hard 297; Lepa 92.
20. Cooling, *Monocacy*, 68.
21. Ibid., 68–69.
22. Moore 2:621.
23. Cooling, *Jubal Early's Raid*, 44.
24. Moore 2:614–615; Vandiver 96–97; Toomey 104.
25. G. Ward Hubbs, ed., *Voices from Company D: Diaries by the Greensboro Guards, Fifth Alabama Infantry Regiment, Army of Northern Virginia* (Athens, GA: University of Georgia Press, 2003), 298; Cooling, *Jubal Early's Raid*, 45; Newcomer 131.
26. Gary W. Gallagher, *Stephen Dodson Ramseur, Lee's Gallant General* (Chapel Hill and London: University of North Carolina Press, 1981), 125–126; David F. Riggs, *13th Virginia Infantry* (Lynchburg, VA: H.E. Howard, 1988), 53; Early, *Autobiographical Sketch*, 385.
27. Moore 2:615; Newcomer 131–132; Cooling, *Monocacy*, 76; Leeke 114–115.
28. Moore 2:615.
29. Hard 297.
30. Moore 2:615.
31. Cooling, *Monocacy*, 78.
32. Ibid., 79.
33. Swisher, "Following Old Jube," 22; Cooling, *Jubal Early's Raid*, 46; Moore 2:619–620.
34. Cooling, *Jubal Early's Raid*, 46; Moore 2:615.
35. Moore 2:621.
36. Cooling, *Jubal Early's Raid*, 274.
37. Ibid., 615, 620.
38. Vandiver 102.
39. Judge 166–167.
40. Lew Wallace, *An Autobiography* (New York and London: Harper and Brothers, 1896), 753–754.

Chapter 17

1. Osborne 221–221.
2. Freeman, *R.E. Lee: A Biography*, 3:60.
3. Faust 396; Goldsborough 189–191, 203; Driver 72.
4. Driver 86; Crist 10:485.

5. Crist 10:443, 10:462; Krick 86–87.
6. Opie 221; Lepa 57–58.
7. Opie 221.
8. Early, *Autobiographical Sketch*, 373–374; E. Miller 193.
9. Strother 263; Lepa 70–71.
10. Lepa 70–71.
11. Osborne 257.
12. Duncan, *Lee's Endangered Left*, 290; Lepa 79.
13. Stark 86–88.
14. Strother 268–269.
15. Early, *Autobiographical Sketch*, 381.
16. Faust 392.
17. Ibid., 456.
18. Early, *Autobiographical Sketch*, 381.
19. Cooling, *Jubal Early's Raid*, 26.
20. Summers 124; Early, *Autobiographical Sketch*, 386.
21. Cooling, *Jubal Early's Raid*, 44.
22. Harry Gilmor, *Four Years in the Saddle* (New York: Harper & Bros, 1866), 188–189; Moore 2:614; Cooling, *Jubal Early's Raid*, 44.
23. Cooling, *Jubal Early's Raid*, 59; Wallace 723–724.
24. Cooling, *Jubal Early's Raid*, 64–65.
25. Ibid., 172.
26. National Park Service, app. H, 26–27.

Chapter 18

1. Stark 88–89.
2. Strother 270–271.
3. E. Miller 213.
4. Ibid., 212- 213; Strother 271.
5. Strother 272.
6. Ibid., 272–273.
7. Stark 89–90.
8. Simon 11:138, 11:143; E. Miller 214.
9. Stark 91.
10. Strother 274; E. Miller 215.
11. Anders 577.
12. Hayes 3:778.
13. Strother 276.
14. E. Miller 217; Strother 276–277.
15. Strother 277.
16. Stark 94.
17. Strother 277.
18. US War Dept., ser. 1, vol. 37, part 2, p. 62.
19. E. Miller 217–218.
20. Ibid., 218.
21. Strother 277.
22. E. Miller 218.
23. Ibid., 219.
24. Cooling, *Jubal Early's Raid*, 36–37.

25. E. Miller 219, 221.
26. Simon 11:230.
27. Strother 279.
28. Simon 11:221, 228, 234, 240.
29. E. Miller 221; Strother 279.
30. Matheny 90; Engle 207; Cooling, *Monocacy*, 182.
31. Wallace 2:754–755.
32. Strother 279.
33. Ibid.
34. US War Dept., ser. I, vol. 37, part 2, pp. 339–341.
35. US War Dept., ser. I, vol. 37, part 2, p. 339.
36. Ibid., 367.
37. US War Dept., ser. I, vol. 37, part 2, p. 337; Simon 11:262.
38. Simon 11:242.
39. Simon 11:256; Strother 280.
40. Simon 11:273.
41. Lepa 121.
42. Ibid., 121–127.
43. US War Dept., ser. I, vol. 37, part 2, p. 423.
44. Ibid., 423–424.
45. Ibid., 463.
46. Simon 11:360.
47. Lepa 129–130.
48. Grant 2:319.
49. Lepa 131.
50. Simon 11:379–380.

Chapter 19

1. John D. Imboden, "Stonewall Jackson in the Shenandoah Valley," in *Battles and Leaders*, Johnson and Buell, eds., 2:297.
2. Early, *Autobiographical Sketch*, 386; Wallace 2:707, 711; Cooling, *Monocacy*, 41–42.
3. Cooling, *Jubal Early's Raid*, 64; Early, *Autobiographical Sketch*, 386.
4. Cooling, *Jubal Early's Raid*, 41–42; Roger S. Keller, *Events of the Civil War in Washington County, Maryland* (Shippensburg, PA: Burd Street Press, 1995), 333–335.
5. Wallace 2:707, 711.
6. Cooling, *Monocacy*, 64, 66.
7. Ibid., 67, 70; Judge 156; Cooling, *Jubal Early's Raid*, 59.
8. Cooling, *Jubal Early's Raid*, 59.
9. Judge 145–146.
10. Cooling, *Monocacy*, 28–29.
11. Ibid., 28.
12. Ibid., 116.
13. Ibid., 116–117.

Chapter 20

1. L.E. Chittenden, *Recollections of President Lincoln and His Administration* (New York: Harper and Bros., 1891), 390; Cooling, *Monocacy*, xiii; Pond 59; Grant 2:306.
2. Worthington 208.
3. Cooling, *Jubal Early's Raid*, 64.
4. Wallace 765–766.
5. Ibid., 749–750.
6. Cooling, *Jubal Early's Raid*, 64.
7. Cooling, *Monocacy*, 115.
8. Ibid., 97–98; Worthington 104–105.
9. Cooling, *Monocacy*, 97.
10. Ibid., 98.
11. Cooling, *Jubal Early's Raid*, 62; Worthington 107.
12. Early, *Autobiographical Sketch*, 387; Lepa 96–97; Moore 2:616.
13. Cooling, *Jubal Early's Raid*, 62, 64; Early, *Autobiographical Sketch*, 387; Worthington 88–92; Moore 2:614–616; Judge 174–176.
14. Moore 2:616; Early, *Autobiographical Sketch*, 387; Cooling, *Monocacy*, 117–118.
15. Jennings Cropper Wise, *The Long Arm of Lee; Or, The History of Artillery in the Army of Northern Virginia* (Lynchburg, VA: J.P. Bell, 1915), 2:817; Cooling, *Monocacy*, 143.
16. Judge 188–190; Cooling, *Monocacy*, 143.
17. Gordon 311–313.
18. Cooling, *Jubal Early's Raid*, 74.
19. Cooling, *Symbol, Sword and Shield*, 191.
20. James A. Hutcheson, "Saved the Day at Monocacy," *Confederate Veteran* 23 (Feb. 1915): 77; Park 379; Early, *Autobiographical Sketch*,388; Thomsen 268.
21. Wallace 791.
22. Moore 2:616–618; Leeke 121–122.
23. Moore 2:624; Leeke 119–122.
24. McKee 53; Reid 2:680.
25. Grant 2:306.
26. Early, *Autobiographical Sketch*, 388.
27. Cooling, *Jubal Early's Raid*, 80–81.
28. Vincent 61.
29. Wallace 2:729.
30. Sorel 248.

Chapter 21

1. Bradley T. Johnson, "Riding a Raid in July, 1864," Laurel, MD, *Leader*, December 26, 1902.
2. Driver 84–86; Crist 10:487; Faust 396.
3. Gordon 316.
4. Cooling, *Jubal Early's Raid*, 39; Robert E. Lee, Jr., 131; Laurel, MD, *Leader*, December 26, 1902.

5. Early, *Autobiographical Sketch*, 385.
6. Driver 87–88.
7. Cooling, *Jubal Early's Raid*, 158; Driver 87.
8. Early, *Autobiographical Sketch*, 386; Driver 87; Gilmor 197–203; Krick 81–82.
9. Driver 88; Cooling, *Jubal Early's Raid*, 158.
10. Gilmor 192.
11. Judge 203; Driver 171.
12. Driver 171; Gilmor 190.
13. Driver 88.
14. Driver 172–173; Gilmor 195–196.
15. Cooling, *Jubal Early's Raid*, 160; Gilmor 191; Toomey 125.
16. Robert E. Michels, *Colonel Harry Gilmor's Ride Around Baltimore, July 10 to July 13, 1864* (Baltimore, MD: Erbe, 1976), 6.
17. Cooling, *Jubal Early's Raid*, 168–169; Driver 172–173; Gilmor 195.
18. Driver 88, 171–174.
19. Cooling, *Jubal Early's Raid*; Jack L. Dickman, *8th Virginia Cavalry* (Lynchburg, VA: H.E. Howard, 1986), 49.
20. Simon 11:229; Driver 88; *Washington Times*, "Early's Summer March Chills Washington," June 5, 2004.
21. Toomey 125; Judge 240; Goldsborough 204.
22. Osborne 287; Toomey 126–137; Goldsborough 204–205; Driver 171.
23. Cooling, *Jubal Early's Raid*, 172; B. Johnson 221–222.
24. Driver 174–175; Tidwell 148; Beitzell 51.
25. Gilmor 203.
26. Daniel D. Harletzer, *Marylanders in the Confederacy* (Silver Spring, MD: Family Line, 1986), 7.

Chapter 22

1. Hardin 130.
2. John Henry Cramer, *Lincoln Under Enemy Fire* (Baton Rouge, LA: Louisiana State University Press, 1948), 9; Hardin 300–301.
3. Cooling, *Monocacy*, 171–173; Moore 2:616–617.
4. Moore 2:617.
5. Ibid., 2:616–617.
6. Ibid., 2:617.
7. Judge 216; Anders 582.
8. Moore 2:622–626.
9. Ibid., 2:617.
10. Cooling, *Monocacy*, 179.

Chapter 23

1. Early, *Autobiographical Sketch*, 373.
2. Cooling, *Jubal Early's Raid*, 255.
3. Ibid., 255.
4. Ibid., 253–254; Osborne 264.
5. Faust 397.
6. Judge 216; Cooling, *Jubal Early's Raid*, 80.
7. Early, *Autobiographical Sketch*, 372.
8. Osborne 257–258.
9. Strother 262; Judge 102.
10. Early, *Autobiographical Sketch*, 379.
11. Crist 10:487 n. 8.
12. Judge 116.
13. Judge 119.
14. Judge 130.
15. Judge 127–127; Cooling, *Jubal Early's Raid*, 40.
16. Vandiver 92.
17. Judge 160.
18. Park 378; Steven Bernstein, "Early's Summer March Chills Washington, *Washington Times*, June 5, 2004.
19. Worsham 221; Judge 214; Osborne 280.
20. Cooling, *Jubal Early's Raid*, 90.
21. Early, *Autobiographical Sketch*, 389.
22. Cooling, *Jubal Early's Raid*, 107.
23. Cooling, *Monocacy*, 186.
24. Early, *Autobiographical Sketch*, 391.
25. Cooling, *Jubal Early's Raid*, 250.

Chapter 24

1. Early, "Early's March to Washington in 1864," 4:497; Cooling, *Jubal Early's Raid*, 102; National Park Service 7:2.
2. Simon 11:199–200.
3. Cooling, *Jubal Early's Raid*, 113; Worsham 241–442; I.G. Bradwell, "Early's Demonstration Against Washington in 1864," *Confederate Veteran* 22.1 (Oct. 1914), 438–439; I.G. Bradwell, "Early's March on Washington in 1864," *Confederate Veteran* 28 (May 1920), 176–177; Worsham 141–142; John C. Cannon, *Record of Service of Company K, One Hundred and Fiftieth Ohio Volunteer Infantry, 1864* (Cleveland, OH: Privately printed, 1903.
4. National Park Service 7:8; Judge 233–237; Cooling, *Jubal Early's Raid*, 113, 148; Early, *Autobiographical Sketch*, 389.

5. Hardin 140; National Park Service 7:8.
6. Opie 246.
7. Early, *Autobiographical Sketch*, 390.
8. Ibid., 391.
9. Douglas 295; A.L. Long, *Memories of Robert E. Lee*, 359–360.
10. Chittenden 405–408.
11. John G. Nicolay and John Hay, *Abraham Lincoln: A History*, (Chicago: University of Chicago Press, 1966), 169; Cramer 47.
12. Cooling, *Jubal Early's Raid*, 123.
13. Gordon 314.
14. Early, *Autobiographical Sketch*, 389.
15. Henry E. Alvord, "Early's Attack Upon Washington, July 1864," in *War Papers* (MOLLUS DC) (Wilmington, NC: Broadfoot, 1993), 478; National Park Service, app. H, 27–28; Leech 341.
16. Cramer 15–16; Worthington 190.
17. Alvord 484.
18. Francis C. Adams, *Seige of Washington, D.C. Written Expressly for Little People* (New York: Dick and Fitzgerald, 1867), 31.
19. Adams 42.
20. Hardin 129.
21. Chittenden 423–424.
22. National Park Service, app. H, 27–28; Simon 11:230–231.
23. National Park Service, app. H, 27–28.
24. Hardin 143.
25. John Warwick Daniel, "Address of John W. Daniel for Jubal Early," *Southern Historical Society Papers* 22 (1894).
26. Pollard 474; Joseph Canty Elliott, *Lieutenant General Richard Heron Anderson: Lee's Noble Soldier* (Dayton, OH: Morningside, 1985), 111–112.

Chapter 25

1. Faust 339–340; Warner, *Generals in Blue*, 205.
2. National Park Service, app. H, 5.
3. National Park Service 7:5.
4. Cooling, *Jubal Early's Raid*, 98.
5. Ibid., 100.
6. Ibid., 100–101.
7. Boatner 870; Faust 780–781.
8. Dyer, s.v. "Veteran Reserve Regiments" in *Compendium* (New York: Thomas Yoseloff, 1959) microfilm.
9. Worsham 241; Judge 237.
10. David Herbert Donald, *Gone*

for *A Soldier: The Civil War Memories of Private Alfred Bellard* (Boston MA: Little Brown, 1975), 270–271.
11. Ibid.
12. Ibid.; Dyer, s.v. "Sixth Veteran Reserve Regiment," 3:1741; National Park Service, app. H, 22–24.
13. Boatner 944.
14. National Park Service, app. H, 22–24.
15. Ibid.; Dyer, s.v. "Ninth Veteran Reserve Regiment," 3:1741.
16. Boatner 342; S.F. Bates 793–795.
17. National Park Service, app. H, 22–24.
18. Ibid.
19. Dyer, s.v. "Twelfth Veteran Reserve Regiment," 3:1741.
20. Ibid.; National Park Service, app. H, 8.
21. Dyer, s.v. "Nineteenth Veteran Reserve Regiment," 3:1742; Boatner 228.
22. Dyer, "Twenty-Fourth Veteran Reserve Regiment," 3:1742.
23. Ibid.
24. Fred Pelka, ed., *The Civil War Letters of Colonel Charles F. Johnson, Invalid Corps* (Amherst, MA: University of Massachusetts Press, 2004), 8–9.
25. Ibid., 26.
26. Ibid.
27. Ibid.
28. National Park Service, app. H, 27–32.
29. Ibid., 22.
30. Cooling, *Jubal Early's Raid*, 99.
31. National Park Service, app. H, 22–24.
32. Ibid., 22.
33. Ibid., 22.
34. Ibid., 31; Cooling, *Jubal Early's Raid*, 109.
35. National Park Service, app. H, 22.
36. Ibid., 22–23; Cooling, *Jubal Early's Raid*, 120.
37. National Park Service, app. H, 22–23.
38. Ibid.
39. Cooling, *Jubal Early's Raid*, 118.
40. Early, *Autobiographical Sketch*, 390.
41. National Park Service, app. H, 22–24.
42. Ibid., 31; Cooling, *Jubal Early's Raid*, 127.
43. National Park Service, app. H, 23.
44. Ibid., 23–24.
45. Ibid.
46. Ibid.

Chapter 26

1. Faust 485.
2. Freeman, *R.E. Lee: A Biography*, 1:141–148.
3. Goodwin 343, quoting entry for March 31, 1861, in the private journal of Montgomery Meigs (copy), container 13, Nicolay papers.
4. David W. Miller, *Second Only to Grant: Quartermaster General Montgomery C. Meigs* (Shippensburg, PA: White Mane, 2000), 230, 247–248.
5. Goodwin 426.
6. Miller, *Second Only to Grant*, xiii, citing James G. Blaine, *Twenty Years in Congress*, vol. 2 (1886), quoted in *Dictionary of American Biography*, Montgomery Cunningham Meigs.
7. National Park Service, app. H, 30.
8. US War Dept., ser. I, vol. 37, part 1, p. 254–255, 258; National Park Service 30.
9. National Park Service, app. H, 30.
10. US War Dept., ser. I, vol. 37, part 1, pp. 258; National Park Service, app. H, 30.
11. US War Dept., ser. I, vol. 37, part 1, p. 254–255; National Park Service, app. H, 30.
12. National Park Service, app. H, 30.
13. Ibid., 254–255; National Park Service, app. H, 30–31.
14. US War Dept., ser. I, vol. 37, part 1, pp. 231; National Park Service, app. H, 31.
15. National Park Service, app. H, 31–32; Park 380.
16. US War Dept., ser. I, vol. 37, part 1, pp. 259–260; National Park Service, app. H, 31–32, 34.
17. US War Dept., ser. I, vol. 37, part 1, p. 257; National Park Service, app. H, 8.
18. National Park Service, app. H, 14–15.

Chapter 27

1. Ann Blackman, *Wild Rose: Rose O'Neale Greenhow, Civil War Spy* (New York: Random House, 2005), 39–46.
2. Tidwell 47; Time-Life Books, *Spies, Scouts and Raiders, Irregular Operations* (Alexandria, VA: Time-Life Books, 1985), 45–46.
3. Tidwell 62.
4. Ibid., 11, 49.
5. Ibid., 87.
6. Time-Life Books 53; Thomas A. Jones, *J. Wilkes Booth* (Chicago IL: Laird and Lee, 1893), 30–32.
7. Tidwell 68–70.
8. Time-Life Books 51; Tidwell 87.
9. Tidwell 87.
10. H.V. Canon, "Confederate Military Intelligence," *Maryland Historical Magazine*, March 1964, 34–51.
11. Donald E. Markle, *Spies and Spymasters of the Civil War* (New York: Hippocrene Books, 1994), 111–112.
12. Tidwell 70–73; Time-Life Books 54–55.
13. Conrad, *Confederate Spy*, 79; Tidwell 67.
14. Thomas Nelson Conrad, *The Rebel Scout: A Thrilling Story of Scouting Life in the Southern Army* (Washington, DC: National, 1904), 127–129.
15. Conrad 291.
16. Tidwell 73.
17. Crist 10:484–486.
18. Early, *Autobiographical Sketch*, 391.
19. Hardin 128.
20. Ibid., 143.
21. Chittenden 412–414.
22. Early, *Autobiographical Sketch*, 391.
23. US War Dept., ser. I, vol. 37, part 1, pp. 253–254.
24. Alexander Hunter, *Johnny Reb and Billy Yank* (New York and Washington: Neale, 1904), 649–652.
25. Early, *Autobiographical Sketch*, 389; Gordon 314.
26. Early, *Autobiographical Sketch*, 391.

Chapter 28

1. Laas, *Wartime Washington*, 400 (Elizabeth Blair Lee to Samuel P. Lee July 6, 1864).
2. Goodwin 630.
3. William Earnest Smith, *The Francis Preston Blair Family in Politics* (New York: Macmillan, 1933), 2:272 (letter from Francis Preston Blair to Gen. Frank Blair, July 4, 1864).
4. Goodwin 640–641.
5. Early, *Autobiographical Sketch*, 385; Moore 2:616–617; Cooling, *Jubal Early's Raid*, 78.
6. Early, *Autobiographical Sketch*, 389.
7. Goodwin 641; Judge 214, 227; Cooling, *Jubal Early's Raid*, 90.
8. Judge 219; Cooling, *Monocacy*, 183–184.
9. Early, *Autobiographical Sketch*, 389; Judge 221.
10. Cooling, *Jubal Early's Raid*, 108.

11. Cooling, *Monocacy*, 185.
12. Early, *Autobiographical Sketch*, 389; Cooling, *Jubal Early's Raid* 108.
13. Leech 345; Goodwin 463–464.
14. Cooling, *Jubal Early's Raid*, 108.
15. W.E. Smith 2:186.
16. Goodwin 312.
17. Ibid., 314; W.E. Smith, 2:90.
18. Ibid., 315.
19. Ibid., 399; W.E. Smith 194.
20. Goodwin 399–400.
21. Ibid., 410–415.
22. Ibid., 583.
23. Miller, *Second Only to Grant*, 195.
24. Cooling, *Jubal Early's Raid*, 152, 164, 218.
25. Laas, *Wartime Washington*, 404, 413; Elizabeth Blair Lee to Stephen P. Lee, July 16, 1864, July 31, 1864 Cornish and Laas, *Lincoln's Lee* (Lawrence, KS: University of Kansas Press, 1986), 135; Dave Scull, descendant of Francis Preston Blair, Sr., and Samuel Phillips Lee, to author, January 12, 2007.
26. Goodwin 642.
27. Laas, *Wartime Washington*, 404–405.
28. Ibid.; Faust 642.
29. Park 379–380.
30. Judge 241.
31. Ibid., 242.
32. Laas, *Wartime Washington*, 405 (Elizabeth Blair Lee to S.P. Lee, July 16, 1864, and July 31, 1864).
33. Early, *Autobiographical Sketch*, 395.
34. Goodwin 644.
35. Ibid., 642.

Chapter 29

1. John H. Eicher and David J. Eicher, *Civil War High Commands* (Palo Alto, CA: Stanford University Press, 2001), 374–375; Charles Whalen and Barbara Whalen, *The Fighting McCooks: America's Famous Fighting Family* (Bethesda, MD: Westmoreland, 2006), frontispiece.
2. Faust 457; Whalen and Whalen 71.
3. Eicher and Eicher 374; Whalen and Whalen 157–168, 177–186; Faust 457, 722–723.
4. Faust 457; US War Dept., ser. I, vol. 37, part 1, p. 230.
5. US War Dept., ser. I, vol. 37, part 1, p. 232.
6. US War Dept., ser. I, vol. 37, part 1, p. 231; Cooling, *Monocacy*, 188.
7. US War Dept., ser. I, vol. 37, part 1, p. 231.
8. National Park Service, app. H, 27.
9. Cooling, *Jubal Early's Raid*, 113.
10. US War Dept., ser. I, vol. 37, part 1, p. 231.
11. Cramer 13–14.
12. Hardin 142.
13. Cooling, *Monocacy*, 188.
14. Hardin 143.
15. George Haven Putnam, *Memories of My Youth, 1844–1865* (New York: G.P. Putnam's Sons, 1914).
16. US War Dept., ser. I, vol. 37, part 2, p. 352.
17. Faust 457; Whalen and Whalen 356–357.
18. Faust 457; Whalen and Whalen 357.

Chapter 30

1. Henry Halleck to George Cadwalader, July 9, 1864 in US War Dept., ser. I, vol. 37, part 2, p. 153.
2. National Park Service, app. H, 8.
3. National Park Service, app. H, 26–27.
4. Ibid., 27.
5. Washington, DC, *Morning Chronicle*, June 7, 1864.
6. Ibid.
7. Ibid.
8. Shirley A. Leckie, *Elizabeth Bacon Custer and the Making of a Myth* (Norman, OK, and London: University of Oklahoma Press, 1984), 50.
9. *Morning Chronicle*.
10. Walt Whitman, *Specimen Days* (Philadelphia PA: Rees Welch, 1882), 716.
11. Cooling, *Jubal Early's Raid*, 127.
12. National Park Service, app. H, 27.
13. National Park Service, app. H, 27.
13. US War Dept., ser. I, vol. 37, part 1, pp. 254–255.
14. Ibid.
15. National Park Service, app. H, 27.
16. National Park Service, app. H, 8.
17. Simon 11:199.

Chapter 31

1. John C. Cannon, comp., *Memorial 150th Ohio, Company K* (Cleveland, July 11, 1907), 8; George T. Stevens, *Three Years in the Sixth Corps: A Narrative of Events in the Army of the Potomac from 1861 to the Close of the Rebellion* (New York: Van Nostrand, 1870), 237–238.
2. National Park Service, app. H, 27.
3. Cramer 46–47, 62–63; Cooling, *Jubal Early's Raid*, 125.
4. National Park Service, app. H, 28.
5. Simon 11:231; Dana 22 (Charles Dana to U.S. Grant July 12, 1864).
6. Judge 251; Cooling, *Jubal Early's Raid*, 125–126, 143, 146.
7. Cramer 17.
8. Ibid., 27.
9. Ibid., 33–34.
10. Ibid., 40.
11. Chittenden 415–416.
12. Cramer 65; Tyler Dennett, ed., *Lincoln and the Civil War: In the Diaries and Letters of John Hay* (New York: Dodd, Mead, 1939), 209.
13. Stevens 382.
14. Ibid.
15. Cramer 102–103.
16. John C. Cannon, *Record of Service of Company K, 150th Ohio Volunteer Infantry* (Cleveland, OH: privately printed, 1903), 16.
17. Cramer 27, 47, 102–103.
18. Cramer 46; Dennett 209.

Chapter 32

1. Trudeau 341.
2. Allan R. Millet and Peter Maslowski, *For the Common Defense: A Military History of the United States of America* (New York: New York Free Press, 1994), 163–168.
3. Jeffrey Record, "External Assistance, Enabler of Insurgent Success," Parameter, US Army War College Quarterly, Autumn 2006, 5.
4. Lynn M. Case and Warren Spencer, *The United States and France: Civil War Diplomacy* (Philadelphia, PA: University of Pennsylvania Press, 1970), 250–270.
5. Goodwin 397–399.
6. Nolan 66.
7. Record 5.
8. McPherson, "No Peace Without Victory," 2.
9. Ibid.
10. Ibid.
11. Record 5.
12. Lee, *Recollections and Letters*, 131; Nolan 73–78; Harsh 59–60.
13. Bonekemper 78; Richard E. Beringer, Herman Hattaway, Archer Jones, and William Still, Jr., *Why the South Lost the Civil War* (Athens, GA: University of Georgia Press, 1986), 169, 179; James M. McPher-

son, *Crossroads of Freedom: Antietam: The Battle that Changed the Course of the Civil War* (New York: Oxford University Press, 2002), 241.
  14. McPherson, "No Peace Without Victory," 2.
  15. D.P. Crook, *Diplomacy During the American Civil War* (New York: John Wiley and Sons, 1975), 93–94, 102–103.
  16. Case and Spencer 355–357.
  17. John Kuhn Bleimaier, "Cassius Marcellus Clay in St. Petersburg," *The Register*, Kentucky Historical Society, July 1975, 263–265.
  18. D.P. Crook 90–91; Bleimaier 265; Case and Spencer 207, 363.
  19. David Donald, ed., *Why the North Won the Civil War* (New York: Collier Books, 1962), 55–78; Gallagher, *Lee and His Generals*, 44.
  20. Brian Jenkins, "The Wise Macaw and the Lion: William Seward and Britain, 1861–1863," *University of Rochester Library Bulletin* 31 (Autumn 1972), 1; Richard Allen Heckman, "British Press Reaction to Emancipation Proclamation," *Lincoln Herald* 16 (1969): 150–153.
  21. Record 5.
  22. Adam Hochschild, *Bury the Chains: Prophets and Rebels in the Fight to Free an Empire's Slaves* (Boston, MA: Houghton Mifflin, 2004).
  23. Cassius Marcellus Clay, *The Life of Cassius Marcellus Clay: Memoirs, Writings and Speeches* (Cincinnati, OH: J.F. Brennon, 1886), 307.
  24. Case and Spencer 207.
  25. D.P. Crook 87.
  26. Bleimaier 270.
  27. Case and Spencer 309, 318.
  28. D.P. Crook 98.
  29. Case and Spencer 363.
  30. McPherson, "No Peace Without Victory," 2; Case and Spencer 384–397.
  31. Case and Spencer 393–395; McPherson, "No Peace Without Victory," 2.
  32. Case and Spencer 398–400; D.P. Crook 159.
  33. Case and Spencer 547.
  34. Case and Spencer 547–548.
  35. Ibid.
  36. Martin Duberman, *Charles Francis Adams, 1807–1886* (Boston, MA: Houghton Mifflin, 1960), 315.
  37. Bleimaier 276–277.
  38. Ibid., 276–277.
  39. Case and Spencer 425–426.
  40. Ibid., 241.
  41. Duberman 315.
  42. Crist 10:132.
  43. Ibid., 10:133 n. 6.
  44. Serge Gavronsky, *The French Liberal Opposition and the American Civil War* (New York: Humanities Press, 1968), 173; Crist 10:134 n. 15.
  45. Case and Spencer 546–547.
  46. Markle 75–76; Crist 10:445.
  47. Crist 10:246.
  48. Gavronsky 207–211.
  49. Case and Spencer 546.
  50. Putnam 339.
  51. Hay 247–248; Goodwin 648.
  52. Goodwin 656; Waugh 354.
  53. Waugh 255.
  54. Ibid., 270.
  55. Ibid., 99.
  56. William Frank Zornow, *Lincoln and the Party Divided* (Norman, OK: University of Oklahoma Press, 1954), 49; Goodwin 606–607.
  57. Waugh 150.
  58. Goodwin 607.
  59. Ibid., 623.
  60. W.E. Smith 2:279.
  61. Ibid., 270–280.
  62. Ibid., 281.
  63. Goodwin 469–470, 624; W.E. Smith 2:207, 262.
  64. Faust 291, 608; Waugh 175–177.
  65. Waugh 179; Goodwin 624.
  66. Waugh 176.
  67. James L. Crouthamel, *Bennett's New York Herald and the Rise of the Popular Press* (Syracuse, NY: Syracuse University Press, 1989), 142–147; Waugh 141.
  68. Goodwin 639–640; Eric Foner, *Reconstruction: America's Unfinished Revolution* (New York: Harper and Row, 1988), 60–62.
  69. Waugh 163.
  70. Ibid.
  71. Crist 10:537.
  72. Crist 10:535–536, 10:536 n. 3, 10:153 n. 5.
  73. Crist 10:537 n. 8; James W. Headley, *Confederate Operations in Canada and New York* (New York and Washington: The Neale Publishing Co., 1906), 238–241.
  74. Crist 10:536 n. 4, 10:537 n. 7.
  75. Goodwin 623–625.
  76. Noah Brooks, *Lincoln Observed, Civil War Dispatches of Noah Brooks*, ed. Michael Burlingame and John R. Turner Etlinger (Baltimore and London: Johns Hopkins University Press, 1998), 129; Waugh 203.
  77. Faust 150, 827; Mottelay and Campbell 2:406.
  78. Wells 2:44, 54–55.
  79. *New York World*, July 12, 1864.
  80. William Tecumseh Sherman, *Memoirs of General W.T. Sherman* (New York: Library of America, 1990), 523.
  81. George Templeton Strong, *The Diary of George Templeton Strong: The Civil War 1860–1865*, ed. Allan Nevins and Milton Halsey Thomas (New York: Macmillan, 1952), 409.
  82. McPherson, "No Peace Without Victory," 3.
  83. Goodwin 648.
  84. Wells 2:68.
  85. Feis, "Union Military Intelligence Failure," 209–225.
  86. Wells 2:77 (entry for July 11, 1864).
  87. Wells 2:78 (entry for July 15, 1864).
  88. Wells 2:77 (entry for July 15, 1864); *New York World*, July 12, 1864.
  89. McPherson, "No Peace Without Victory," 4–5.
  90. Waugh 209–211.
  91. Ibid., 250–257; Crist 10:559–561.
  92. Waugh 89; Goodwin 654.
  93. Simon 11:362–363.
  94. Sherman 583.
  95. Freeman, *Lee's Lieutenants*, 3:598.

Chapter 33

  1. Faust 128.
  2. Ibid., 233, 288.
  3. Bushong 60–62.
  4. Connelly 52.
  5. Pollard 477.
  6. Osborne 116; Cooling, *Jubal Early's Raid*, 10.
  7. Bushong 191; Cooling 10; Osborne 57.
  8. Gordon 314–319.
  9. Ibid.
  10. Sorrel 338–339.
  11. Bushong 169.
  12. Faust 233; Gallagher, *Lee and His Army*, 222; Pollard 478.
  13. Faust 613, 640.
  14. Osborne 390.
  15. Faust 835.
  16. Osborne 345.
  17. Ibid; Faust 121.
  18. Faust 678; Sheridan 485–487; Worthington 11.
  19. Dana 205.
  20. Wells 2:76 (entry for July 13, 1864).
  21. Faust 415.
  22. Cooling, *Jubal Early's Raid*, 218.
  23. Ibid., 250; Bushong 192.
  24. Worthington 244–245.
  25. Faust 306.
  26. Osborne 191; Bushong 147.
  27. Lepa 114–115.
  28. Duncan, *Lee's Endangered Left*, 256–258.
  29. Early, *Autobiographical Sketch*, 373.
  30. Osborne 257.
  31. Ibid., 255–259.

Notes—Chapter 33

32. Wittenberg, *Little Phil,* 258–259.
33. Feis, "Union Military Intelligence Failure," 219; Strother 267–275; Lepa 80–83.
34. Feis, "Union Military Intelligence Failure," 215–223.
35. Early, *Autobiographical Sketch,* 382–383.
36. Cooling, *Monocacy,* 13; Early, *Autobiographical Sketch,* 371; Cooling, *Jubal Early's Raid,* 25.
37. Cooling, *Jubal Early's Raid,* 126; Matheny 87–89.
38. Judge 141–153; Cooling, *Jubal Early's Raid,* 27–41.
39. Wallace 759.
40. Cooling, *Jubal Early's Raid,* 44.
41. Ibid., 64.
42. Worthington 128–143, 244–248.
43. Early, *Autobiographical Sketch,* 385.
44. Cooling, *Jubal Early's Raid,* 49.
45. Shingleton 116–117.
46. Crist 10:488, 493, 497.
47. Cooling, *Jubal Early's Raid,* 173; Crist 10:514–515.
48. Early, *Autobiographical Sketch,* 389.

Bibliography

Archival Sources

National Archives. War Records, Quartermaster General's Office. Letter Book No. 61, June 26, 1862, to August 14, 1862, Montgomery Meigs to W.A. Hammond. July 17, 1862 Washington, D.C.

National Archives. Records of the Office of the Quartermaster General. Record Group No. 92, "Lists of Confederate Soldiers and Sailors of War Deaths—Northern Prisons." Vol. I. 1914, Washington, D.C.

National Archives. Records of Events of the 10th West Virginia Infantry Regiment. Washington, D.C.

Newspapers

Baltimore Sun
Detroit Free Press
Laurel Leader
New York Herald
New York Times
New York World
Staunton Vindicator
Union Bridge Pilot
Washington Morning Chronicle
Washington Times

Primary Sources

Adams, Francis C. *Siege of Washington DC Written Expressly for Little People.* New York, NY: Fitzgerald, 1867.

Alexander, Edward Porter. *Fighting for the Confederacy: Personal Recollections of General Edward Porter Alexander.* Edited by Gary W. Gallagher. Chapel Hill, NC: University of North Carolina Press, 1989.

_____. *Military Memoirs of a Confederate.* New York: Charles Scribner's Sons, 1907.

Allen, George H. *Forty-Six Months with the Fourth Rhode Island Volunteers.* Providence, RI: J.A. and E.A. Reid, 1887.

Alvord, Henry E. "Early's Attack Upon Washington, July 1864." In *War Papers.* Washington DC: Military Order of the Loyal Legion (MOLLUS), paper 26.

Bain, William E., ed. *B&O in the Civil War: From the Papers of Wm. Prescott Smith.* Denver, CO: Sage Books, 1966.

Baker, Lafayette C. *The United States Secret Service in the Late War.* St. Louis, MO: J.H. Chambers and Co., 1889.

Barnard, John Gross. *A Report on the Defenses of Washington to the Chief of Engineers.* US Army Corps of Engineers, Corps of Engineers, Professional Paper No. 20. Washington, DC: The Government Printing Office, 1871.

Bartlett, A.W. *History of the 12th Regiment of N.H. Volunteers.* Concord, NH: Ira C. Cross, 1887.

Bates, Edward. *The Diary of Edward Bates, 1859–1865.* New York: Da Capo Press, 1971.

Booth, George W. *A Maryland Boy in Lee's Army: Personal Reminiscences of a Maryland Soldier in the War Between the States, 1861–1865.* Reprint, Lincoln, NE: University of Nebraska Press, 2000.

Bradwell, I.G. "Early's Demonstration Against Washington in 1864." *Confederate Veteran* 28 (May 1920).

_____. "Early's March on Washington in 1864." *Confederate Veteran* 22 (October 1914).

Butler, Benjamin F. *Private and Official Correspondence of Gen. Benjamin F. Butler.* 5 vols. Norwood, MA: Plimpton Press, 1917.

Butler, Matthew C. "The Cavalry Fight at Trevilian Station." In *Battles and Leaders of the Civil War,* ed. Robert Underwood Johnson and Clarence Clough Buell, vol. 4. New York: Thomas Yoseloff, Inc., 1956.

Cannon, John C. *Memorial 150th Ohio, Company K.* Cleveland, July 11, 1907.

_____. *Record of Service of Company K, 150th Ohio Volunteer Infantry.* Cleveland, OH: Privately printed, 1903.

Casler, John O. *Four Years in the Stonewall Brigade.* Dayton, OH: Morningside, 1971.

Chittenden, L.E. *Recollections of President Lincoln and His Administration.* New York: Harper and Bros., 1891.

Colvin, E.M. "A Visit to Point Lookout Prison." *Confederate Veteran* 22 (December 1914).

_____. "Prison Experience at Point Lookout." *Confederate Veteran* 15 (September 1907).

Conrad, Thomas Nelson. *A Confederate Spy.* New York: J.S. Ogilvie, 1892.

_____. *The Rebel Scout: A Thrilling History of Scouting Life in the Southern Army.* Washington, DC: The National Publishing Co., 1904.

Crist, Lynda Lasswell, ed. *The Papers of Jefferson Davis.* Vol. 10. Baton Rouge, LA: Louisiana State University Press, 1999.

Crook, George. *General George Crook: His Autobiography.* Edited by Martin F. Schmitt. Norman, OK: University of Oklahoma Press, 1946.

Dana, Charles H. *Recollections of the Civil War.* New York, NY: D. Appleton and Company, 1898.

Daniel, John Warwick. "Address of John W. Daniel for Jubal Early." *Southern Historical Society Papers* 22, Richmond, VA, 1894.

Deichmann, Catherine Lynch. *Rogues and Runners: Bermuda and the American Civil War*. Hamilton, Bermuda: Bermuda National Trust, 2003.

Douglas, Henry Kyd. *I Rode with Stonewall*. Edited by Fletcher M. Green. Chapel Hill, NC: University of North Carolina Press, 1940.

Drickamer, Lee C., and Karen D. Drickamer, eds. *Fort Lyon to Harper's Ferry; On the Border of North and South with "Ramblin' Jour": The Letters and Dispatches of Charles H. Moulton (34th Mass. Volunteer Infantry)*. Shippensburg, PA: White Mane Publishing Company, Inc., 1987.

Du Pont, H.A. *The Campaign of 1864 in the Valley of Virginia and Expedition to Lynchburg*. New York, NY: National Americana Society, 1925.

Dudley, Edgar S. "Early's Attack: A Reminiscence of Early's Attack on Washington in 1864." In *Sketches of Civil War History, 1861–1865*. MOLLUS. vol. 1. Reprint, Wilmington, NC: Broadfoot Publishing Company, 1991.

Early, Jubal. *Autobiographical Sketch and Narrative of the War Between the States*. Reprint, Wilmington, NC: Broadfoot Publishing Company, 1989.

_____. *A Memoir of the Last Year of the War for Independence in the Confederate States of America*. New Orleans, LA: Blalock and Co., 1867.

Elliott, Joseph Canty. *Lieutenant General Richard Heron Anderson: Lee's Noble Soldier*. Dayton, OH: Morningside, 1985.

FitzSimons, Charles. "The Hunter Raid." In *Military Essays and Recollections*. MOLLUS. Chicago, IL: Cosseno and Beaton, 1907.

Gilmor, Harry. *Four Years in the Saddle*. New York: Harper & Bros, 1866.

Gilson, J.H. (Co.D) *Concise History of the One Hundred Twenty-Sixth Regiment of Ohio Volunteer Infantry*. Reprint, Huntington, WV: Blue Acorn Press, 2000.

Gordon, John B. *Reminiscences of the Civil War*. New York, NY: Charles Scribner's Sons, 1904.

Grant, Ulysses S. *Memoirs of Ulysses S. Grant*. 2 vols. New York: Charles Webster and Company, 1885.

Hard, Abner. *History of the Eighth Cavalry Regiment, Illinois Volunteers, During the Great Rebellion*. Aurora, IL: 1868.

Hay, John. *Inside Lincoln's White House: The Complete Civil War Diary of John Hay*. Edited by Michael Burlingame and John R. Turner Etlinger. Carbondale, IL: Southern Illinois University Press, 1999.

Hayes, Rutherford B. *Diary and Letters of Rutherford B. Hayes*. 5 vols. Edited by Charles R. Williams. Columbus, OH: Ohio State Archeological and Historical Society, 1922–1926.

Headley, James W. *Confederate Operations in Canada and New York*. New York and Washington: The Neale Publishing Co., 1906.

Hubbs, G. Ward, ed. *Voices from Company D: Diaries by the Greensboro Guards, Fifth Alabama Infantry Regiment, Army of Northern Virginia*. Athens, GA, and London: University of Georgia Press, 2003.

Hunter, Alexander. *Johnny Reb and Billy Yank*. New York and Washington: Neale and Co., 1904.

Hunter, Major General David. "The Opposing Forces in the Lynchburg Expedition — The Union Army." In *Battles and Leaders of the Civil War*, ed. Robert Underwood Johnson and Clarence Clough Buell, vol. 4. New York: Thomas Yoseloff, Inc., 1956.

Hyde, Thomas W. *Following the Greek Cross; Or, Memories of the Sixth Army Corp*. Boston, MA, and New York: Houghton, Mifflin and Company, 1894.

Imboden, John D. "The Battle of New Market Va., May 15, 1864." In *Battles and Leaders of the Civil War*, eds. Robert Underwood Johnson and Clarence Clough Buell, vol. 4. New York: Thomas Yoseloff, Inc., 1956.

Isham, Asa B. *Historical Sketch of the Seventh Michigan Volunteer Cavalry*, New York: Town Topics Publishing Co., 1893.

Johnson, Bradley T. "My Ride Around Baltimore in 1864." In *Southern Historical Society Papers*, vol. 30 (1902), pp. 215–225.

Johnson, Robert U., and Clarence C. Buell, eds. "Early's March to Washington in 1864." In *Battles and Leaders of the Civil War*, ed. Robert Underwood Johnson and Clarence Clough Buell, vol. 4. New York: The Century Company, 1887–88.

_____, and _____, eds. "Sigel, Franz, Major-General U.S.V., Sigel in the Shenandoah Valley in 1864." In *Battles and Leaders of the Civil War*, vol. 4. Reprint, New York: Thomas Yoseloff, Inc., 1956.

Jones, J.B. *A Rebel War Clerk's Diary at the Confederate State Capital*, vol. 2. Philadelphia, PA: J.B. Lippincott and Co., 1866.

Jones, J. William. "The Kilpatrick-Dahlgren Raid Against Richmond." In *Southern Historical Society Papers*, vol. 30. Richmond, VA: 1889.

Jones, Thomas A. *J. Wilkes Booth*. Chicago IL: Laird and Lee, 1893.

Junior, Josephus. *The Annals of Harper's Ferry, West Virginia*. Harper's Ferry, WVA: printed at the Offices of the Beckley Union, 1872.

Keiley, Anthony M. *In Vinculis, or the Prisoner of War*. New York: Bleilock and Co., 1866.

Kennon, Lieutenant L.W.V. "The Valley Campaign of 1864: A Military Study." In *Papers of the Military Historical Society of Massachusetts*, vol. 6. Boston, 1907.

Kidd, J.H. *Personal Recollections of a Cavalryman*. Iona, MI: Sentinel Printing Co., 1908.

Lee, R.E. *Lee's Dispatches: Unpublished Letters of General Robert E. Lee C.S.A. to Jefferson Davis and War Department of the Confederate States of America*. Edited by Douglas Southall Freeman and Grady McWhiney. New York: Putnam, 1957.

Lincoln, Abraham. *The Collected Works of Abraham Lincoln*. Edited by Roy Basler. New Brunswick, NJ: Rutgers University Press, 1953.

Lincoln, William Server. *Life with the 34th Massachusetts Infantry in the War of the Rebellion*. Worcester, MA: Press of Noyes, Snow and Co., 1879.

Long, A.L. "General Early's Valley Campaign," in *Southern Historical Society Papers*, vol. 30 (Richmond, VA: 1877), 112.

_____. *Memoirs of Robert E. Lee*. New York, Philadelphia and Washington: J.M. Stoddard and Co., 1876.

Lowell, Charles Russell. *Life and Letters of Charles Russell Lowell*. Columbia, SC: University of South Carolina Press, 2005.

Malone, Bartlett Yancy. *Whipt 'Em Every Time: The Diary of Bartlett Yancey Malone*. Jackson, TN: McCowat-Mercer Press, 1960.

M'chesny, James Z. "Scouting on Hunter's Raid to Lynchburg, Va." *Confederate Veteran* 28 (May 1920).

Mettan, Henry Clay. "Civil War Memories of First Maryland Cavalry, C.S.A." *Maryland Historical Magazine* 58 (1963).

Mosby, John S. *Memoirs of John Singleton Mosby*. Norwood, MA: Little Brown and Co., 1917.

Munson, John W. *Reminiscences of a Mosby Guerilla*. New York: Moffet, Yard and Company, 1906.

National Park Service. Appendix E: "General Reports about the Defenses." Appendix H: "A Sampling of Correspondence, Reports, Orders, Etc., Relating to the Battle of Fort Stevens." In *Civil War Defenses of Washington: A Historic Resource Study*, part I. Washington, DC.

Newcomer, C. Armour. *Cole's Cavalry; or, Three Years in the Saddle in the Shenandoah Valley*. Freeport, NY: Books for Libraries Press, 1970.

Opie, John N. *A Rebel Cavalryman with Lee, Stuart and Jackson*. Chicago, IL: W.B. Conkey Company, 1999.

Pendleton, William Nelson. *Memoirs of William Nelson Pendleton*. Philadelphia, PA: J.P. Lippincott Company, 1893.

Perkins, George A. (Co.D) *A Summer in Maryland and Virginia; Or, Campaigning with the 149th Ohio Volunteers*. Chillicothe, OH: Scholl Printing Co., 1911.

Porter, Captain Charles H. "Operations of Generals Sigel and Hunter in the Shenandoah Valley in May and June, 1864." Vol. 8. Boston, MA: Military History Society of Massachusetts, 1907.

Porter, Horace. *Campaigning with Grant*. New York: Century, 1899.

Putnam, George Haven. *Memories of My Youth, 1844–1865*. New York: G.P. Putnam Sons, 1914.

Rawling, C.J. *History of the First Regiment of Virginia Infantry*. Philadelphia, PA: J.B. Lippincott Company, 1897.

Rodenbough, Theo. F. "Sheridan's Trevilian Raid." In *Battles and Leaders of the Civil War*, ed. Robert Underwood Johnson and Clarence Clough Buell, vol. 4. New York: Thomas Yoseloff, Inc., 1956.

Scott, Major John, C.S.A. *Partisan Life with Col. John S. Mosby*. New York: Harper and Brothers, 1867.

Setchell, George Case. "A Sergeant's View of the Battle of Piedmont." *Civil War Times Illustrated* 2 (May 1963).

Sheridan, Philip H. *Personal Memoirs of P.H. Sheridan*. New York: Charles Webster and Co., 1888.

Sherman, William Tecumseh. *Memoirs of General W.T. Sherman*. New York: Library of America, 1990.

Simon, John, ed. *The Papers of Ulysses S. Grant*. 18 vols. Carbondale and Edwardsville, IL: Southern Illinois University Press, 1982.

Sorrel, Moxley. *Recollections of a Confederate Staff Officer*. Edited by Bell Irvin Wiley. Jackson, TN: McCowat-Mercer Press, Inc., 1958.

Stark, William B. "The Great Skedaddle." *Atlantic Monthly*, July 1938.

Stevens, George T. *Three Years in the Sixth Corps: A Narrative of Events in the Army of the Potomac from 1861 to the Close of the Rebellion*. New York: D. Van Nostrand, 1870.

Stevenson, James Hunter. *Boots and Saddles: A History of the First Volunteer Cavalry of the War Known as the First New York (Lincoln) Cavalry*. Harrisburg, PA: Patriot Publishing Co., 1879.

Stiles, Robert. *Four Years Under Marse Robert*. New York and Washington: The Neale Publishing Co., 1903.

Stribling, Robert M. *The Gettysburg Campaign and the Campaigns of 1864 and 1865 in Virginia*. Petersburg, VA: The Franklin Press Co., 1905.

Strong, George Templeton, *The Diary of George Templeton Strong: The Civil War 1860–1865*. Edited by Allan Nevins and Milton Halsey Thomas. New York: Macmillan, 1952.

Taylor, Walter H. *Four Years with Lee*. Bloomington, IN: University of Indiana Press, 1962.

Thayer, William Roscoe, ed. *The Life and Letters of John Hay*. 2 vols. Boston, MA: Houghton Mifflin Co., 1915.

Thompson, Magnus S. "Plan to Release Our Men at Point Lookout." *Confederate Veteran* 20 (February 1912).

United States War Department. *The War of the Rebellion: A Compilation of the Official Records of the Union and Confederate Armies*. 4 series, 129 volumes. Washington, DC: Government Printing Office, 1880–1900.

Vincent, Thomas McCurdy. "Early's March on Washington." In *Washington During War Time: A Series of Papers Showing the Military, Political and Social Phases During 1861–1865*. Official Souvenir of the Thirty-Sixth Annual Encampment of the Grand Army of the Republic. Collected and edited by Marcus Benjamin, the director of the Committee on Literature for the Encampment. Washington, DC: National Tribune Co., n.d.

Wallace, Lew. *An Autobiography*. New York and London: Harper and Brothers, 1896.

Wells, Gideon. *Diary of Gideon Wells*. Vol. II, April 1, 1864–December 31, 1866. Boston and New York: Houghton Mifflin Co., 1911.

Wildes, Thomas Francis. *Record of the One Hundred Sixteenth Ohio Volunteer Infantry in the War of the Rebellion*. Sandusky, OH: I.F. Mack and Bros., 1874.

Williamson, James J. (Co. A). *Mosby's Rangers: A Record of the Operations of the Forty-Third Battalion of Virginia Cavalry from Its Organization to Surrender*. 2nd ed. New York: Sturgis and Walton, 1909.

Wilson, Edmund S. "The Lynchburg Campaign." In *Sketches of War History, 1861–1865*. Reprint, Wilmington, NC: The Broadfoot Publishing Company, 1991.

Wilson, John M. *The Defenses of Washington, 1861–1865*. Washington, DC: Military Order of the Loyal Legion, December 1901.

Wing, Henry E. *When Lincoln Kissed Me: A Story of the Wilderness Campaign*. New York: Eaton and Mains, 1913.

Worsham, John H. *One of "Jackson's foot Cavalry": His Experiences and What He Saw, 1861–1865*. New York: The Neale Publishing Co., 1912.

Worthington, Glenn H. *Fighting for Time: The Battle That Saved Washington and Maybe the Union*. Frederick, MD: Frederick County Historical Society, 1932.

Secondary Sources

Ambrose, Stephen E. *Halleck, Lincoln's Chief of Staff*. Baton Rouge, LA: Louisiana State University Press, 1962.

Anders, Curt. *Henry Halleck's War: A Fresh Look at Lincoln's Controversial General in Chief*. Indianapolis: Guild Press of Indiana, 1999.

Armstrong, Richard L. *19th and 20th Virginia*. Lynchburg, VA: H.E. Howard, Inc., 1994.

_____. *25th Virginia Infantry and 9th Battalion Virginia Infantry*. Lynchburg, VA: H.E. Howard, Inc., 1990.

Armstrong, William H. *Major McKinley: William McKinley and the Civil War*. Kent, OH, and London: Kent State University Press, 2000.

Ashdown, Paul, and Edward Caudell. *The Mosby Myth: A Confederate Hero in Life and Legend*. Wilmington, DE: Scholarly Resources, 2002.

Bartlett, A.W. *History of the 12th Regiment N.H. Volunteers*. Concord, NH: Ira Cross, 1887.

Bates, Samuel F. *Martial Deeds of Pennsylvania*. Philadelphia, PA: T.H. Davis, 1876.

Beitzell, Edwin W. *Point Lookout Prison Camp for Confederates*. Leonardtown, MD: St. Mary's County Historical Society, 1983.

Bell, John. *Confederate Seadog: John Taylor Wood in War and in Exile*. Jefferson, NC: McFarland, 2002.

Beringer, Richard E., Herman Hattaway, Archer Jones, and William N. Still, Jr. *Why the South Lost the Civil War*. Athens, GA: University of Georgia Press, 1986.

Black, Robert C., III. *The Railroads of the Confederacy*. Chapel Hill, NC: University of North Carolina Press, 1952.

Blackman, Ann. *Wild Rose: Rose O'Neale Greenhow, Civil War Spy*. New York: Random House, 2005.

Bleimaier, John Kuhn. "Cassius Marcellus Clay in St. Petersburg." *The Register*, Kentucky Historical Society, July 1975.

Boatner, Mark. *The Civil War Dictionary*. New York: David McKay, 1959.

Bonekemper, Edward H., IV. *How Robert E. Lee Lost the Civil War*. Fredericksburg, VA: Sergeant Kirkland's Press, 1998.

Bonnell, John C. *Sabres in the Shenandoah: The 21st New York Cavalry, 1863–1866*, Shippensburg, PA: Burd Street Press, 1996.

Bowery, Charles, Jr. *Lee and Grant: Profiles in Leadership from the Battlefields of Virginia*. New York: Amacom, 2005.

Brice, Marshall Moore. *Conquest of a Valley*. Charlottesville, VA: University Press of Virginia, 1965.

Brooks, Noah. *Lincoln Observed: Civil War Dispatches of Noah Brooks*. Edited by Michael Burlingame and John R. Turner Etlinger. Baltimore and London: Johns Hopkins University Press, 1998.

_____. *Mr. Lincoln's Washington: Selections from the Writings of Noah Brooks, Civil War Correspondent*. Edited by P.J. Staudenhaus. South Brunswick, NJ: Thomas Yoseleff, Inc., 1967.

Brown, James Earl. "Life of Brigadier General John McCausland." *West Virginia History* 4.4 (July 1943), 239–293.

Browning, Robert M., Jr. *From Cape Fear to Cape Charles: The North Atlantic Blockading Squadron During the Civil War*. Tuscaloosa and London: University of Alabama Press, 1993.

Bruce, Philip Alexander. *Robert E. Lee*. Philadelphia, PA: George W. Jacobs, 1907.

Bushong, Millard Kessler. *Old Jube: A Biography of General Jubal A. Early*. Boyce, VA: Carr Publishing, 1955.

_____, and Dean McKoin Bushong. *Fightin' Tom Rosser, C.S.A*. Shippensburg, PA: Beidel Printing House, 1983.

Canon, H.V. "Confederate Military Intelligence." *Maryland Historical Magazine*, March 1964.

Cantor, George. *Confederate Generals: Life Portraits*. Dallas, TX: Taylor Trade Publications, 2000.

Carmichael, Peter S., ed. *Audacity Personified: The Generalship of Robert E. Lee*. Baton Rouge, LA: Louisiana State University Press, 2004.

Case, Lynn M., and W. Spencer. *The United States and France: Civil War Diplomacy*. Philadelphia, PA: University of Pennsylvania Press, 1970.

Casstevens, Francis H. *Out of the Mouth of Hell: Civil War Prisons and Escapes*. Jefferson, NC, and London: McFarland, 2005.

Catton, Bruce. *Civil War*. New York: Fairfax Press, 1984.

_____. *Grant Takes Command*. Boston: Little, Brown & Co., 1969.

Censer, Jane Turner, ed. *The Papers of Frederick Law Olmstead*. Vol. 4: *Defending Union: The Civil War and the U.S. Sanitary Commission 1861–1863*. Baltimore, MD: Johns Hopkins University Press, 1986.

Coffin, Howard. *Full Duty: Vermonters in the Civil War*. Woodstock, VT: The Countryman Press, 1993.

Connelly, Thomas L. *The Marble Man: Robert E. Lee and His Image in American Society*. New York: Alfred A. Knopf, 1977.

Cooling, Benjamin Franklin. *Jubal Early's Raid on Washington in 1864*. Baltimore, MD: Nautical and Aviation Publishing Co., 1989.

_____. *Monocacy: The Battle That Saved Washington*. Shippensburg, PA: White Mane, 1988.

_____. *Symbol, Sword and Shield: Defending Washington During the Civil War*. Shippensburg, PA: White Mane, 1991.

_____, and Walter B. Owen. *Mr. Lincoln's Forts: A Guide to the Civil War Defenses of Washington*. Shippensburg, PA: White Mane, 1984.

Cornish, Dudley Taylor, and Virginia Jeans Laas. *Lincoln's Lee*. Lawrence, KS: University of Kansas Press, 1986.

Cowen, B.R. "The Battle of the Monocacy." In *Sketches in War History*, vol. 5 (MOLLUS) Reprint, Wilmington, NC: Broadfoot Publishing Company, 1992.

Cox, William Van Zandt. "Fort Stevens Where Lincoln Was Under Fire." In *Washington During War Time: A Series of Papers Showing the Military, Political and Social Phases During 1861 to 1865*. Official Souvenir of the Thirty-Sixth Encampment of the Grand Army of the Republic. Collected and edited by Marcus Benjamin under the Direction of the Committee on Literature for the Encampment. Washington, DC: National Tribune Co., n.d.

Cramer, Henry. *Lincoln Under Enemy Fire: The Complete Account of His Experiences During Early's Attack on Washington*. Baton Rouge, LA: Louisiana State University Press, 1948.

Crook, D.P. *Diplomacy During the American Civil War*. New York: John Wiley and Sons, 1975.

Crouthamel, James L. *Bennett's New York Herald and the Rise of the Popular Press*. Syracuse, NY: Syracuse University Press, 1989.

Daniel, Edward M. *Speeches and Orations of John Warwick Daniel*. Lynchburg, VA: J.P. Bell, 1911.

Delauter, Roger, Jr. *McNeill's Rangers*. Lynchburg, VA: H.E. Howard, 1986.

Dennett, Tyler, ed. *Lincoln in the Civil War: In the Diaries and Letters of John Hay*. New York: Dodd, Mead and Company, 1939.

Dickman, Jack L. *8th Virginia Cavalry*. Lynchburg, VA: H.E. Howard, 1986.

Dixon, Joan M. "The Civil War Years, July 1, 1863—December 31, 1865." In *National Intelligencer Newspaper Abstracts*, Special Edition, vol. 2. Bowie, MD: Heritage Books, 2001.

Donald, David Herbert. *Gone for a Soldier: The Civil War Memories of Private Alfred Bellard*. Boston, MA: Little Brown, 1975.

Donald, David, ed. *Why the North Won the Civil War*. New York: Collier Books, 1962.

Donnelly, Ralph W. *History of the Confederate States Marine Corps*. Wilmington, NC: privately printed, 1976.

Drake, Mike, and Mark Travis. *My Brave Boys: To War with Colonel Cross and the Fighting Fifth*. Hanover and London: University Press of New England, 2001.

Driver, Robert, Jr. *First and Second Maryland Cavalry, C.S.A*. Charlottesville, VA: Rockbridge Publishing, 1999.

Duberman, Martin. *Charles Francis Adams, 1807–1886*. Boston, MA: Houghton Mifflin, 1960.

Duncan, Richard R. *Lee's Endangered Left*. Baton Rouge, LA: Louisiana State University Press, 1998.

_____. "Maryland's Reaction to Early's Raid." *Maryland Historical Magazine* 64.3 (Fall 1969): 248–270.
DuPont, H.A. *The Campaign of 1864 in the Valley of Virginia and the Expedition to Lynchburg.* New York: J.J. Little, 1925.
Dyer, Frederick H. *A Compendium of the War of the Rebellion.* Des Moines, IA: Dyer Publishing, 1868.
Eby, Cecil D., Jr. *A Virginia Yankee in the Civil War: The Diaries of David Hunter Strother.* Chapel Hill, NC: University of North Carolina Press, 1961.
Eicher, John H., and David J. Eicher. *Civil War High Commands.* Palo Alto, CA: Stanford University Press, 2001.
Emerson, Edward W. *Life and Letters of Charles Russell Lowell.* Boston and New York: Houghton Mifflin, 1907.
Engle, Stephen D. *Yankee Dutchman: The Life of Franz Sigel.* Fayetteville, AK: University of Arkansas Press, 1993.
Farrar, Samuel Clark. *The 22nd Pennsylvania Cavalry.* Pittsburg, PA, 1911.
Faust, Patricia L., ed. *Historical Times Illustrated Encyclopedia of the Civil War.* New York: Harper and Row, 1986.
Feis, William B. "Neutralizing the Valley: The Role of Military Intelligence in the Defeat of Jubal Early's Army of the Valley, 1864–1865." *Civil War History*, vol. 39, no. 3. Kent, OH: Kent State University Press, Sept. 1993.
_____. *Grant's Secret Service.* Lincoln and London: University of Nebraska Press, 2002.
_____. "A Union Military Intelligence Failure: Jubal Early's Raid June 12–July 14, 1864." *Civil War History*, vol. 36, no. 3. Kent, OH: Kent State University Press, Sept. 1990.
Flood, Charles Bracelon. *Grant and Sherman: The Friendship That Won the Civil War.* New York: Farrar, Straus and Giroux, 2005.
Flower, Frank Abial. *Edwin McMasters Stanton: The Autocrat of Rebellion Emancipation and Reconstruction.* Akron, OH: Soalfield, 1905.
Foner, Eric. *Reconstruction: America's Unfinished Revolution.* New York: Harper and Row, 1988.
Freeman, Douglas Southall. *Lee's Lieutenants: A Study in Command.* 3 vols. New York: Charles Scribner's Sons, 1942–1945.
_____. *R.E. Lee: A Biography.* 4 vols. New York: Charles Scribner's Sons, 1934–35.
Gallagher, Gary W. *Lee and His Army in Confederate History.* Chapel Hill, NC: University of North Carolina Press, 2001.
_____. *Lee and His Generals in War and in Memory.* Baton Rouge, LA: Louisiana State University Press, 1998.
_____. *Stephen Dodson Ramseur, Lee's Gallant General.* Chapel Hill and London: University of North Carolina Press, 1981.
Gannon, James P. *Irish Rebels, Confederate Tigers: The 6th Louisiana, 1861–1865.* Campbell, CA: Sovas Publishing Company, 1998.
Gavronsky, Serge. *The French Liberal Opposition and the American Civil War.* New York: Humanities Press, 1968.
Goff, Richard D. *Confederate Supply.* Durham, NC: Duke University Press, 1969.
Goldsborough, W.W. *The Maryland Line in the Confederate Army, 1861–1865.* Port Washington, NY: Kennekat Press, 1972.
Goodwin, Doris Kearns. *Team of Rivals: The Political Genius of Abraham Lincoln.* New York, London, Toronto and Sydney: Simon and Schuster, 2005.
Hall, James O. "The Dahlgren Papers." *Civil War Times Illustrated*, November 1983.

Hall, Laura Virginia. *Four Violent Years in the Shenandoah Valley, 1861–1865.* Strasburg, VA: Shenandoah Publishing House, 1968.
Harletzer, Daniel D. *Marylanders in the Confederacy.* Silver Spring, MD: Family Line, 1986.
Harris, Nelson. *17th Virginia Cavalry.* Lynchburg, VA: H.E. Howard, Inc., 1994.
Harsh, Joseph L. *Confederate Tide Rising: Robert E. Lee and the Making of Southern Strategy, 1861–1862.* Kent, OH: Kent State University Press, 1998.
Hartzler, Daniel D. *Marylanders in the Confederacy.* Silver Spring, MD: Family Line Publications, 1986.
Haynes, Martin A. *History of the Second Regiment New Hampshire Volunteers: Its Camps, Marches and Battles.* Manchester, NH: C.F. Livingston, 1865.
Heckman, Richard Allen. "British Press Reaction to the Emancipation Proclamation." *Lincoln Herald* 16 (1969).
Heitman, Francis. *Historical Register and Dictionary of the United States Army, 1789–1903.* Washington, DC: U.S. Government Printing Office, 1903.
Hochschild, Adam. *Bury the Chains: Prophets and Rebels in the Fight to Free the Empire's Slaves.* Boston: Houghton Mifflin, 2004.
Humphries, Milton W. *A History of the Lynchburg Campaign.* Charlottesville, VA: Michie, 1921.
Jenkins, Brian. "The Wise Macaw and the Lion: William Seward and Britain 1861–1863." *University of Rochester Library Bulletin* 31 (autumn 1972).
Johnson, Robert Underwood, and Clarence Clough Buell, eds. *Battles and Leaders of the Civil War.* 4 vols. New York: Thomas Yoseloff, 1956.
Jones, J. William. *Personal Reminiscences, Anecdotes and Letters of Gen. Robert E. Lee.* New York: D. Appleton and Company, 1875.
Jones, Thomas J. *J. Wilkes Booth.* Chicago, IL: Laird and Lee, 1893.
Jones, Virgil Carrington. *Ranger Mosby.* Reprint, McLean, VA: EMP Publications, 1987.
Judge, Joseph. *Season of Fire: The Confederate Strike on Washington.* Berryville, VA: Rockbridge, 1994.
Kaufman, Wilhelm. *The Germans in the American Civil War.* Carlisle, PA: John Kallmann, 1999.
Keller, Roger S. *Events of the Civil War in Washington County, Maryland.* Shippensburg, PA: Burd Street Press, 1995.
_____, ed. *Col. Thomas L. Rosser: Riding with Rosser.* Shippensburg, PA: Burd Street Press, 1997.
Kellogg, Sanford A. *The Shenandoah Valley and Virginia 1861–1865: A War Sketch.* New York and Washington: The Neale Publishing Company, 1903.
Kirk, Hyland C. *Heavy Guns and Light: A History of the Fourth New York Heavy Artillery.* New York: C.T. Dillingham, 1890.
Kleese, Robert B. *Shenandoah County in the Civil War: The Turbulent Years.* Lynchburg, TN: H.E. Howard, 1992.
Korda, Michael. *Ulysses S. Grant: The Unlikely Hero.* New York: Harper Collins, 2004.
Krick, Robert H. "The Cause of All My Disaster: Jubal A. Early and the Undisiplined Valley Cavalry." In *The Struggles for the Shenandoah: Essays on the 1864 Valley Campaign*, edited by Gary W. Gallagher. Kent, OH: Kent State University Press, 1991.
Laas, Virginia Jeans, ed. *Wartime Washington: The Civil War Letters of Elizabeth Blair Lee.* Urbana, IL: Illini Books, 1999.
Law, E.M. "From the Wilderness to Cold Harbor." In *Battles and Leaders of the Civil War*, ed. Robert Under-

wood Johnson and Clarence Clough Buell, vol. 4. New York: Thomas Yoseloff, 1956.

Leckie, Shirley A. *Elizabeth Bacon Custer and the Making of a Myth*. Norman, OK, and London: University of Oklahoma Press, 1984.

Lee, Robert E., Jr. *Recollections and Letters of General Robert E. Lee*. New York: Doubleday, Page & Co., 1904.

Leech, Margaret. *Reveille in Washington, 1860–1865*. New York and London: Harper and Brothers, 1941.

Leeke, J., ed. *A Hundred Days to Richmond: Ohio's "Hundred Days" Men in the Civil War*. Bloomington and Indianapolis, Indiana: Indiana University Press, 1999.

Lepa, Jack. *The Shenandoah Valley Campaign of 1864*. Jefferson, NC, and London: McFarland, 2004.

Livermore, Thomas L. *Numbers and Losses in the Civil War in America*. Bloomington, IN: Kessinger Press, 2006, reprint.

Long, David E. *Jewel of Liberty: Abraham Lincoln's Reelection and the End of Slavery*. New York: Da Capo, 1997.

Longacre, Edward G. *Gentleman and Soldier: A Biography of Wade Hampton III*. Nashville, TN: Rutledge Hill Press, 2003.

_____. *The Life and Wars of James H. Wilson*. Mechanicsburg, PA: Stackpole Books, 2000.

_____. *A Regiment of Slaves: The Fourth United States Colored Regiment, 1863–1866*. Mechanicsburg, PA: Stackpole Books, 2003.

Luraghi, Raimondo. *A History of the Confederate Navy*. Annapolis, MD: Naval Institute Press, 1996.

Mahon, Michael G. *The Shenandoah Valley, 1861–1865: The Destruction of the Granary of the Confederacy*. Mechanicsburg, PA: Stackpole Books, 1999.

Markle, Donald E. *Spies and Spymasters in the Civil War*. New York: Hippocene Books, 1994.

Marszalek, John F. *Commander of All Lincoln's Armies: A Life of General Henry W. Halleck*. Cambridge, MA, and London: Belknap Press, 2004.

Martinez, J. Michael. *Life and Death in Civil War Prisons*. Nashville, TN: Rutledge Hill Press, 2004.

Massachusetts Adjutant General's Office. *Soldiers, Sailors and Marines in the Civil War*. Vol. 6. Norwood, MA: The Norwood Press, 1932.

Matheny, H.E. *Major-General Thomas Maley Harris*. Parsons, WV: McClain, 1963.

McClure, Alexander. *Lincoln and Men of War Times* (Lincoln, NE: University of Nebraska Press, 1997).

McFeely, William. *Grant*. London: W.W. Norton, 1982.

McKee, Irving. *"Ben Hur" Wallace: The Life of General Lew Wallace*. Berkeley and Los Angeles: University of California Press, 1947.

McKenzie, John. *Uncertain Glory: Lee's Generalship Re-examined*. New York: Hippocrene Books, 1997.

McPherson, James M. *Battle Cry of Freedom: The Civil War Era*. New York: Oxford University Press, 1988.

_____. *Crossroads of Freedom: Antietam, the Battle that Changed the Course of the Civil War*. New York: Oxford University Press, 2002.

_____. "No Peace Without Victory." Presidential address at the 118th annual meeting of the American Historical Association, Washington, DC, January 3, 2003.

McWhiney, Grady, and Perry D. Jamieson. *Attack and Die: Civil War Military Tactics and the Southern Heritage*. Tuscaloosa, AL: University of Alabama Press, 1982.

Michels, Robert E. *Colonel Harry Gilmor's Ride Around Baltimore, July 10th to July 13th, 1864*. Baltimore, MD: Erbe Publishers, 1976.

Miller, David W. *Second Only to Grant: Quartermaster General Montgomery C. Meigs*. Shippensburg, PA: White Mane, 2000.

Miller, Edward A., Jr. *Lincoln's Abolitionist General: A Biography of General David Hunter*. Columbia, SC: University of South Carolina Press, 1997.

Millet, Allan R., and Peter Maslowski. *For the Common Defense: A Military History of the United States of America*. New York: New York Free Press, 1994.

Moore, Frank, ed. *The Rebellion Record: A Diary of American Events*. Vol. 11. New York: Van Nostrand, 1868.

Morris, George S., and Susan L. Foutz. *Lynchburg in the Civil War*. Lynchburg, VA: H.E. Howard, 1984.

Mottelay, Paul, and Copeland T. Campbell. *The Soldier in Our Civil War*. 2 vols. New York: Stanley Bradley Publishing Co., 1880.

National Park Service. Part 1, chapter 6, "Maintenance of the Defenses"; and part 1, chapter 7, "Jubal Early's Raid on Washington DC/Battle of Fort Stevens." In *The Civil War Defenses of Washington: A Historic Resource Study*. Washington, DC: U.S. Dept. of Interior, National Park Service, National Capital Region; Chevy Chase, MD: CEHP, Inc., 2004.

Nolan, Alan T. *Lee Considered: General Robert E. Lee and Civil War History*. Chapel Hill, NC: University of North Carolina Press, 2001.

Official Souvenir and Program of Monument First Connecticut Heavy Artillery and Dedicatory Exercises. Hartford, CT: R.S. Peck, 1902.

Offutt, William. *Bethesda: A Social History of the Area Through World War Two*. Bethesda, MD: McNaughton, 1985.

Olson, John E. *21st Virginia Cavalry*. Lynchburg, VA: H.E. Howard, 1989.

Osborne, Charles C. *Jubal: The Life and Times of General Jubal A. Early, C.S.A., Defender of the Lost Cause*. Chapel Hill, NC: Algonquin Books, 1992.

Palmer, Michael. *Lee Moves North: Robert E. Lee on the Offensive*. New York: John Wiley and Sons, 1998.

Park, Robert E. "The Twelfth Alabama Infantry, Confederate States Army." Southern Historical Society Papers. Richmond, VA: Virginia Historical Society, 1905.

Patchan, Scott. *The Forgotten Fury: The Battle of Piedmont, VA*. Fredericksburg: Sgt. Kirkland's Museum and Historical Society, 1996.

Pauley, Michael J. *Unreconstructed Rebel: The Life of General John McCausland, C.S.A.* Charleston, WV: Pictorial Histories, 1993.

Pelka, Fred, ed. *The Civil War Letters of Colonel Charles F. Johnson, Invalid Corps*. Amherst, MA: University of Massachusetts Press, 2004.

Philips, Edward H. *The Shenandoah Valley in 1864: An Episode in the History of Warfare*. Charleston, SC: The Citadel, The Military College of South Carolina, May 1995.

Pollard, Edward A. *Lee and His Lieutenants*. New York: E.B. Treat, 1867.

Pond, George E. *The Shenandoah Valley in 1864*. Reprint, Wilmington, NC: Broadfoot, 1989.

Porter, Charles H. "Operation of Generals Sigel and Hunter in the Shenandoah Valley in May and June of 1864." *Papers of the Military Historical Society of Massachusetts*. Vol 6. Boston, MA: 1907.

Pratt, Fletcher. *Stanton: Lincoln's Secretary of War*. New York: W.W. Norton, 1953.

Ramage, James. *Gray Ghost*. Lexington, KY: University Press of Kentucky, 1999.

Record, Jeffrey. "External Assistance, Enabler of Insurgent Success." *US Army War College Quarterly*, Autumn 2006.

Reed, Thomas J. *Tibbitts Boys — A History of the 21st New*

York Cavalry. Lanham, MD: University Press of America, 1997.

Reich, Robert R. "Lee at Chancellorsville." In *Lee, the Soldier*, ed. Gary W. Gallagher. Lincoln, NE: University of Nebraska Press, 1996.

Reid, Whitelaw. *Ohio in the War: Her Statesmen, Generals and Soldiers*. Vol. 2. Cincinnati, OH, and New York: Moore, Wilstack and Baldwin, 1868.

Riggs, David F. *13th Virginia Infantry*. Lynchburg, VA: H.E. Howard, 1988.

Roe, Alfred Seelye, and Charles Nutt. *History of the First Regiment of Heavy Artillery, Massachusetts Volunteers*. Worchester and Boston: Commonwealth Press, 1917.

Sanders, Charles W., Jr. *While in the Hands of the Enemy: Military Prisons in the Civil War*. Baton Rouge, LA: Louisiana State University Press, 2005.

Scharf, Thomas J. *A History of the Confederate States Navy from Its Organization to the Surrender of Its Last Vessel*. New York: Rogers and Sherwood, 1957.

Seipel, Kevin. *The Life and Times of John Singleton Mosby*. New York: St. Martin's Press, 1983.

Shaw, Horace J., and Charles House. *First Maine Heavy Artillery: A Regimental History*. Portland, ME: Charles House, 1903.

Shingleton, Royce Gordon. *John Taylor Wood: Sea Ghost of the Confederacy*. Athens, GA: University of Georgia Press, 1979.

Sibley, F. Ray, Jr. *The Confederate Order of Battle*. Volume I, *The Army of Northern Virginia*. Shippensburg, PA: White Mane, 1997.

Smith, Jean Edward. *Grant*. New York: Simon and Schuster, 2001.

Smith, William Earnest. *The Francis Preston Blair Family in Politics*. New York: Macmillan, 1933.

Speer, Emory. *Lincoln, Lee, Grant and Other Biographical Addresses*. New York and Washington: The Neale Publishing Co., 1909.

Speer, Lonnie R. *Portals to Hell: Military Prisons in the Civil War*. Lincoln, NE: University of Nebraska Press, 1997.

Summers, Festus P. *The Baltimore and Ohio in the Civil War*. New York: G.P. Putnam's Sons, 1939.

Swisher, James R. "Following Old Jube: Richmond to Washington." *Confederate Veteran* 5 (2000): 16–23.

_____. *Warrior in Gray: General Robert Rodes of Lee's Army*. Shippensburg, PA: White Mane Books, 2000.

Tankersley, Allen P. *John B. Gordon: A Study in Gallantry*. Atlanta, GA: Whitehall, 1955.

Thomsen, Brian M., ed. *Commanding Voices of Blue and Gray*. New York: Tom Doherty Associates, 2002.

Tidwell, William H., with James O. Hall and David Winfred Gaddy. *Come Retribution: The Confederate Secret Service and the Assassination of President Lincoln*. Jackson, MS: University of Mississippi Press, 1988.

Time-Life Books. *Spies, Scouts and Raiders: Irregular Operations*. Alexandria, VA: Time-Life Books, 1985.

Toomey, Daniel Carroll. *The Civil War in Maryland*. Baltimore, MD: Toomey Press, 1983.

Trudeau, Noah Andre. *Bloody Roads South: The Wilderness and Cold Harbor, May–June, 1864*. Baton Rouge, LA: Louisiana State University Press, 1989.

Tucker, Spencer C. *Brigadier General John D. Imboden: Confederate Commander in the Shenandoah*. Lexington, KY: University Press of Kentucky, 2003.

Vail, Dudley Landon. *The County Regiment: A Sketch of the Second Connecticut Volunteer Heavy Artillery*. Litchfield County University Club, 1908.

Vandiver, Frank E. *Jubal's Raid: General Early's Famous Attack on Washington*. MD: Old Soldier Books, Gaithersburg, 1988.

Waddell, J. Addison. *Annals of Augusta County*. Staunton, VA: C. Russell Caldwell, 1902.

Walker, Aldace F. *The Vermont Brigade in the Shenandoah Valley, 1864*. Burlington, VT: The Free Press Association, 1869.

Walker, Gary C. *Hunter's Fiery Raid Through Virginia's Valley*. Roanoke, VA: A and W Enterprise, 1989.

Walker, William C. *History of the Eighteenth Regiment Connecticut Volunteers in the War for the Union*. Norwalk, CT, 1885.

Ward, George W. *History of the Second Pennsylvania Heavy Artillery (112th Regiment Pennsylvania Volunteers) from 1861–1866*. Philadelphia, PA: G.W. Ward, 1904.

Warner, Ezra. *Generals in Blue*. Baton Rouge, LA: Louisiana State University Press, 1964.

_____. *Generals in Gray*. Baton Rouge, LA: Louisiana State University Press, 1959.

Waugh, John C. *Reelecting Lincoln: The Battle for the 1864 Presidency*. New York: Crown Publishers, 1997.

Wert, Jeffrey D. *From Winchester to Cedar Creek: The Shenandoah Campaign of 1864*. Carlisle, PA: South Mountain, 1987.

_____. "Jubal A. Early and the Confederate Leadership." In *Struggles for the Shenandoah: Essays on the Valley Campaign of 1864*, edited by Gary W. Gallagher. Kent, OH: Kent State University Press, 1991.

_____. *Mosby's Rangers*. New York: Simon and Schuster, 1990.

Whalen, Charles, and Barbara Whalen. *The Fighting McCooks: America's Famous Fighting Family*. Bethesda, MD: Westmoreland Press, 2006.

White, Gregory C. *"The Most Bloody and Cruel Drama": A History of the 31st Georgia Volunteer Infantry, Lawton-Gordon-Evans Brigade, Army of Northern Virginia, Confederate States of America, 1861–1865*. Baltimore, MD: Butternut and Blue, 1989.

Whitman, Walt. *Specimen Days*. Philadelphia, PA: Rees Welch, 1882.

Wise, Jennings Cropper. *The Long Arm of Lee; Or, The History of Artillery in the Army of Northern Virginia*. Vol. 2. Lynchburg, VA: J.P. Bell, 1915.

_____. *Military History of the Virginia Military Institute*. Lynchburg, VA: J.P. Bell, 1912.

Wittenberg, Eric J. *Glory Enough for All: Sheridan's Second Raid and the Battle of Trevelian Station*. Washington, DC: Brussy's, 2001.

_____. *Little Phil: A Reassessment of the Civil War Legacy of General Philip H. Sheridan*. Dulles, VA: Brassey's, 2002.

Woodward, Harold R., Jr. *Defender of the Valley: John Daniel Imboden, C.S.A.* Berryville VA: Rockbridge, 1996.

Young, James C. *Marse Robert: Knight of the Confederacy*. New York: Rae D. Hinckle, 1929.

Zornow, William Frank. *Lincoln and the Party Divided*. Norman, OK: University of Oklahoma Press, 1954.

Index

Abbott, Henry L. 86
Alabama regiments: 12th Alabama Infantry 98, 103, 162, 174, 195, 203
Alexander, C.T. 95
Alexander, Edward Porter 8, 21, 196
Alexander, Frederic 106, 136, 139
Alexandria, Virginia 75, 85, 193, 195–196, 207–208
Allan, William 159
Alleganian 132
Alvord, Henry 181
Anaconda Plan 213
Anderson, Richard 18–19, 55, 117, 183–184
Armistead, Lewis 20
Armory Square Hospital 207–208
Army of Northern Virginia 3, 40, 55, 70, 110, 130, 133, 137, 164
Army of the James 3, 23, 46, 95, 189
Army of the Potomac 3, 6, 12, 14, 16, 18, 29, 35, 37, 44, 46–47, 78, 84–86, 92, 117, 189, 205, 207, 209
Army of the Valley 27, 54, 70, 135
Augur, Christopher 86, 129, 176, 189, 193
Averell, William 36–37, 39, 41–42, 44, 48, 50–51, 57–58, 60–61, 65, 67, 118, 144

Bacon, Peter 87
Baker, Lafayette C. 24, 198
Baltimore, Maryland 7, 23, 27–28, 53, 72, 106, 108, 119–120, 123, 129, 132, 135, 138, 141, 143, 145–146, 154–155, 164–167, 169–172, 189, 200, 217–218, 224
Baltimore and Ohio Railroad 36, 54, 68–70, 72, 98–100, 102, 105–106, 118–119, 123, 126, 129, 136–137, 148, 150, 154, 167, 170, 186, 188
Baltimore Sun 166
Banks 108, 155, 159
Banks, Nathaniel 14, 86
Barksdale, William 20
Barlow, S.M.L. 217
Barnard, John G. 74–75, 77, 79, 83–84, 129

Barnes, James 94, 96
Barton, William 196
Bates, Edward 113
Battery Alexander 74
Battery Cameron 76, 78
Battery Garesche 71, 77, 84
Battery Jameson 78
Battery Kemble 75, 78
Battery Parrott 78
Battery Smead 80, 189
Battery Vermont 75, 78
Battle, Cullen 162
Beauregard, Pierre 3, 46, 116–117, 196
Bellard, Alfred 187
Benjamin, Judah P. 196
Benton, R.C. 80
Blair, Francis P., Sr. 177, 200, 202–203, 217
Blair, Frank 202, 217
Blair, Montgomery 117, 200–204, 217
Bogden, Harry 197
Booth, George 33, 72, 122
Booth, John Wilkes 28
Bowie, Wat 123
Boyle, Cornelius 196
Bradbury, Albert 129
Bradford, Augustus 167, 202
Bradwell, Isaac 176–177
Brady, Allen G. 96
Bragg, Braxton 47, 53
USS *Brandywine* 131
Breckinridge, John C. 3, 36 40, 46–49, 52–53, 57–61, 64, 98, 102, 105, 109, 111, 118–119, 127, 137, 139, 141, 153, 160, 202–203
Briggs, George 179, 205
Brown, A.L. 136, 155, 159–160, 162
Brown, Ridgely 26–27
Browne, W.H. 42
Bryan, E. Pliney 196, 198
Buckeystown Road (near Monocacy, Maryland) 6, 141, 146, 156–157, 159–160, 223
Bull, David 210
Bureau of Military Information 57, 69, 117–118
Burnside, Ambrose 17–18, 27, 92, 95
Butler, Benjamin 23, 25, 46, 95–96, 113, 117, 133, 217

Butler, Matthew 31–34
Buttermilk Rangers 63, 144

Cadwalader, George 10, 86, 207
Cadwallader, Sylvanus 179
Cameron, Simon 202
Camp, E.E. 195
Camp Hoffman, Maryland 91
Camp Nicholls, Virginia 57
Campbell, Jacob 43, 64
Cannon, James C. 210
Cape Fear River, North Carolina 110, 135, 168
Carroll, John N. 167
Carver Hospital 207
Casler, John O. 69, 112
Catoctin Mountain, Maryland 107, 123, 138–140, 148, 150, 156, 165
Cawood, Charles 196–197
Cedar Creek, Battle of 222
Cedar Creek, Virginia 36–37, 39–40, 100
Cedar Mountain, Battle of 14, 54, 86, 145
Cemetary Hill (Gettysburg), Pennsylvania 19, 54, 222
Cerro Gordo, Mexico 8
Chain Bridge, D.C. 78, 84
Chambersburg, Pennsylvania 153–154, 202, 222
Chancellorsville, Virginia 8, 16, 18–19, 54, 65, 92, 105, 128, 139, 143, 215, 221
Chaplin, Daniel 78
Chapultepec, Mexico 12
Charleston, West Virginia 68–69, 147–149
Charlottesville, Virginia 14, 29–30, 35–37, 39–40, 43–46, 48–49, 57–61, 64–65, 110, 115–116, 118, 147, 152, 173, 183, 222–223
Chase, Salmon P. 217
Chesapeake and Ohio Canal 69–70, 72, 75, 93–94, 98, 123, 137
Chesapeake Bay 5, 89–92, 117, 132, 135
Chicago Tribune 217
Chittenden, L.E. 179, 181, 198, 211
Clay, Cassius Marcellus 214
Clay, Clement C. 219
Clendenin, David 107, 123–124, 129, 137–141, 145, 154, 159, 170

251

Index

Cochrane, John 218
Cold Harbor, Virginia 7, 20, 23, 46–47, 54, 56–57, 61, 78–79, 84, 86, 95, 115–116, 173, 183, 213, 219, 221, 223
Cole's Cavalry 49, 99, 107, 138–140
Colfax, Schuyler 115
Columbia Hospital 207
Colvin, E.M. 91
Confederate Quartermaster Department 110
Confederate Secret Service 31, 196
Confederate Signal Corps 28, 130, 196
Congressional Medal of Honor 31 39, 95, 140
Connecticut regiments: 1st Connecticut Heavy Artillery 84; 2nd Connecticut Heavy Artillery 84; 18th Connecticut Infantry 42, 43
Conrad, Thomas Nelson 28, 31, 198
Cook, Giles 117
Copperheads 220
Coquette 132
Couch, Darius 107, 117
Cox, Fleet 133
Crawford, C.V. 211
Crook, George 36–37, 39, 41–42, 44–46, 48, 50–51, 58, 61, 63–65, 67, 144, 147–148, 152–153, 222
Crosby, T.R. 207
Custer, Elizabeth Bacon 208
Custer, George Armstrong 27, 31–34, 122, 208

Dahlgren, Ulric 24–26
Dana, Charles 119, 150, 152, 182, 210, 222
Dana, D.D. 83
Daniel, John Warwick 63, 183
Daniel, Junius 56, 173
Daniel, Townsend 49
Davies, Henry E. 31
Davis, George 140
Davis, Jefferson 5, 7, 19, 21, 47, 53, 55, 57, 68–69, 89, 96, 102, 109, 130–131, 133–135, 164, 168, 198, 203, 218, 224
Davis, Thomas 41
Dayton, O.V. 79, 188–189
De Lhuys, Drouyn 215
DeMarres Hospital 207
DeRussy, Gustavus A. 70–71, 80, 86
Devin, Thomas C. 30, 32–34
District of Columbia regiments: 1st District of Columbia Cavalry 24; 2nd District of Columbia Infantry 87, 189, 194–195
District of St. Mary's (Maryland) 96
Doles, George 56, 173
Douglas, Henry Kyd 55, 105, 137, 149
Douglas Hospital 207
Douthat, Henry 49, 59–60
Draper, Alonzo 96
Ducalet, H.W. 208

Duffie, Alfred 39, 48–50, 57–58, 60, 63–67, 144
Dugan, R.H. 173
DuPont, Charles 87, 188
DuPont, Henry 39, 42, 50–51, 64–65, 67

Early, Jubal A. 1, 3, 5, 6–7; background 53–55; on Cavalry 143–144; Cemetary Hill 19, 54, 222; Chambersburg 153; Frederick 136–141; on Lee 12–13, 15–19; Leetown-Harpers Ferry 5, 98, 100, 102, 104–109, 120, 145, 223; Lynchburg 21, 29–30, 46–47, 49–50, 57–61, 64–67, 130; march North 21, 69–70, 89, 117–119, 126–127, 130, 147–149, 164, 174, 223; Monocacy 146, 154–157, 159–160, 162; Mosby 70, 120, 123–125, 138; move on Washington 6–7, 22, 28, 55, 75, 77–81, 117, 128–129, 150–151, 167–170, 172–173, 176, 178–179, 182–183, 185–186, 190, 193, 198–204, 207, 210; plan Point Lookout 108–109, 130, 133, 138, 141, 143, 165; plan Washington 3, 27, 53, 56, 68–70; relieved of command 221; Retreat and Valley operations 152–153, 184, 195; route to Washington 70–73; shoes 110–112
Echols, John 47, 52, 57, 60–61, 162, 200
Edwards Ferry, Maryland 73, 142, 223
Eldridge, Daniel 33
Ely, William 63
Emancipation Proclamation 17, 214
Emerson, W. 144
Emory Hospital 208
England 7, 16, 110, 117, 201, 214–216
Evans, Clement 69, 100, 105, 107, 161, 173
Ewell, Richard 5, 21, 47, 55, 58, 65, 117–120, 163, 183, 222

Fackler, George 177
Falklands Estate (Maryland) 200–203
Farmers and Mechanics Bank 159
Farnsworth, Addison 88, 187, 189, 194
Ferguson, J.B. 110
Finley Hospital 208
Fitts, Nelson 199
Fleetwood, Christian 95
Florie 133
Flying Cloud 123
Forrest, Bedford 219
Fort Albany 77, 85
Fort Baker 70, 75, 83
Fort Barnard 71, 77, 84
Fort Bayard 75, 79, 87
Fort Bennett 77, 86
Fort Berry 71, 77, 84

Fort Buffalo 77
Fort Bunker Hill 70, 75, 78, 82
Fort Carroll 75
Fort Cass 71, 77, 85
Fort C.F. Smith 71, 77, 86
Fort Chaplin 75
Fort Corcoran 71, 77, 86
Fort Craig 71, 77, 85
Fort Davis 70, 75, 83
Fort DeRussy 75, 78–79
Fort DuPont 70, 75
Fort Ellsworth 71, 77, 84
Fort Ethan Allen 71, 74, 78
Fort Farnesworth 71, 77
Fort Foote 70, 75, 83, 86
Fort Gaines 75, 80
Fort Greble 70, 75, 83
Fort Haggerty 77, 86
Fort Jackson 77
Fort Kearny 75, 80, 87, 189–190
Fort Lincoln 70, 75, 78, 82, 88, 180
Fort Lincoln (Maryland) 93–94
Fort Lyon 71, 77
Fort Mahan 70, 82
Fort Mansfield 75, 78–79
Fort Marcy 71, 74, 78
Fort McPherson 77
Fort Meigs 70, 75
Fort Morton 77
Fort Munson 77
Fort O'Rourke 71, 77
Fort Ramsey 77
Fort Reno 70, 75, 79, 87, 178, 185, 189–191, 201
Fort Reynolds 71, 77, 84
Fort Richardson 71, 77, 84–85
Fort Ricketts 70, 75, 83
Fort Rodgers 71, 75
Fort Runyon 72
Fort Saratoga 75, 78, 82
Fort Scott 71, 77, 85
Fort Simmons 75, 78–79, 87
Fort Slemner 75, 78
Fort Slocum 70, 75, 80–82, 190, 193–194, 209
Fort Snyder 70, 75, 83
Fort Stanton 71, 75, 83
Fort Stevens 6, 71, 75, 78, 80–82, 87–88, 150, 173–174, 176–180, 182, 186–187, 189–190, 193–195, 199–201, 205, 207, 209–211, 222, 224
Fort Strong 77, 86
Fort Sumner 71, 74, 78–79, 87, 185, 190
Fort Taylor 77
Fort Thayer 75, 78, 82, 185
Fort Tillinghast 71, 77, 85
Fort Totten 71, 75, 81–82, 187, 189–190, 194
Fort Wagner 71, 75, 83
Fort Ward 71, 77, 84
Fort Washington 75
Fort Weed 71
Fort Whipple 71, 77, 85
Fort Willard 71, 77
Fort Williams 71, 77, 84
Fort Woodbury 71, 77, 85
Fort Worth 71, 77

Index

France 7, 16, 117, 214–215
Frances Elmore 132
Franklin, William 15, 18, 28, 167
Franklin Savings Bank 159
Frederick, Maryland 5, 6, 16, 28, 72–73, 98, 104–107, 109, 112, 119–120, 123, 129, 136–141, 145, 150, 154, 156–157, 159, 165, 174–175, 185
Frederick Central Bank 159
Frederick County Bank 159
Frederick Town Savings Bank 159
Fredericksburg, Virginia 14, 18–19, 24, 84, 92, 95, 102, 139, 143, 145, 192, 196, 215, 221
Fremont, John C. 12, 36, 99, 217
Fry, William 176, 201

Gaines Mill, Virginia 5, 14, 56, 11, 173–174
Garnett, Dick 20
Garrett, John 69, 106–107, 118, 127–128, 136, 150, 170
George Leary 95
Georgetown, D.C. 23, 79, 179
Georgia regiments: 12th Georgia Infantry 107; 31st Georgia Infantry 69, 176–177; 38th Georgia Infantry 100, 103
Gettysburg, Pennsylvania 3, 5, 19–20, 54, 63, 89, 92, 110, 143, 183, 202, 209, 213, 215, 222, 224
Gibbon, John 15
Gibbs, Frank C. 129
Gibson, Augustus 78
Gile, George 79, 187, 189–191
Gillmore, Quincy 36, 157, 182, 195, 206
Gilmor, Harry 7, 28, 41, 139–140, 165–169, 172
Gilpin, Charles 136, 139–140, 154–155, 159
Gladstone, William 213
Glennan, R. 208
Golden Rod 132
Goldsborough, Louis 87–88, 180–181
Gordon, John B. 20 55–56, 61, 63–64, 105, 107, 141, 160, 162–164, 173, 176–177, 179, 199–200 203, 221
Gordonsville, Virginia 14, 27, 29, 35, 37, 43, 48, 116
Grant, Ulysses S. 3, 5–7, 19–21, 27, 34, 36–37, 40, 44, 47, 53, 55–57, 66, 102, 103, 105, 113, 115; Hunter/Shenandoah Valley operations 29, 35, 39, 41, 45–46, 48, 50, 52 69; intelligence failure 106, 113, 116–121, 129; invasion of Maryland 106–107; Petersburg 116; troops from Point Lookout 95; troops for Washington 119–20, 176; troops from Washington 77–80, 82–84, 86, 88; Wallace 129, 137, 157, 162; war of attrition 190, 213; Wilderness Campaign 113, 115–116, 186, 219
Greeley, Horace 217

Green, E.M. 194
Green, Thomas 198
Greenhow, Rose 196
Gregg, David M. 31–32, 48
Gregg, J.I. 31
Griffith, William 212
Gunpowder River Bridge (Maryland) 165–168

Hagerstown, Maryland 6, 16–17, 106–108, 112, 137–138, 141, 155–156
Hagerstown Bank 108, 155
Hagerstown Savings Bank 108, 155
Hall, L.K. 141
Halleck, Henry 5, 36–37, 39, 69, 74, 86, 88, 90, 103, 106–107, 113, 116–120, 123, 126–129, 137, 147, 149–153, 162, 170–171, 176, 189, 193, 204, 209
Hammond, W.A. 89–90
Hammond General Hospital (Maryland) 89, 92
Hampton, Wade 3, 21, 23, 25–27, 29–35, 47–48, 143, 145, 164, 168
Hancock, Winfield S. 116
Hanging Rock, Virginia 67, 110, 144, 147
Hanover Junction, Virginia 20, 24, 26, 40, 115
Hardin, John J. 185
Hardin, Martin D. 22, 79, 86–88, 170, 178, 181–182, 185, 191, 198, 205
Harewood Hospital 208
Harmon, John 122, 159
Harpers Ferry, West Virginia 5, 16–17, 49, 57, 66, 70–73, 98–100, 102–107, 112, 118–120, 123, 126–129, 136–137, 140, 145, 149, 151, 154, 175, 189, 223
Harper's Weekly 217
Harris, Thomas Maley 72, 99–100, 104, 127
Haskins, Joseph 70, 86, 185
Hawks, Wells J. 122, 159
Hay, John 212
Hayes, Rutherford B. 51, 60–61, 148
Hays, Harry Thompson 56, 173
Hayward, William 71, 86
Heat 6, 173, 200
Heaton, Henry 124
Henry, William 140, 155
Herring, William 166
Heth, Henry 89, 110
Hildreth, J.S. 207
Hill, A.P. 14, 55, 117
Hill, D.H. 57–60–61
Hilton, Alfred 95
Hincks, Edward 96
Hitchcock, Ethan A. 119
Hliss, D.W. 207
Hoffman, William 90–91, 94
Hoke Robert 40
Holly, J.N. 81
Holmes, Oliver Wendell, Jr. 211–212
Hooker, Joseph 8, 18–19, 92, 221

Howe, Albion 74–76, 78, 117, 120, 123, 126, 128–129, 137, 140, 150–151, 189
Humphreys, Andrew 85, 117
Hundson, Charles 82
Hunter, Alexander 179
Hunter, David: background 36; communications with Grant and Washington 118, 129, 147–153; and Early 129, 149–150, 152; Grant's directions 45–48; lack of ammunition 46, 52; Lexington 49–51; Lynchburg campaign 57–61, 64–67; Piedmont campaign 37, 39, 40–44; retreat to West Virginia 67–69, 106, 111, 117–118, 126, 136, 144–145, 147–150, 173
Hutcheson, James 162

Illinois regiments: 8th Illinois Cavalry 107, 123–124, 137–139, 148, 156, 159, 170; 23d Illinois Infantry 99, 127
Imboden, John D. 3, 39–43, 46, 49–50, 52, 57, 60–61, 63, 67, 100, 127, 144–145
Indiana regiments: 17th Indiana Light Artillery 72
Ingram, Alex 208
Intelligence failure *see* Grant, Ulysses S.
Iron Brigade 15
Ives, Joseph 8, 12

Jackson, Thomas J. "Stonewall" 3, 6, 8, 12–19, 27–28, 41, 51, 54–56, 65, 98, 107, 110, 126, 143, 145, 154, 174
Jackson, William L. "Mudwall" 27, 39, 41, 47, 60, 119, 145, 156, 164, 188
James River Canal (Virginia) 29, 33–34, 44, 48, 52
John Brooks 90
Johnson, Bradley T. 5–7, 72, 122; attack on Point Lookout 23, 26–28, 130–133, 141, 143, 164–166; Baltimore raid 96–97, 135, 138, 146, 157, 166–167, 168, 169, 172, 202, 224; Chambersburg 222; Frederick area 139–140, 145, 149, 223; Leetown 69, 98–100, 109, 145; response to Dahlgren-Kilpatrick raid 24–26
Johnson, Charles F. 188
Johnson, Edward 173
Johnston, Joseph E. 12, 116
Johnston, R.D. 56, 173
Johnston, R.E. 189
Jonas Powell 149
Jones, Buehring 42
Jones, J.M. 56, 173
Jones, John B. 134
Jones, William "Grumble" 27, 40–43, 47, 60–61, 119, 122, 131, 144–145
Judiciary Square Hospital 208
USS *Juniata* 166

Kaiser, Peter H. 210
Kearny, Phil 10, 15
Keiley, Anthony M. 92
Kenly, John 72
Kershaw, Joseph 183
Kidd, James 32–33
Kilpatrick, Judson 24–25
King of Spades 8

Landstreet, William 106, 135, 146, 154, 159
Lane, Joseph 155
Lawrence, Samuel 106, 135
Lee, Edwin G. 43
Lee, Elizabeth Blair 200, 202
Lee, Fitzhugh 18, 27, 31–34, 47–48, 143, 145
Lee, G.W. Custis 26, 28, 56, 130, 132–135, 168, 169
Lee, J.G.C. 195
Lee, John 71
Lee, Robert E.: Antietam 16–17; audacity 8–10, 12–17, 19–21, 102, 143, 212; background 8, 192, 200, 202; Chancellorsville 18–19, 222; Fredericksburg 18; Gettysburg 19–20; heat 174; Mexican War 8–12; move to Washington 44–47, 52–58, 62, 65–70, 72, 89, 96, 98, 102, 104–105, 108, 112, 117, 145, 183, 219, 226; Petersburg 220; plans for Point Lookout 130–132, 141, 143, 154, 164, 173, 175, 198, 224; Second Bull Run (Manassas) 14–15, 213; Seven Days 12–14, 213; Wilderness, Spottsylvania, North Anna, Cold Harbor 20–21, 113, 115–117 213
Lee, Robert E., Jr. 5, 7, 21, 108, 133, 137
Lee, Rooney 31
Lee, S.P. 177, 202
Leesburg, Virginia 5, 70–71, 137, 222
Leetown, Battle of 27, 69, 72, 98–101, 106, 174, 223
Leib, Edward 154, 171
Lester, George H. 100, 103
Let-Her-B 133
Letcher, John 51, 167, 196, 202
Lewis, George Cornwall 214
Lewis, William 105, 107
Lexington, Virginia 35, 48–53, 58, 61, 117, 144, 202
Lexington Home Guard 50
Liddell, J.H. 208
Lilley, Robert 159
Lincoln, Abraham 6–7, 23–24, 26–28, 36, 67, 81, 129, 152–153, 164, 179, 192, 198, 201–202, 221; affected by War 113–115; diplomacy 214; reelection 116, 213, 216–220; under fire at Stevens 210–211; Wade-Davis Bill 218
Lincoln Hospital 208
Lomax, Lunsford 27, 34, 143
Long, Armistead 20, 56–57, 179
Longstreet, James 15–17, 20, 55
Loudon Rangers 70, 72, 107, 123, 137–139
Louisiana regiments: 1st Louisiana Infantry 173; 2nd Louisiana Infantry 173; 5th Louisiana Infantry 173; 6th Louisiana Infantry 173; 7th Louisiana Infantry 173; 8th Louisiana Infantry 173; 9th Louisiana Infantry 100, 173; 10th Louisiana Infantry 173; 14th Louisiana Infantry 173; 15th Louisiana Infantry 173
Lowell, Charles R., Jr. 70, 79, 91
Lynchburg, Virginia 3, 5, 21, 37, 29–30, 33, 35, 37, 39–40, 44, 46–50, 52, 55, 57–61, 63–67, 69–70, 98, 111, 117, 118–119, 144–145, 149, 183, 222–223

Maine regiments: 1st Maine Battery 88, 129; 1st Maine Cavalry 24, 31; 1st Maine Heavy Artillery 78, 86
Malone, Yancey Bartlett 95–96
Manassas Junction, Virginia 15
Marble, John 71, 79, 86
Marble, Manton 217
Marston, Gilman 90–92, 95–96
Martinsburg, West Virginia 5, 36, 44, 52, 65–66, 69–73, 98–100, 102–105, 107, 112, 119–120
Maryland Heights, Maryland 5, 27, 98–99, 101–107, 123–124, 126–129, 137, 140, 145, 149, 151, 154, 174, 223
Maryland Line 24
Maryland regiments: Baltimore Battery (Union) 106, 154, 159, 161; Baltimore Light Artillery (Conf.) 24, 26–27; 1st Maryland Cavalry (Conf.) 23–24, 26–27, 139, 167; 1st Maryland Cavalry (Union) 155; 1st Maryland Potomac Home Brigade (Union) 49, 64, 72, 136, 159, 171; 2nd Maryland Cavalry (Conf.) 139, 166; 2nd Maryland Eastern Shore Infantry (Union) 63; 2nd Maryland Infantry (Conf.) 24, 26; 3d Maryland Potomac Home Brigade (Union) 106, 135, 139, 155, 159; 5th Maryland Infantry (Union) 170; 11th Maryland Infantry (Union) 106, 135, 140, 146, 154, 159
Mason, James 21, 201, 213
Massachusetts regiments: 1st Massachusetts Cavalry 31; 1st Massachusetts Heavy Artillery 85–86; 2nd Massachusetts Cavalry 23, 70, 124, 137; 3d Massachusetts Heavy Artillery 71, 86; 5th Massachusetts (Colored) Dismounted Cavalry 96; 6th Massachusetts Unattached Heavy Artillery 83; 7th Unattached Massachusetts Heavy Artillery 83; 9th Unattached Massachusetts Heavy Artillery 83; 12th Unattached Massachusetts Heavy Artillery 83; 34th Massachusetts Infantry 40, 42–43, 63, 66–68, 102, 149
Maximilian 215–216
McCall, C.A. 208
McCann, Thomas 151
McCausland, John 27, 39, 44, 47–48, 50–52, 57–58, 60, 63–65, 67, 69, 98, 100, 105–108, 112, 137–138, 144–145, 153–157, 160, 176, 178, 180, 201–201, 223
McClellan, George B. 8, 12–16, 92, 198, 213, 217, 220–221
McClennan, Matthew 141
McClure, Alexander 113
McCook, Alexander McD. 6, 87–88, 128, 181–182, 185, 189–190, 193–195, 205–207 209–210
McDowell, Irwin 12, 14, 36
McEntee, John 51, 69, 118
McGuire, Hunter 159
McKee, J.C. 208
McKinley, William 63
McLaws, Lafayette 18–19
McLean, Hancock 108, 155
Meade, George G. 68, 107, 119–120, 174
Meigs, Montgomery 6, 81, 88, 90, 190–191, 193–195, 206
Merritt, Wesley 31, 33–34
Mettan, Henry Clay 27
Mexico City, Mexico 9, 12
Michigan regiments: 1st Michigan Cavalry 31–33; 5th Michigan Cavalry 24, 31–32; 6th Michigan Cavalry 31–33; 7th Michigan Cavalry 31–33, 88, 179; 13th Michigan Battery 71, 86–87, 178; 14th Michigan Battery 71, 86
Miles, Dixon S. 17, 126
Miller, Samuel 140
Monocacy, Battle of 5–6, 141, 150–151, 154, 157–158, 198, 223
Monocacy Junction, Maryland 6, 106–108, 136, 138, 141, 151, 154, 159–160
Moor, Augustus 42–43
Morris, Lewis O. 72, 79
Morrow, T. 100, 161
Mosby, John Singleton 28, 37, 39, 70, 72, 107, 119, 137–138; and Early 122, 124–125, 138–139, 223; Point of Rocks attack 122–124, 126–127
Mosby's Confederacy 70, 122
Moulton, Charles H. 102
Mount Pleasant Hospital 208
Mule Shoe Salient 20, 26, 115, 173
Mulligan, James 5, 72, 99–100, 107, 145, 174, 223
Mumford, Thomas 34
Murphy, J.M. 79

National Intelligencer 123
New Hampshire regiments: 1st New Hampshire Heavy Artillery 79; 2nd New Hampshire In-

fantry 90, 92–93, 95; 5th New Hampshire Infantry 92, 94–95; 12th New Hampshire Infantry 90, 92–93, 95
New Jersey regiments: 1st New Jersey Cavalry 31; 3d New Jersey Infantry 188; 4th New Jersey Infantry 188; 5th New Jersey Infantry 187; 7th New Jersey Infantry 194, 207, 209; 14th New Jersey Infantry 141, 159; 28th New Jersey Infantry 187
New Market, Virginia 36, 40–42, 61
New York Herald 218
New York regiments: 1st New York (Lincoln) Cavalry 39, 64; 1st New York (Veteran) Cavalry 64; 2nd New York Cavalry 24, 31; 2nd New York Heavy Artillery 86; 4th New York Cavalry 31, 33; 4th New York Heavy Artillery 42, 80, 86; 5th New York Cavalry 24; 5th New York Heavy Artillery 63, 102, 104, 127; 6th New York Cavalry 31, 33; 7th New York Heavy Artillery 79–80, 86; 9th New York Cavalry 31; 9th New York Heavy Artillery 79–80, 141; 10th New York Cavalry 31; 10th New York Heavy Artillery 84, 86; 13th New York Cavalry 70, 124, 137; 16th New York Cavalry 70; 19th New York Cavalry 31; 21st New York Cavalry 42, 64; 25th New York Cavalry 87, 178, 189–190, 206 ; 30th Battery New York Light Artillery 64; 32nd New York Independent Battery A 72; 77th New York Infantry 210; 106th New York Infantry 141, 159; 151st New York Infantry 141, 159
New York Times 218
New York Tribune 217
New York World 217–218, 226
Newtown, Virginia 39
Nicholls, Francis 47
Nichols, C.H. 208
Nineteenth Corps 3, 79, 88, 120, 157, 177, 183, 195
Norris, John 80
Norris, William 196
North Ana, Virginia 7, 20, 40, 54, 79, 84, 86, 115, 173, 185, 213, 219
North Carolina regiments: 11th North Carolina Infantry 92; 26th North Carolina (Colored) Infantry (Union) 95
North Mountain Depot, West Virginia 69, 98, 100

Ohio regiments: 1st Ohio Battery 88; 1st Ohio Infantry 205; 1st Ohio Light Artillery 71, 86, 129; 6th Ohio Cavalry 31; 13th Ohio Infantry 64; 23d Ohio Infantry 63; 28th Ohio Infantry 42, 63; 34th Ohio Mounted Infantry 64; 36th Ohio Infantry 63; 91st Ohio Infantry 64; 110th Ohio Infantry 159; 116th Ohio Infantry 42–43, 63, 65; 122nd Ohio Infantry 159, 170; 123d Ohio Infantry 63; 126th Ohio Infantry 141, 159; 135th Ohio Infantry 72, 100; 136th Ohio Infantry 84; 139th Ohio Infantry 96; 144th Ohio Infantry 106, 136, 139–140, 155, 159; 147th Ohio Infantry 78, 80, 84, 88; 149th Ohio Infantry 106, 136, 139, 155, 159, 162; 150th Ohio Infantry 71, 80–82, 87, 177–178; 151st Ohio Infantry 71, 79–80, 86–87, 185; 152nd Ohio Infantry 72; 159th Ohio Infantry 139, 154–155, 159, 167; 160th Ohio Infantry 72, 100, 103; 161st Ohio Infantry 72, 100; 163d Ohio Infantry 80; 166th Ohio Infantry 85; 169th Ohio Infantry 78; 170th Ohio Infantry 71, 87, 129
Olmstead, Frederick Law 95
Olney, John 64
Opie, John 178
Orange and Alexandria Railroad 30, 49, 59, 111, 144
Ord, E.O.C. 172
Oswalt, Francis 89, 92
Otey, Van 47
Overland Campaign 20–21, 23, 47, 54, 110, 116, 173, 198, 221
Ox Hill, Virginia, Battle of 15

Paine, E.M. 141
Paine, Halbert E. 194–195
Palmer, F.S. 187, 189–190
Palmer, J. 86
Palmerston, Lord 16, 213–215
Park, Robert 98, 103, 162, 174, 194, 203
Parkersburg, West Virginia 69, 148–150
Parkersburg Gazette 149
Peck, W.R. 173
Pedregal (Mexico) 10, 12
Pegram, John 56, 102, 173
Peninsular Campaign 8, 10, 54, 92, 95, 128, 185, 198, 213, 221
Pennsylvania regiments: 1st Pennsylvania Artillery Battalion 71; 1st Pennsylvania Cavalry 31; 1st Pennsylvania Light Artillery72; 2nd Pennsylvania Cavalry 31; 2nd Pennsylvania Heavy Artillery 78, 81, 87; 3d Pennsylvania Reserve Infantry 64; 4th Pennsylvania Cavalry 31; 4th Pennsylvania Reserve Infantry 64; 6th Pennsylvania Cavalry 31; 8th Pennsylvania Cavalry 31; 12th Pennsylvania Cavalry 107, 138; 13th Pennsylvania Cavalry 31; 14th Pennsylvania Cavalry 42–43, 50; 16th Pennsylvania Cavalry 31, 176; 22nd Pennsylvania Cavalry 100, 155; 23d Pennsylvania Infantry 72; 54th Pennsylvania Infantry 42–42, 64; 67th Pennsylvania Infantry 170; 81st Pennsylvania Infantry 188; 87th Pennsylvania Infantry 141, 159; 102nd Pennsylvania Infantry 211; 138th Pennsylvania Infantry 141
Peters, William 58
Petersburg, Virginia 3, 7, 20, 29–30, 49, 71, 79, 82, 85, 95–96, 116–117, 119, 121, 132, 148, 220
Pettigrew, James J. 89
Peyton, George Quinn 102, 105
Philadelphia, Wilmington and Baltimore Railroad 166
Phillips, R.H. 49
Phillips, Wendell 217
Pickett, George 20, 40, 132
Piedmont, Battle of 27, 39, 42–44, 47, 52, 122, 131, 143, 154
Pierce, Franklin 9–10
Pillow, Gideon 10
Pimpero 215
Podierna, Mexico 10
Point Lookout Prison Camp (Maryland) 3, 5–7, 21–23, 27–30, 83, 89; authorization and construction 90–92; defenses 94–97; conditions 95; naval expedition 109, 130–131; planned attack 96, 105, 108, 117, 120, 129–131, 133–135, 138, 141, 143, 146, 163–166, 173, 198, 223–224; raid 167
Point of Rocks, Maryland 23, 72, 107, 123, 126–127, 132, 138
Pope, John 8, 14–15, 92, 213
Popov, A. 215
Porter, Charles 59
Porter, David Dixon 192
Potomac River 5, 23, 28, 37, 68–72, 74–79, 84, 86, 89–92, 100, 102–103, 105, 107, 112, 120, 123, 127, 130, 132, 137, 142, 149, 152, 183, 192, 196, 198–200, 222
Price, Francis 81, 190, 194, 207, 209
Price, Robert 166
Price's Provisional Brigade 6, 81, 88 128, 190, 194–195, 206–207
Putnam, George Haven 217

Quaker Meeting House (Lynchburg, Virginia) 60–61, 63, 144
Quartermaster Employees (Union) 6, 88, 128, 192, 195
Quartermaster General 189, 193
Quinn, Timothy 39

Ramseur, Stephen D. 55–56, 61, 63–64, 67, 100, 102, 104–105, 107, 109, 139, 141, 145, 159–160, 174, 200, 203, 221
Ransom, Robert 6, 27, 56, 65, 99, 102, 110–120, 139, 143, 145–146, 223
Raymond, Henry C. 217
Raymond, Henry J. 218
USS *Reliance* 132
Reno, Jesse 79

Republican Convention 115–116
Rhode Island regiments: 1st Rhode Island Light Artillery 71, 86; 4th Rhode Island Infantry 95
Richmond, Virginia 3, 5, 8, 12–14, 21, 23–29, 45–49, 53, 55–56, 58–59, 66, 68–69, 77–78, 80, 84, 86, 95, 106, 110–113, 115–117, 119, 133, 143, 147–149, 184, 189, 219–220, 222
Richmond, Fredericksburg and Potomac Railroad 20, 40, 115
Ricketts, James B. 6, 73, 98, 120, 140–141, 151, 154–155, 157, 159–160, 162–163, 165, 171, 176, 193
Roberts, Robert 188
Robertson, James M. 31
Rodenbough, Theophilus 31
Rodes, Robert 56, 61, 64–65, 100, 102–107, 109, 139, 145, 174, 177–178, 180, 200–201
Rosser, Thomas 30–33, 143
Rucker, D.H. 193–194
Russell, Lord John 213–214
Russia 214–216
Rynders, John 194

Sabine, George 78
Saint Elizabeth's Hospital 208
San Antonio, Mexico 10
Sanders, Miles 129
Santa Anna, Antonio López de 8
USS *Satellite* 132
Schenck, Robert 164
Schermer, L. 86
Schoomaker, John M. 50
Schwartz, Hugh 72, 122
Scorpion 215
Scott, Alexander 140
Scott, Winfield 8–12, 110, 116, 118, 213
Second Bull Run (Manassas) Campaign 16, 27, 54, 95, 143, 145, 164, 185, 187, 213
Seddon, James 47, 196
Seminary Hospital 208
Seven Days Battle 8, 12–14, 16, 143, 145, 185, 188, 213
Seventh Street Rd (Maryland/D.C.) 75, 78, 80, 176, 182, 193, 198–201, 205, 210
Seward, William 192, 201, 213, 215–216
Sharpe, George 117–118
Shaw, Frederick 78
Shearer, George 155
Shenandoah Valley, Virginia 3, 5, 14, 21, 24, 27, 29, 36–37, 40–41, 45–48, 52, 56–57, 66, 68–70, 72, 98, 106, 108, 11, 116–117, 119, 143, 147, 174, 200
Sheridan, Philip H. 3, 21, 26–27, 29–35, 40, 44–45, 47–48, 52, 58–59, 87, 117, 143, 153, 183, 188, 221–223
Sherman, William Tecumseh 113, 116, 192, 206, 213, 216, 219
Shields, James 10, 12, 58
Shock, W.W. 126

Shoes 40, 73, 98, 11–112, 156
Sickles, Daniel 92
Sigel, Franz 5, 36–37, 42, 52, 61, 66, 69, 71–73, 98–100, 102–105, 107, 112, 119, 126–129, 137, 140, 145, 147, 149, 151, 154, 223
Sigler, Sam 99
Silver Spring Estate (Maryland) 177, 200, 202–204
Simms, John 132
Sixth Corps 3, 80, 88, 107, 120, 140, 142, 157, 159, 165, 171, 183, 189, 193, 209–211
Slidell, John 201, 213, 216
Slocum, John 8
Smith, Francis 50–52
Smith, George 177
Smith, Percival 10
Smith, William "Baldy" 3, 30, 96, 116–117
Smith, William Prescott 119, 129
Sons of Liberty 220
Sorel, Moxley 55
South Carolina regiments: 4th South Carolina Cavalry 32
South Side Railroad 49
Spottsylvania, Virginia 7, 20–21, 26, 40, 54–55, 86, 105, 115, 173, 213, 219
Stafford, Leroy 56, 173
Stahel, Julius 39–40, 44, 48–49, 99, 107, 129, 147
Stahle, J.A. 141
Stanton, Edwin 13, 36, 69, 90, 92, 96, 106–107, 115, 127, 149–150, 152–153, 193, 202
Stanton, Elizabeth Cady 217
Stanton, J.F. 172
Stanton Hospital 208
Stark, William 66–68, 147, 149
Staunton, Virginia 25, 35–37, 39–41, 43–44, 46–48, 52, 58–59, 68–70, 73, 110–112, 117, 119, 174, 183
Stearns, Joseph 39
Stelden, A.F. 207
Stevens, George 210–211
Stevens, Isaac 15, 20
Stewart, G.H. 56
Stickney, James 188–189
Stiles, Robert 55
Stoughton, Edwin 122
Stribling, Robert 117
Stringfellow, Benjamin 198
Strong, George Templeton 219
Strother, David Hunter 36, 39–40, 44–46, 50–51, 57, 60, 64–65, 67–68, 147–149, 173
Stuart, J.E.B. 15, 18–19, 26–27, 122, 143
Sullivan, Jeremiah 39, 42, 48, 58, 60, 63–65, 67, 149–150
Sumner, Edwin V. 79, 102

Talbot, Thomas 78
CSS *Tallahassee* 135
Tannatt, Henry L. 86
Taylor, Walter 19
Tennallytown, D.C. 79, 176, 179, 185, 189, 201

Tennessee regiments: 1st Tennessee Cavalry 41; 3d Tennessee Mounted Infantry 41; 12th Tennessee Cavalry 41; 16th Tennessee Cavalry 41; 39th Tennessee Mounted Infantry 41; 43d Tennessee Mounted Infantry 41; 59th Tennessee Mounted Infantry 41; 60th Tennessee Infantry 41; 61st Tennessee Infantry 41; 62nd Tennessee Infantry 41
Terry, William 100, 102, 105, 162
Thoburn, Joseph 42–43, 64
Thomas, Charles 197
Thomas Morgan 95
Thompson, Jacob 218–219
Thompson, James 95
Tibbetts, William 64
Tidball, John C. 86
Tompkins, Charles 195
Tom's Brook, Battle of 222
Torbert, Alfred 30, 33, 47
Totten, Joseph 81
Trent Affair 201, 213, 214
Trevilian Station, Virginia 3, 21, 27–34, 47, 52, 57, 143, 188, 223
Truex, William 140–141, 154–155, 159
Turnbull, William 8
Turner, Henry 189
Twenty-Second Corps 80, 86, 129, 176, 185
Twiggs, David 8–10
Tye River Railroad Bridge (Virginia) 49–50, 57, 144
Tyler, Erastus 72, 106, 137, 139–140, 145, 154–156, 159–160, 162

Underwriter 132
U.S. Capitol 194
U.S. Colored Troops: 1st U.S. Colored 94; 4th U.S. Colored 94; 29th U.S. Colored 96; 36th U.S. Colored 95–96
U.S. Regular Army: 1st U.S. Artillery 31; 1st U.S. Cavalry 31; 2nd U.S. Artillery 31, 71; 2nd U.S. Cavalry 31; 4th U.S. Artillery 71, 86; 5th U.S. Artillery 64; 5th U.S. Cavalry 31, 138, 154, 171; 6th U.S. Cavalry 106–107, 137, 155
U.S. Sanitary Commission 95
Upton, Emory 84

Vallandigham, Clement 219
Vaughn, John C. 3, 40–43, 46, 52, 57, 102, 143–144
Venable, Charles 198
Vermont regiments: 1st Vermont Heavy Artillery 80–82, 86, 185; 2nd Vermont Infantry 88, 189; 3d Vermont Infantry 88, 189; 10th Vermont Infantry 140, 155, 159
Veteran reserve regiments: 1st Veteran Reserve Infantry 79, 186–187, 190; 6th Veteran Reserve In-

fantry 79, 186–187, 189–190; 9th Veteran Reserve Infantry 88, 186–188, 191; 10th Veteran Reserve Infantry 95, 189; 12th Veteran Reserve Infantry 88, 186–187, 189, 194–195; 18th Veteran Reserve Infantry 186; 19th Veteran Reserve Infantry 79, 186, 188–191; 20th Veteran Reserve Infantry 96; 22nd Veteran Reserve Infantry 186, 189–190; 24th Veteran Reserve Infantry 79, 186, 188–190
Veul, Charles 95
Virginia Central Railroad 20, 24, 29–30, 33–35, 40, 46, 48 111, 115
Virginia Military Institute 29, 50–52, 59, 202
Virginia regiments: 1st Virginia Cavalry 122; 2nd Virginia Infantry 165, 173; 3d Virginia Cavalry 31; 4th Virginia Infantry 105, 173; 5th Virginia Cavalry 26, 173; 5th Virginia Infantry 105; 8th Virginia Cavalry 27; 9th Virginia Battalion 107; 9th Virginia Cavalry 26; 10th Virginia Infantry 105; 12th Virginia Infantry 92; 13th Virginia Infantry 102, 105; 14th Virginia Cavalry 100, 108; 14th Virginia Infantry 105; 16th Virginia Cavalry 100, 108; 16th Virginia Infantry 108; 17th Virginia Cavalry 100, 108; 18th Virginia Cavalry 40; 19th Virginia Cavalry 47; 20th Virginia Cavalry 199; 21st Virginia Infantry 60, 100, 102, 105, 112, 173–174, 176, 186; 22nd Virginia Cavalry 100; 22nd Virginia Infantry Battalion (Infantry) 57; 23d Virginia Battalion (Infantry) 57, 70; 23d Virginia Cavalry 40; 23d Virginia Infantry 105; 24th Virginia Cavalry 27; 24th Virginia Infantry 54; 25th Virginia Cavalry 108; 25th Virginia Infantry 105, 107, 173; 26th Virginia Battalion (Infantry) 57; 27th Virginia Infantry 173; 30th Virginia Battalion Sharpshooters 57; 33d Virginia Infantry 112, 173; 34th Virginia Battalion 27; 36th Virginia Battalion 27, 41–42; 37th Virginia Battalion 27; 37th Virginia Cavalry 108; 37th Virginia Infantry 105; 40th Virginia Cavalry 133; 42nd Virginia Infantry 105, 173; 43d Virginia Battalion (Cavalry) 39, 122–124, 137; 44th Virginia Infantry 105, 173; 45th Virginia Battalion 41–42; 45th Virginia Infantry 42, 57; 48th Virginia Infantry 105, 173; 50th Virginia Infantry 105, 173; 51st Virginia Infantry 57; 60th Virginia Battalion 41–42; 62nd Virginia Mounted Infantry 177
VMI Cadets 50, 60–61
Volck, A.J. 196

Walker, J.A. 56, 173
Wallace, Lew 5–6, 72–73, 98, 117, 223; Frederick 106–108, 123, 127, 129, 135–142, 146; Monocacy 151, 154–157, 159, 162, 165, 187, 193, 200; retreat to Baltimore 170–172
War weariness 116
Warner, J.M. 86, 185
Washington, D.C. 3, 5–8, 13–16, 21–23, 27–30, 36, 44, 53, 66–83, 86–87, 89, 96, 98, 102, 104–108, 112–113, 115–117, 119–120, 123–129, 132, 135, 137, 141–143, 145–146, 148, 150–152, 154, 157, 160, 162–163, 166, 169, 171–174, 176, 178, 181–190, 192–193, 195–196, 198–201, 205, 207–210, 213, 216, 219–220, 222–224
Washington Chronicle 87
Washington County Bank of Williamsport 108, 155
Washington Navy Yard 87
Watson, William 66
Weber, Max 5, 66, 69, 71 100, 102–104, 107, 119, 123, 126–129, 145, 149, 151, 223
Weddell, Jacob 43
Welles, Gideon 94, 113, 115, 120, 149, 151, 219, 222
Wells, George 40
West Virginia regiments: 1st West Virginia Cavalry 64; 1st West Virginia Light Artillery 72; 2nd West Virginia Cavalry 64; 3d West Virginia Cavalry 64; 5th West Virginia Infantry 63 ; 7th West Virginia Cavalry 64; 9th West Virginia Infantry 64 ; 10th West Virginia Infantry 72, 99, 127; 11th West Virginia Infantry 64; 12th West Virginia Infantry 42, 63; 13th West Virginia Infantry 48, 63; 14th West Virginia Infantry 64; 15th West Virginia Infantry 64; West Virginia Light Artillery, Battery D 64
Wharton, Gabriel 47, 52, 57
Wharton, James 149
White, Carr B. 64
Whiting, William 89, 133–134
Whitman, Walt 208
Wickham, Williams 27, 34
Wiegel, William 106
Wilcox, Cadmus 19
Wilderness, Virginia 7, 20–21, 23, 26, 30 40, 46, 54–56, 113, 115, 173, 213, 215, 219, 221–222
Williams, Seth 118
Williamson, James 137
Williamson, Thomas 51
Wilmington, North Carolina 5–6, 89, 97, 110, 132–133, 168
Wilson, John 79, 82
Winchester, Virginia 5, 28, 69–70, 72, 98, 111–112, 145, 147, 174, 183, 200
Wisconsin regiments: 1st Wisconsin Heavy Artillery 80
Wistar, Isaac 23–24
Wiswell, Moses 187
Wivern 215
Wood, John Taylor 5–6, 89, 96–97, 109; Point Lookout Operation 130–135, 141, 146, 164, 168, 169, 224; raid in Chesapeake 132
Woodhull, Max 119
Woodward, John K. 78
Worsham, John H. 60, 100, 102, 105, 112, 174, 176, 186
Worth, William 10
Wright, Horatio G. 151–153, 157, 179, 182–183 205, 209–212

Yellow Tavern, Virginia 26
York, Zebulon 161–162

www.ingramcontent.com/pod-product-compliance
Lightning Source LLC
Chambersburg PA
CBHW060259240426
43661CB00060B/2834